Journey

The Beautiful World

1

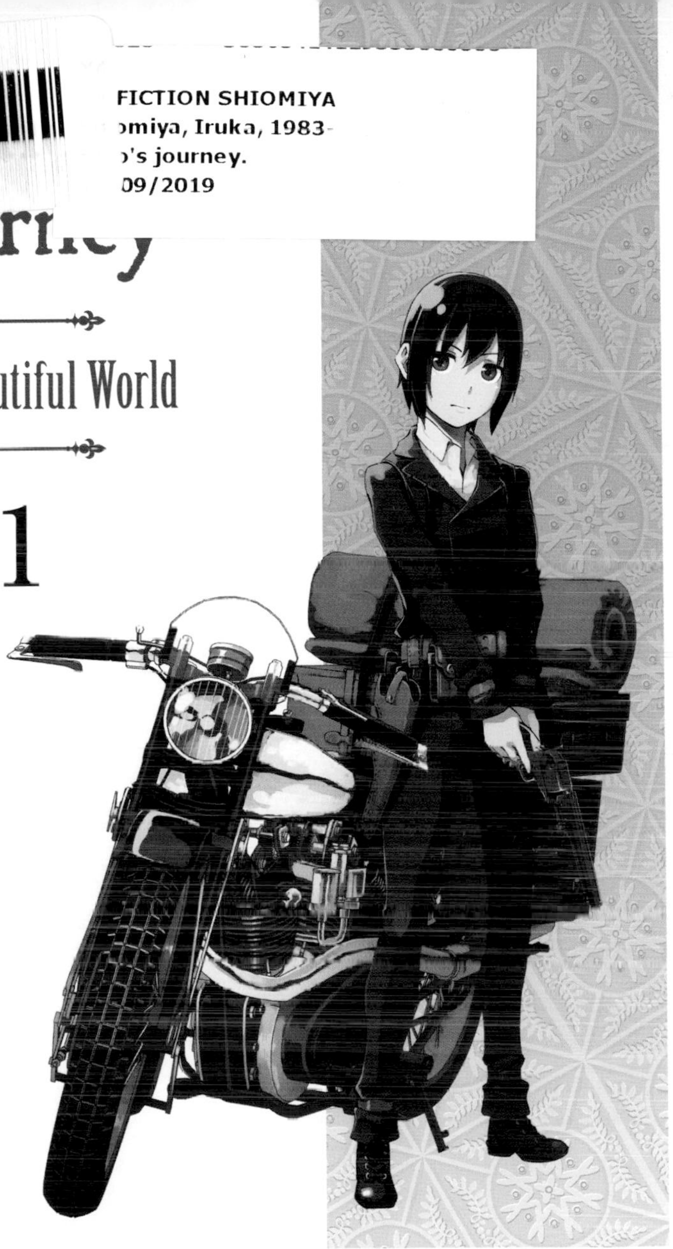

Iruka Shiomiya

Original Story:
Keiichi Sigsawa

Original Character Design:
Kouhaku Kuroboshi

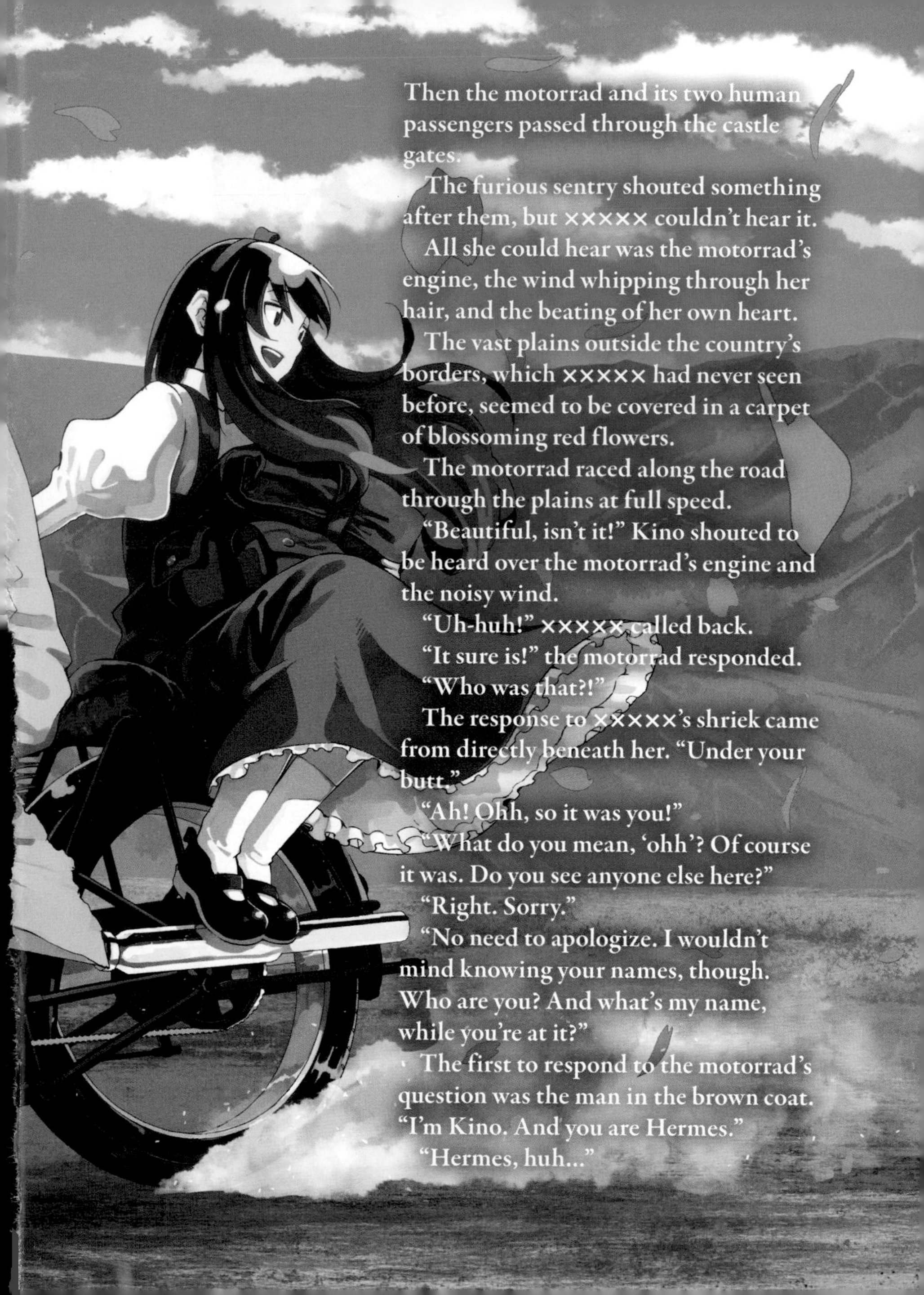

Then the motorrad and its two human passengers passed through the castle gates.

The furious sentry shouted something after them, but ××××× couldn't hear it.

All she could hear was the motorrad's engine, the wind whipping through her hair, and the beating of her own heart.

The vast plains outside the country's borders, which ××××× had never seen before, seemed to be covered in a carpet of blossoming red flowers.

The motorrad raced along the road through the plains at full speed.

"Beautiful, isn't it!" Kino shouted to be heard over the motorrad's engine and the noisy wind.

"Uh-huh!" ××××× called back.

"It sure is!" the motorrad responded.

"Who was that?!"

The response to ×××××'s shriek came from directly beneath her. "Under your butt."

"Ah! Ohh, so it was you!"

"What do you mean, 'ohh'? Of course it was. Do you see anyone else here?"

"Right. Sorry."

"No need to apologize. I wouldn't mind knowing your names, though. Who are you? And what's my name, while you're at it?"

The first to respond to the motorrad's question was the man in the brown coat. "I'm Kino. And you are Hermes."

"Hermes, huh..."

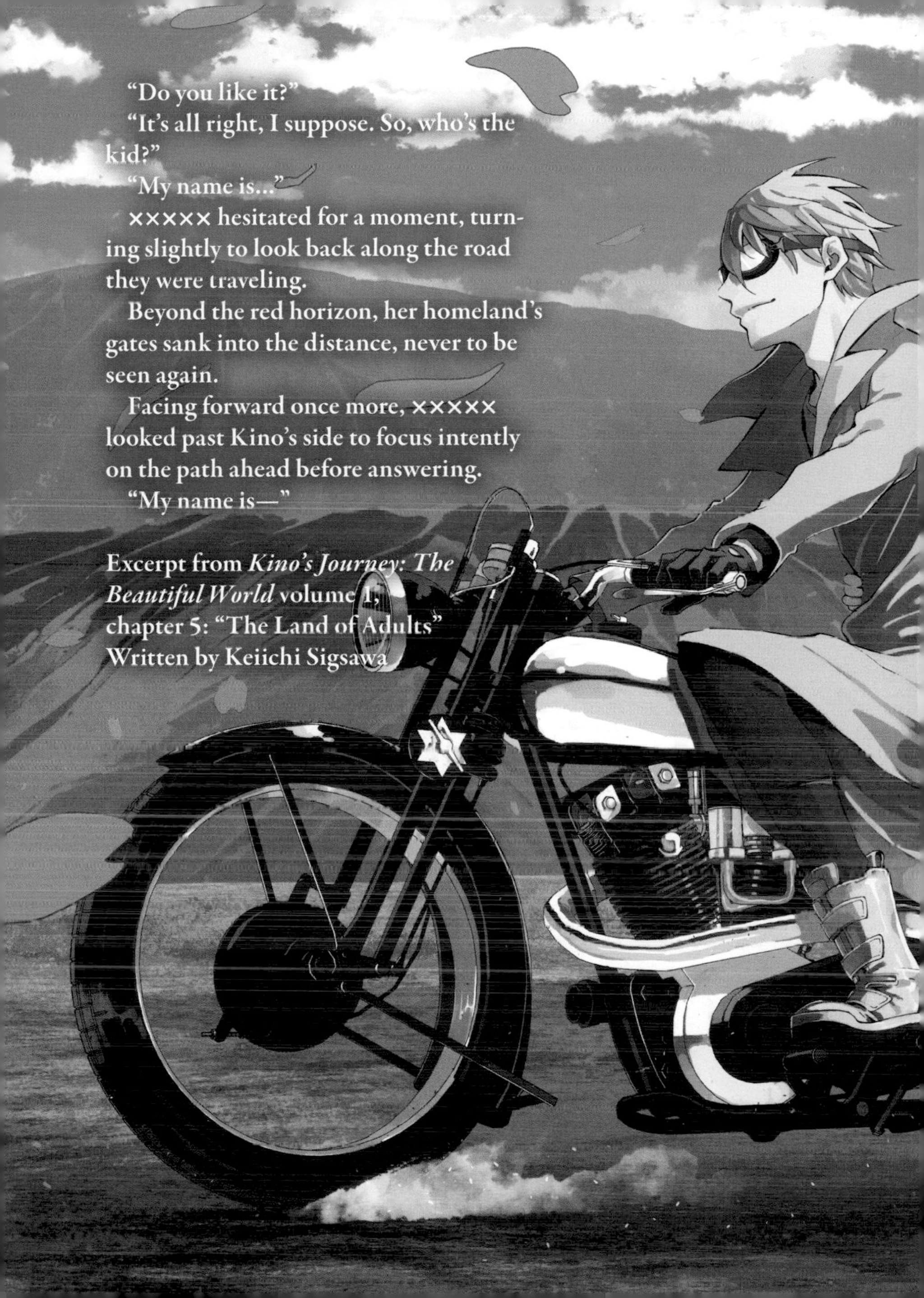

"Do you like it?"

"It's all right, I suppose. So, who's the kid?"

"My name is..."

××××× hesitated for a moment, turning slightly to look back along the road they were traveling.

Beyond the red horizon, her homeland's gates sank into the distance, never to be seen again.

Facing forward once more, ××××× looked past Kino's side to focus intently on the path ahead before answering.

"My name is—"

Excerpt from *Kino's Journey: The Beautiful World* volume 1,
chapter 5: "The Land of Adults"
Written by Keiichi Sigsawa

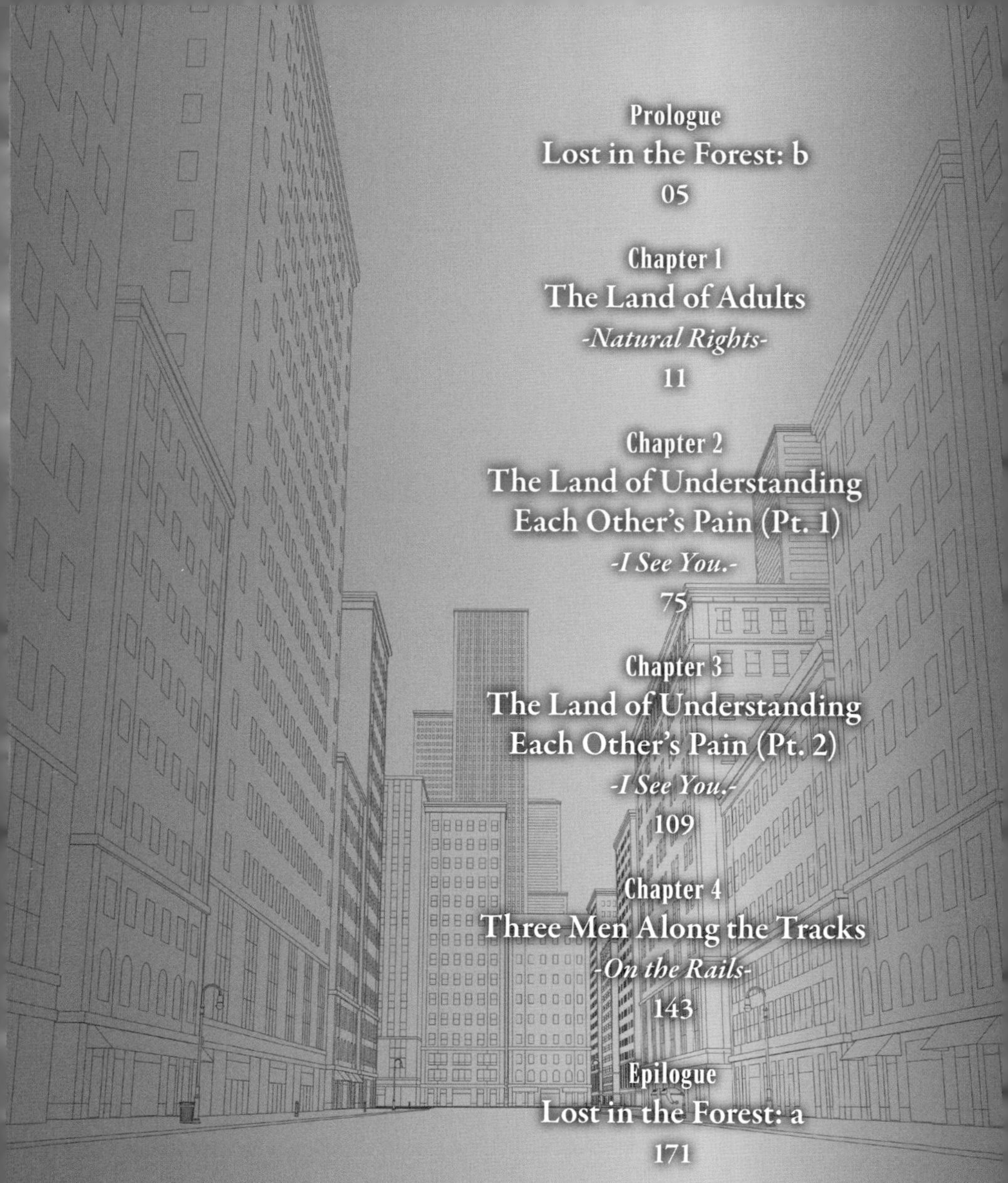

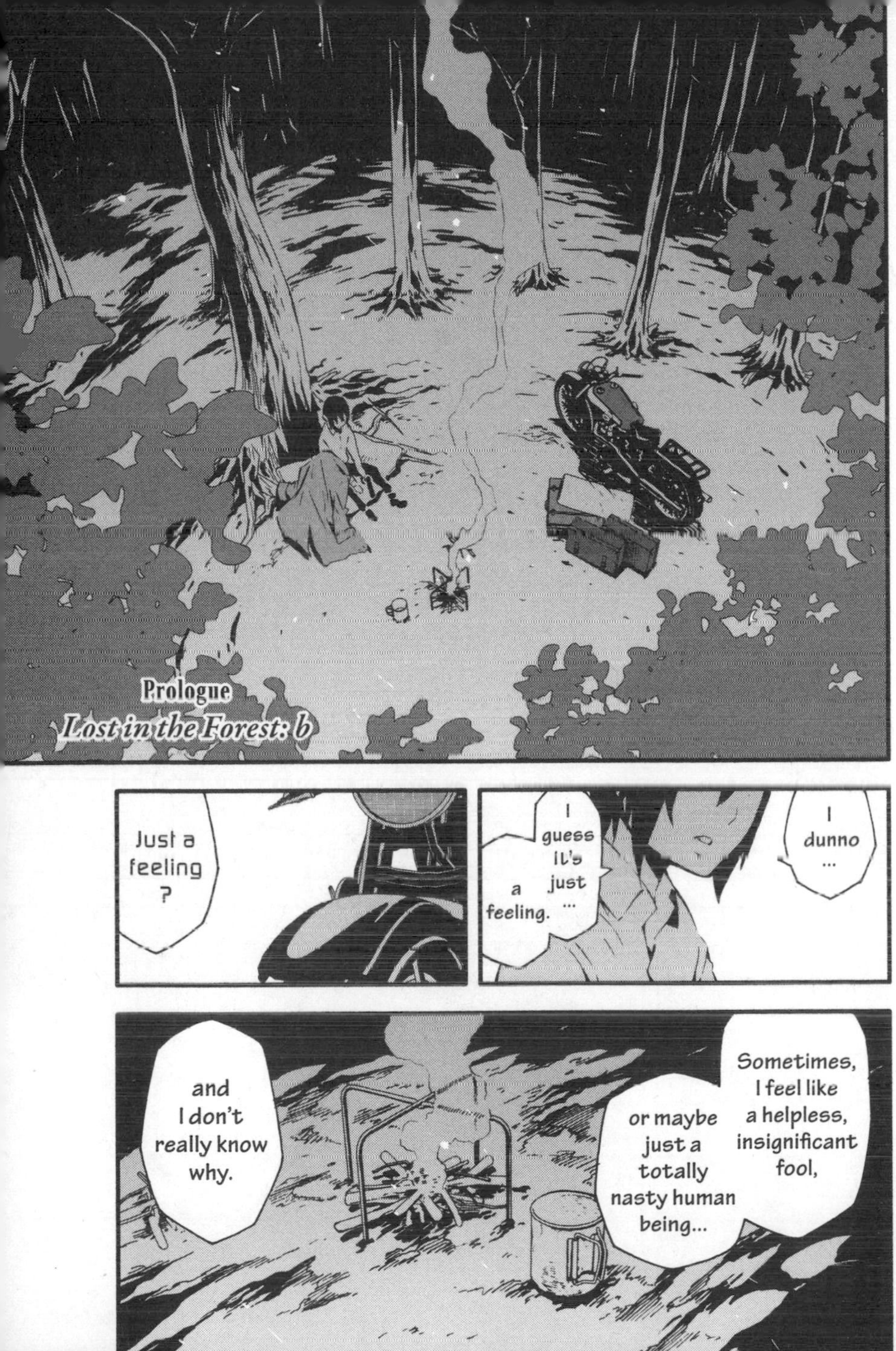
Prologue
Lost in the Forest: b
I dunno ...
I guess it's just ... a feeling.
Just a feeling ?
Sometimes, I feel like a helpless, insignificant fool,
or maybe just a totally nasty human being...
and I don't really know why.

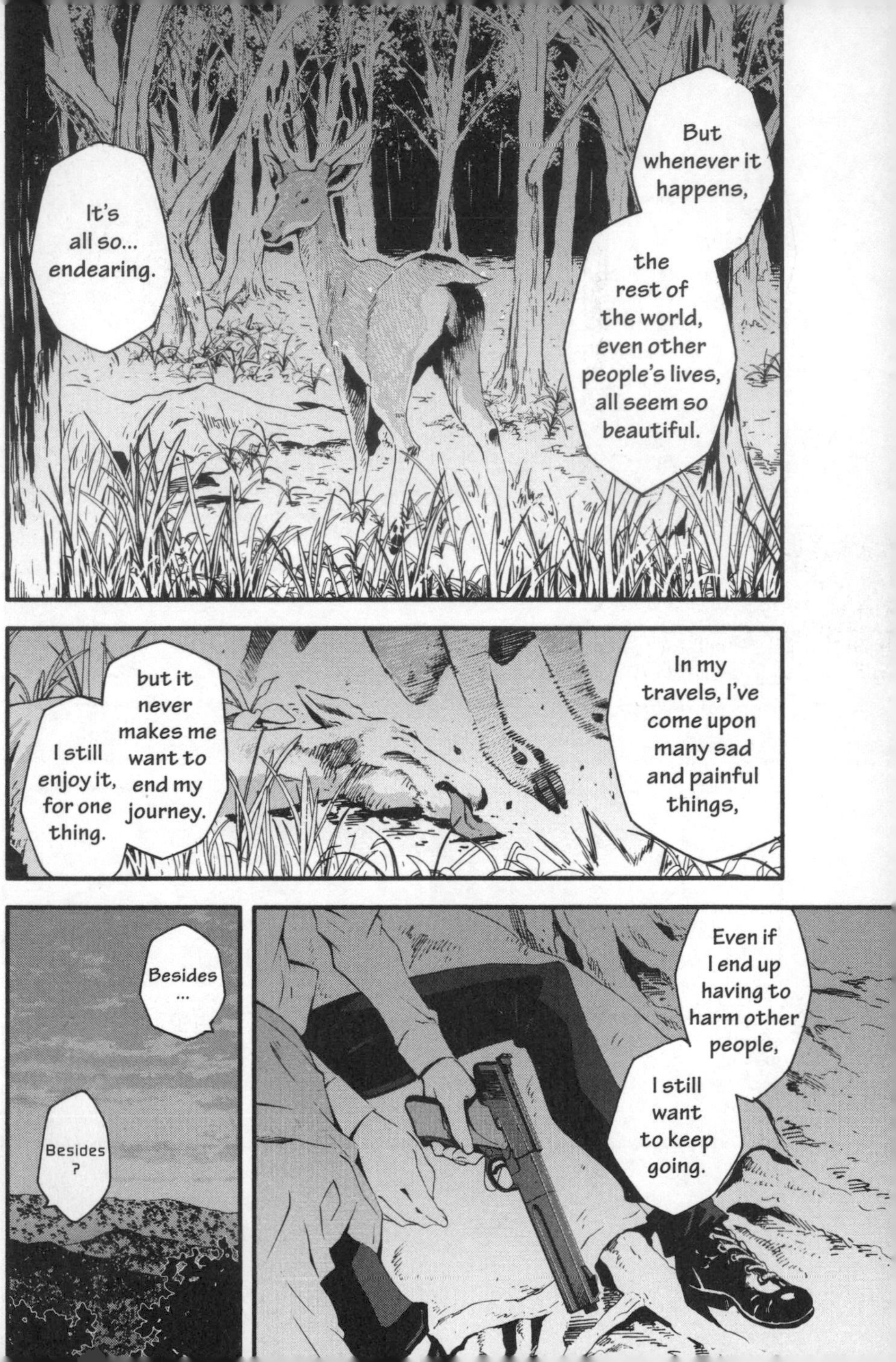
But whenever it happens,
the rest of the world, even other people's lives, all seem so beautiful.
It's all so... endearing.
In my travels, I've come upon many sad and painful things,
but it never makes me want to end my journey.
I still enjoy it, for one thing.
Even if I end up having to harm other people,
I still want to keep going.
Besides ...
Besides ?

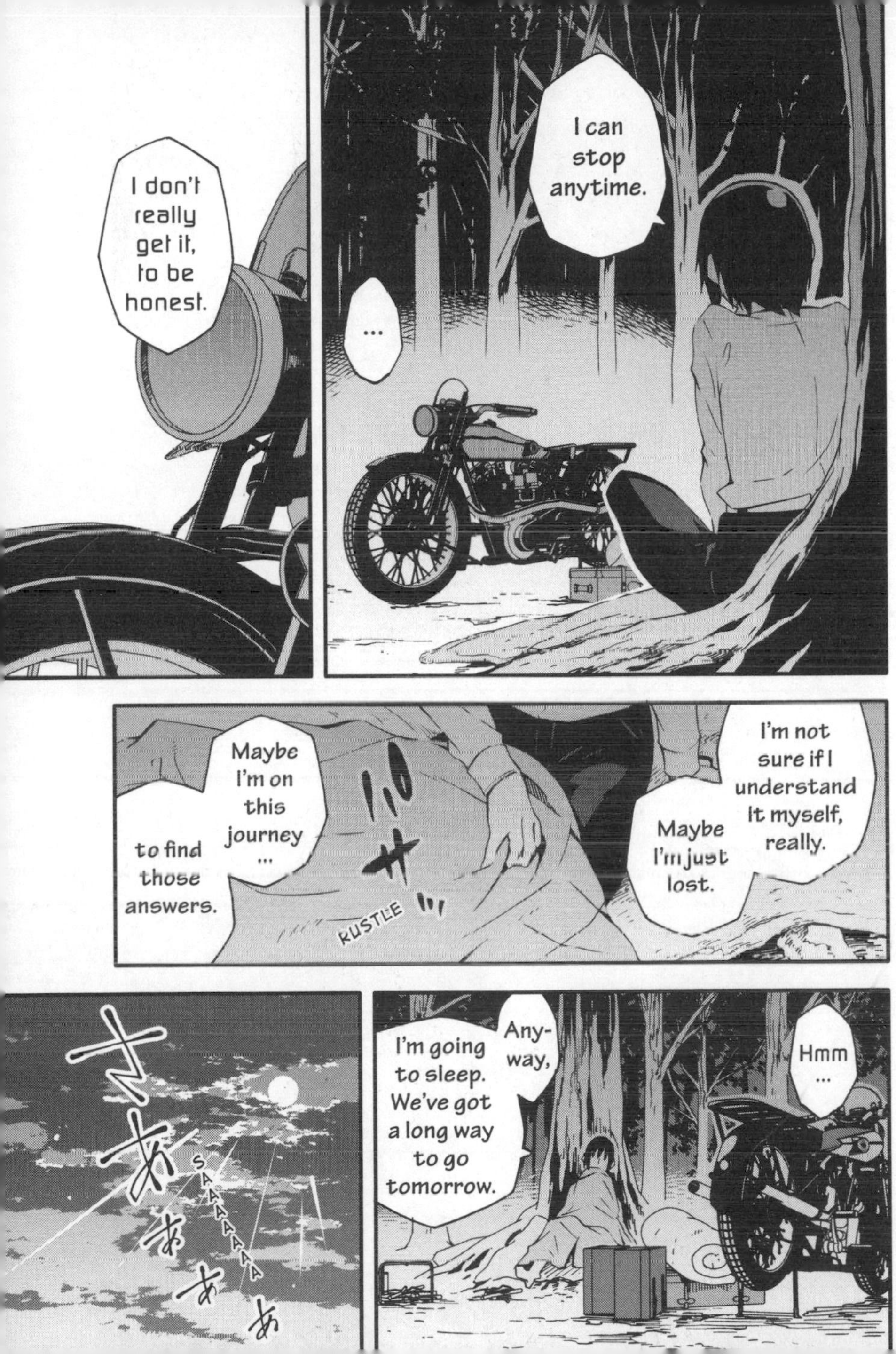
I can stop anytime.
...
I don't really get it, to be honest.
I'm not sure if I understand it myself, really.
Maybe I'm just lost.
Maybe I'm on this journey ...
to find those answers.
RUSTLE
Hmm ...
Any-way,
I'm going to sleep. We've got a long way to go tomorrow.
SAAAAAAA

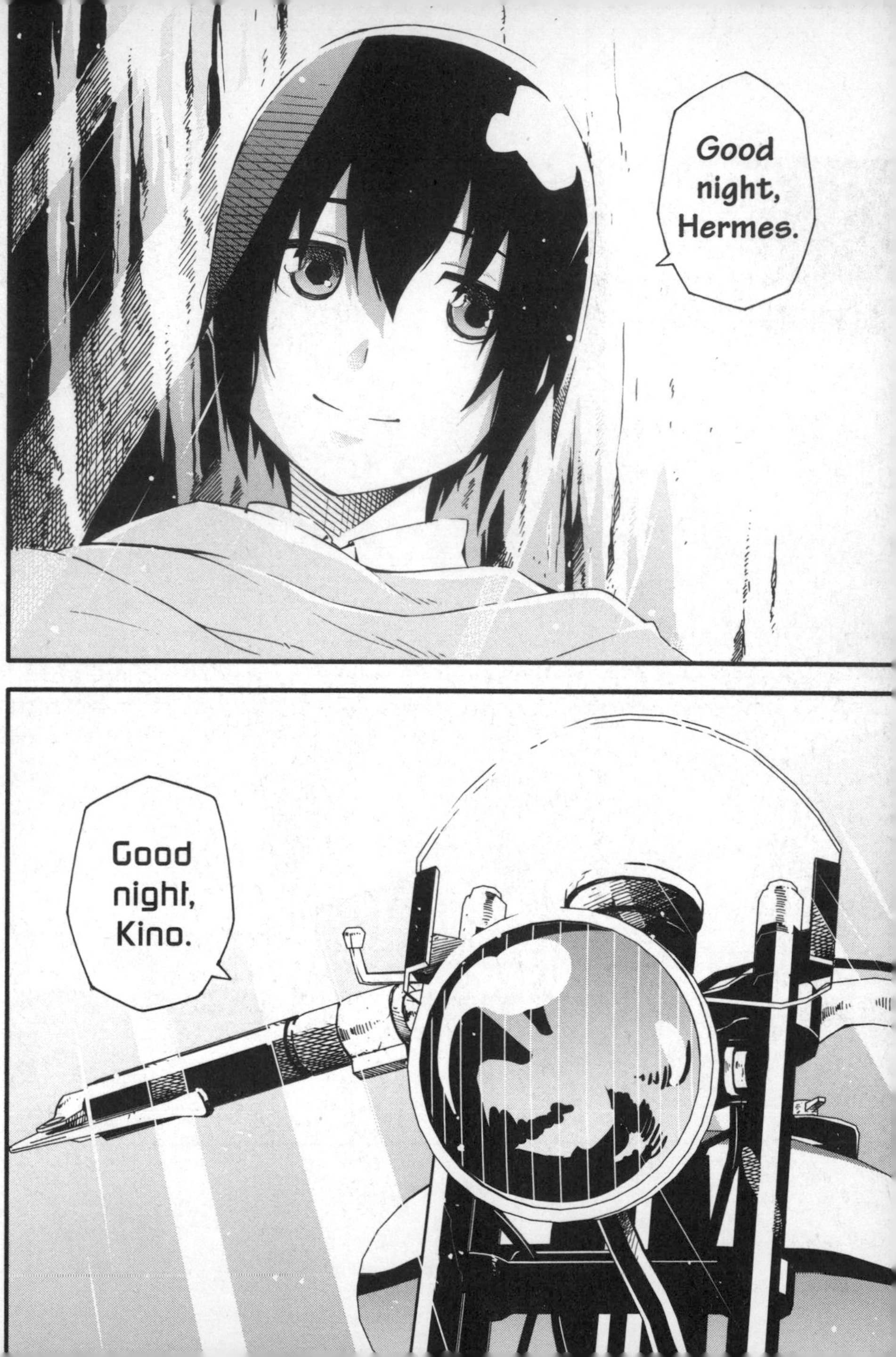
Good night, Hermes.
Good night, Kino.

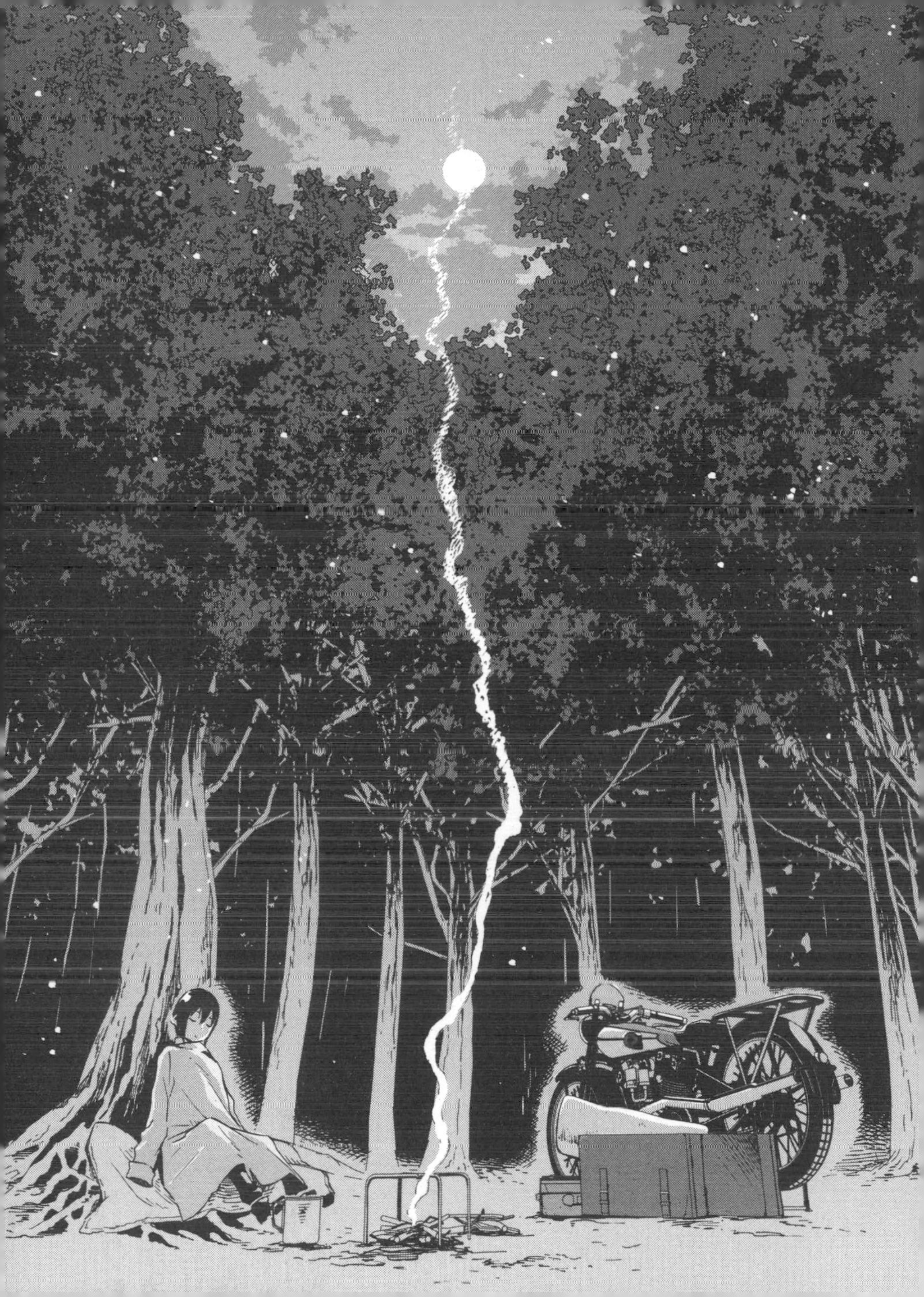

Kino's Journey

—→ The Beautiful World ←—

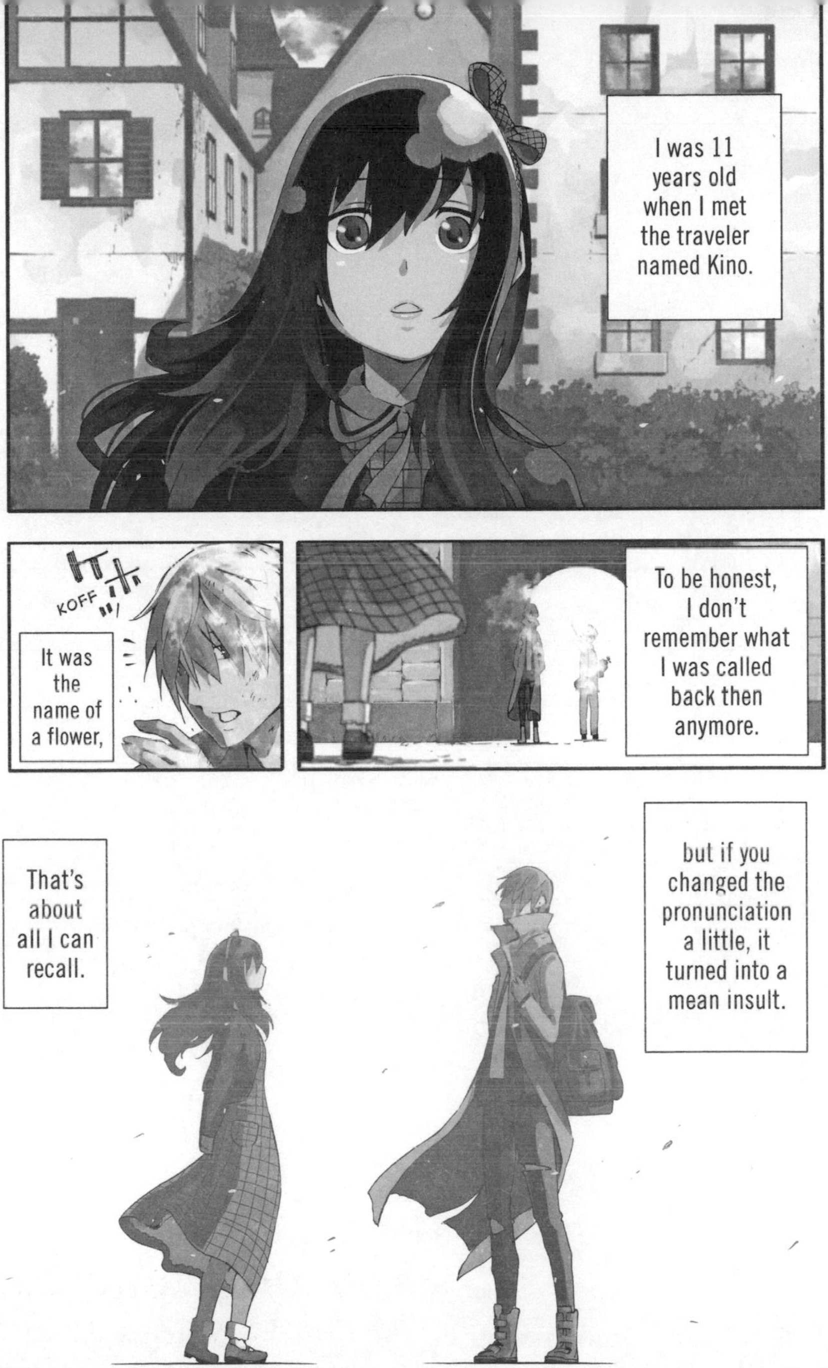
I was 11 years old when I met the traveler named Kino.
To be honest, I don't remember what I was called back then anymore.
KOFF
It was the name of a flower,
but if you changed the pronunciation a little, it turned into a mean insult.
That's about all I can recall.

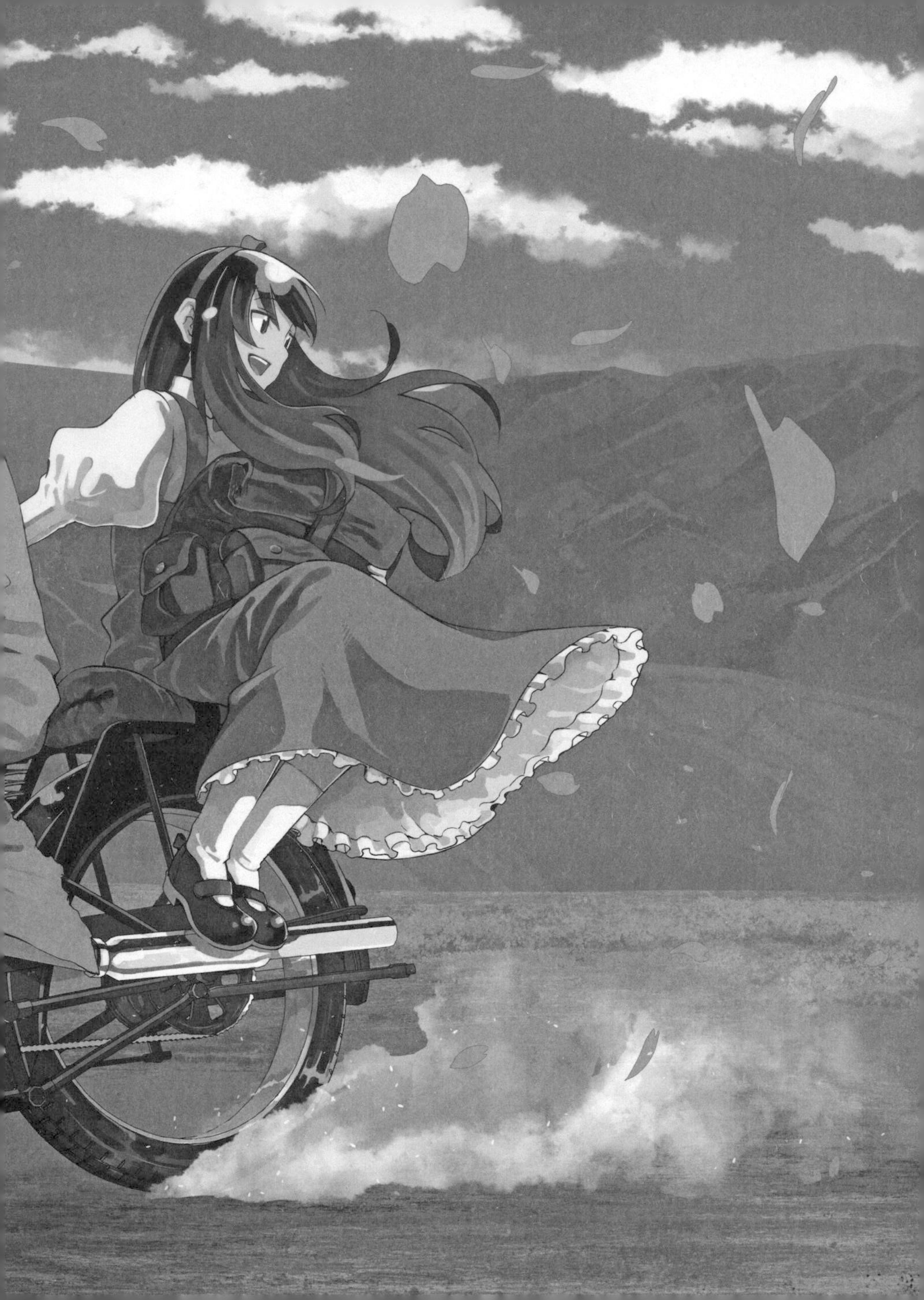

Chapter 1

The Land of Adults

-Natural Rights-

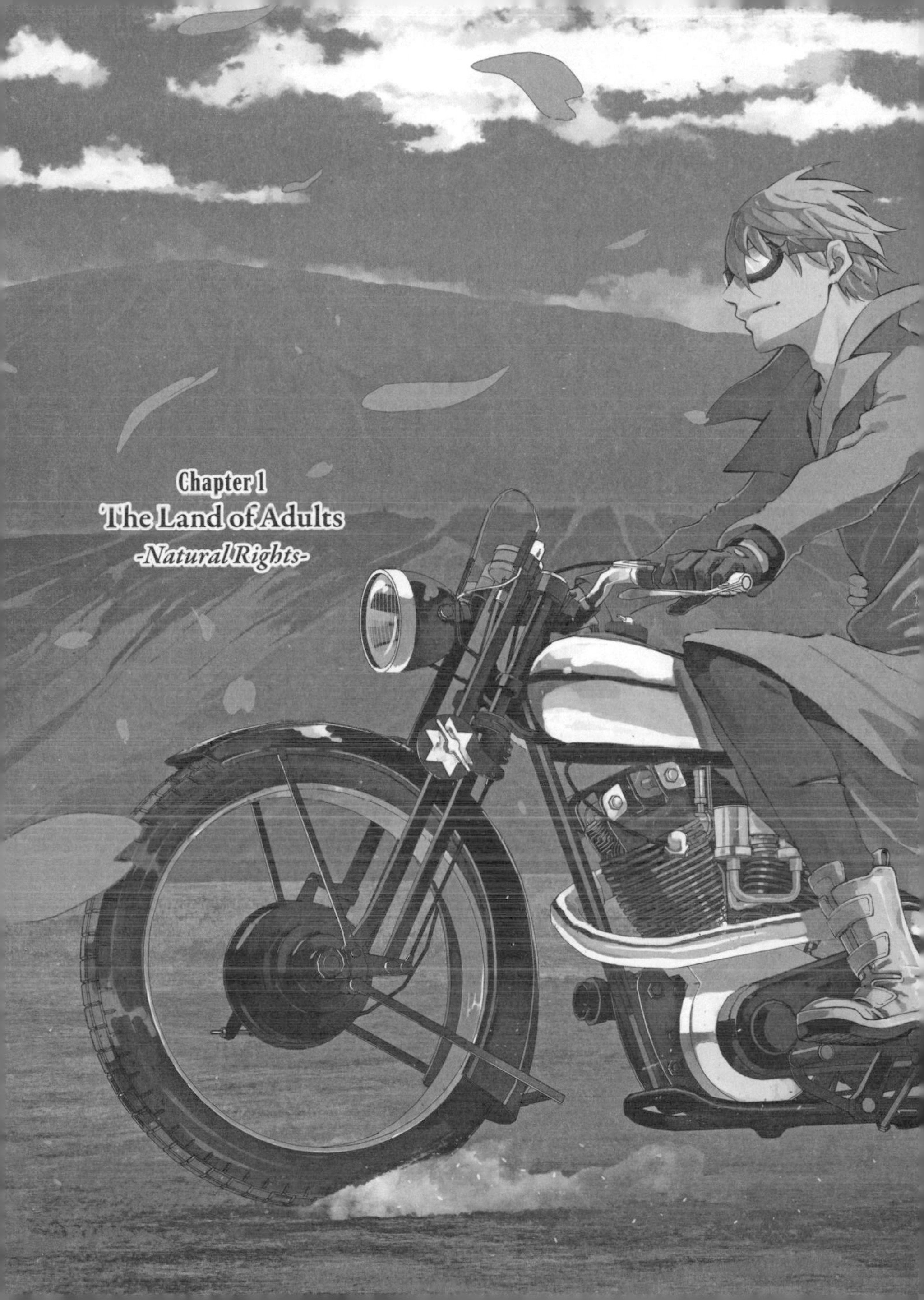

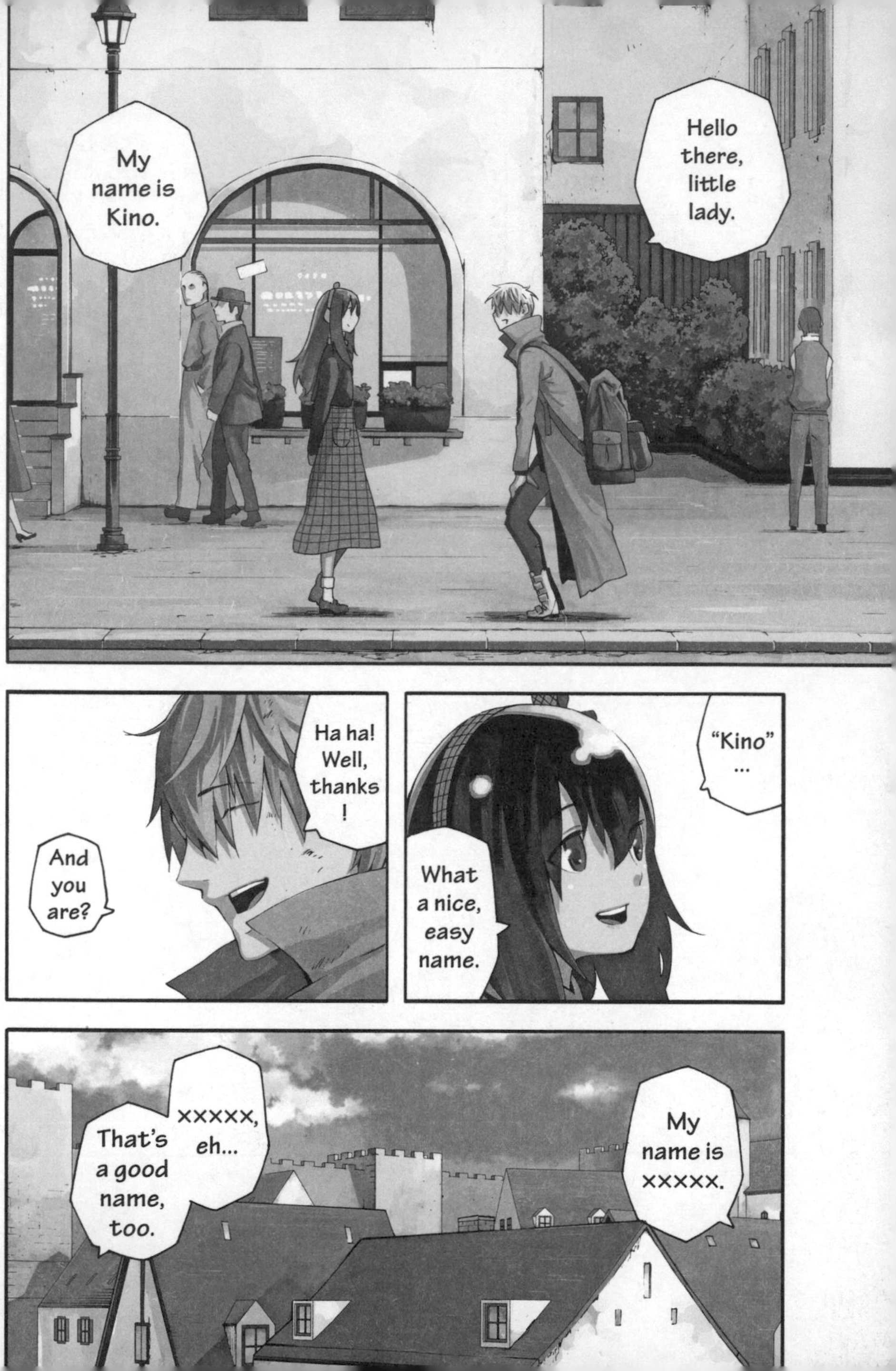
Hello there, little lady.
My name is Kino.
“Kino” ...
What a nice, easy name.
Ha ha! Well, thanks!
And you are?
My name is xxxxx.
xxxxx, eh...
That’s a good name, too.

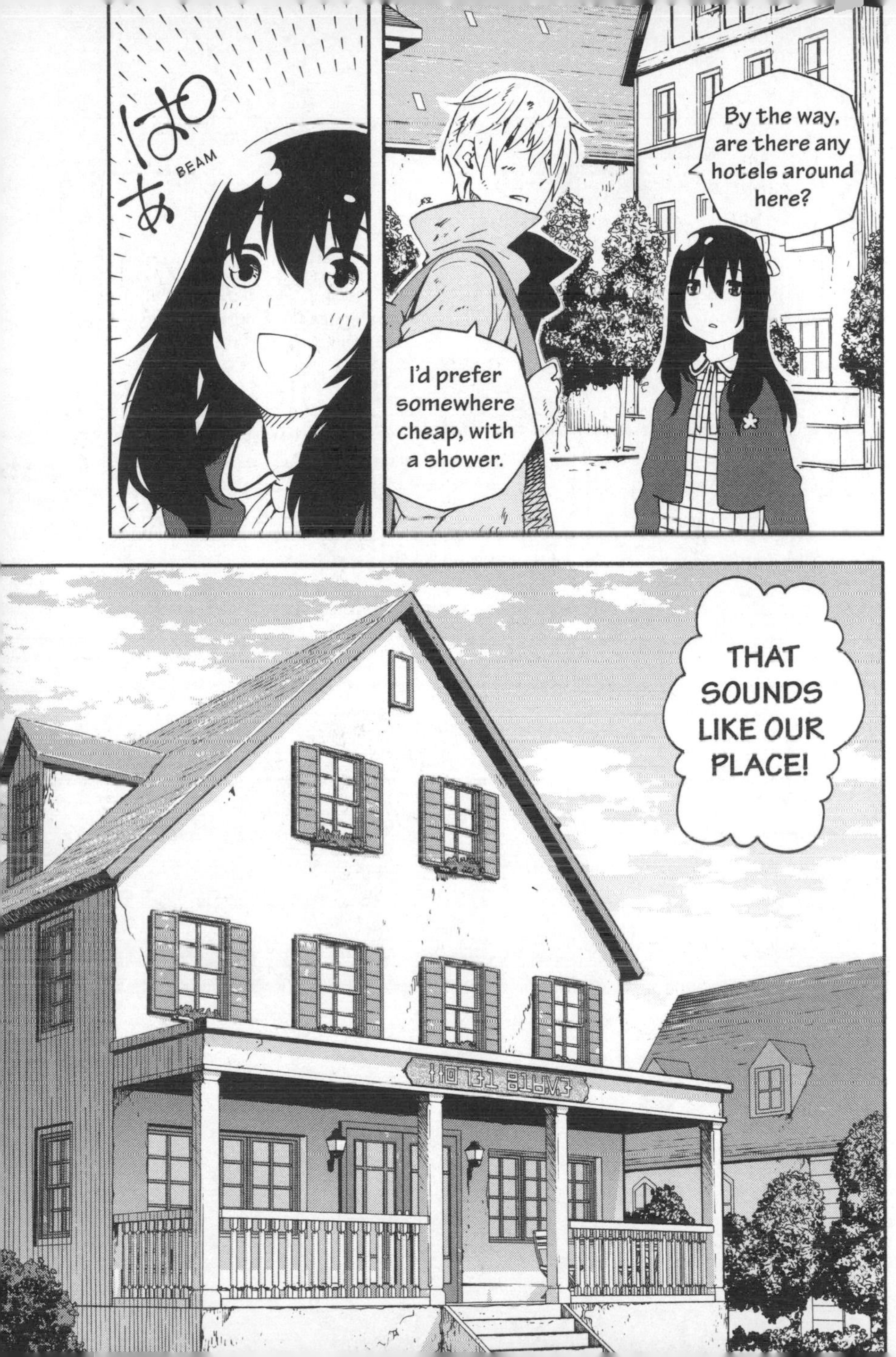
By the way, are there any hotels around here?
I'd prefer somewhere cheap, with a shower.
はぁ
BEAM
THAT SOUNDS LIKE OUR PLACE!

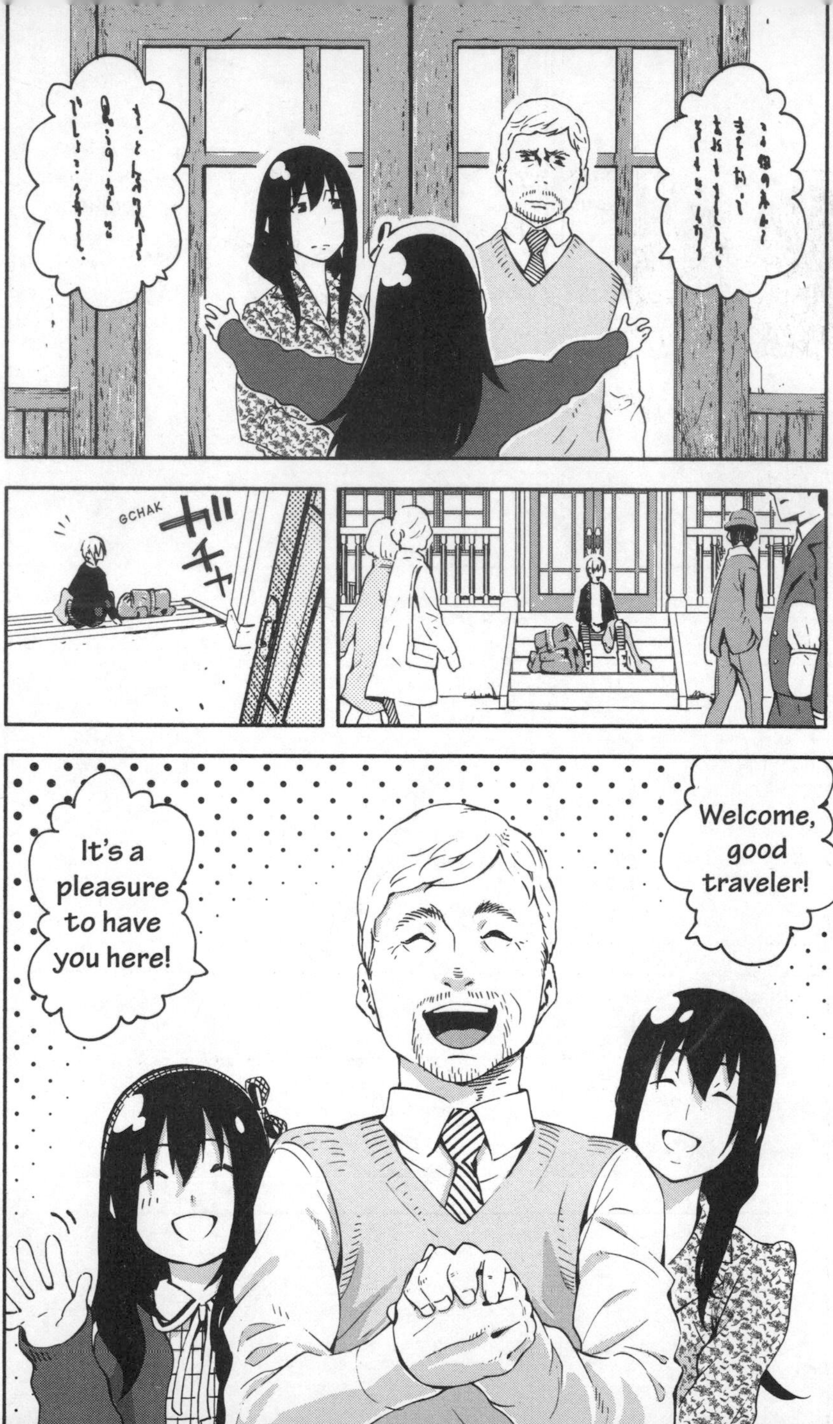
GCHAK
ガチャ
Welcome, good traveler!
It's a pleasure to have you here!

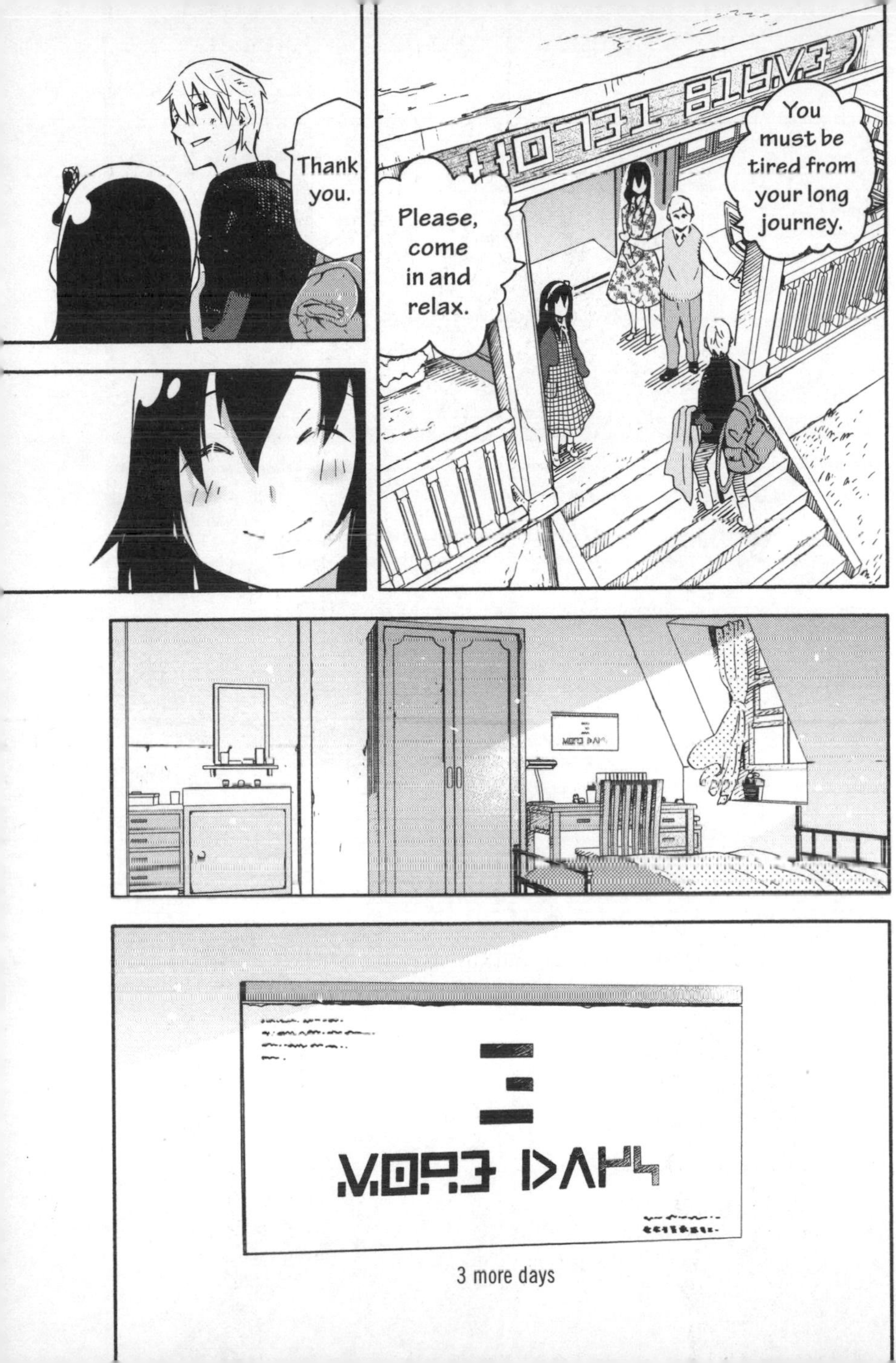
You must be tired from your long journey.
Please, come in and relax.
Thank you.
3 more days

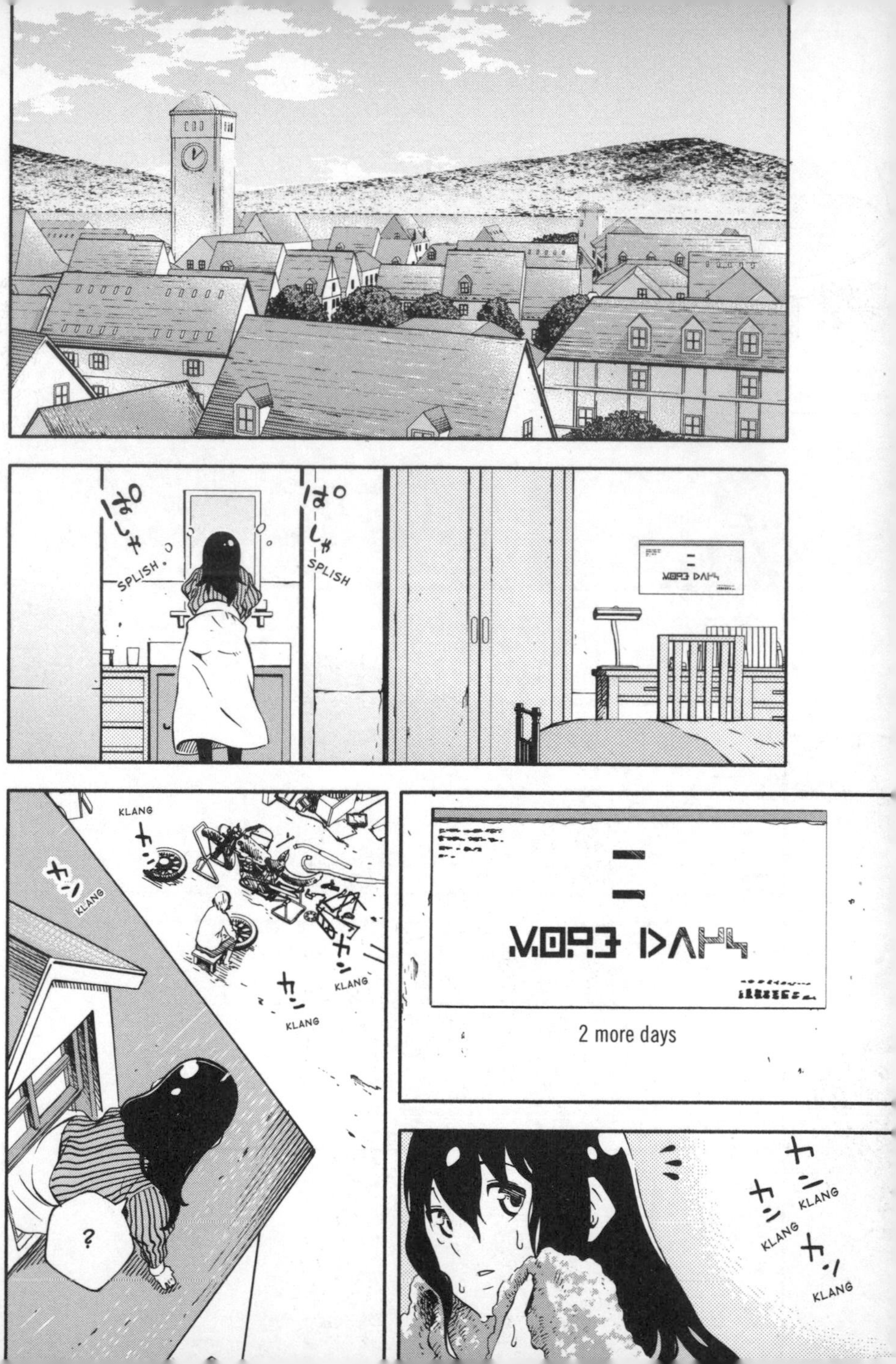
ぱしゃ
SPLISH
ぱしゃ
SPLISH
2 more days
カン
KLANG
カン
KLANG
カン
KLANG
カン
KLANG
カン
KLANG
カン
KLANG
カン
KLANG
?

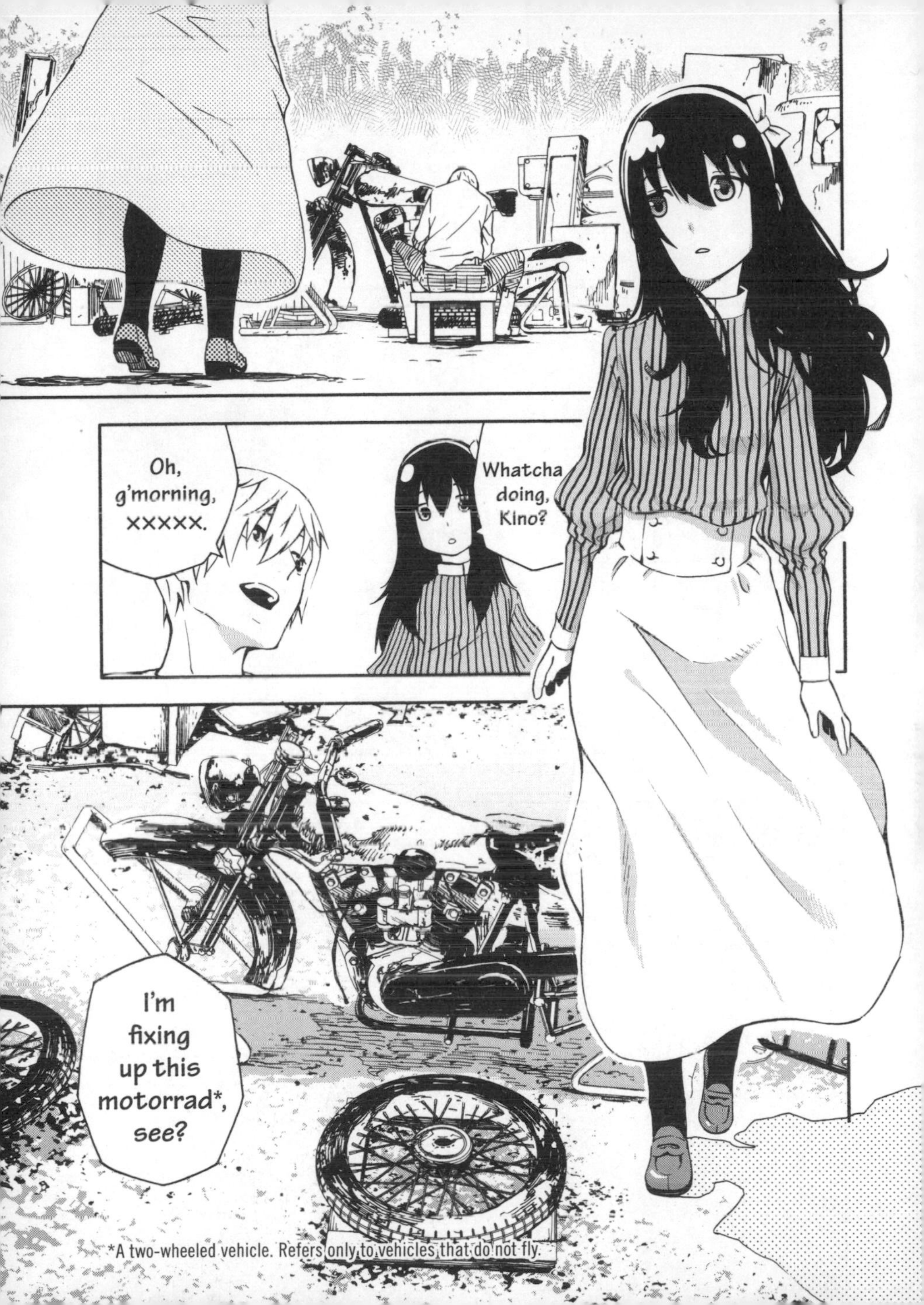
Whatcha doing, Kino?
Oh, g'morning, xxxxx.
I'm fixing up this motorrad*, see?

*A two-wheeled vehicle. Refers only to vehicles that do not fly.

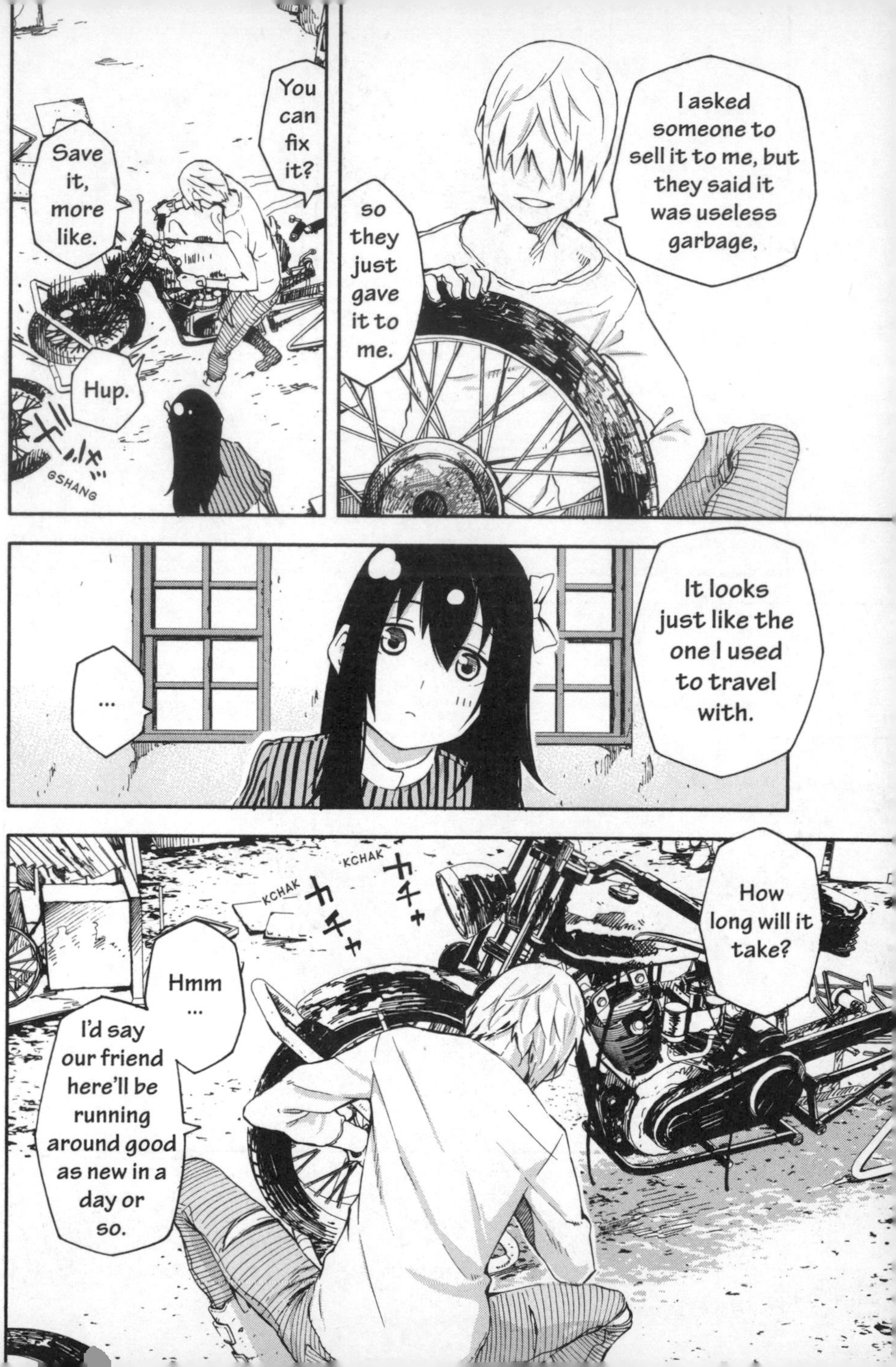
I asked someone to sell it to me, but they said it was useless garbage,
so they just gave it to me.
You can fix it?
Save it, more like.
Hup.
GSHANG
It looks just like the one I used to travel with.
...
How long will it take?
KCHAK
KCHAK
Hmm...
I'd say our friend here'll be running around good as new in a day or so.

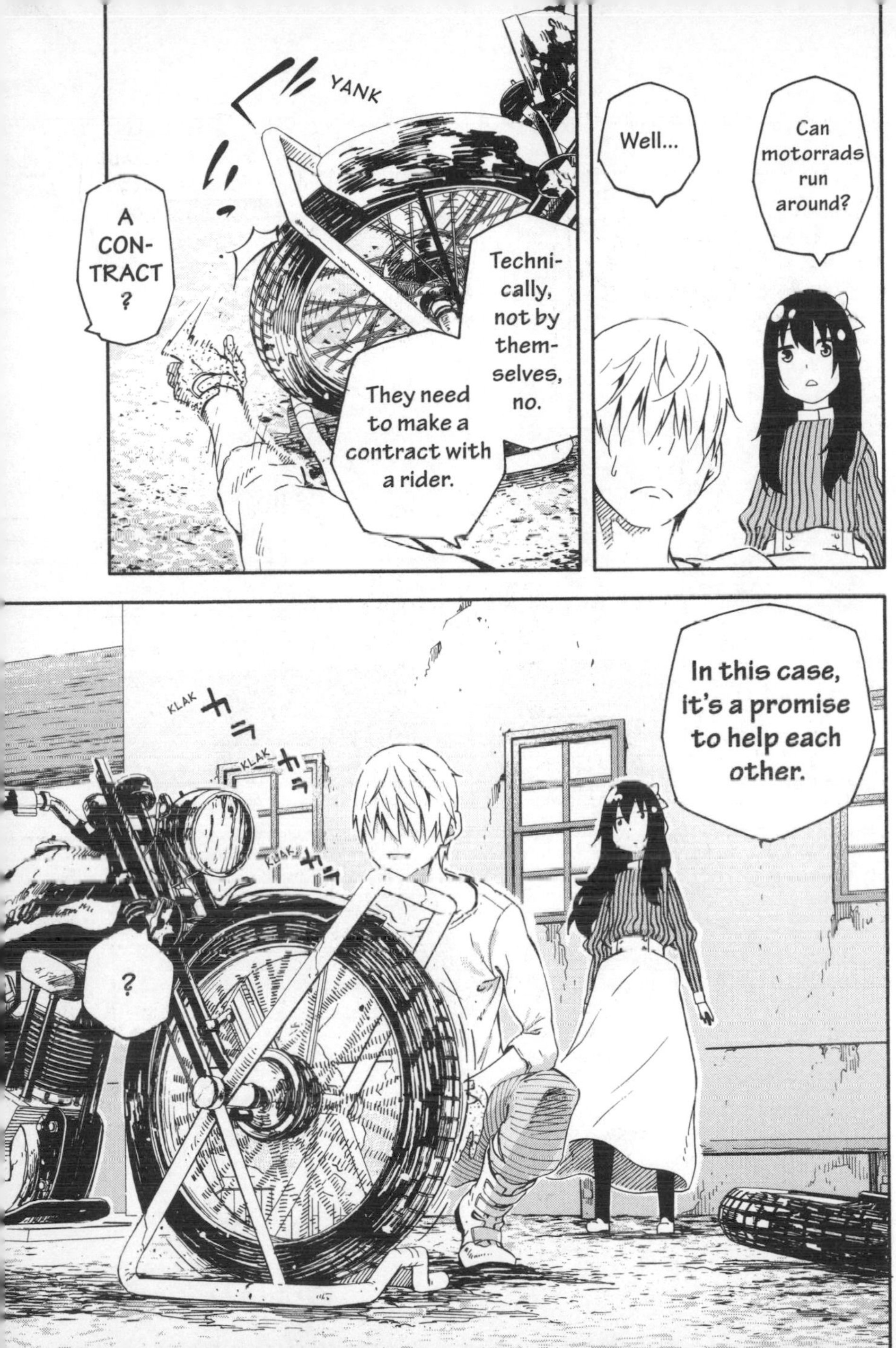
Can motorrads run around?
Well...
YANK
Technically, not by themselves, no.
They need to make a contract with a rider.
A CONTRACT?
In this case, it's a promise to help each other.
KLAK
KLAK
KLAK
?

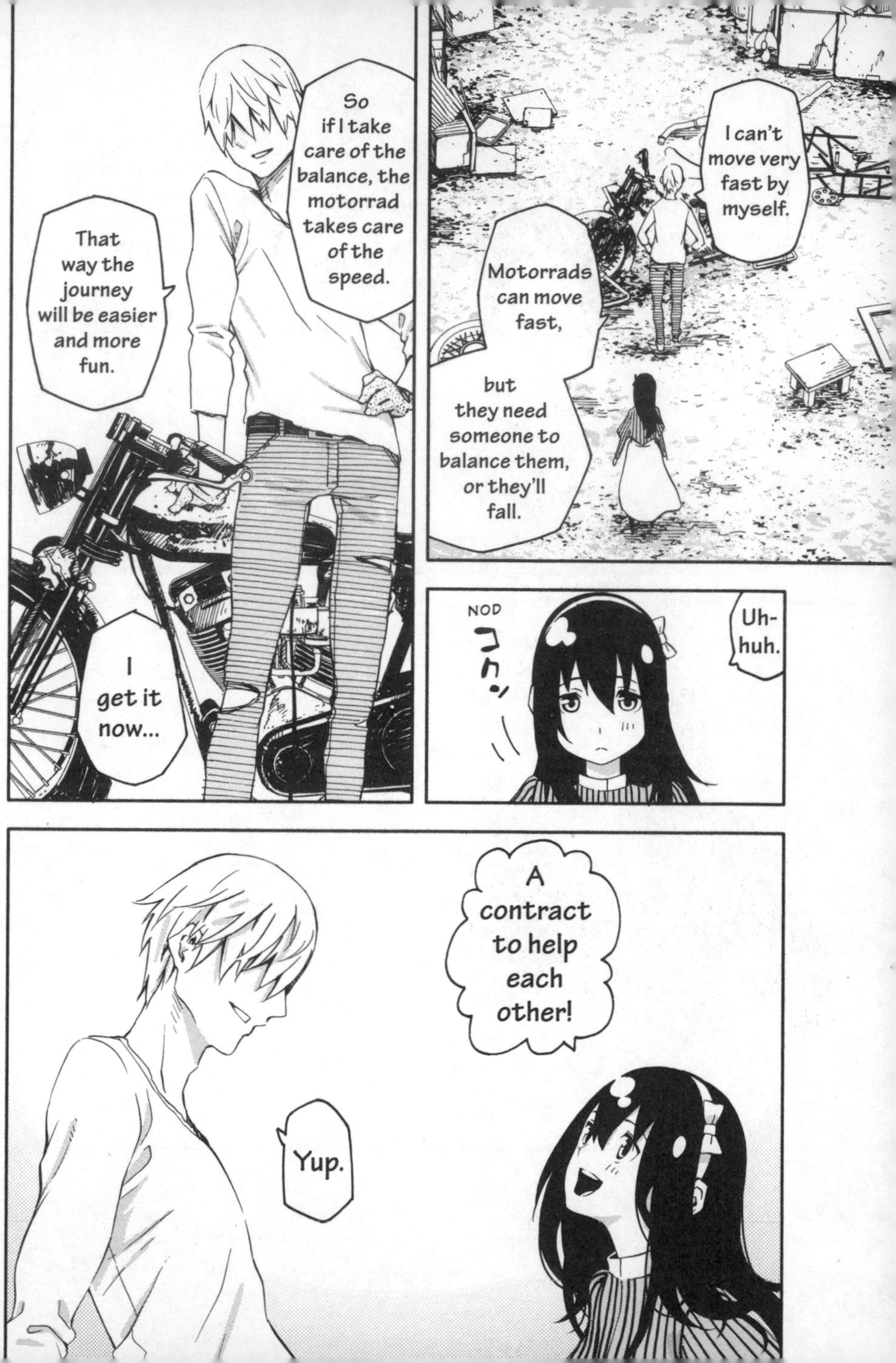
I can't move very fast by myself.
Motorrads can move fast,
but they need someone to balance them, or they'll fall.
NOD
コクッ
Uh-huh.
So if I take care of the balance, the motorrad takes care of the speed.
That way the journey will be easier and more fun.
I get it now...
A contract to help each other!
Yup.

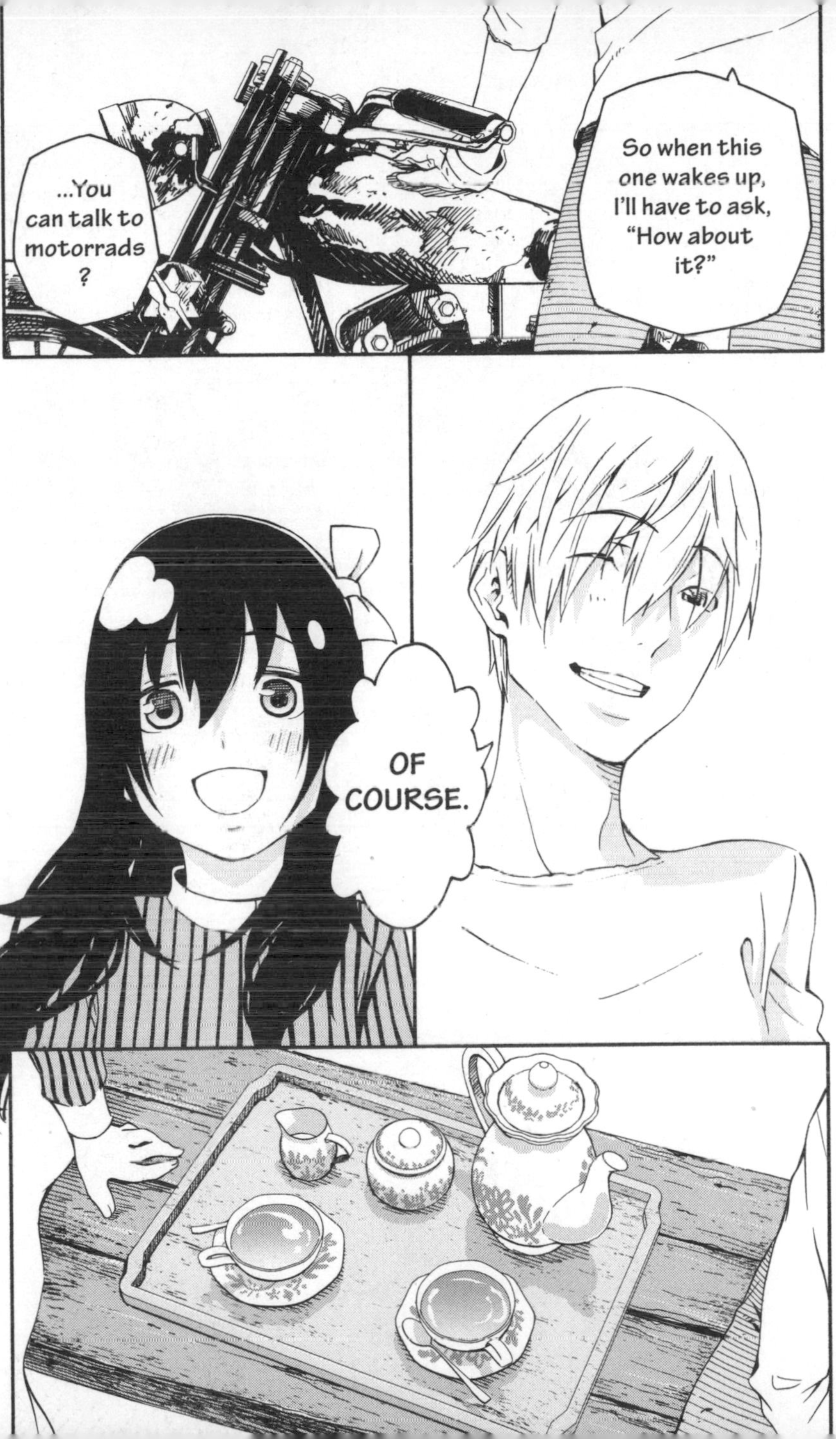
So when this one wakes up, I'll have to ask, "How about it?"
...You can talk to motorrads ?
OF COURSE.

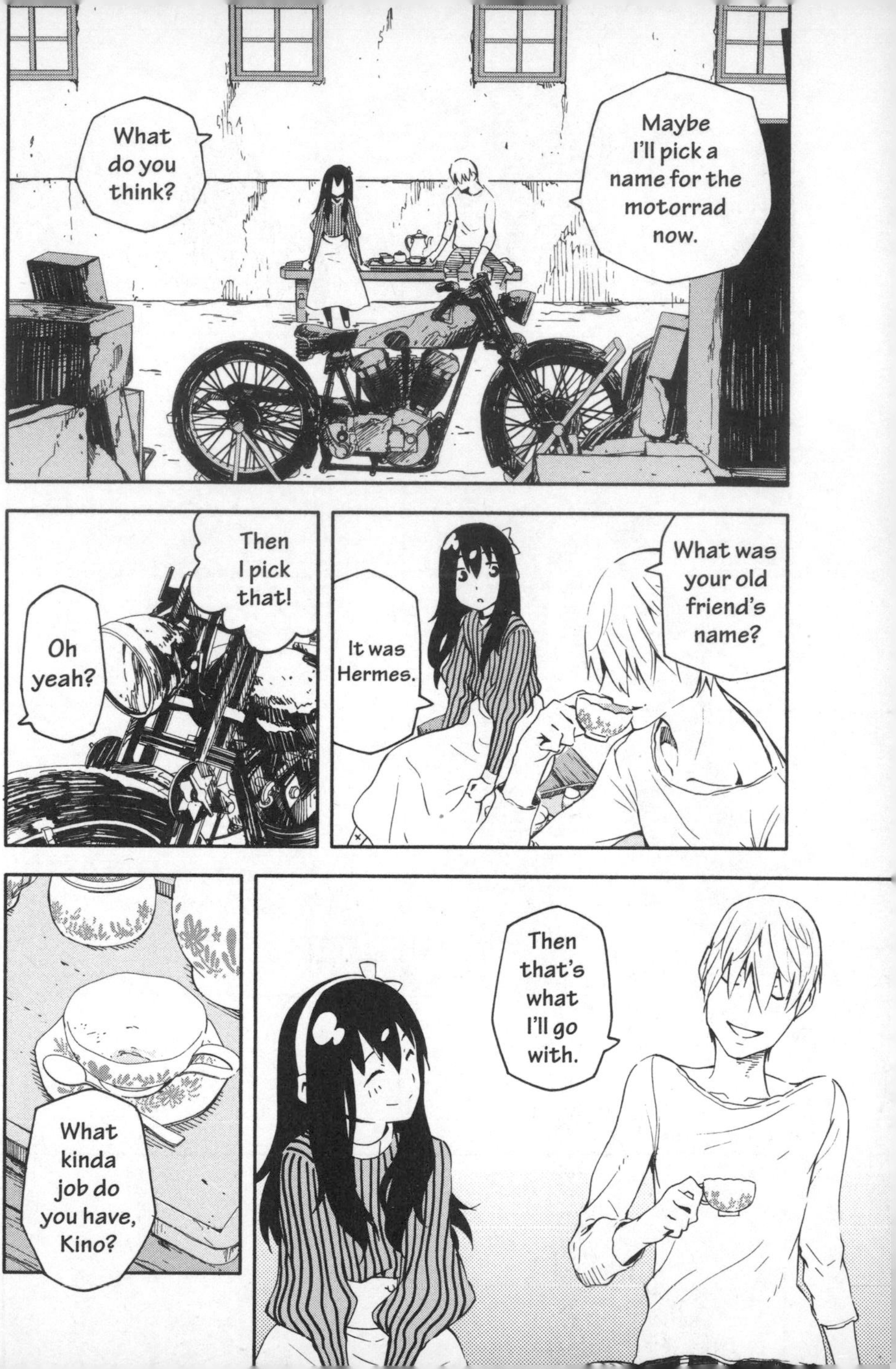
Maybe I'll pick a name for the motorrad now.
What do you think?
What was your old friend's name?
It was Hermes.
Then I pick that!
Oh yeah?
Then that's what I'll go with.
What kinda job do you have, Kino?

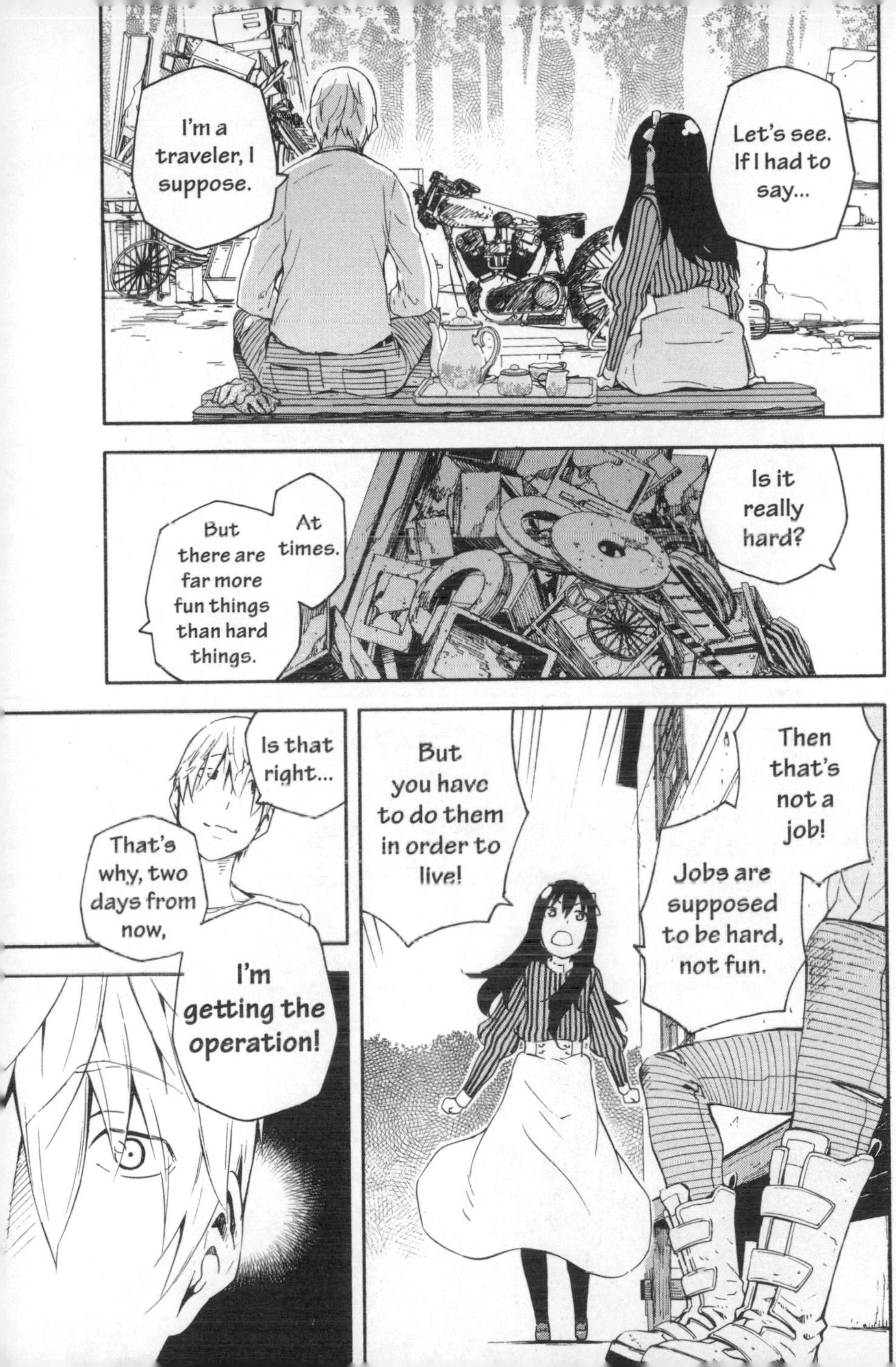
Let's see. If I had to say...
I'm a traveler, I suppose.
Is it really hard?
At times.
But there are far more fun things than hard things.
Then that's not a job!
Jobs are supposed to be hard, not fun.
But you have to do them in order to live!
Is that right...
That's why, two days from now,
I'm getting the operation!

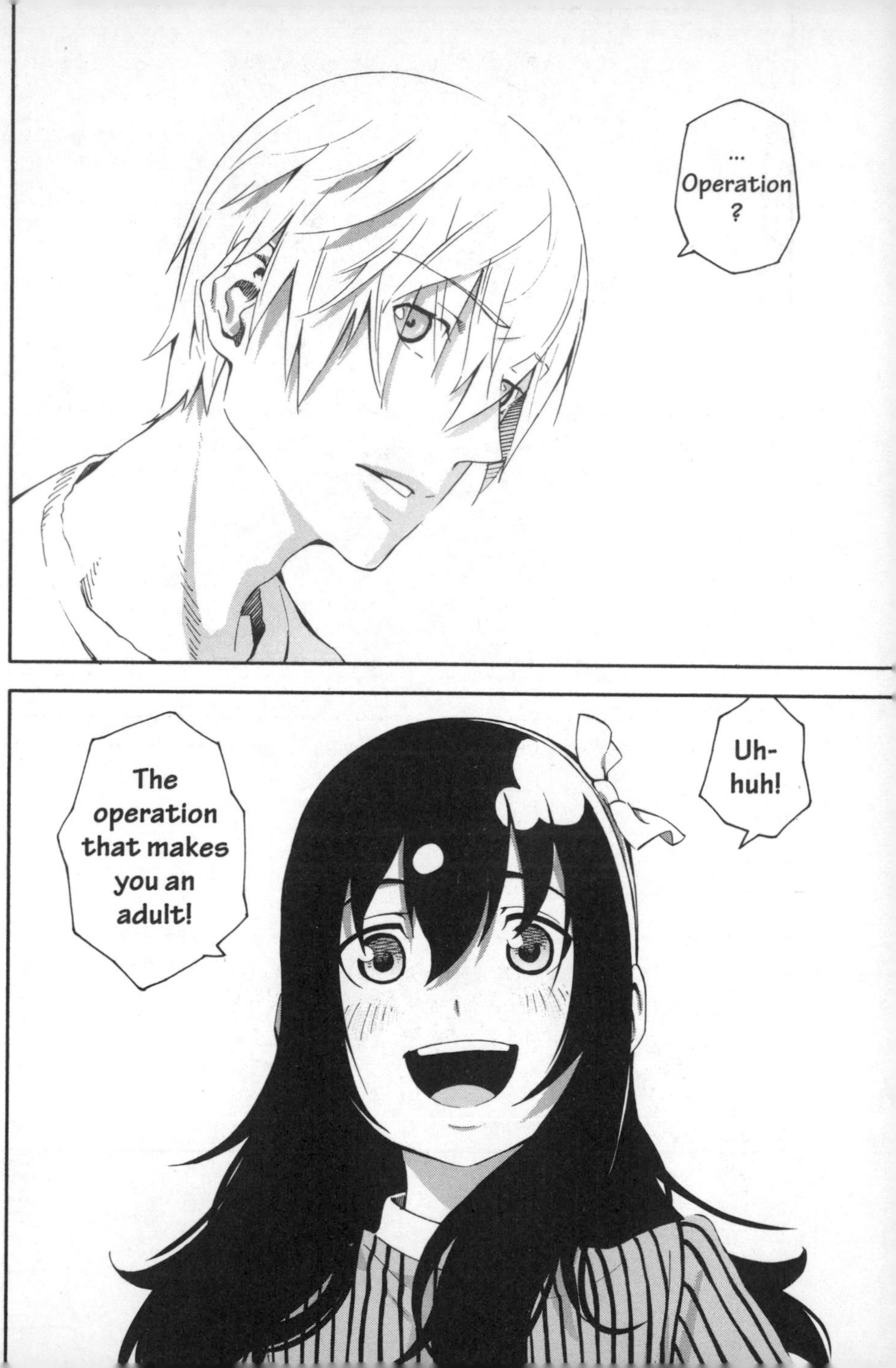
... Operation?
Uh-huh!
The operation that makes you an adult!

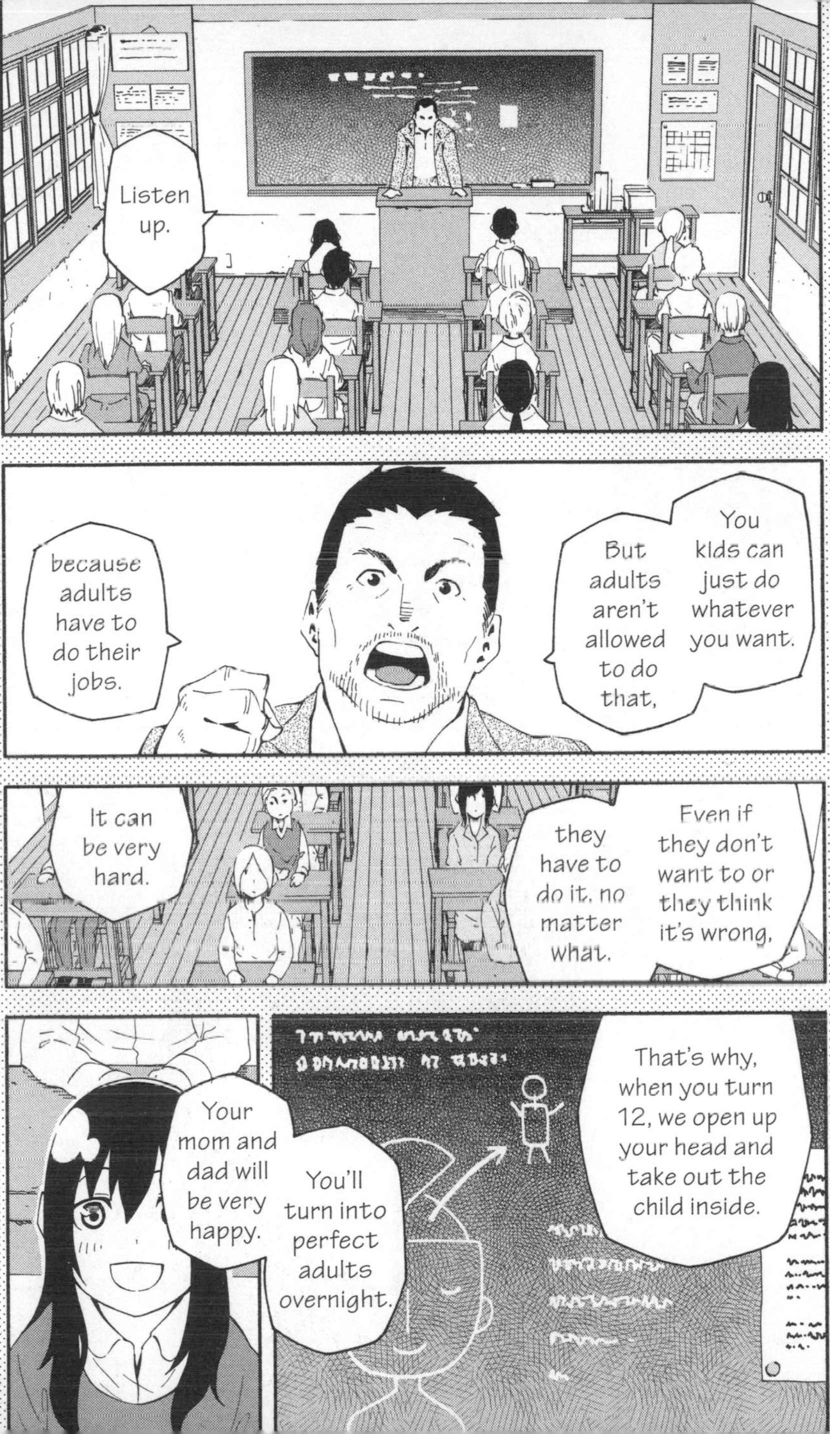
Listen up.
You kids can just do whatever you want.
But adults aren't allowed to do that,
because adults have to do their jobs.
Even if they don't want to or they think it's wrong,
they have to do it, no matter what.
It can be very hard.
That's why, when you turn 12, we open up your head and take out the child inside.
You'll turn into perfect adults overnight.
Your mom and dad will be very happy.

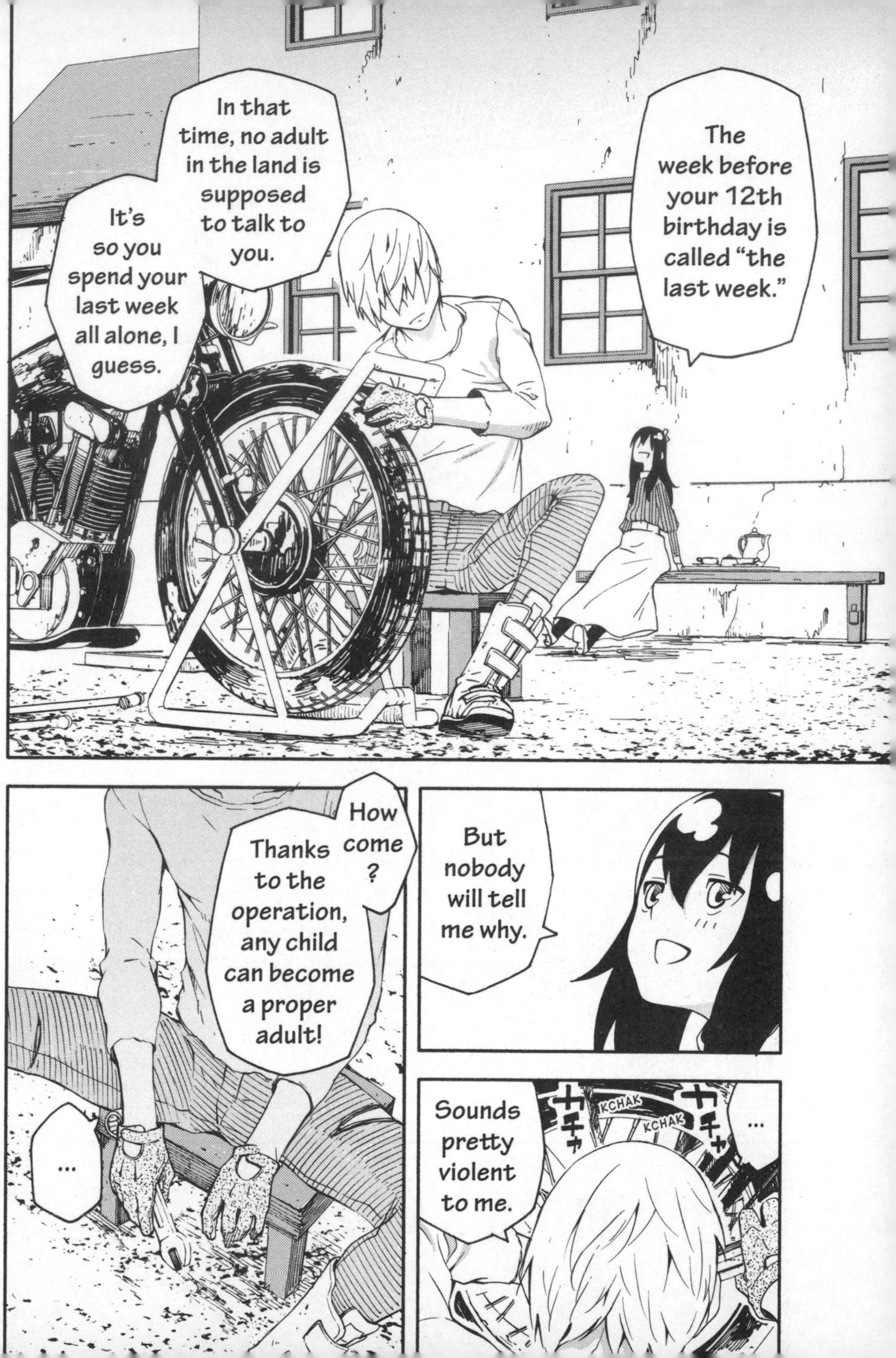
The week before your 12th birthday is called "the last week."
In that time, no adult in the land is supposed to talk to you.
It's so you spend your last week all alone, I guess.
But nobody will tell me why.
How come?
Thanks to the operation, any child can become a proper adult!
...
...
カチャ
KCHAK
カチャ
KCHAK
Sounds pretty violent to me.

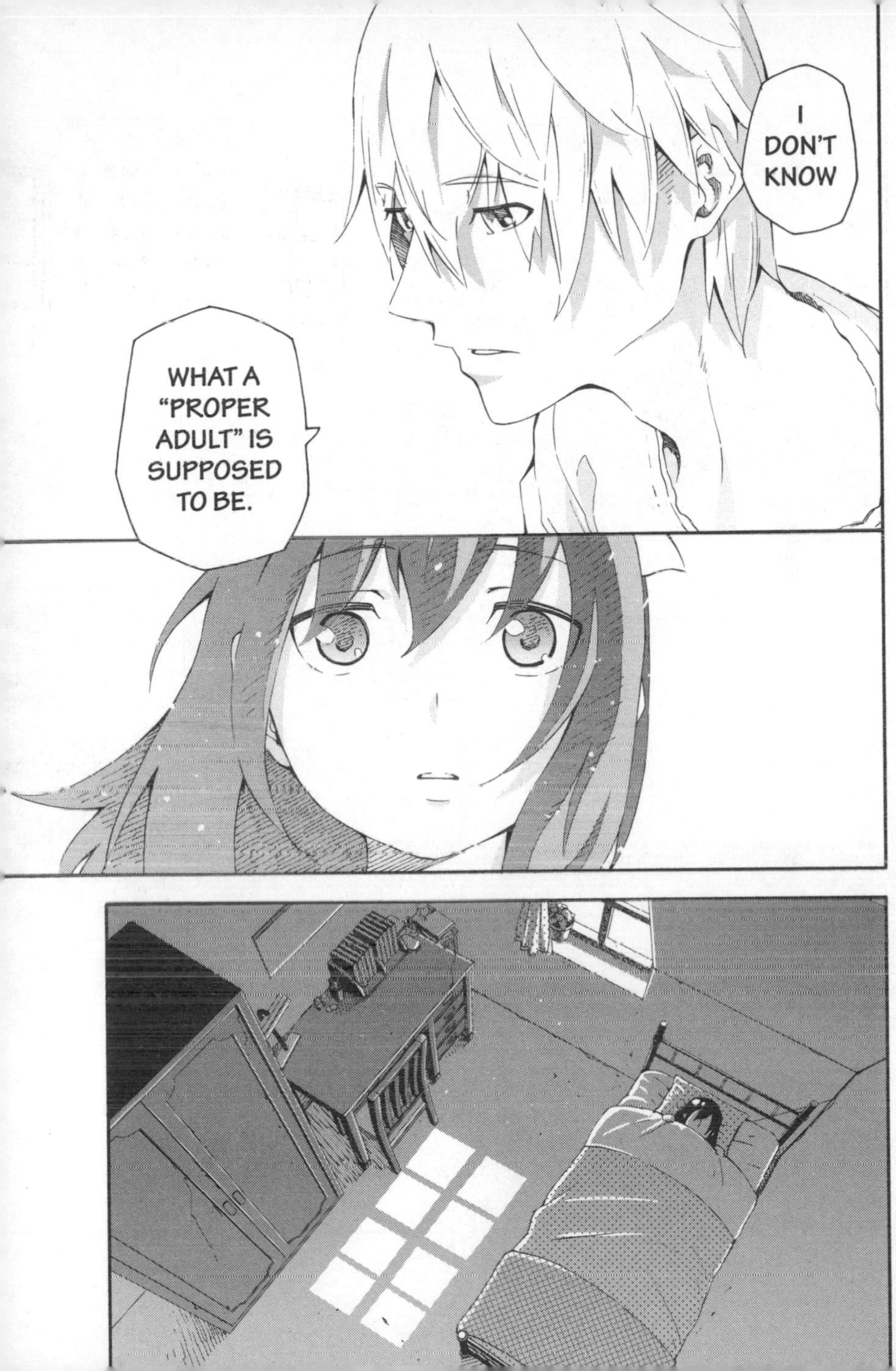
I DON'T KNOW
WHAT A "PROPER ADULT" IS SUPPOSED TO BE.

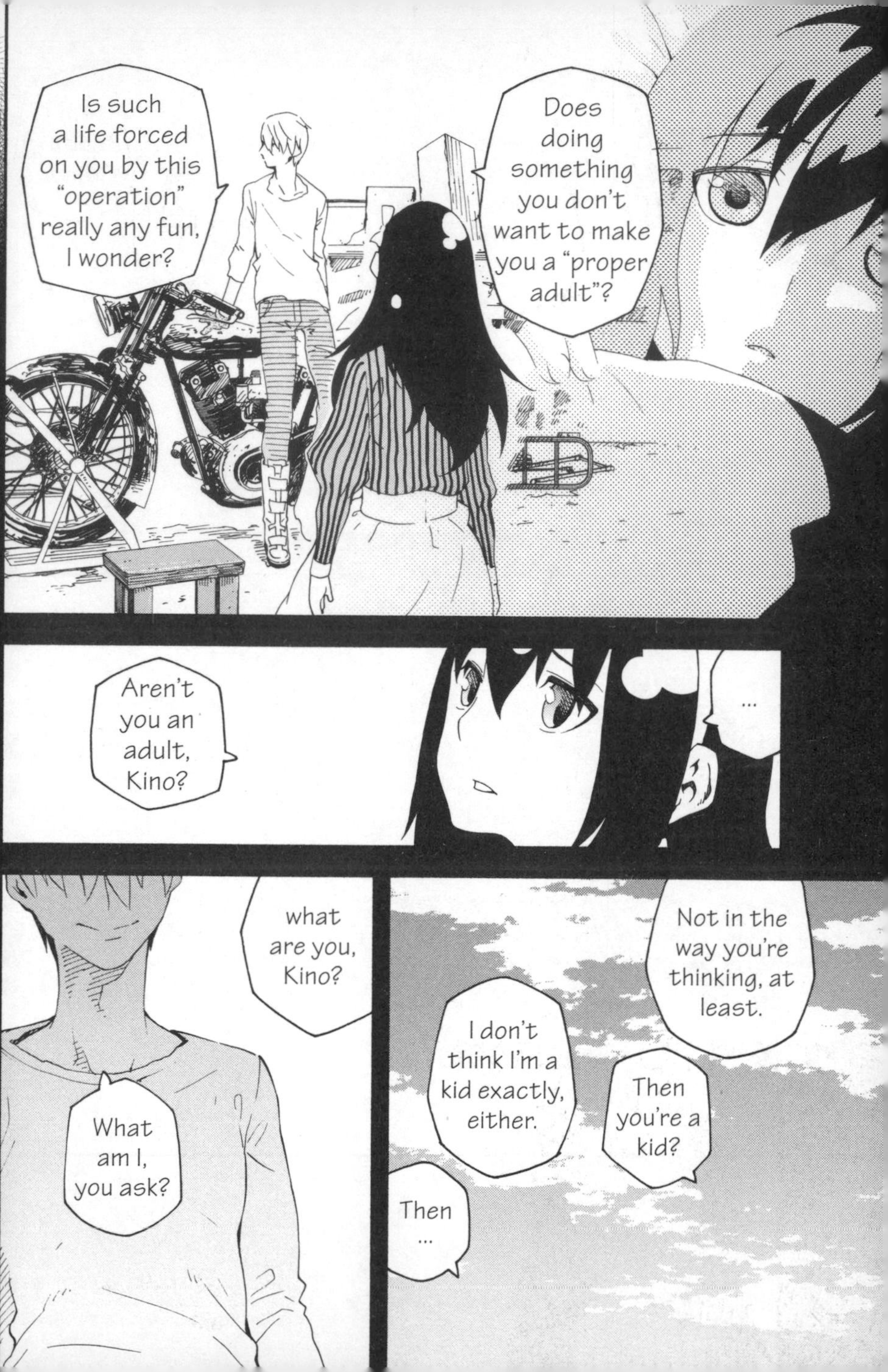
Does doing something you don't want to make you a "proper adult"?
Is such a life forced on you by this "operation" really any fun, I wonder?
...
Aren't you an adult, Kino?
Not in the way you're thinking, at least.
Then you're a kid?
I don't think I'm a kid exactly, either.
Then ...
what are you, Kino?
What am I, you ask?

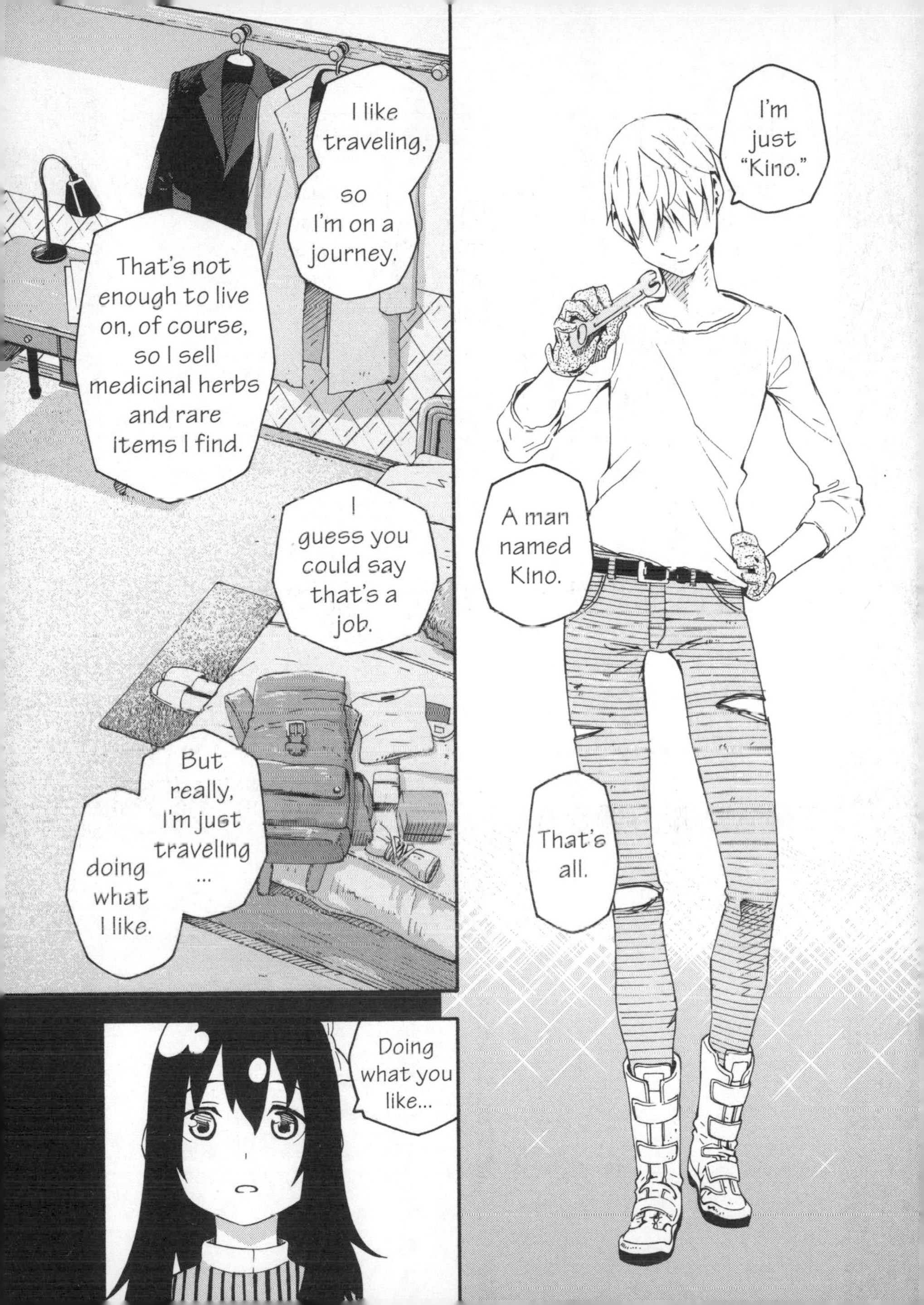
I'm just "Kino."
A man named Kino.
That's all.
I like traveling,
so I'm on a journey.
That's not enough to live on, of course, so I sell medicinal herbs and rare items I find.
I guess you could say that's a job.
But really, I'm just traveling...
doing what I like.
Doing what you like...

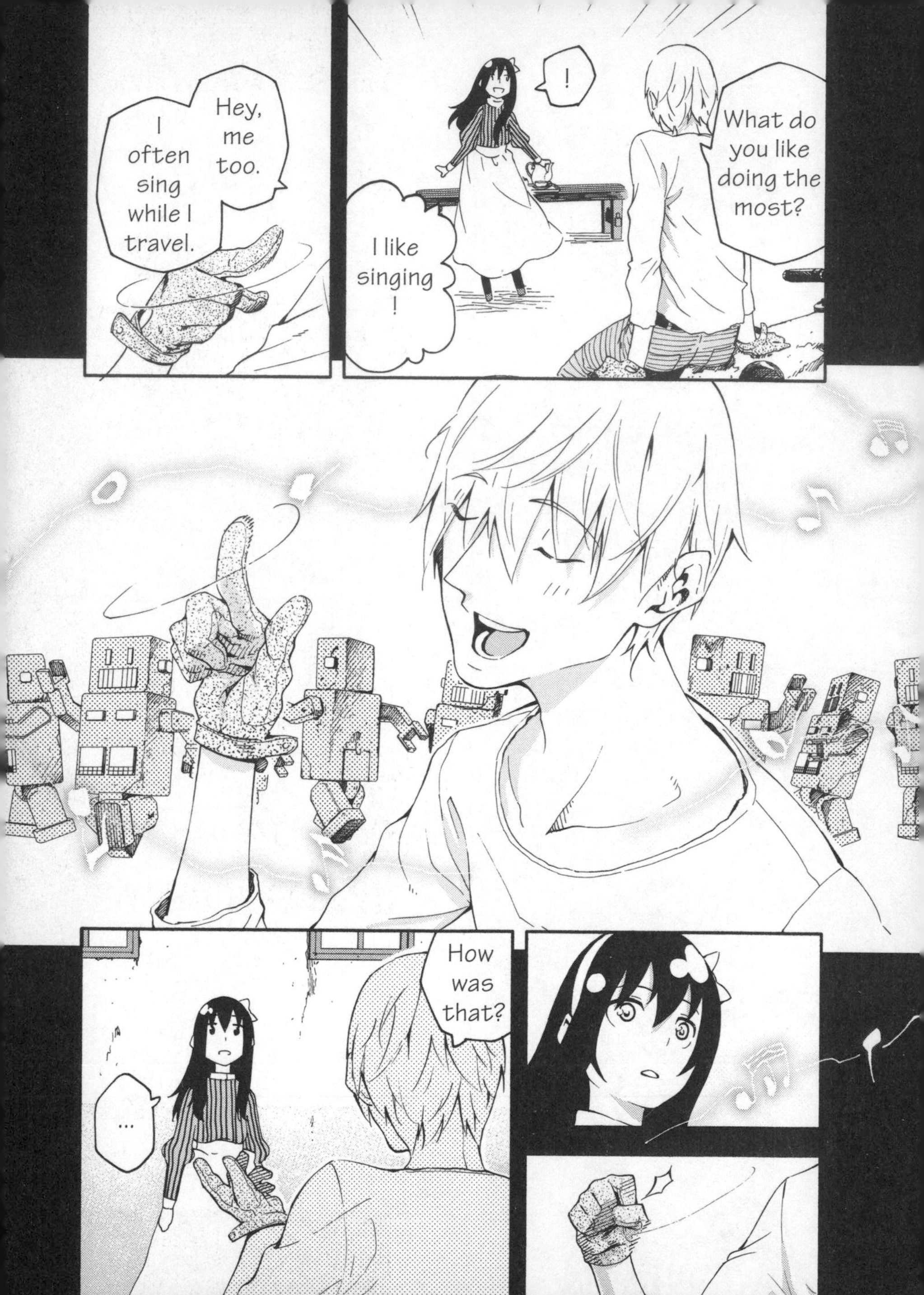
What do you like doing the most?
!
I like singing!
Hey, me too.
I often sing while I travel.
How was that?
...

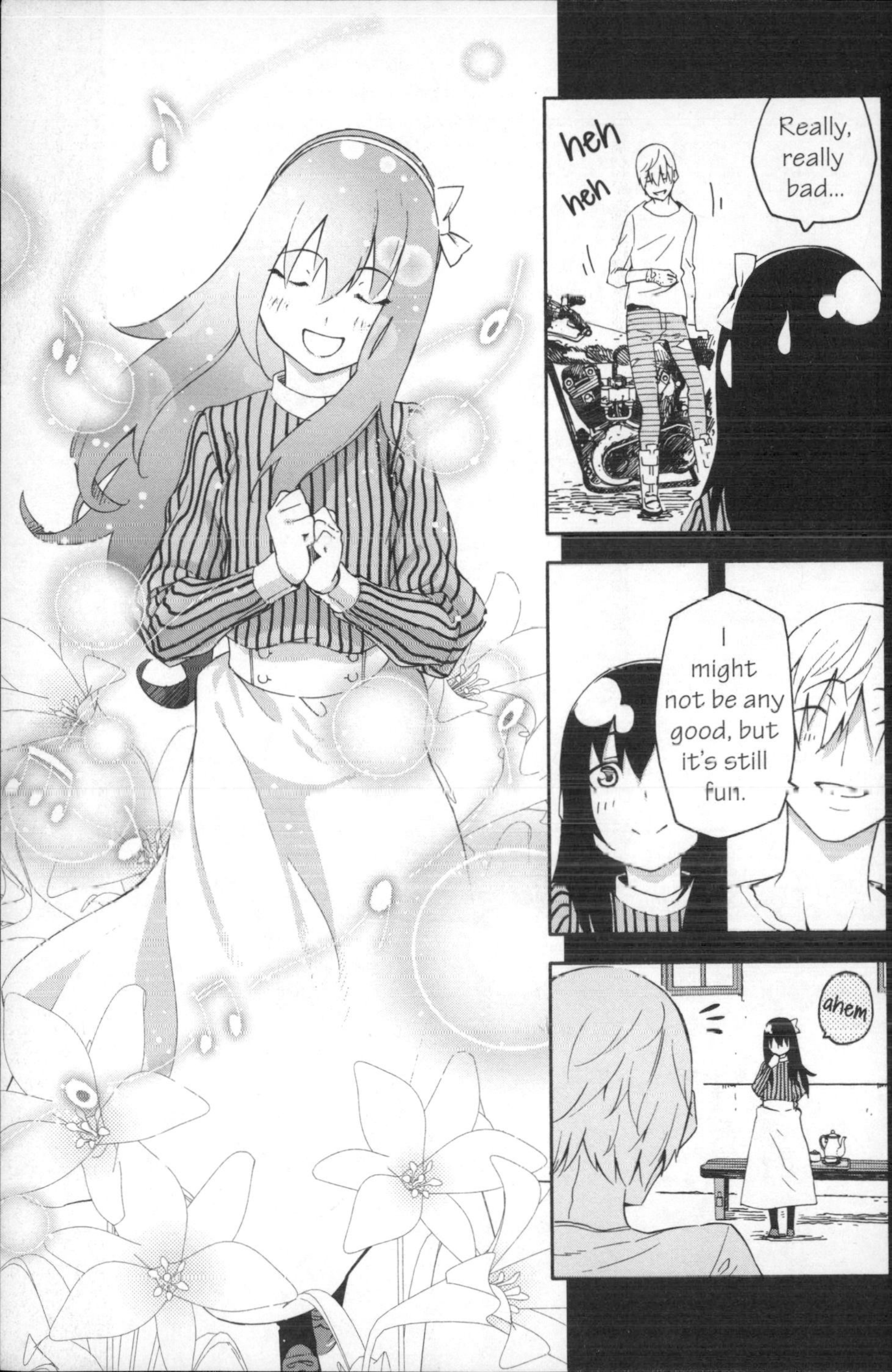
Really, really bad...
heh heh
I might not be any good, but it's still fun.
ahem

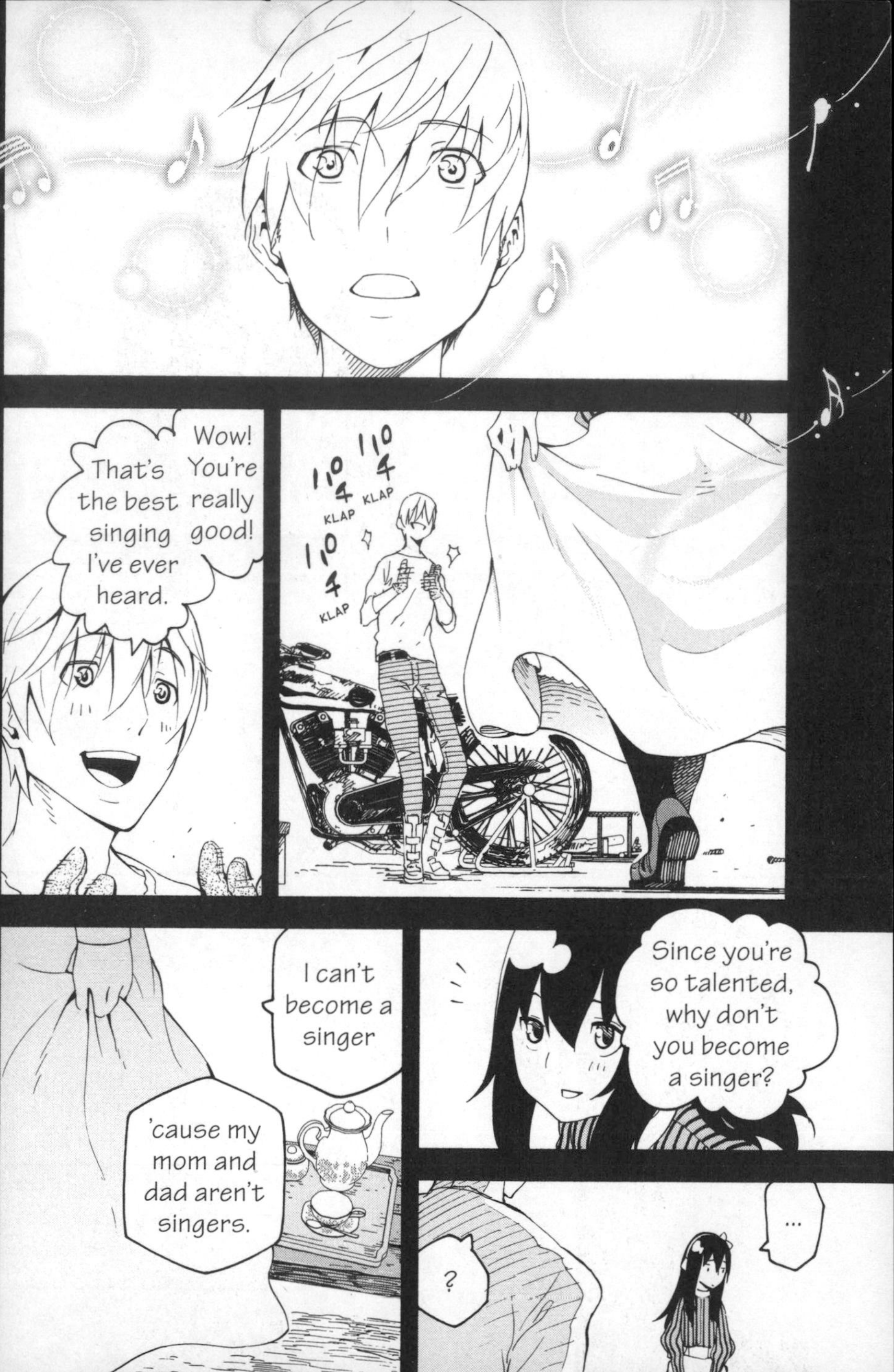
KLAP
KLAP
KLAP
Wow! You're really good!
That's the best singing I've ever heard.
Since you're so talented, why don't you become a singer?
...
?
I can't become a singer
'cause my mom and dad aren't singers.

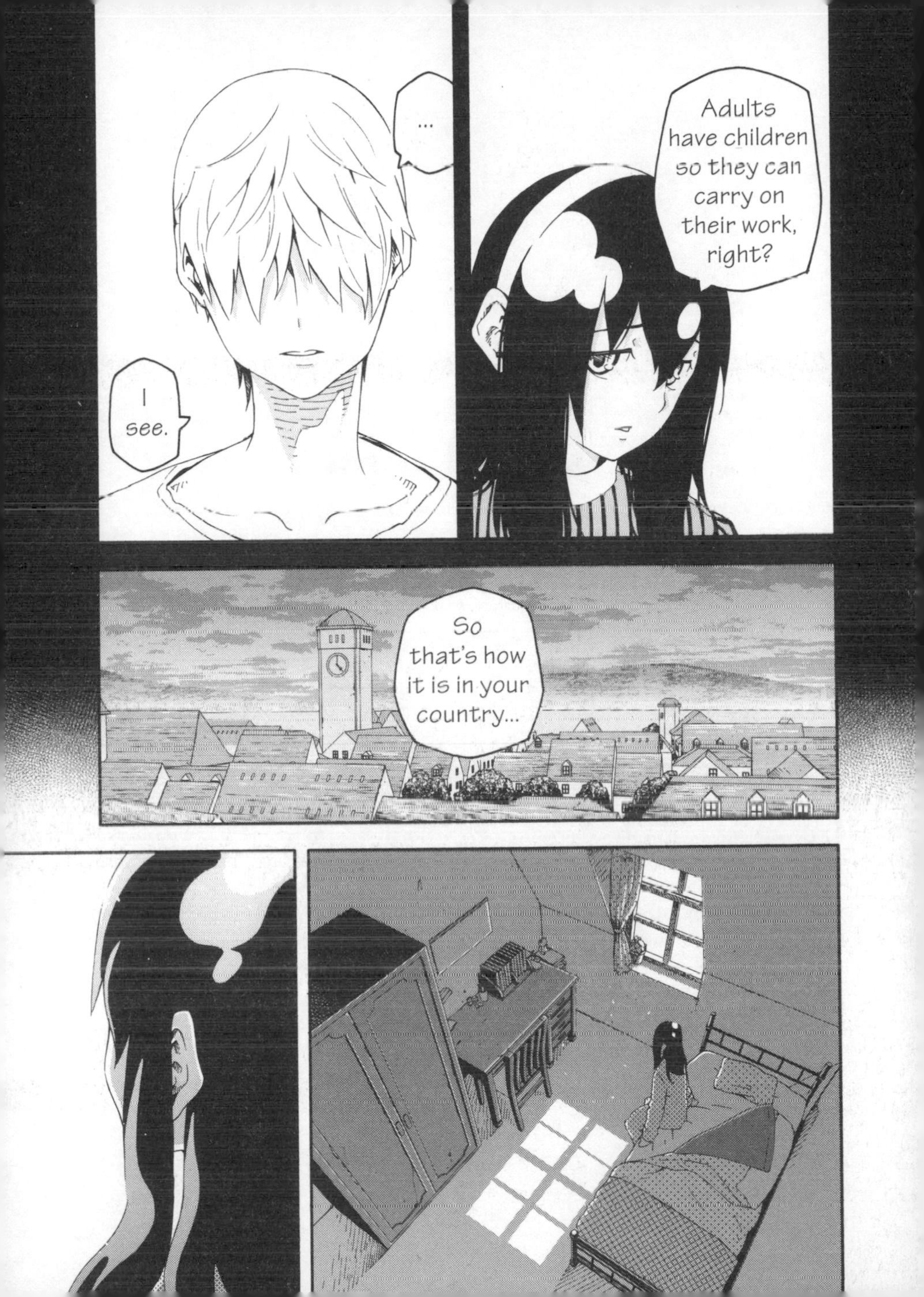
Adults have children so they can carry on their work, right?
...
I see.
So that's how it is in your country...

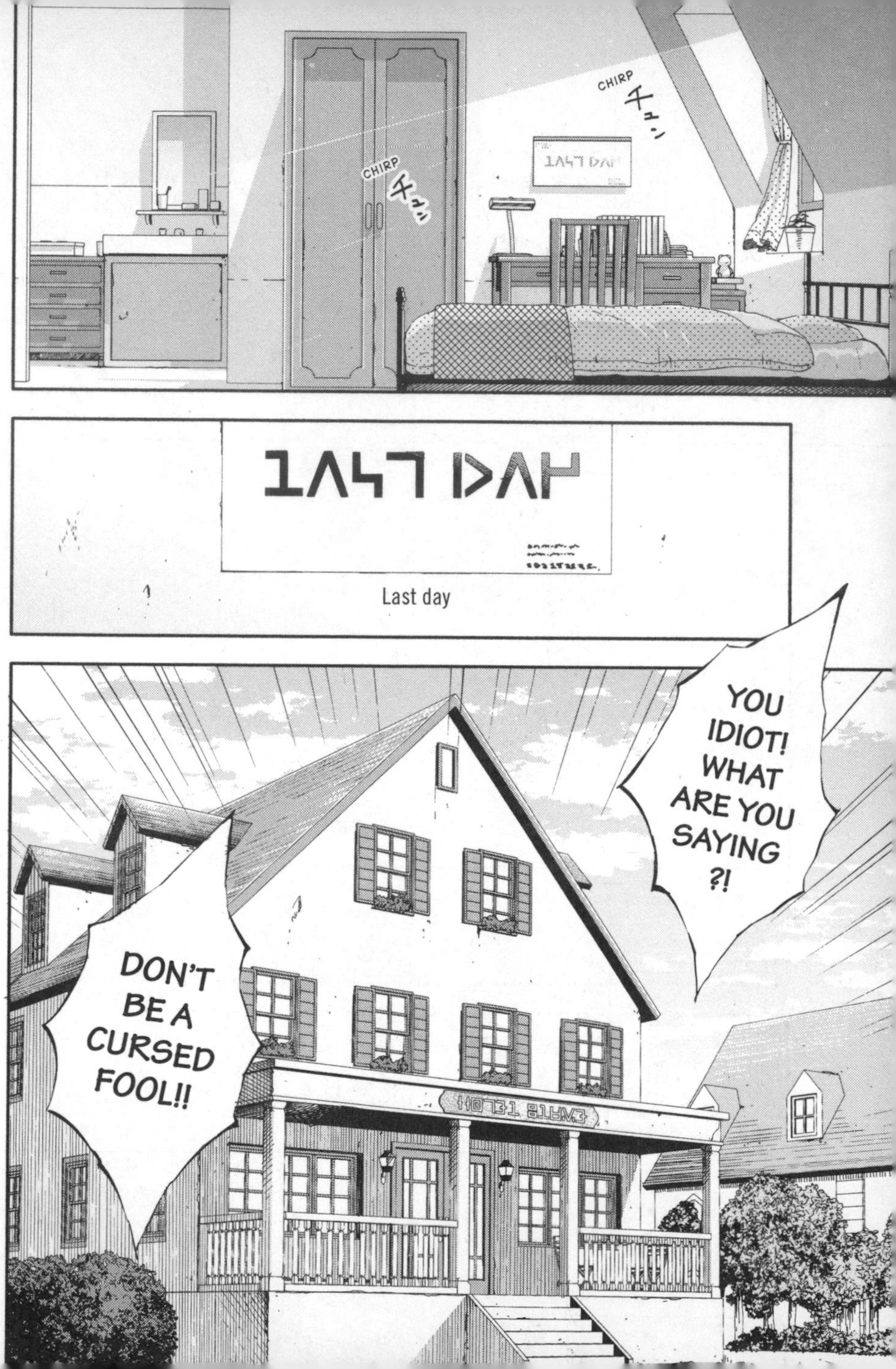
CHIRP チュン
CHIRP チュン
Last day
YOU IDIOT! WHAT ARE YOU SAYING?!
DON'T BE A CURSED FOOL!!

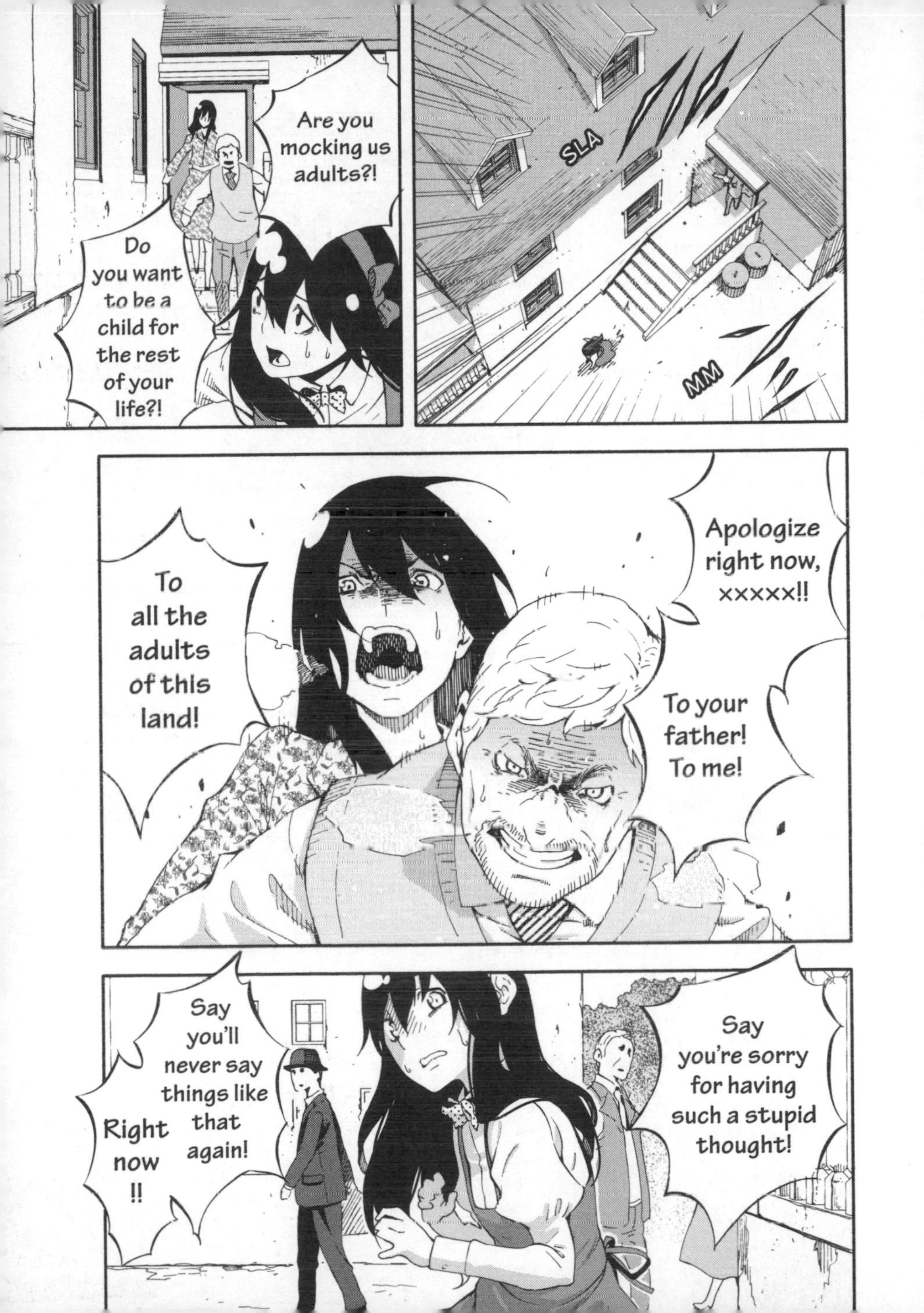
SLA
MM
Are you mocking us adults?!
Do you want to be a child for the rest of your life?!
Apologize right now, xxxxx!!
To your father! To me!
To all the adults of this land!
Say you're sorry for having such a stupid thought!
Say you'll never say things like that again!
Right now !!

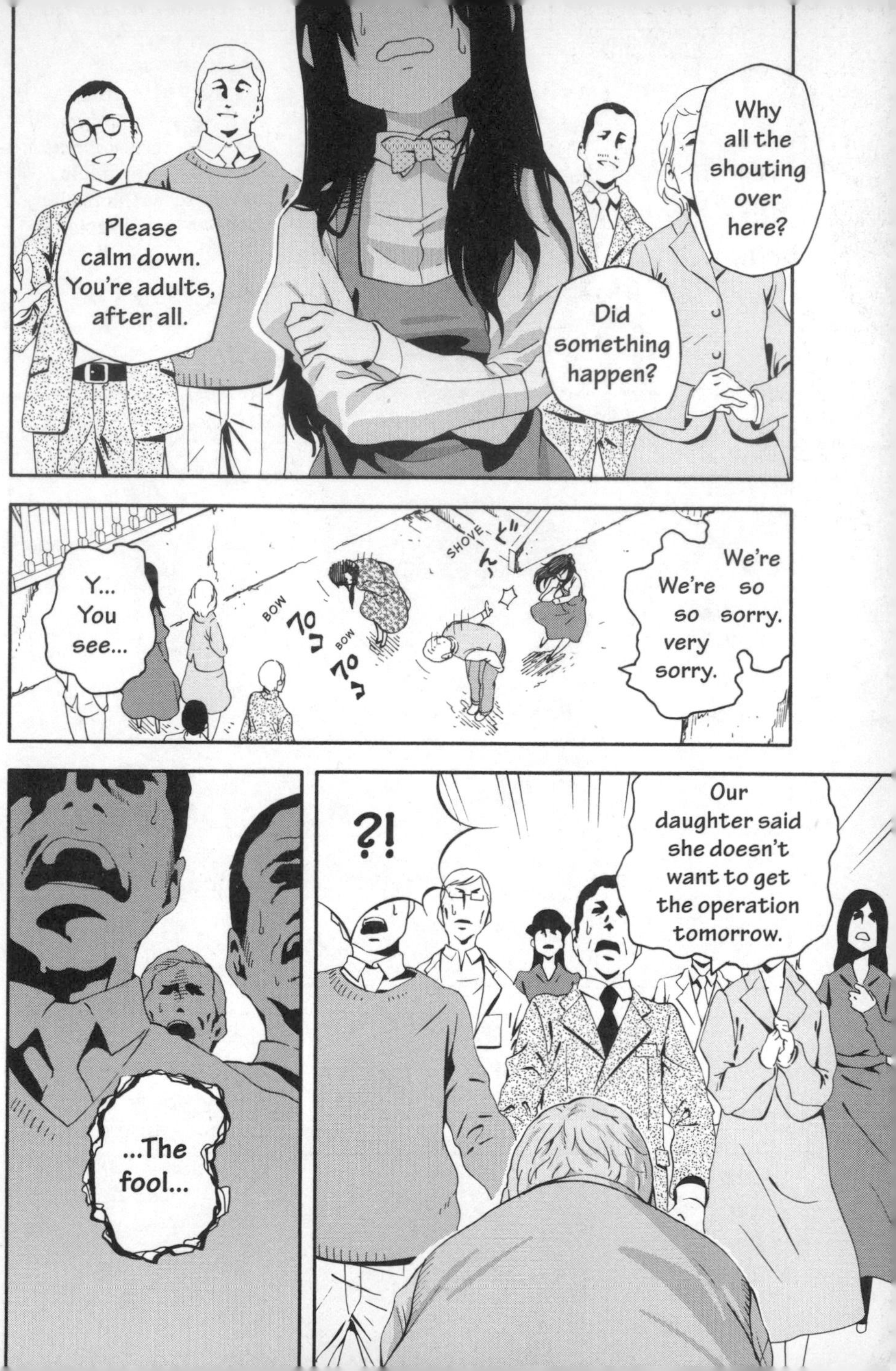
Why all the shouting over here?
Did something happen?
Please calm down. You're adults, after all.
We're so sorry.
We're so very sorry.
SHOVE
BOW
BOW
Y... You see...
Our daughter said she doesn't want to get the operation tomorrow.
?!
...The fool...

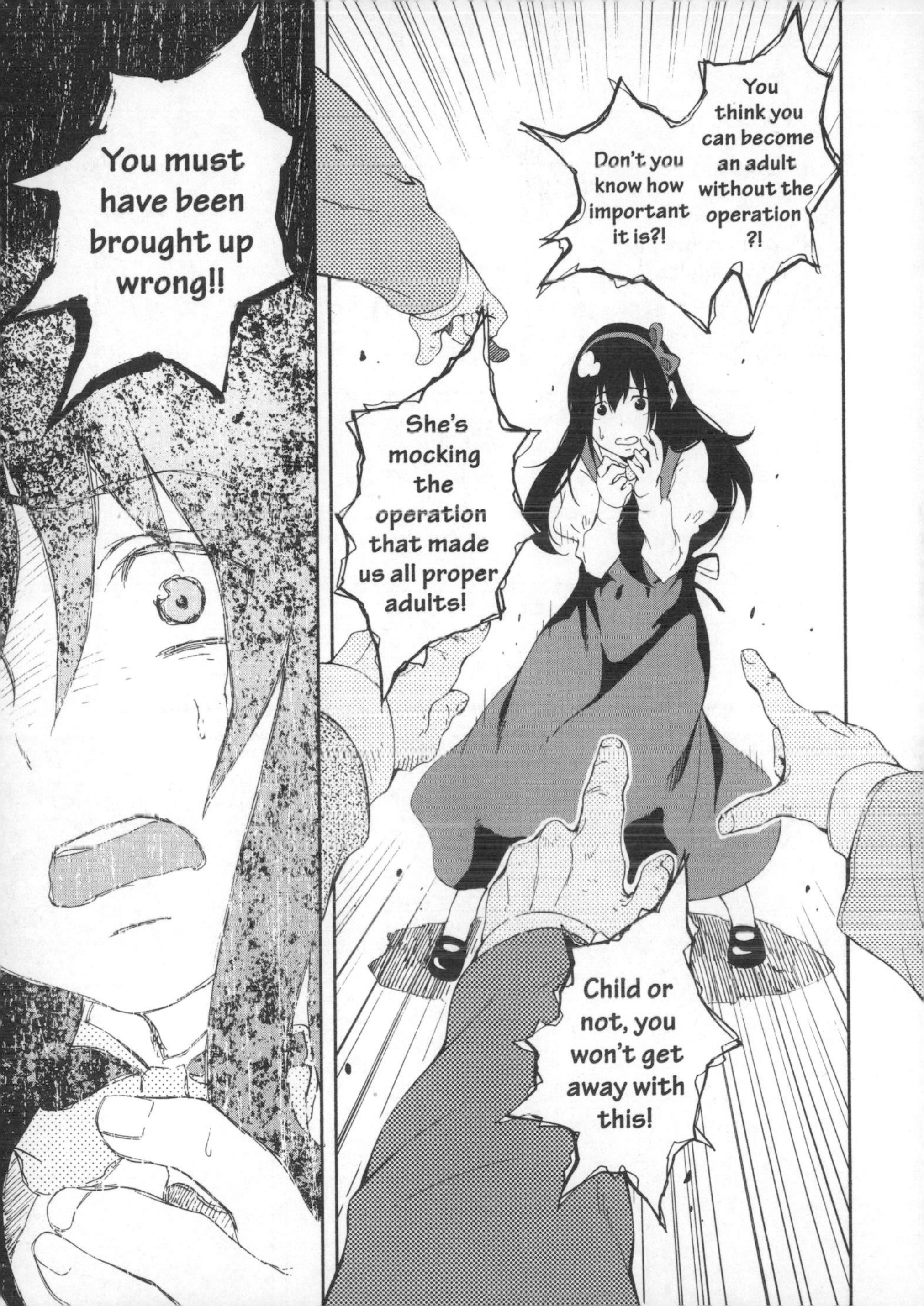
You think you can become an adult without the operation?!
Don't you know how important it is?!
She's mocking the operation that made us all proper adults!
Child or not, you won't get away with this!
You must have been brought up wrong!!

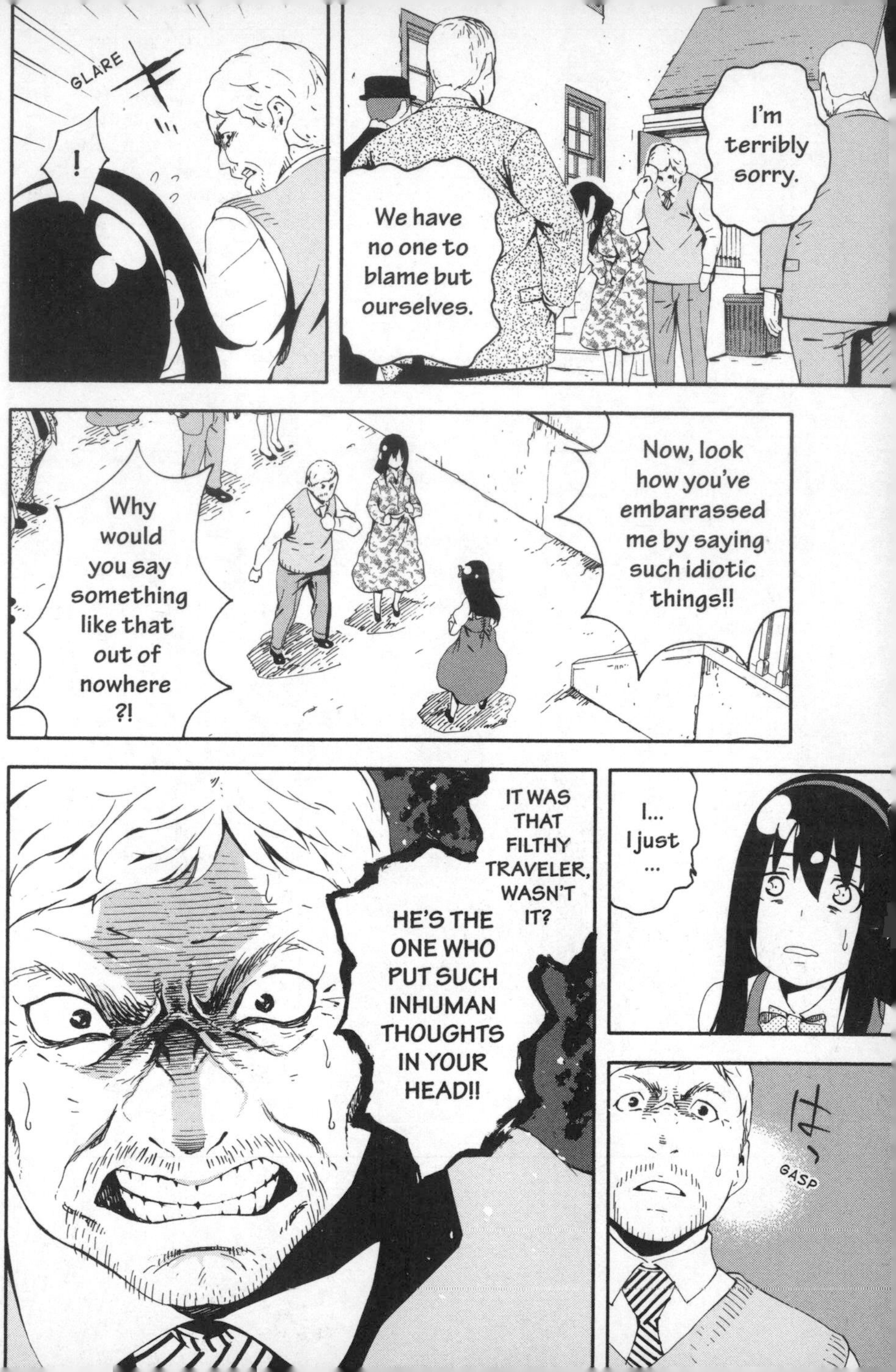
I'm terribly sorry.
We have no one to blame but ourselves.
GLARE
!
Now, look how you've embarrassed me by saying such idiotic things!!
Why would you say something like that out of nowhere?!
I... I just ...
GASP
IT WAS THAT FILTHY TRAVELER, WASN'T IT?
HE'S THE ONE WHO PUT SUCH INHUMAN THOUGHTS IN YOUR HEAD!!

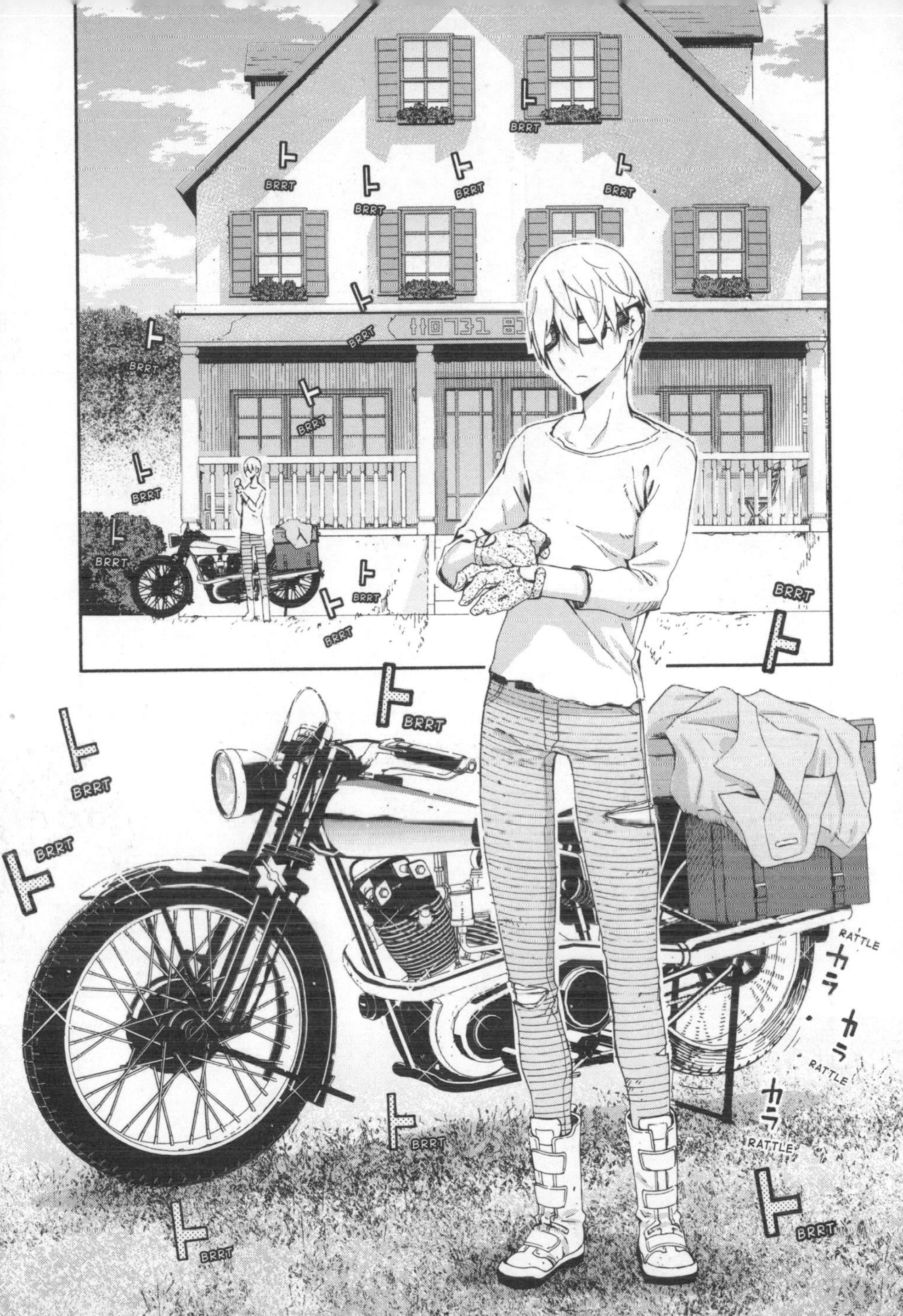

ト BRRT
ト BRRT
ト BRRT
ト BRRT
ト BRRT
ト BRRT
ト BRRT
ト BRRT
ト BRRT
ト BRRT
ト BRRT
ト BRRT
ト BRRT
ト BRRT
ト BRRT
ト BRRT
カラ RATTLE
カラ RATTLE
カラ RATTLE
ト BRRT
ト BRRT
ト BRRT

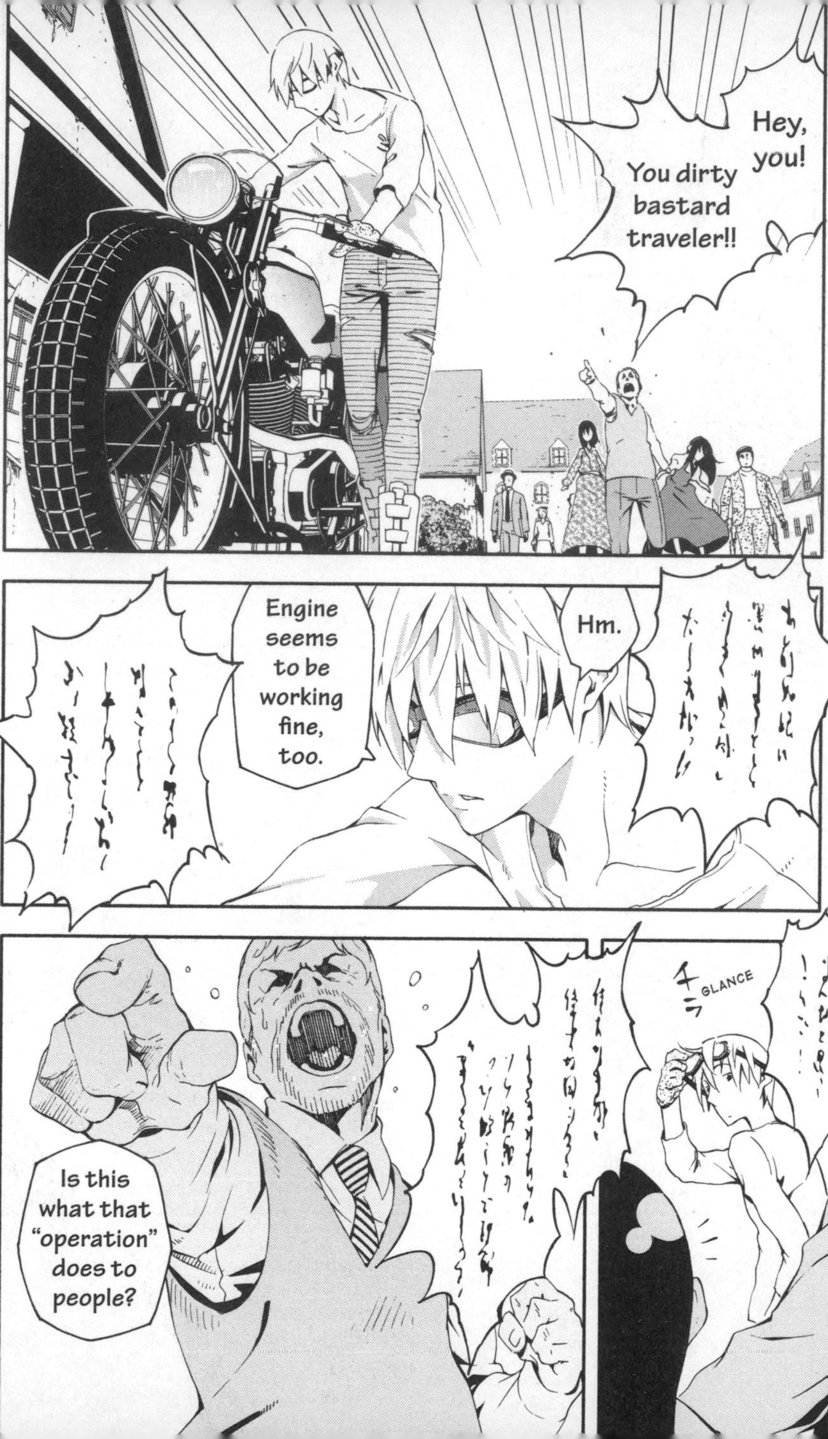
Hey, you!
You dirty bastard traveler!!
Hm.
Engine seems to be working fine, too.
チラ GLANCE
Is this what that "operation" does to people?

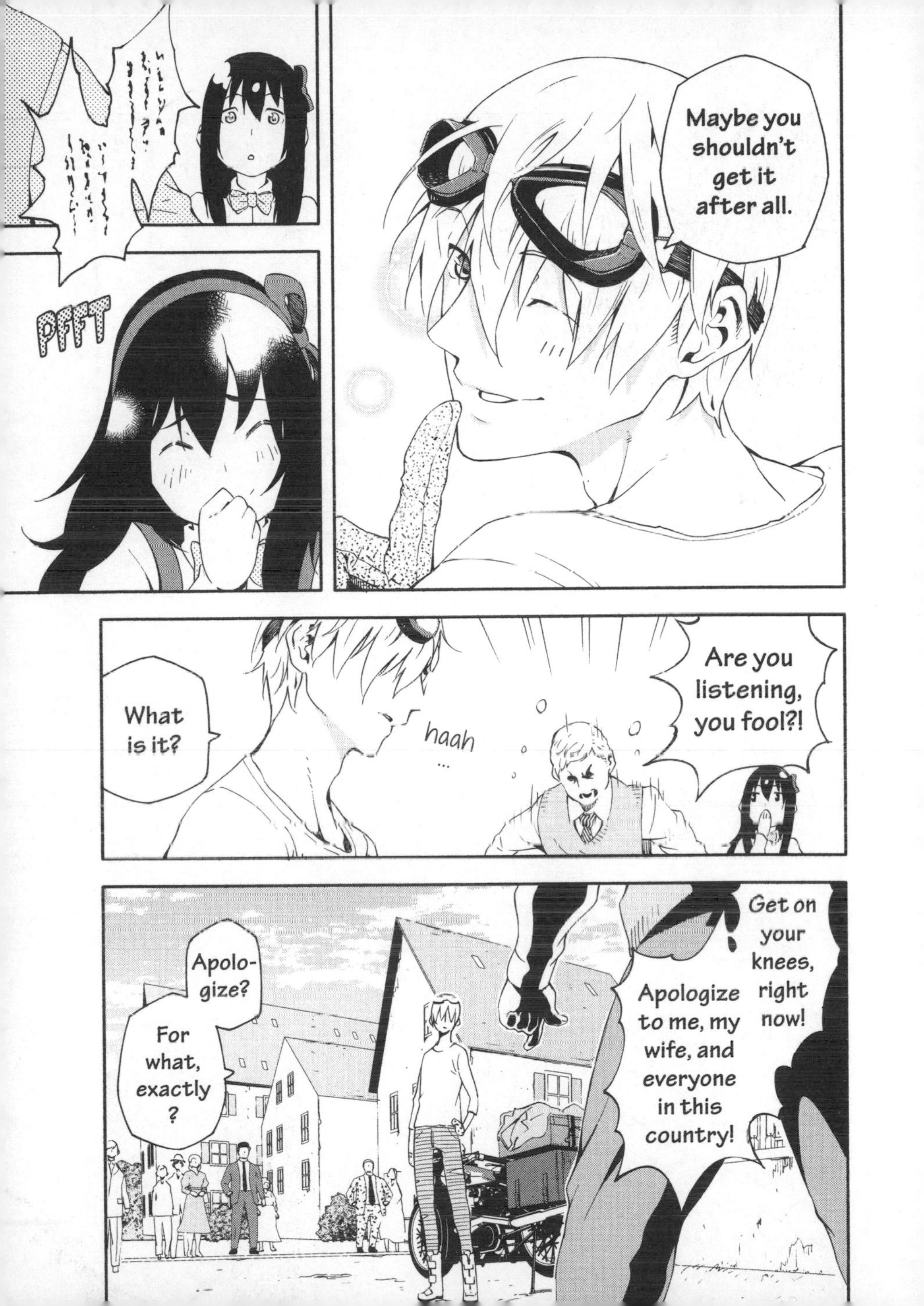

Maybe you shouldn't get it after all.
PFFT
Are you listening, you fool?!
haah ...
What is it?
Get on your knees, right now!
Apologize to me, my wife, and everyone in this country!
Apologize?
For what, exactly?

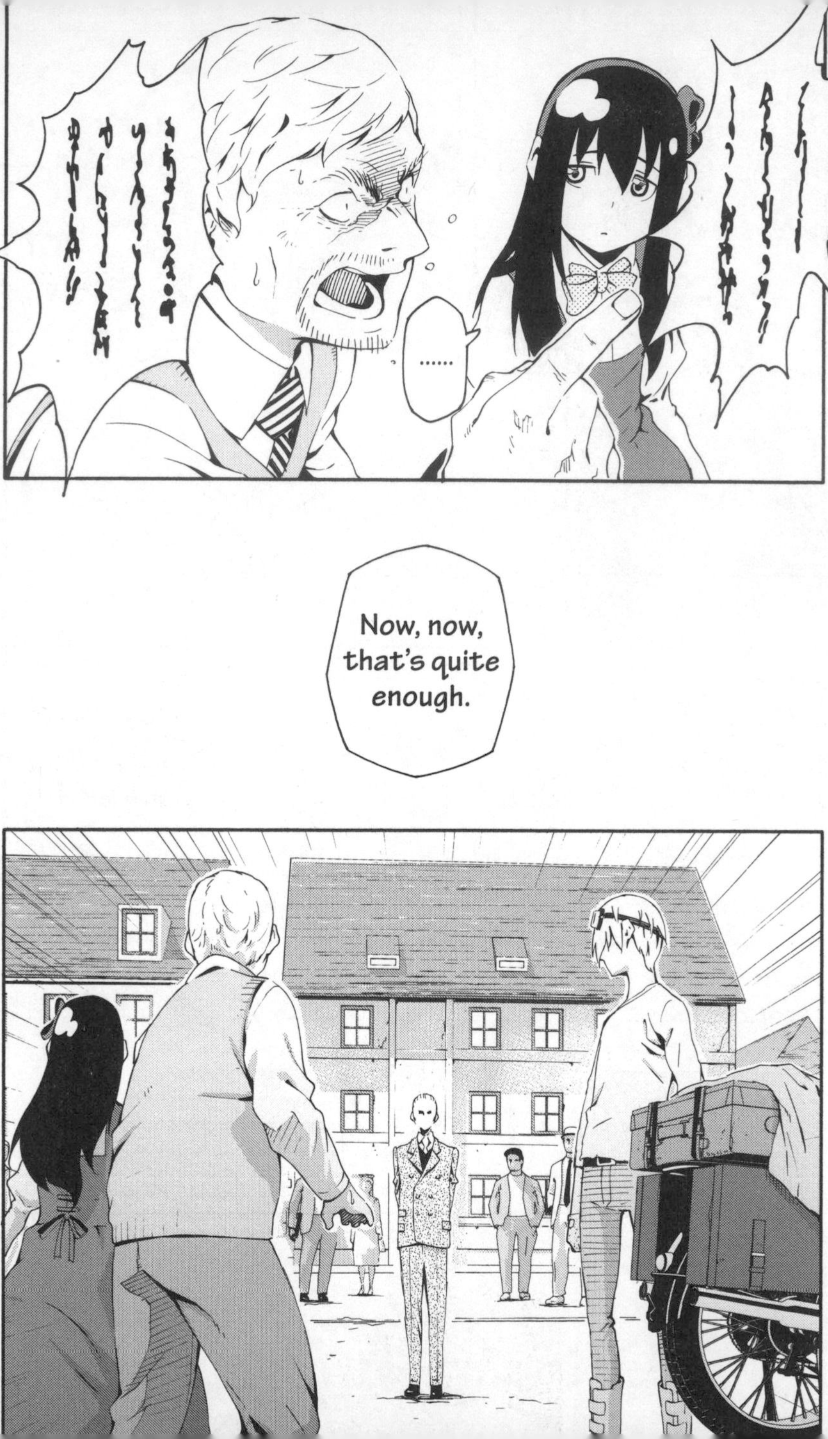
......
Now, now, that's quite enough.

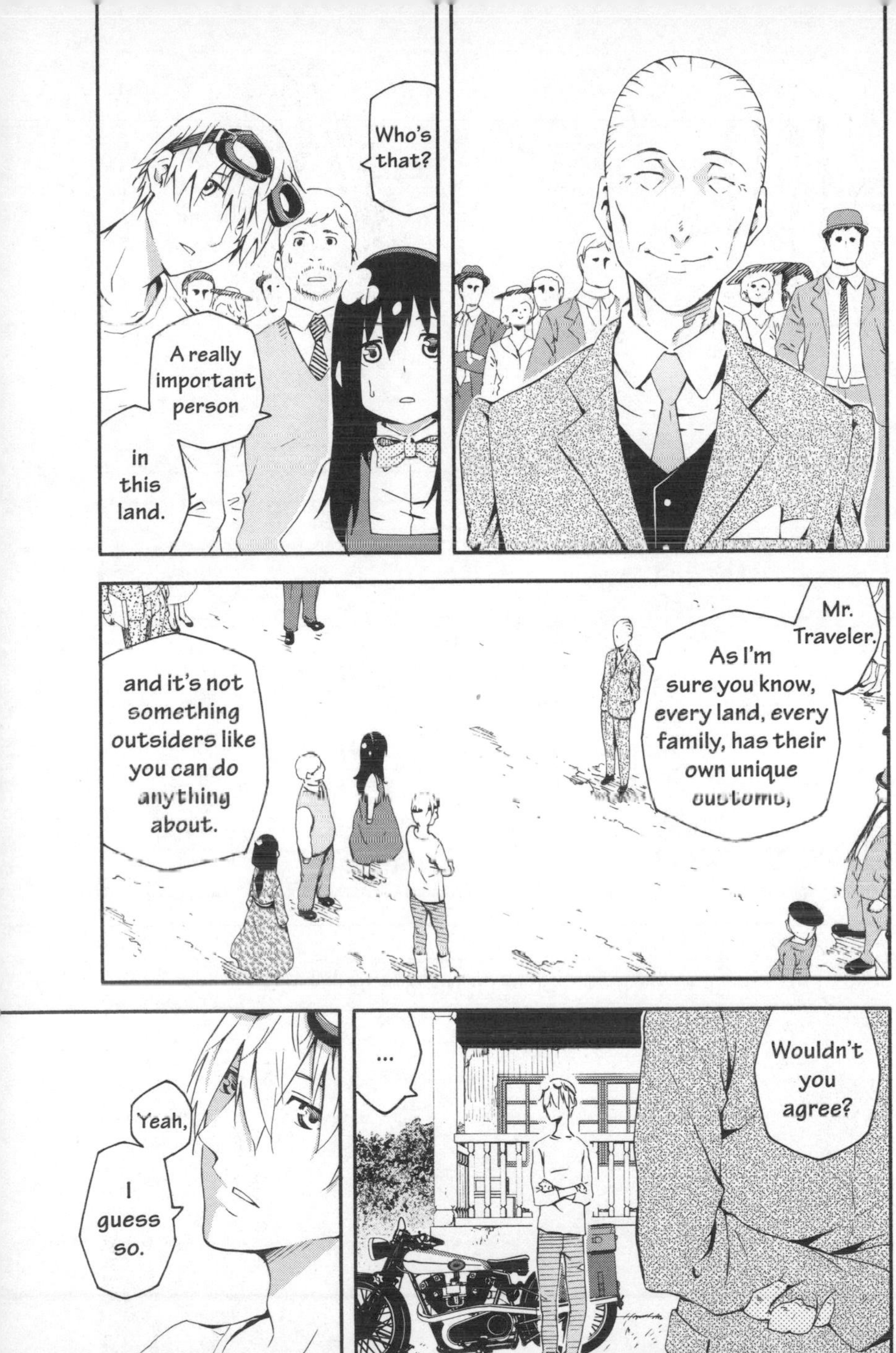
Who's that?
A really important person
in this land.
Mr. Traveler.
As I'm sure you know, every land, every family, has their own unique customs,
and it's not something outsiders like you can do anything about.
Wouldn't you agree?
...
Yeah,
I guess so.

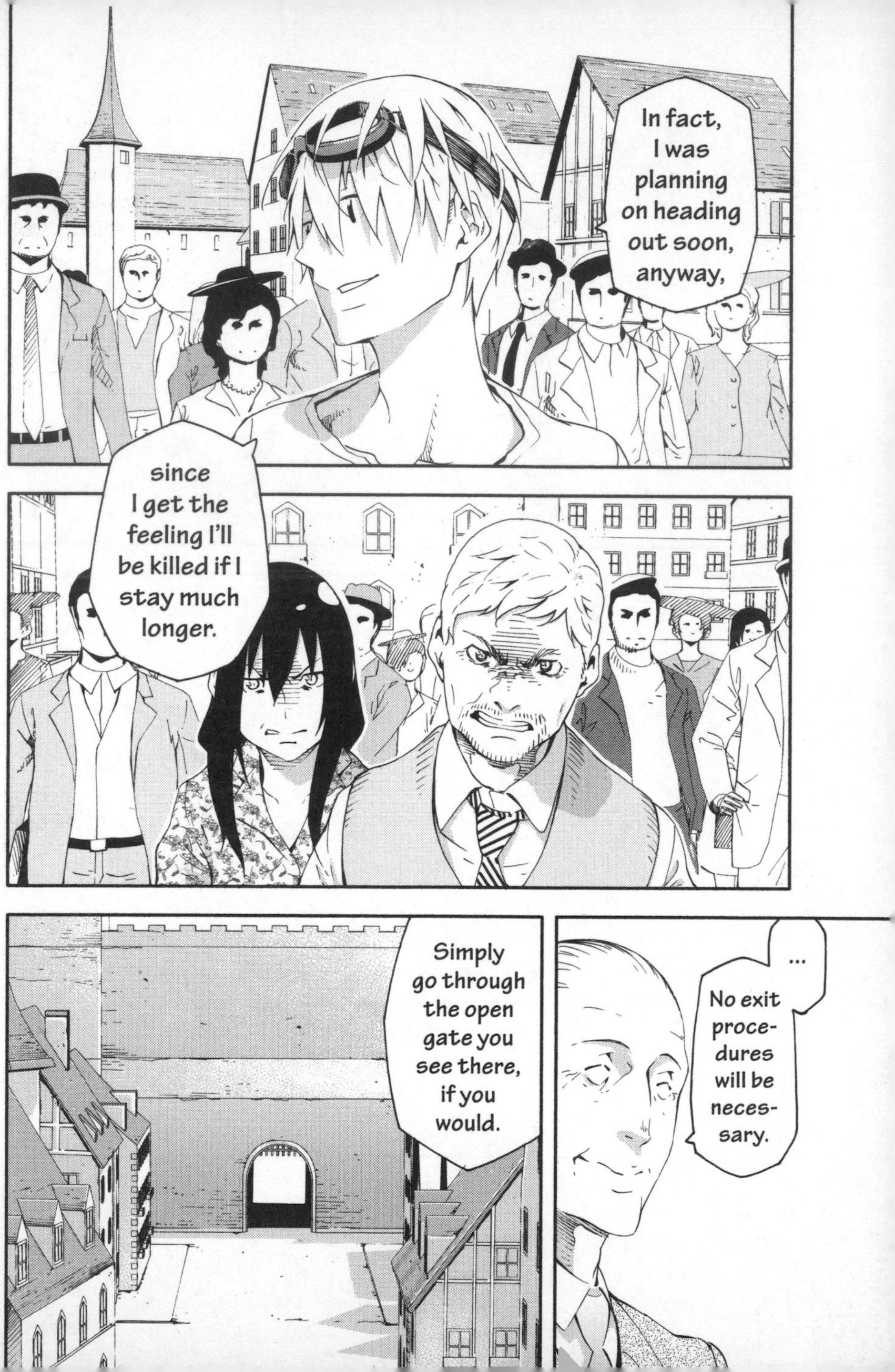
In fact, I was planning on heading out soon, anyway,
since I get the feeling I'll be killed if I stay much longer.
...
No exit proce-dures will be neces-sary.
Simply go through the open gate you see there, if you would.

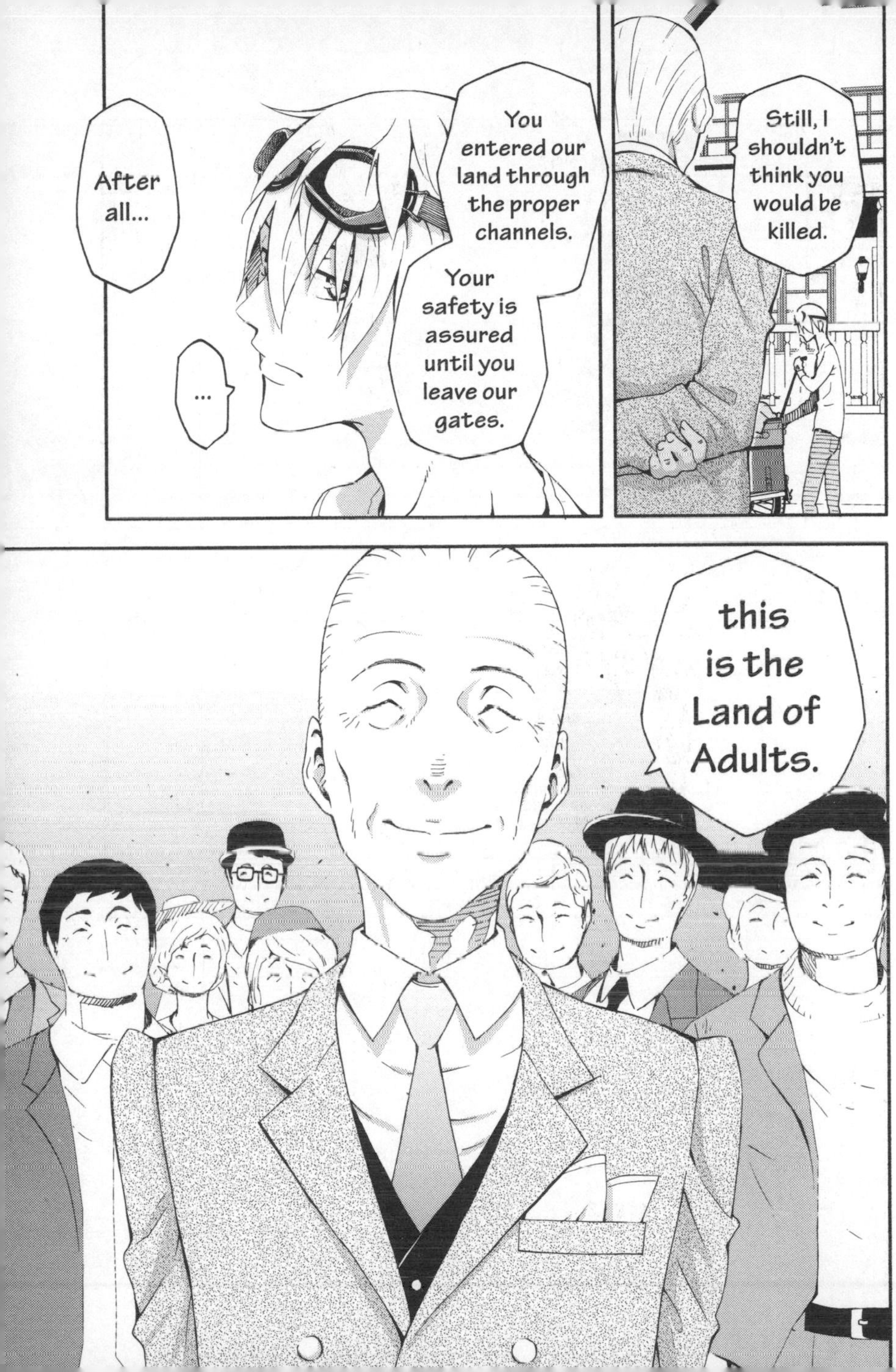
Still, I shouldn't think you would be killed.
You entered our land through the proper channels.
Your safety is assured until you leave our gates.
After all...
...
this is the Land of Adults.

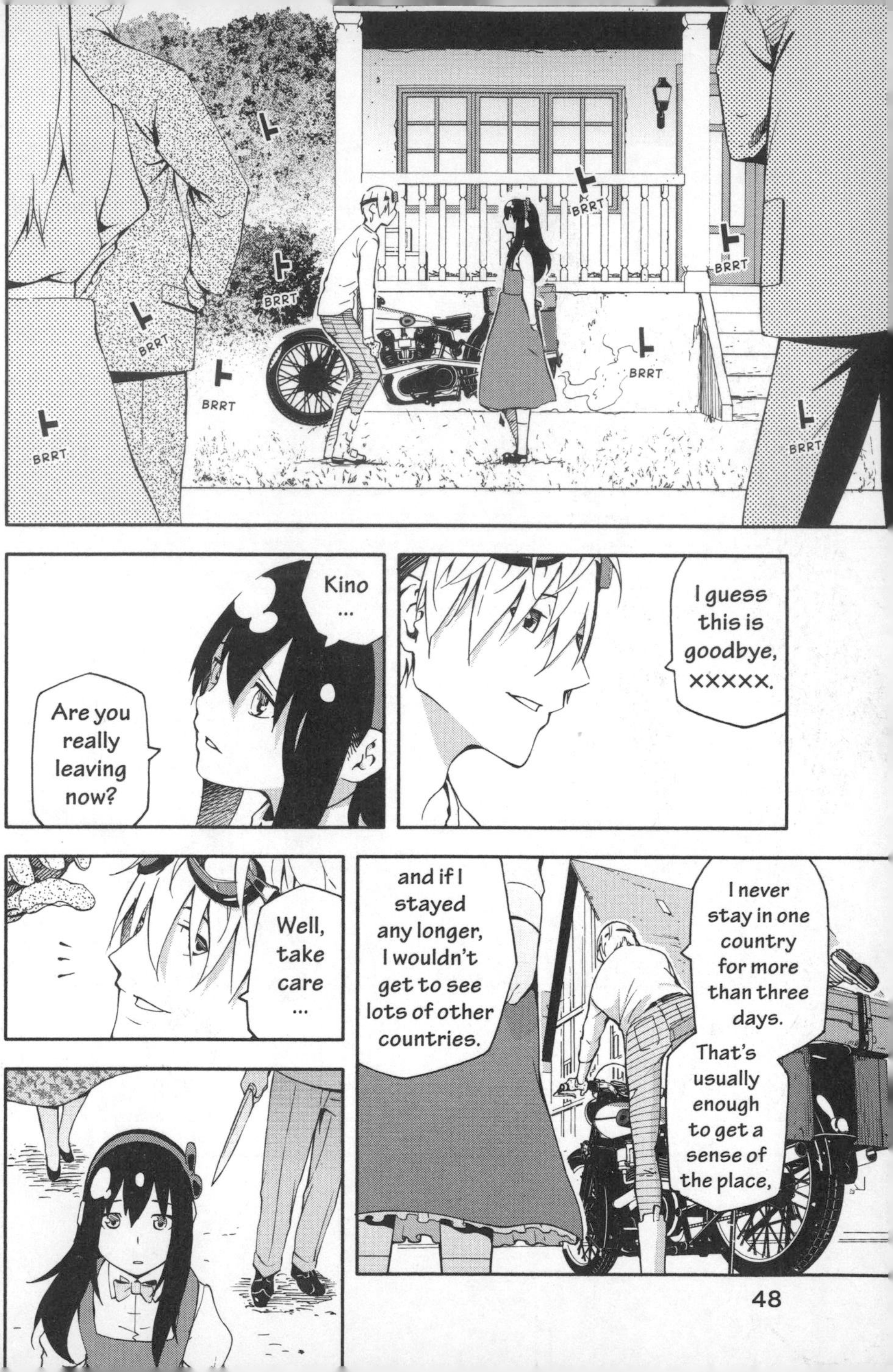
ト BRRT
ト BRRT
ト BRRT
ト BRRT
ト BRRT
ト BRRT
ト BRRT
ト BRRT
I guess this is goodbye, XXXXX.
Kino ...
Are you really leaving now?
I never stay in one country for more than three days.
That's usually enough to get a sense of the place,
and if I stayed any longer, I wouldn't get to see lots of other countries.
Well, take care ...

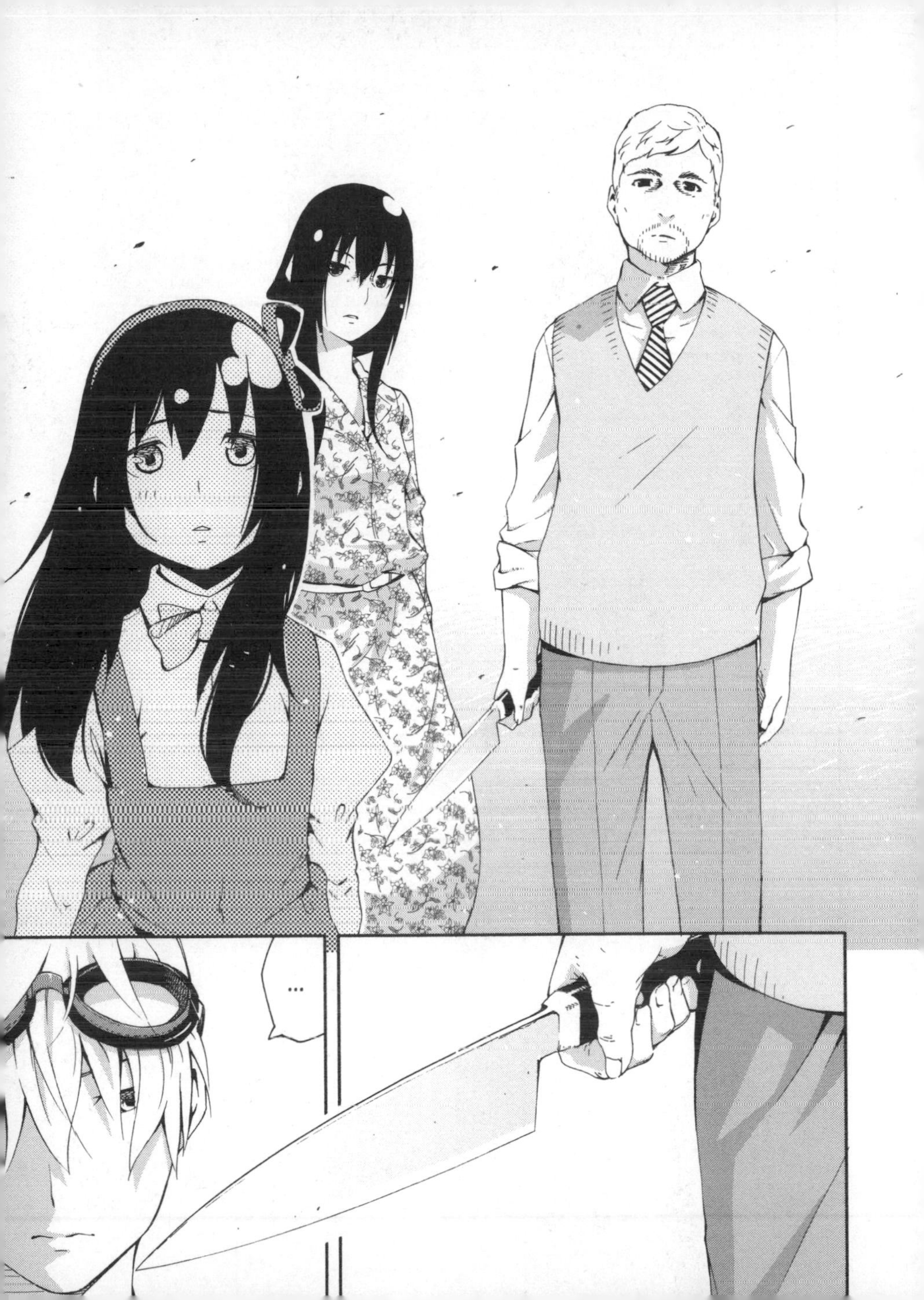
...

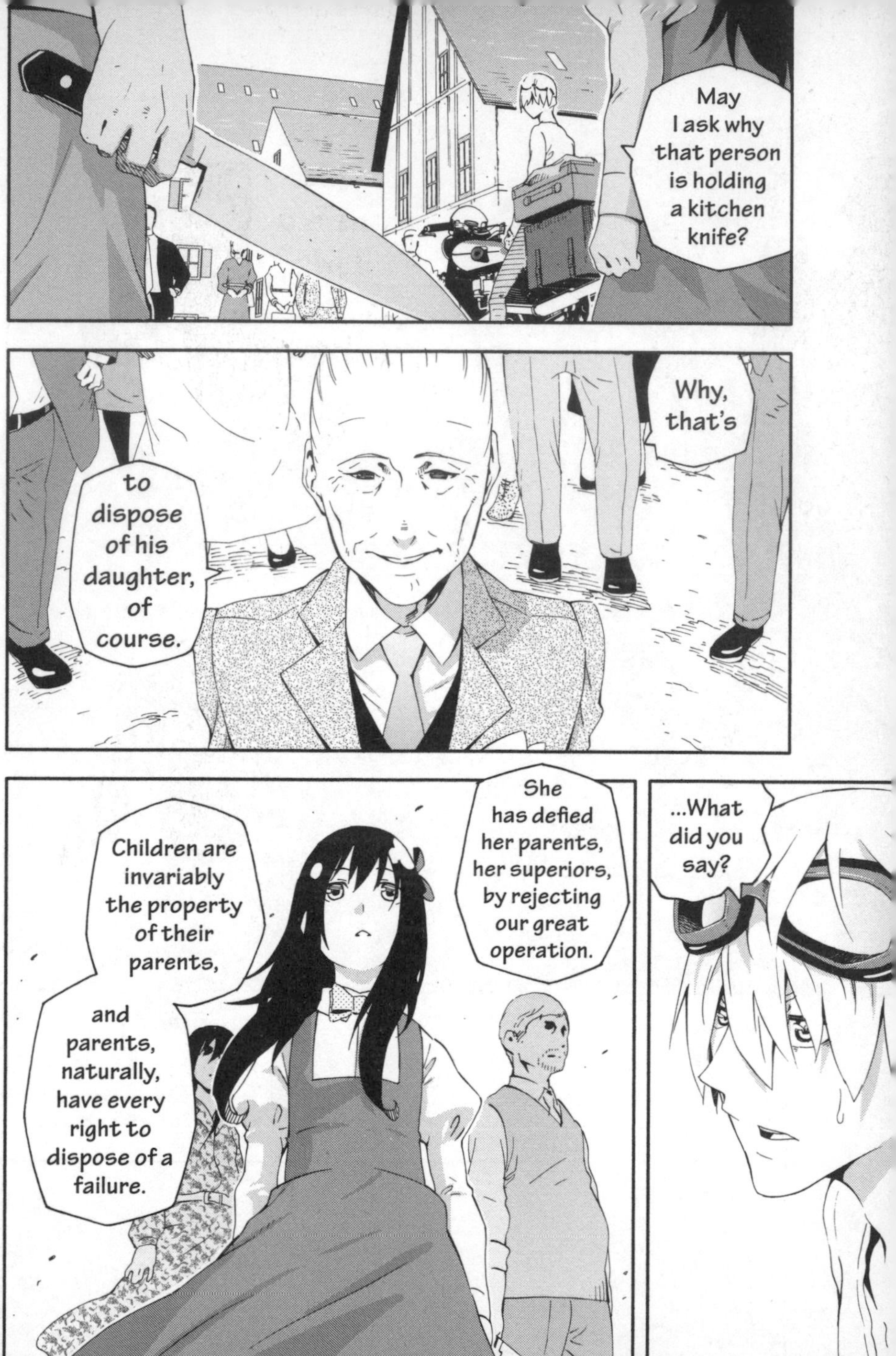
May I ask why that person is holding a kitchen knife?
Why, that's
to dispose of his daughter, of course.
...What did you say?
She has defied her parents, her superiors, by rejecting our great operation.
Children are invariably the property of their parents,
and parents, naturally, have every right to dispose of a failure.

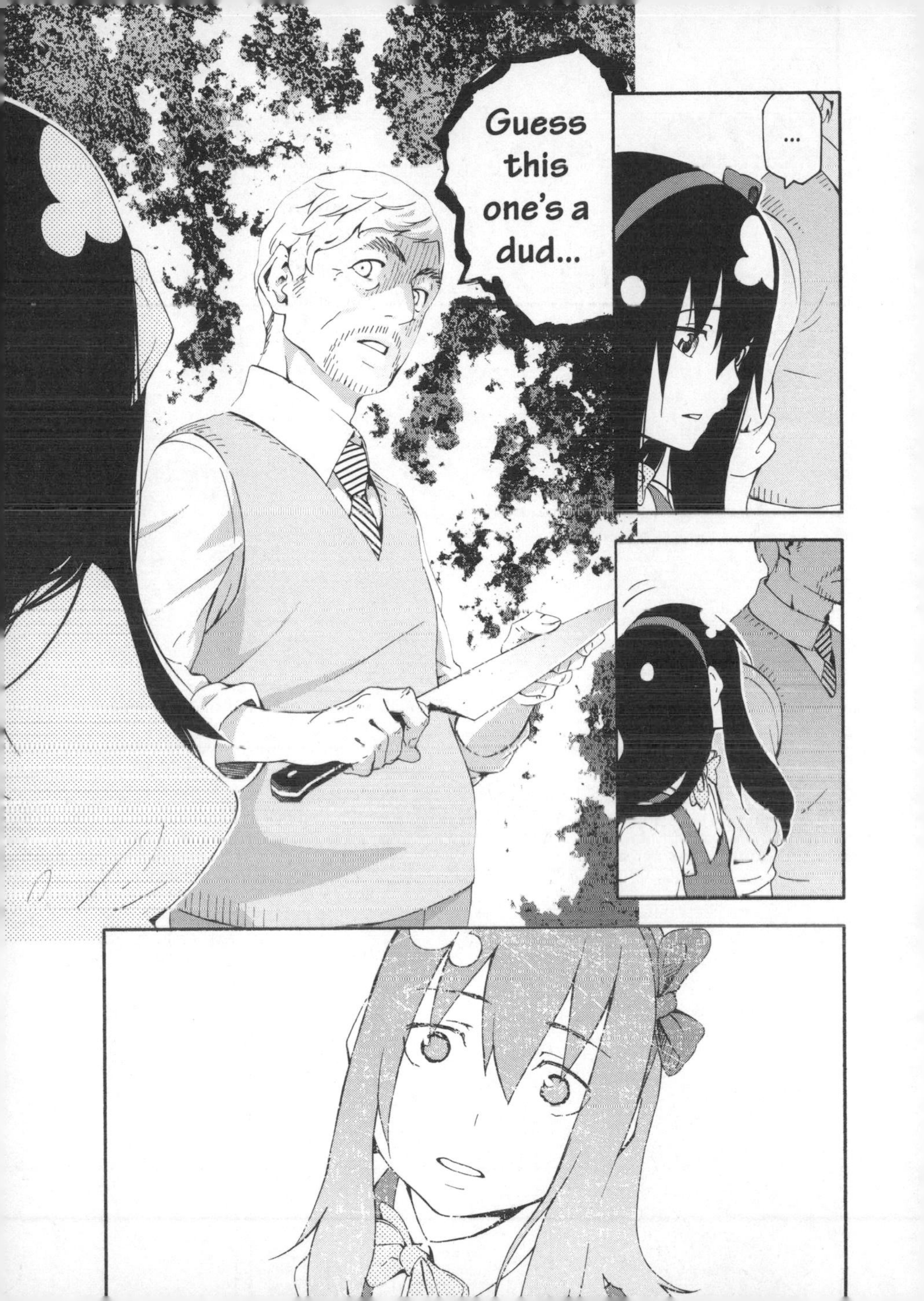
...
Guess this one's a dud...

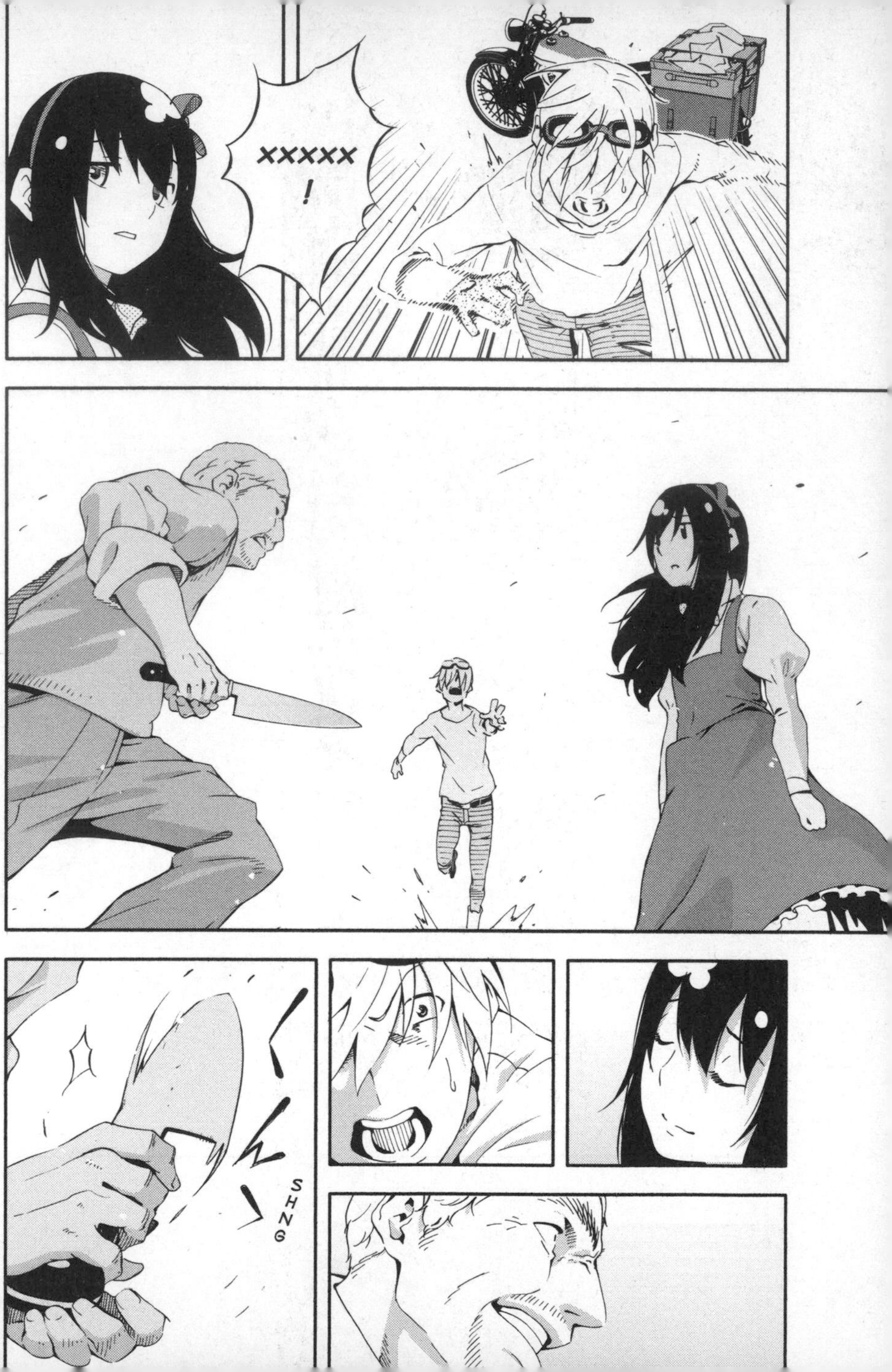
XXXXX
!
SHNG

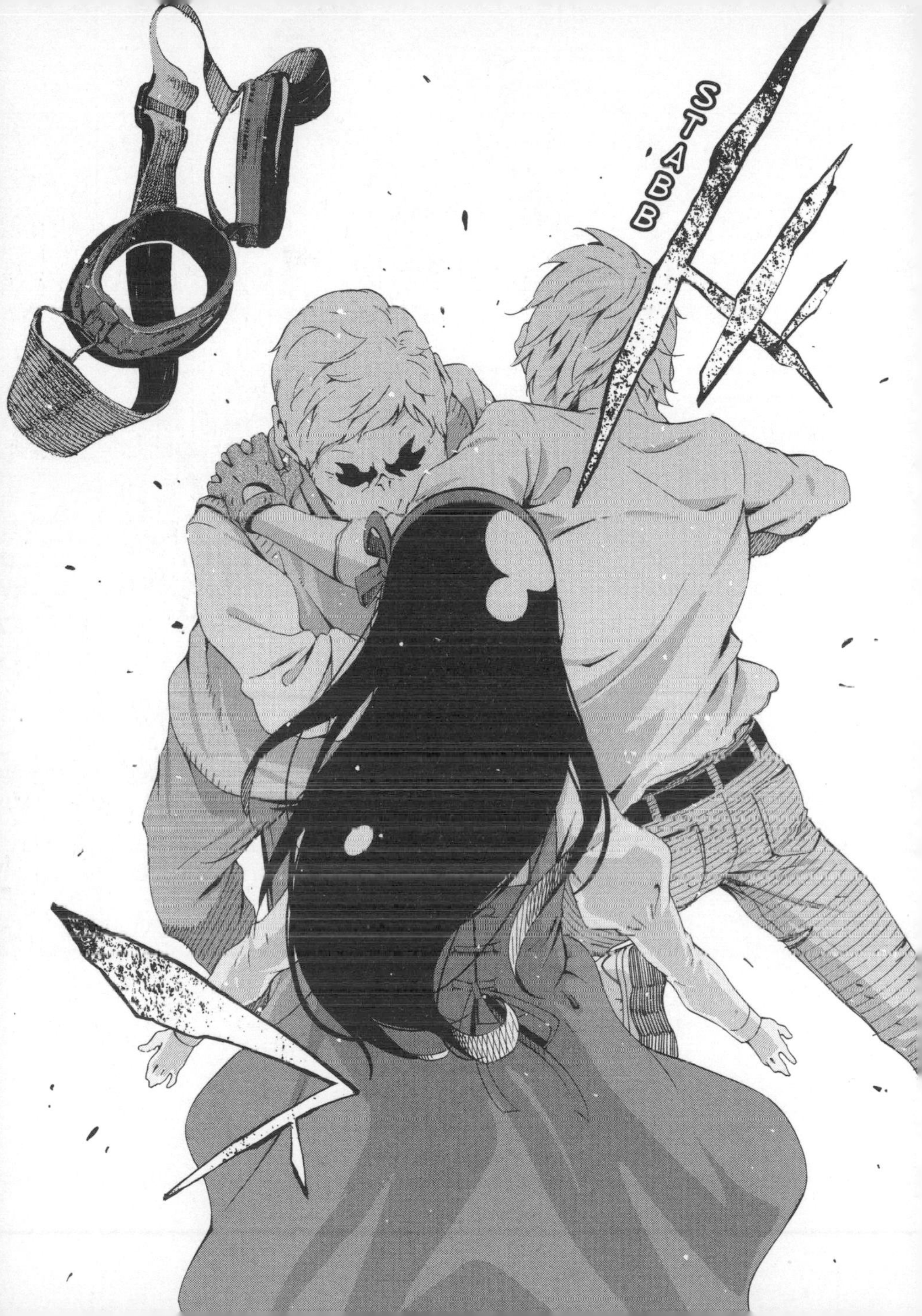
STABB

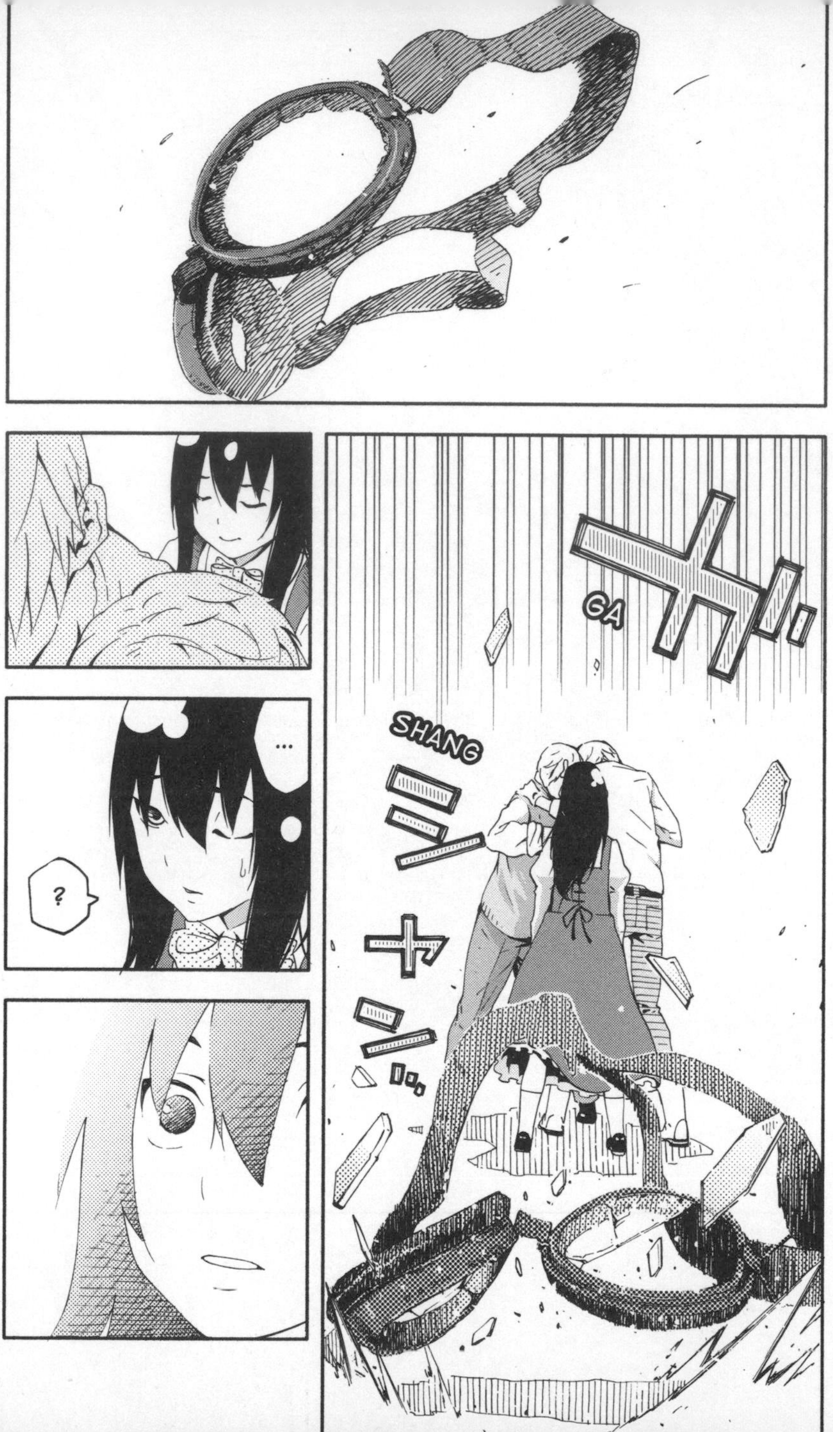
GA
SHANG
...
?

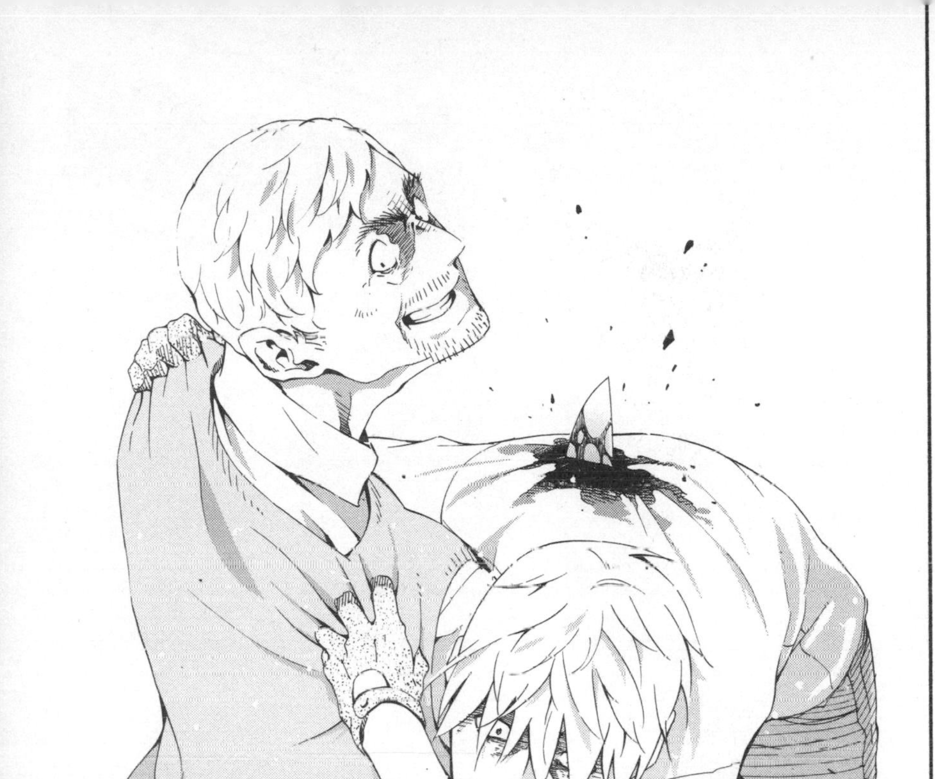
Gah...
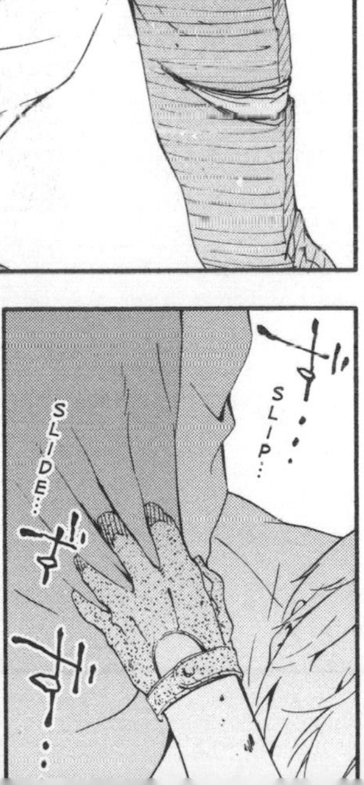
SLIP...
SLIDE...
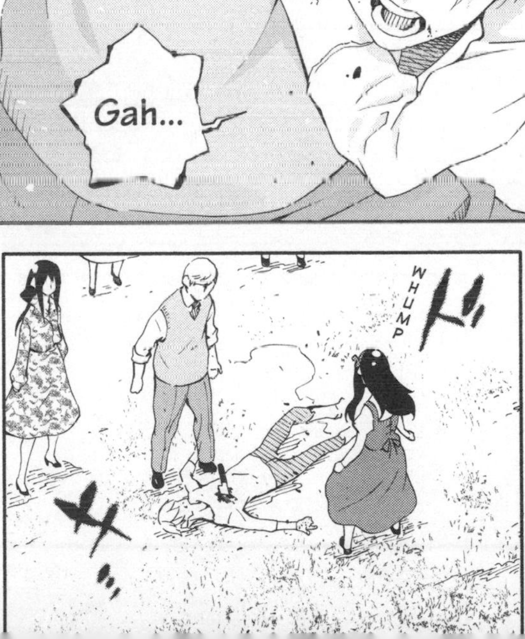
WHUMP

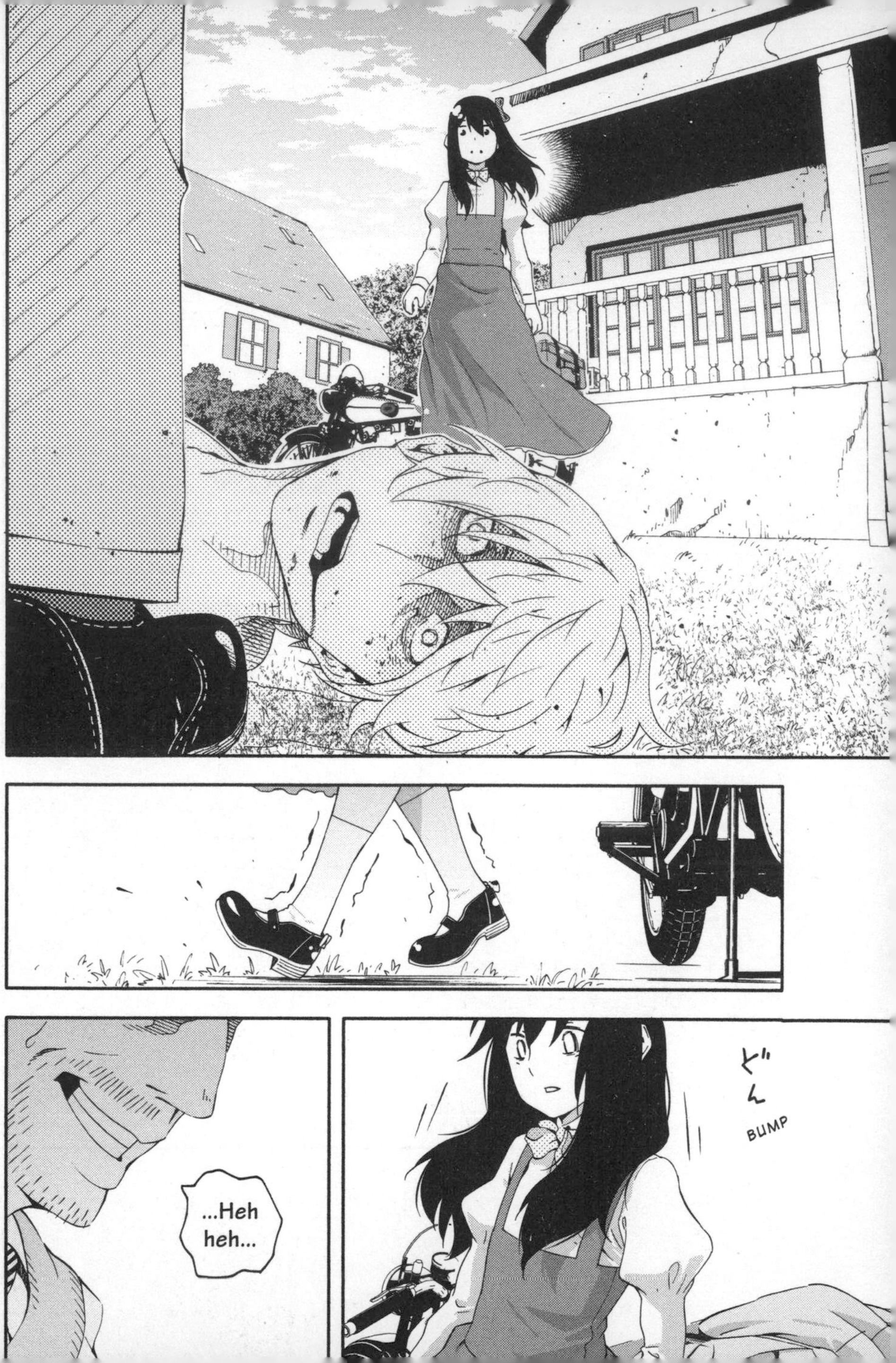
どん
BUMP
...Heh heh...

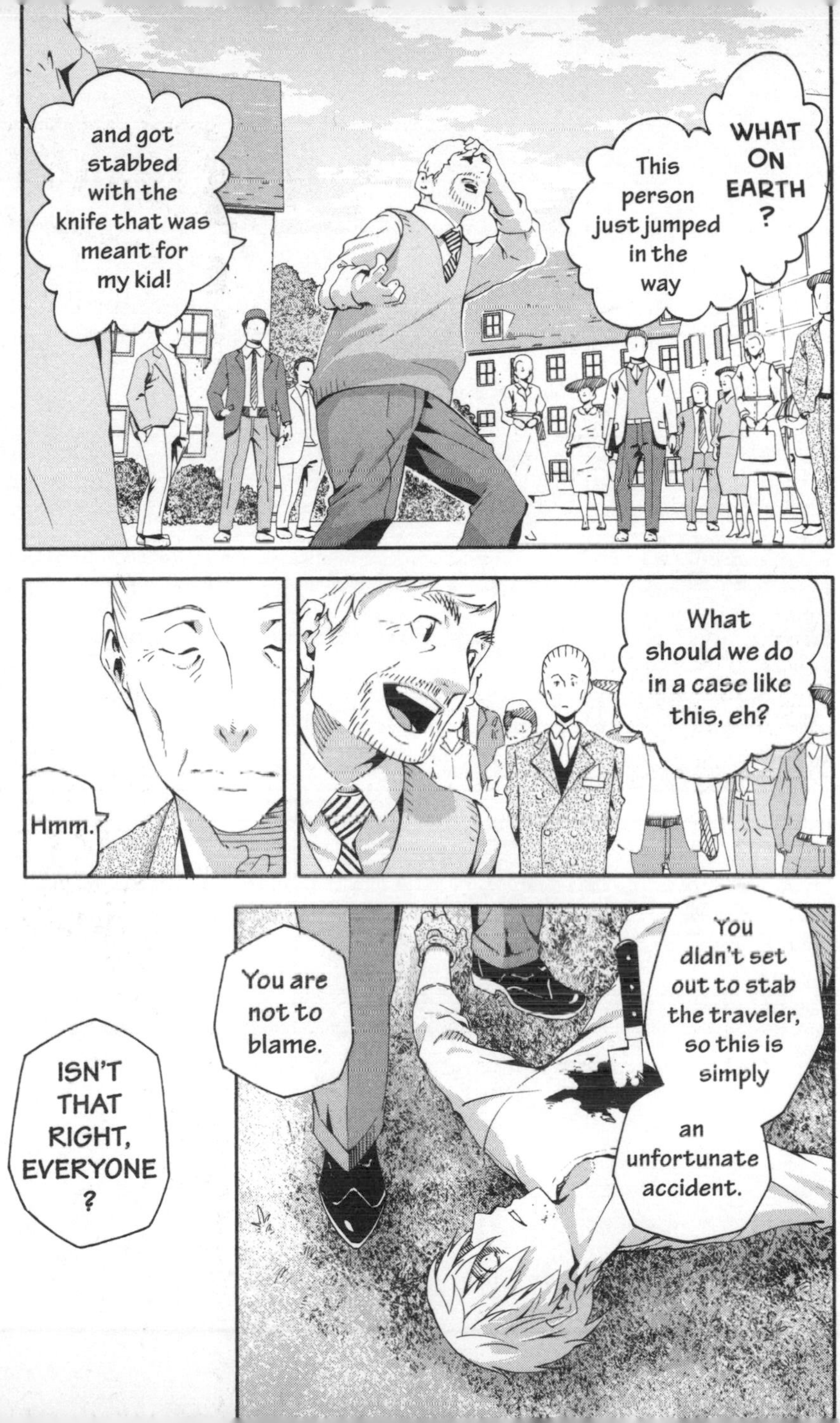
WHAT ON EARTH?
This person just jumped in the way
and got stabbed with the knife that was meant for my kid!
What should we do in a case like this, eh?
Hmm.
You didn't set out to stab the traveler, so this is simply
an unfortunate accident.
You are not to blame.
ISN'T THAT RIGHT, EVERYONE?

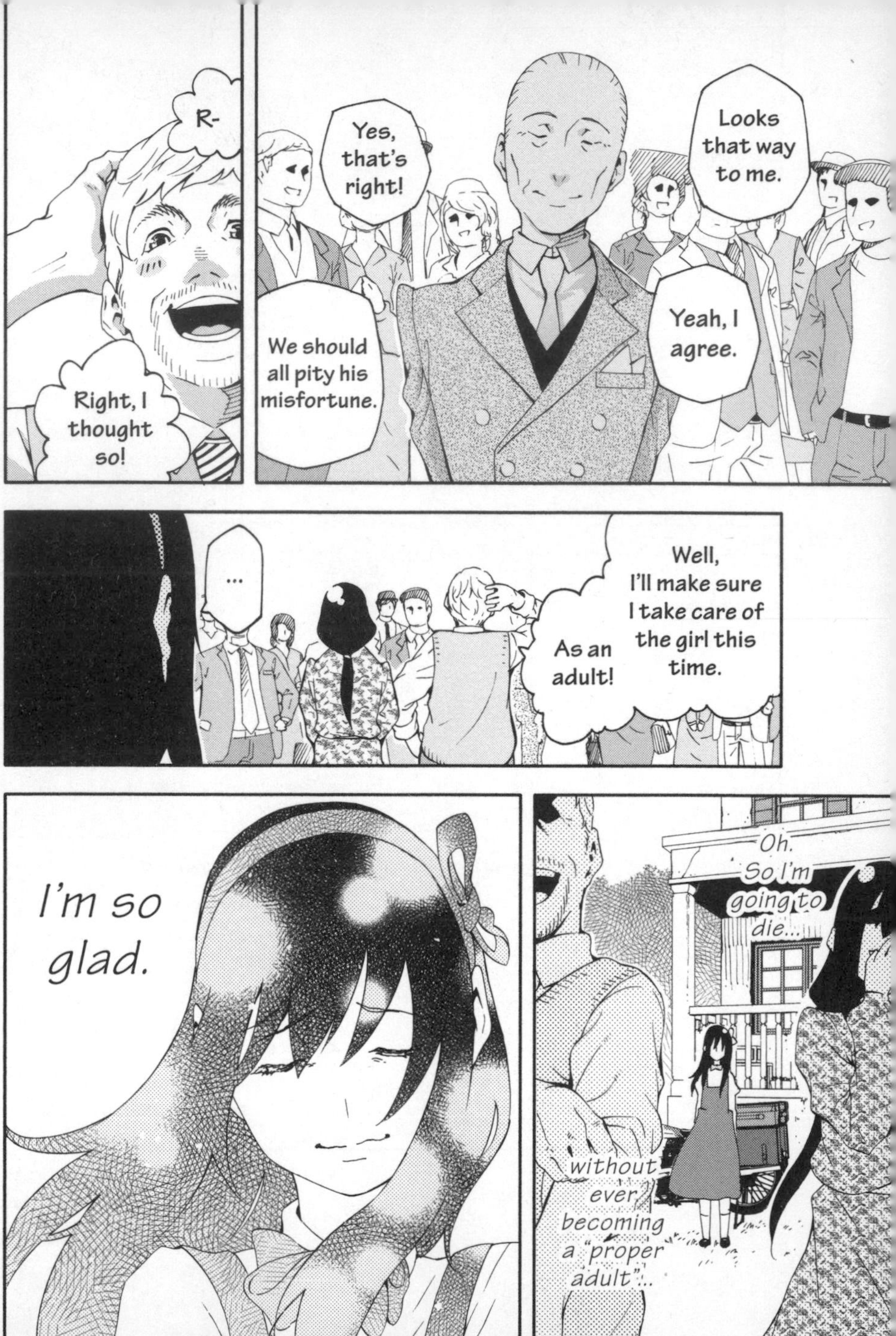
Looks that way to me.
Yes, that's right!
Yeah, I agree.
We should all pity his misfortune.
R-
Right, I thought so!
Well, I'll make sure I take care of the girl this time.
As an adult!
...
Oh. So I'm going to die...
without ever becoming a "proper adult"...
I'm so glad.

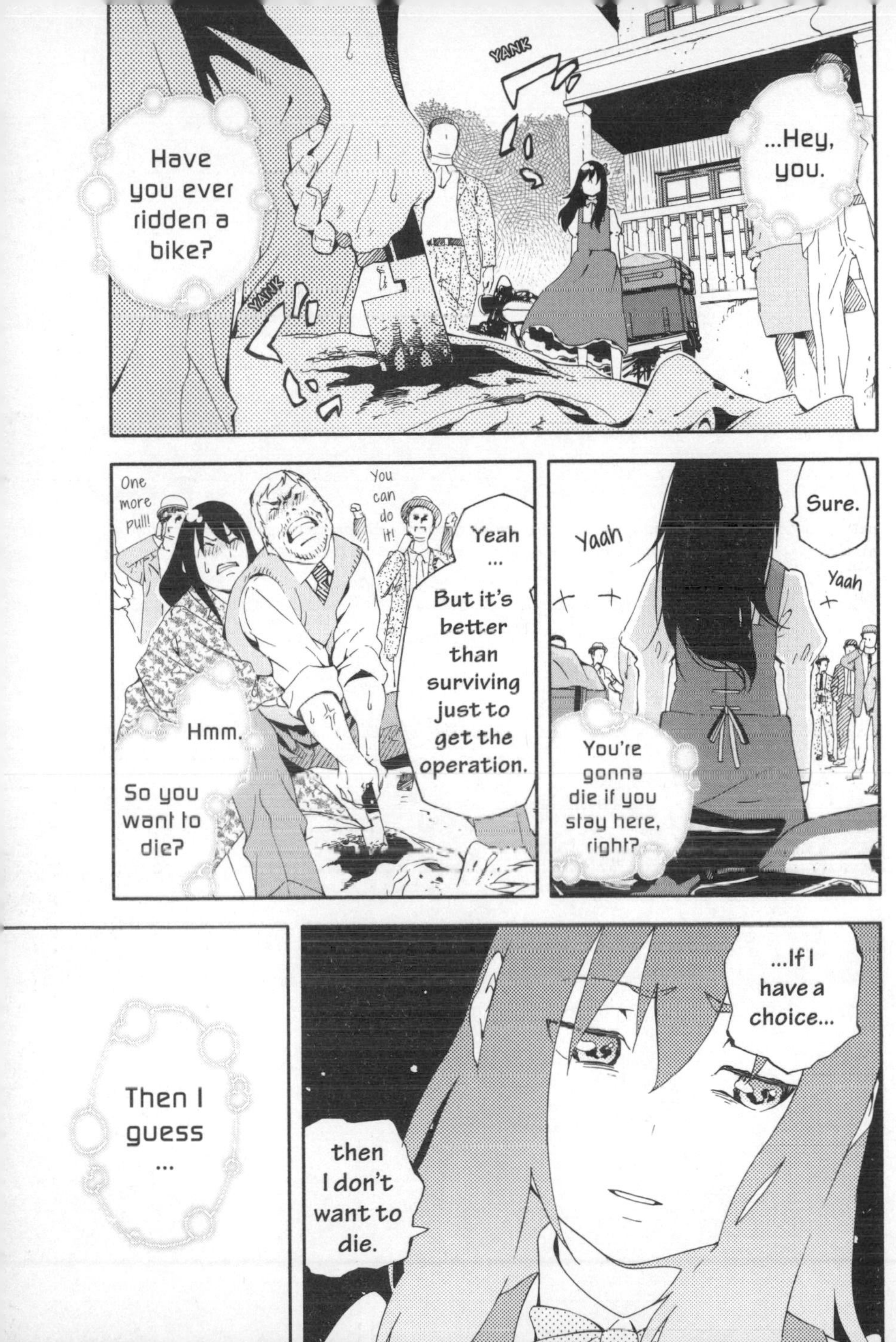
YANK
...Hey, you.
Have you ever ridden a bike?
YANK
Sure.
Yaah
Yaah
You're gonna die if you stay here, right?
You can do it!
One more pull!
Yeah ... But it's better than surviving just to get the operation.
Hmm.
So you want to die?
...If I have a choice...
then I don't want to die.
Then I guess ...

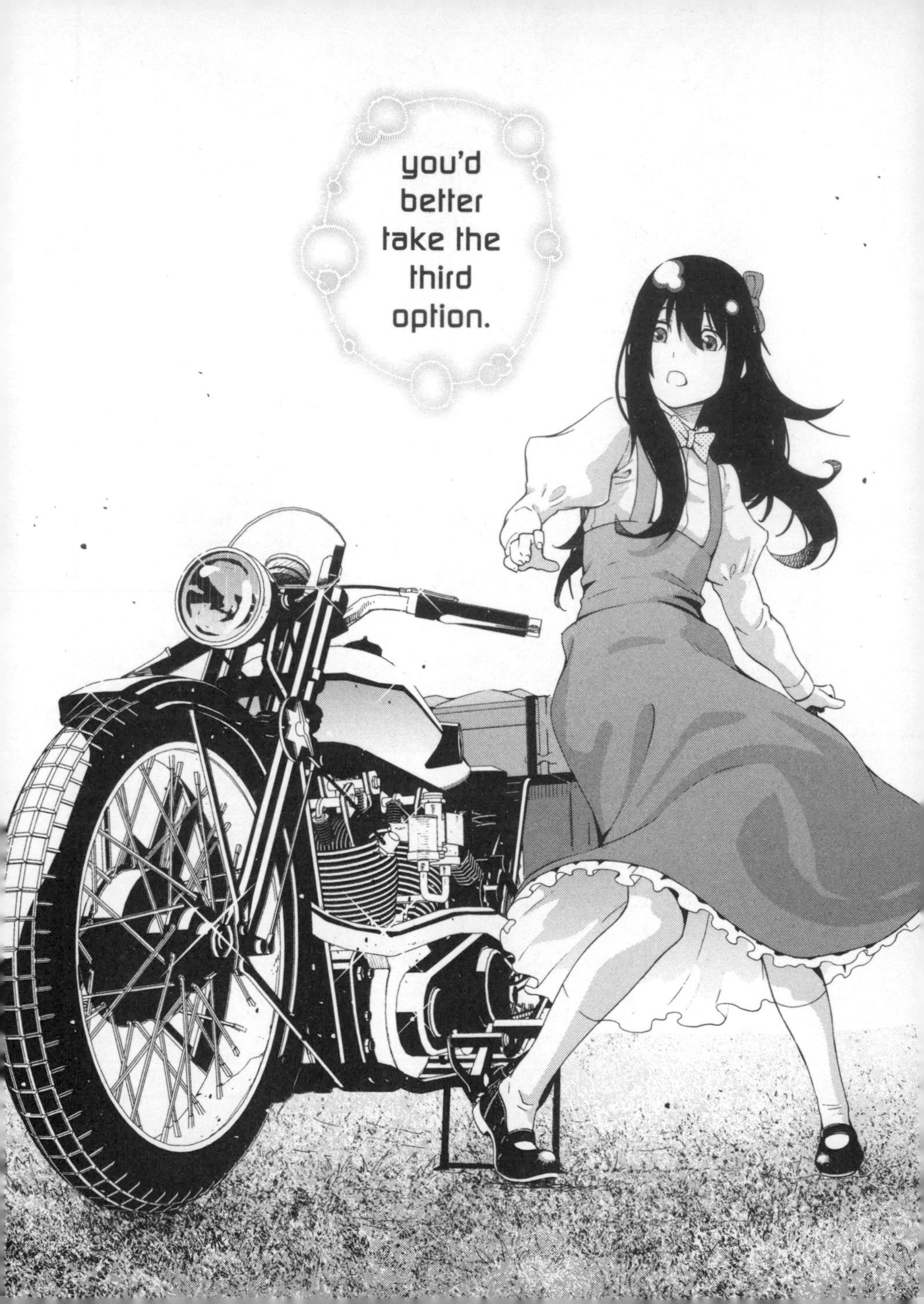
you'd better take the third option.

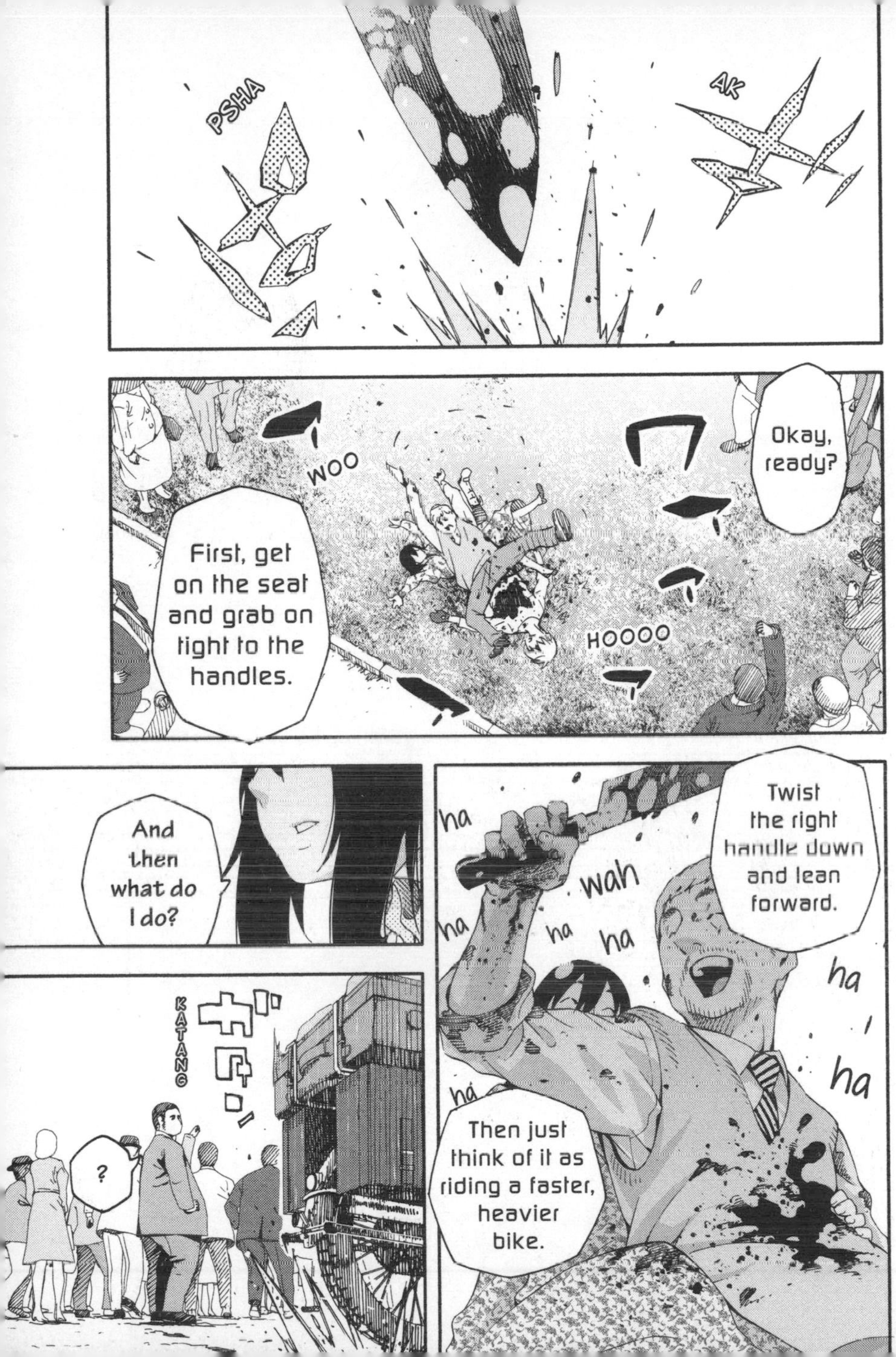
AK
PSHA
Okay, ready?
WOO
First, get on the seat and grab on tight to the handles.
HOOOO
Twist the right handle down and lean forward.
ha
wah
ha
ha
ha
ha
ha
ha
Then just think of it as riding a faster, heavier bike.
And then what do I do?
KATANG
?

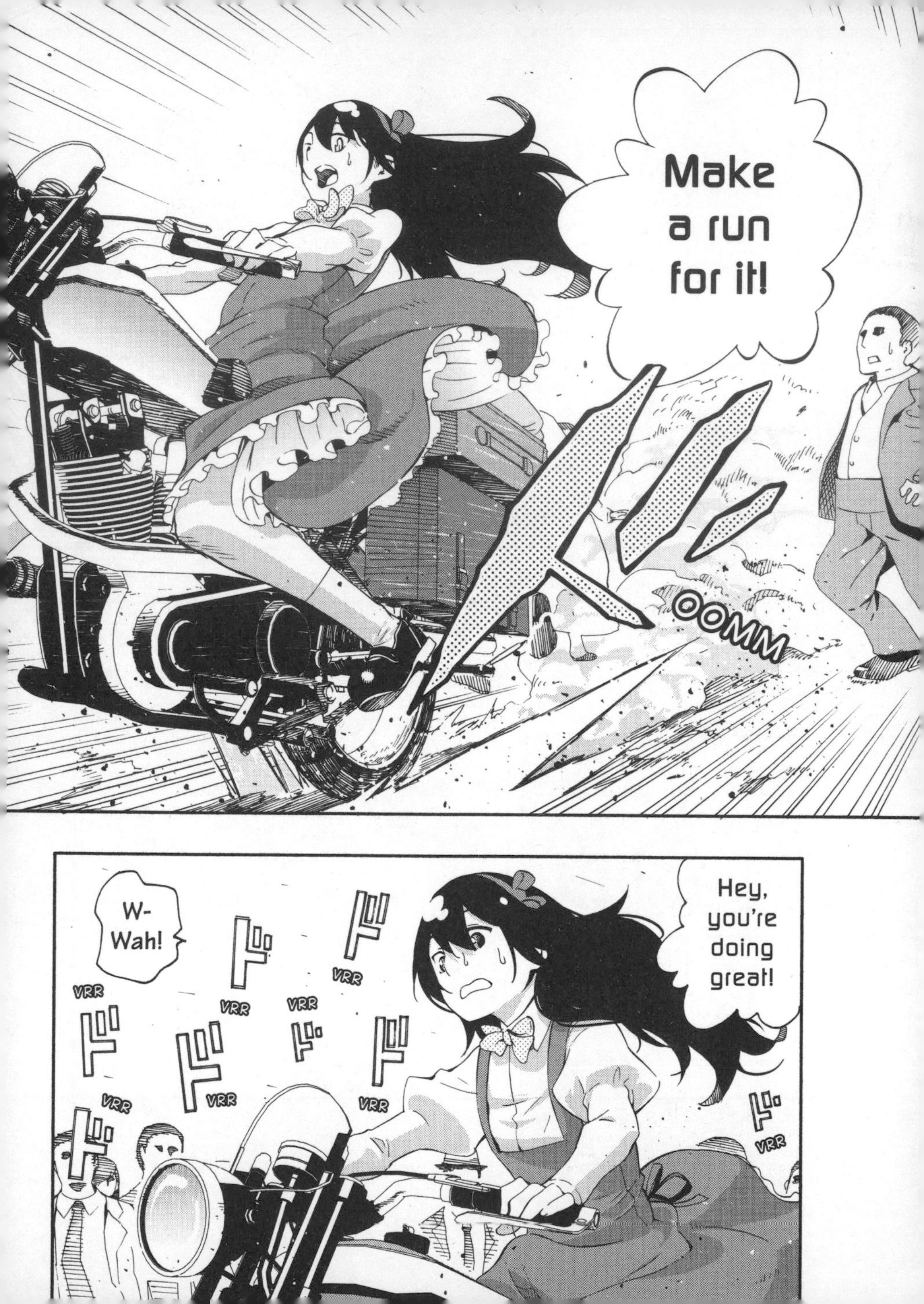
Make a run for it!
OOMM
Hey, you're doing great!
VRR
W-Wah!
VRR
VRR
VRR
VRR
VRR
VRR
VRR
VRR

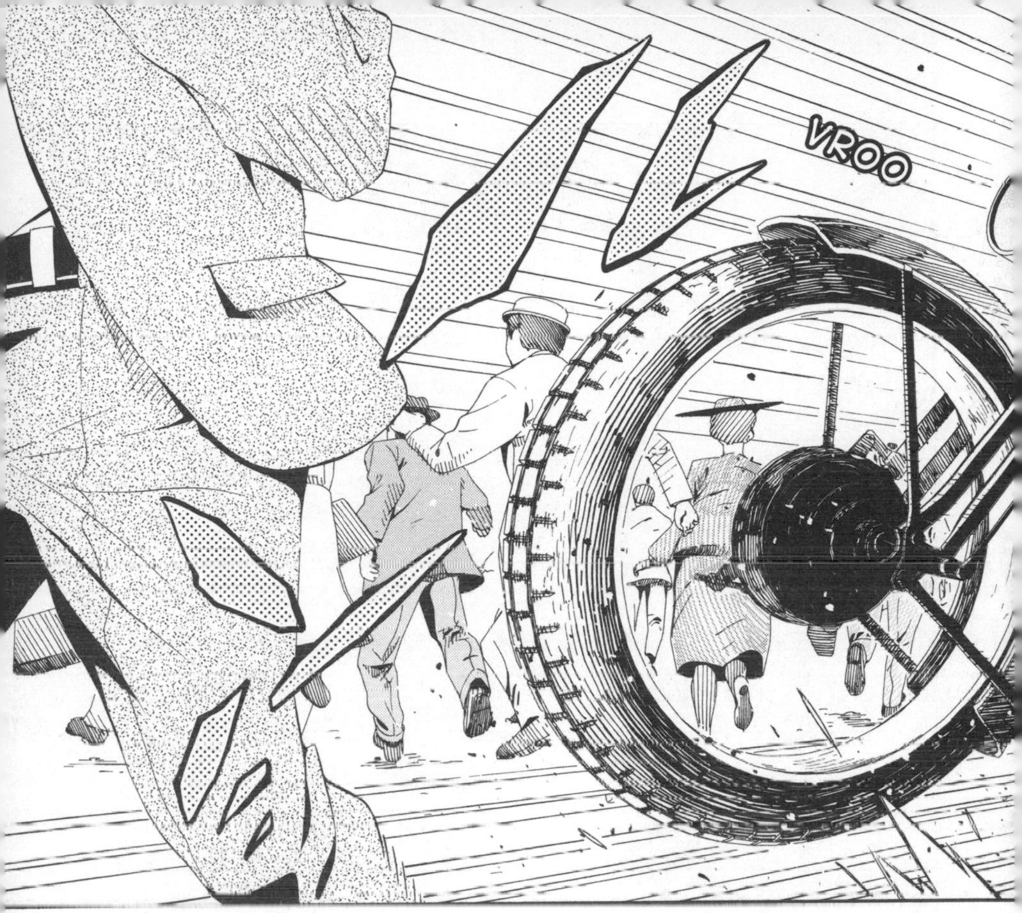
VROO

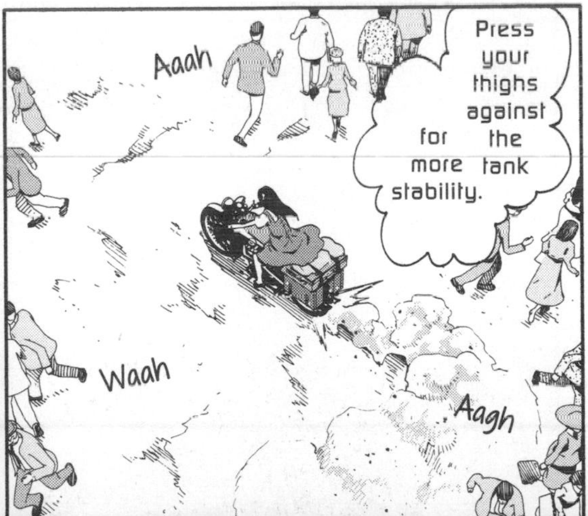
Aaah
Press your thighs against the tank for more stability.
Waah
Aagh

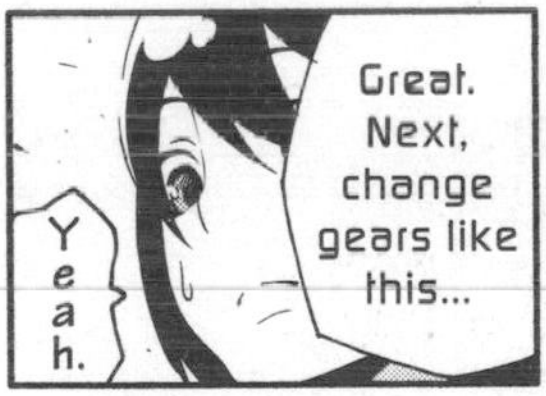
Great. Next, change gears like this...
Yeah.

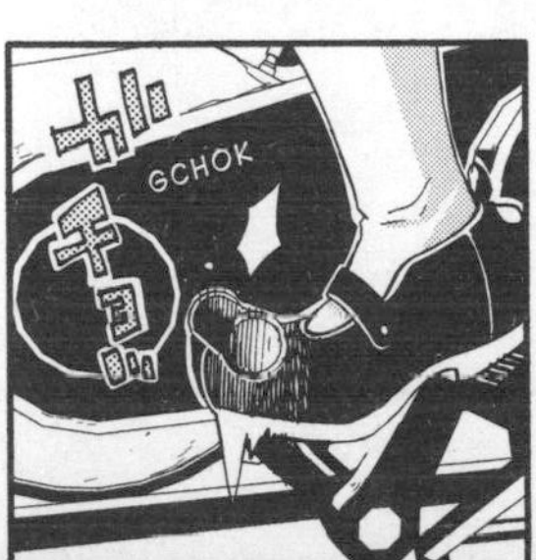
GCHOK

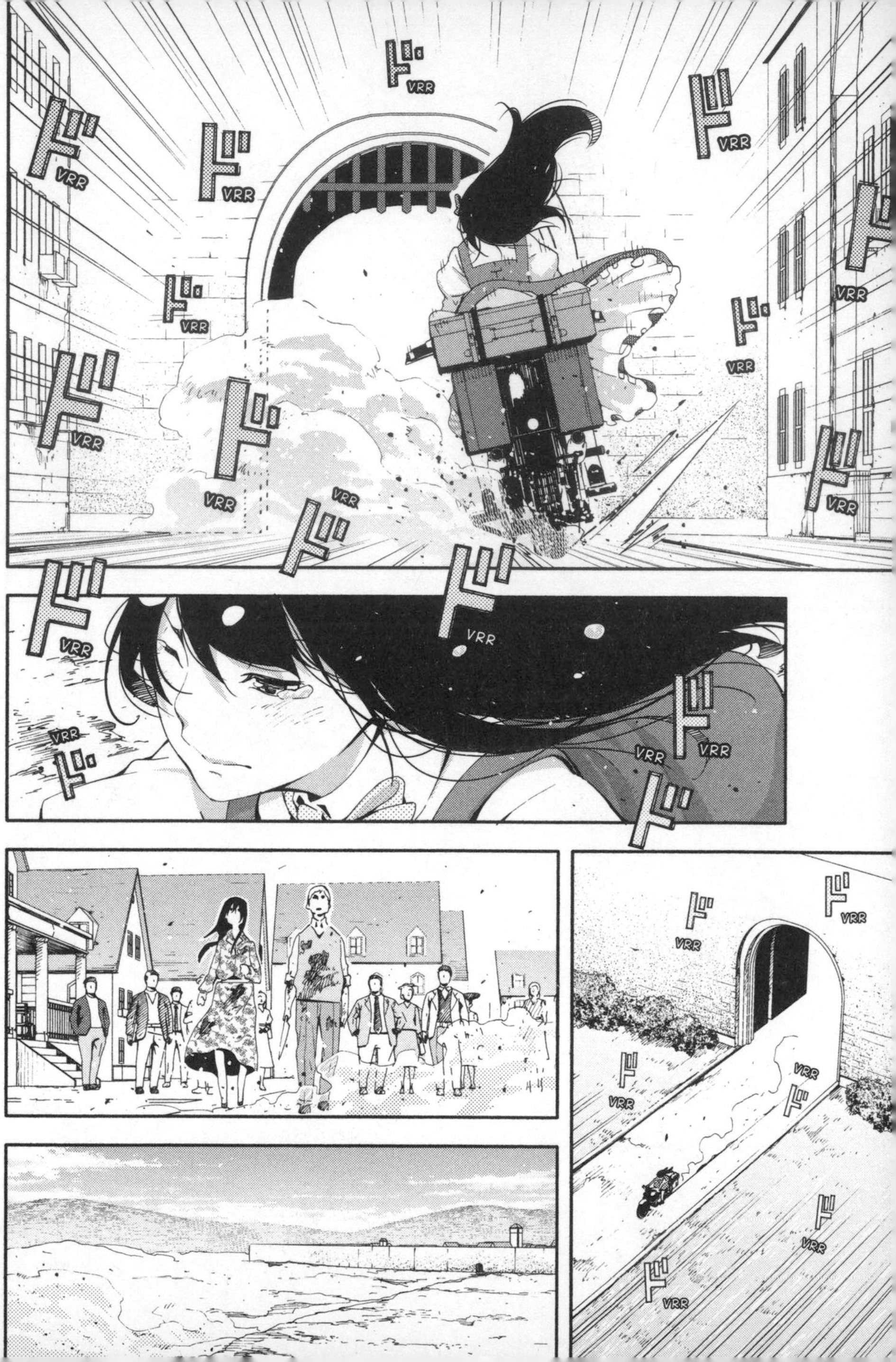
ド VRR
ド VRR
ド VRR
ド VRR
ド VRR
ド VRR
ド VRR
ド VRR
ド VRR
ド VRR

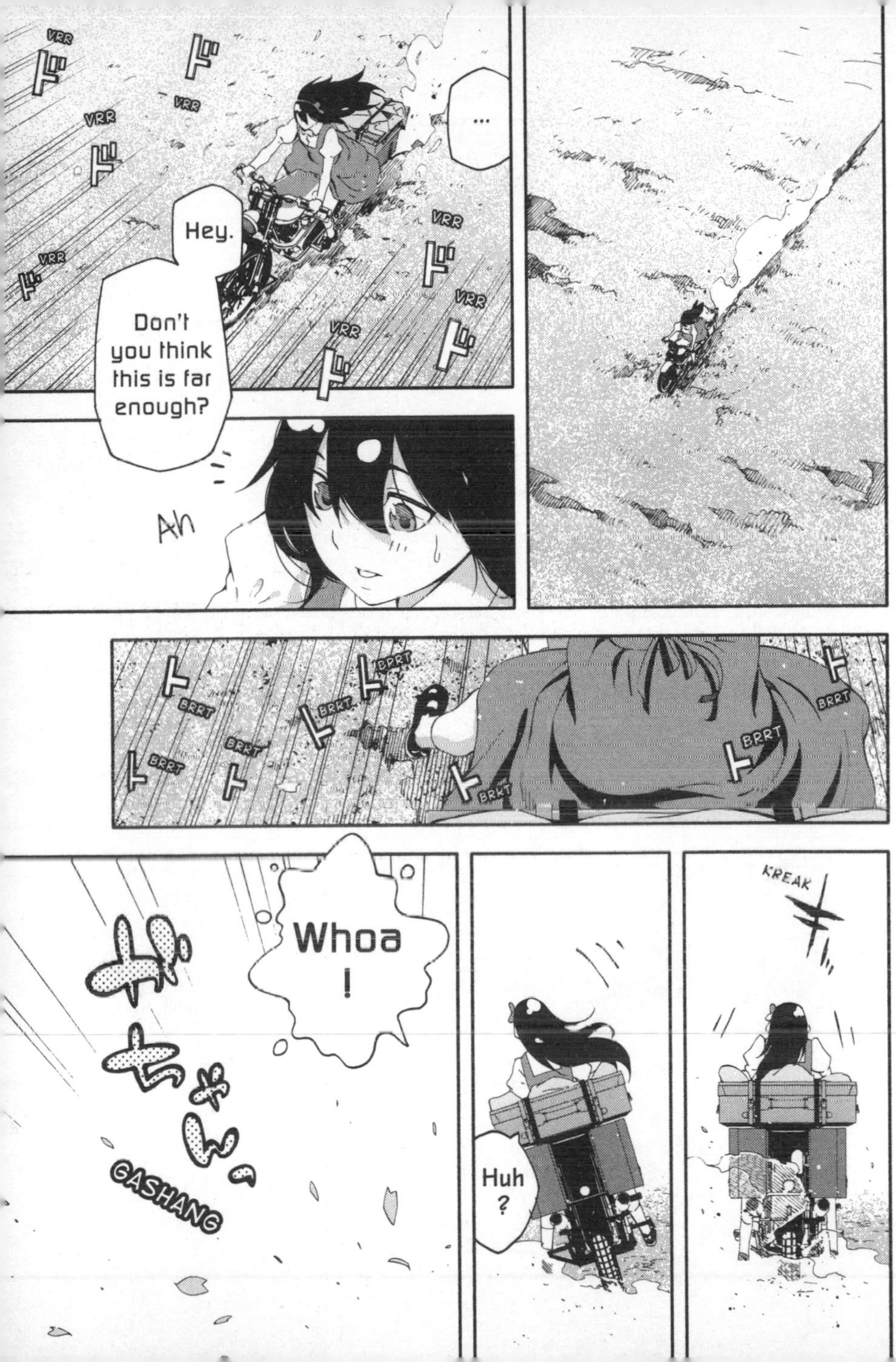

VRR
VRR
VRR
VRR
VRR
VRR
VRR
...
Hey.
Don't you think this is far enough?
Ah
BRRT
BRRT
BRRT
BRRT
BRRT
BRRT
BRRT
BRRT
KREAK
Huh?
Whoa!
GASHANG

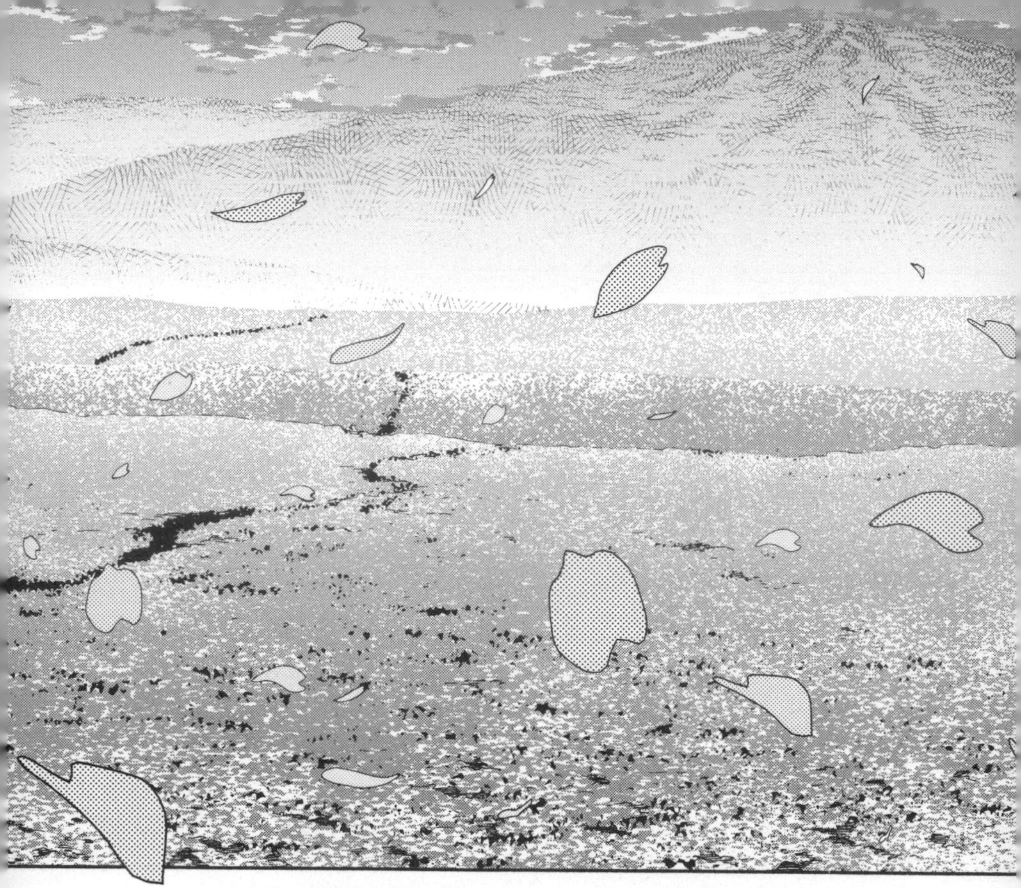

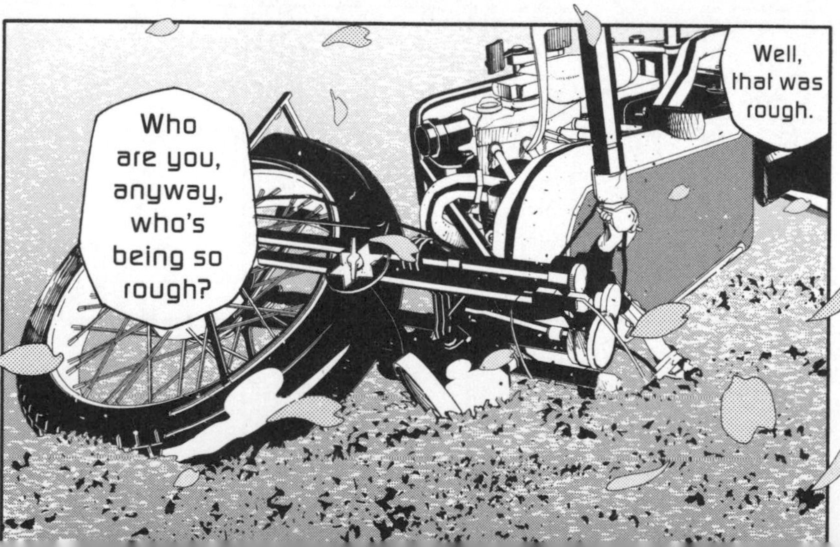
Well, that was rough.
Who are you, anyway, who's being so rough?

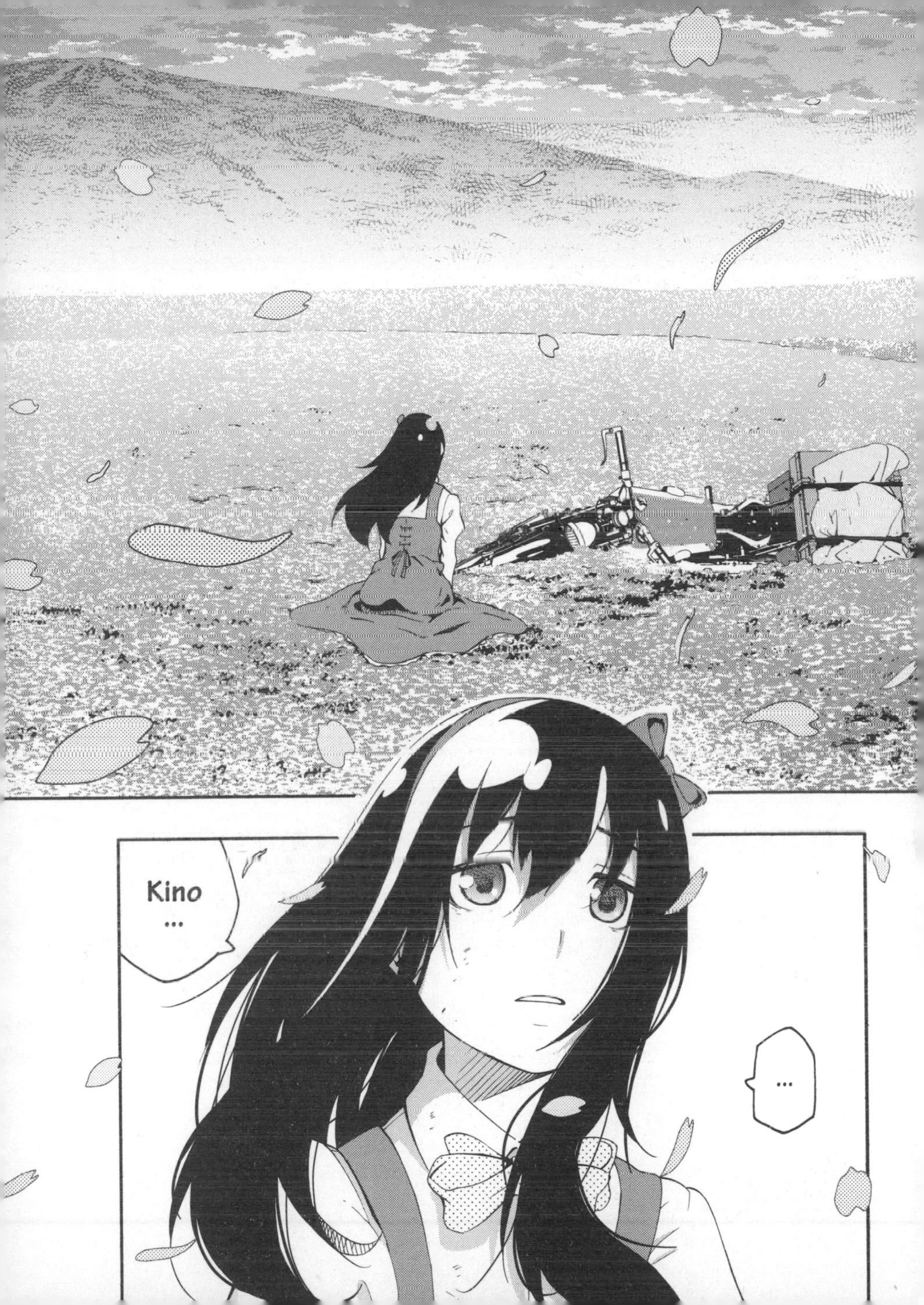
...
Kino ...

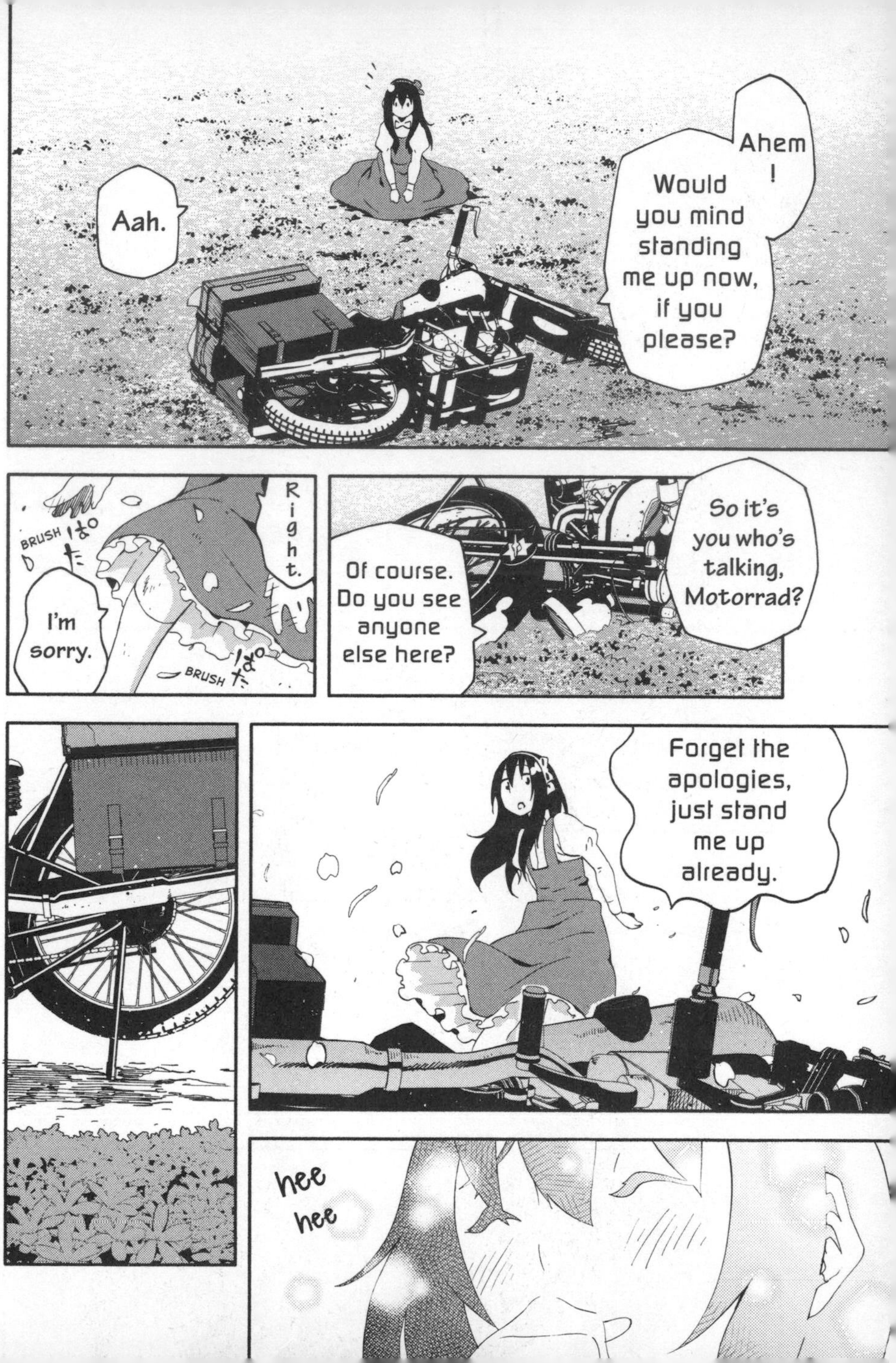
Ahem! Would you mind standing me up now, if you please?
Aah.
So it's you who's talking, Motorrad?
Of course. Do you see anyone else here?
Right.
BRUSH
I'm sorry.
BRUSH
Forget the apologies, just stand me up already.
hee hee

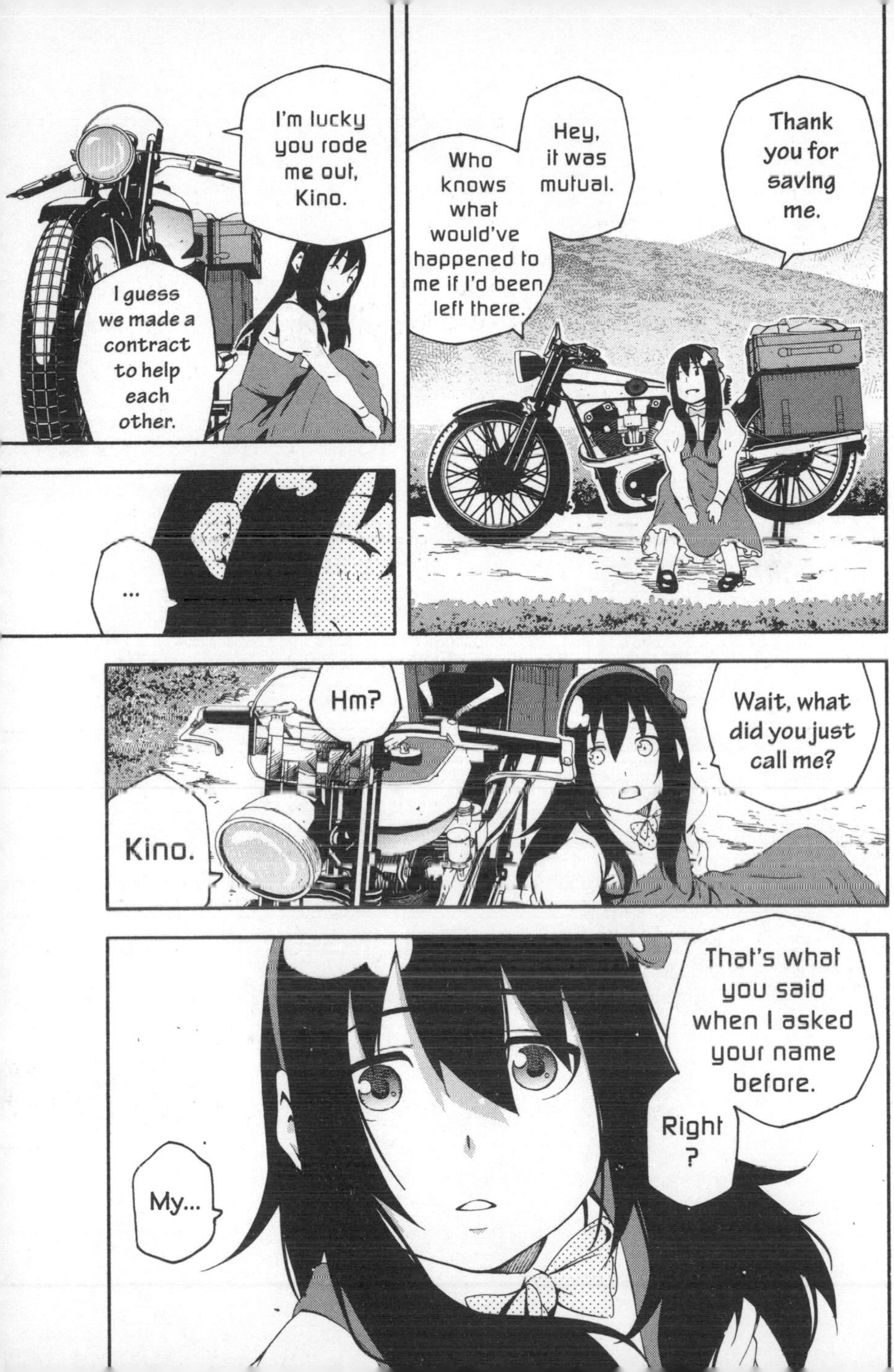
Thank you for saving me.
Hey, it was mutual.
Who knows what would've happened to me if I'd been left there.
I'm lucky you rode me out, Kino.
I guess we made a contract to help each other.
...
Wait, what did you just call me?
Hm?
Kino.
That's what you said when I asked your name before.
Right?
My...

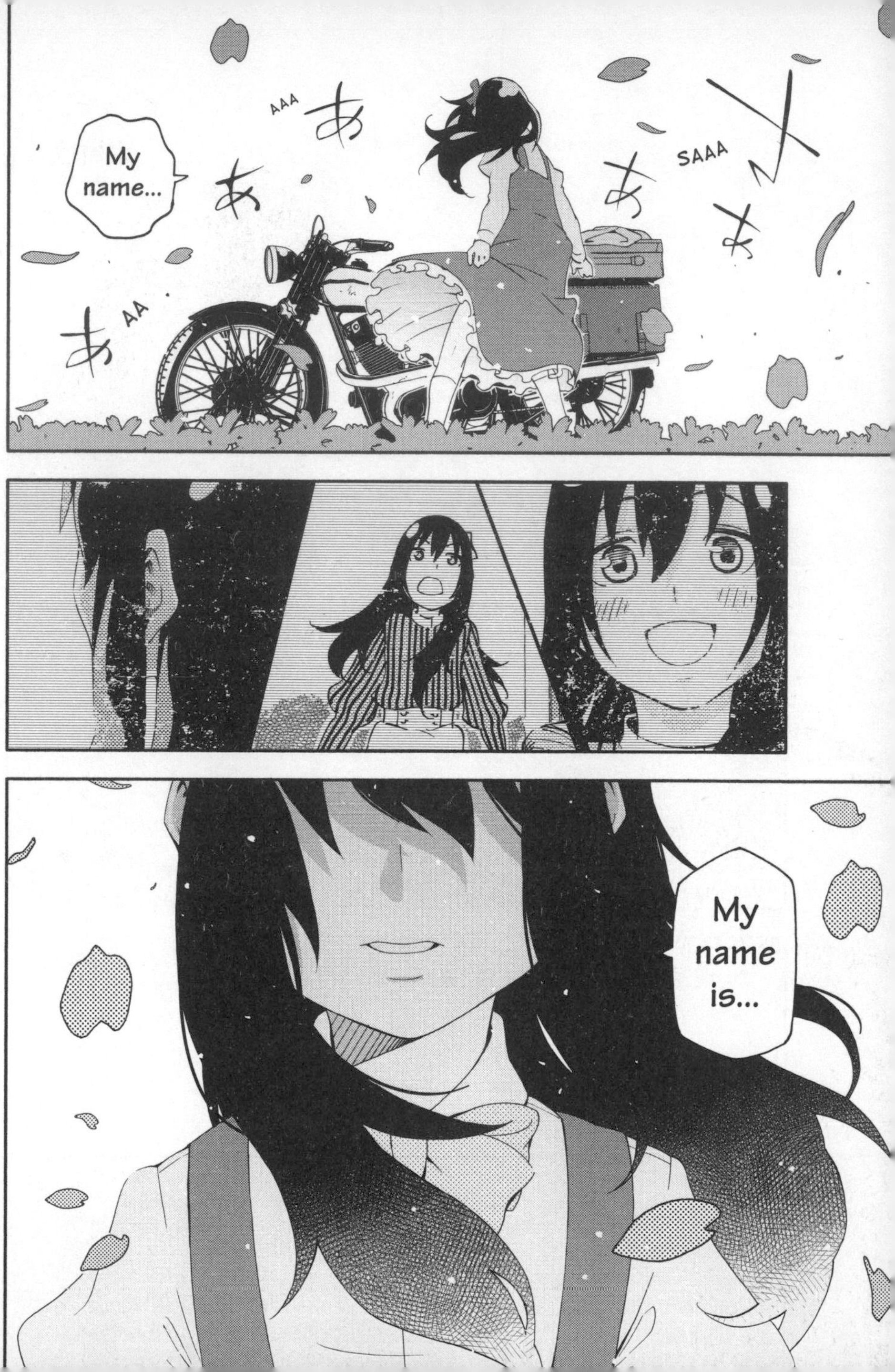
SAAA
AAA
My name...
AA
My name is...

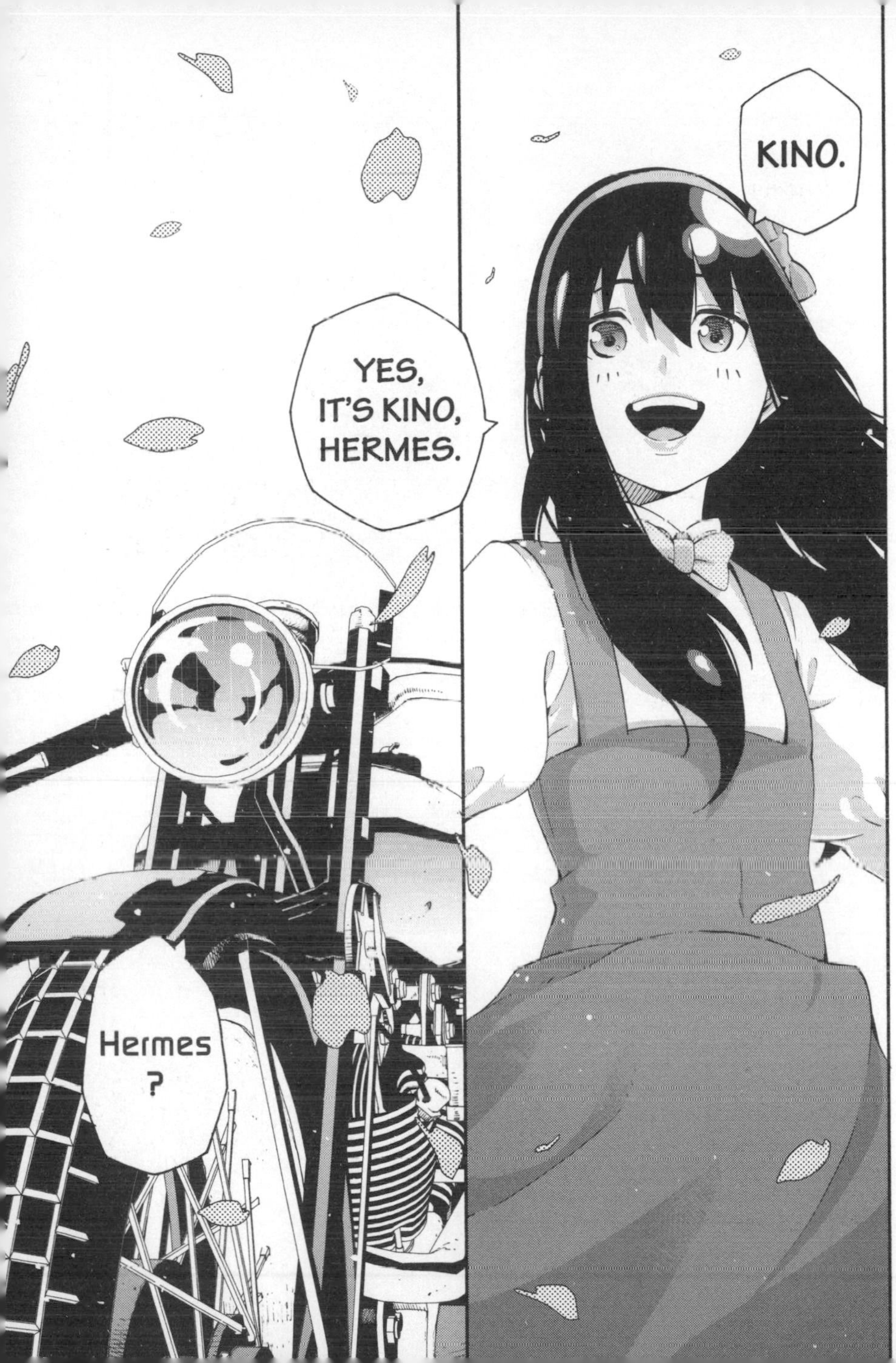
KINO.
YES, IT'S KINO, HERMES.
Hermes ?

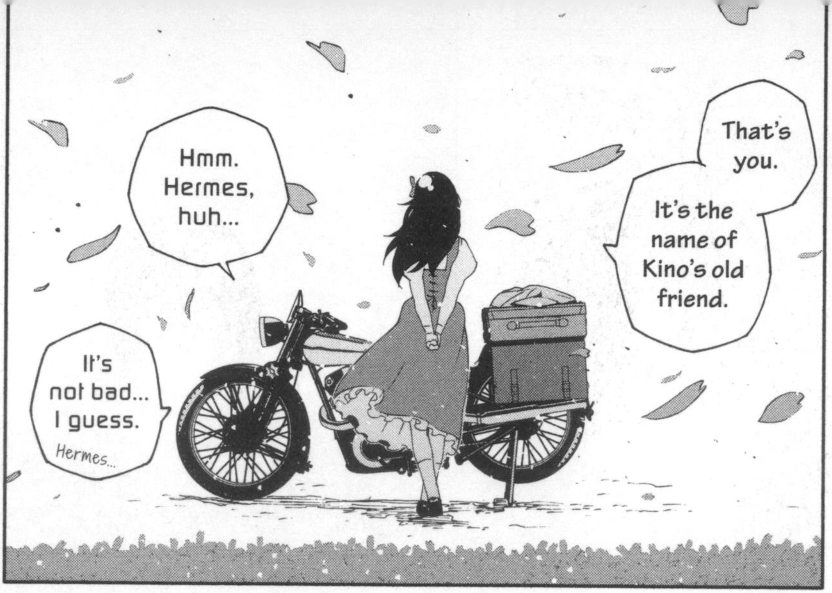
That's you.
It's the name of Kino's old friend.
Hmm. Hermes, huh...
It's not bad... I guess.
Hermes...

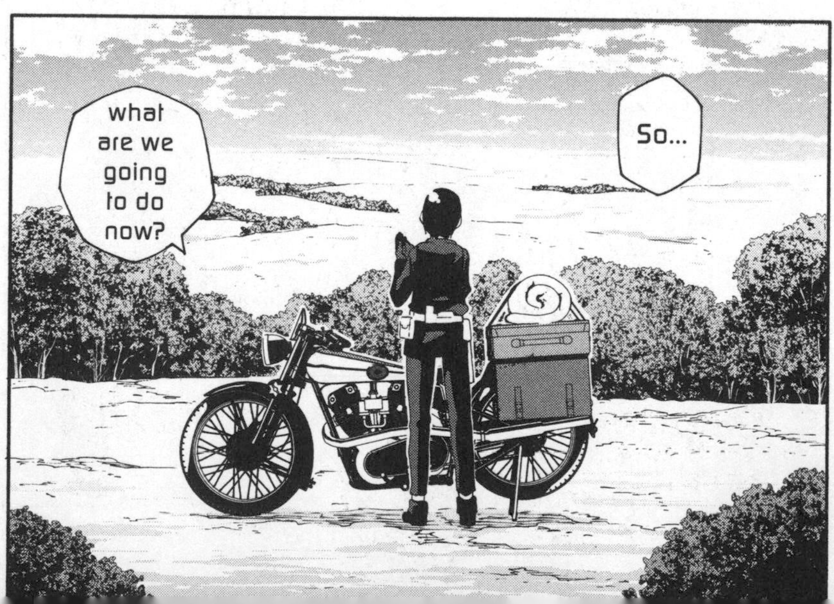
So...
what are we going to do now?

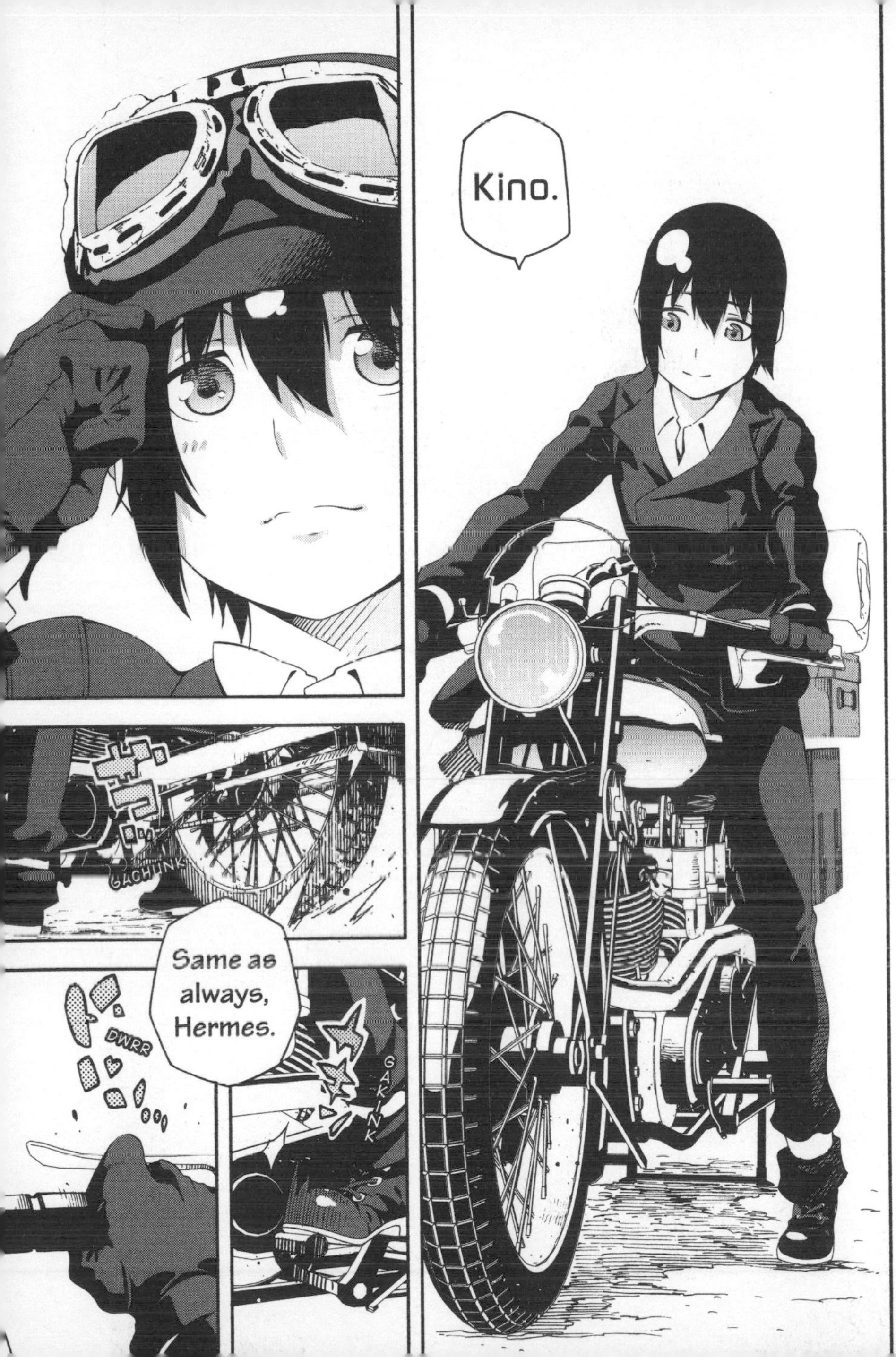
Kino.
GACHUNK
Same as always, Hermes.
DWRR
GAKINK

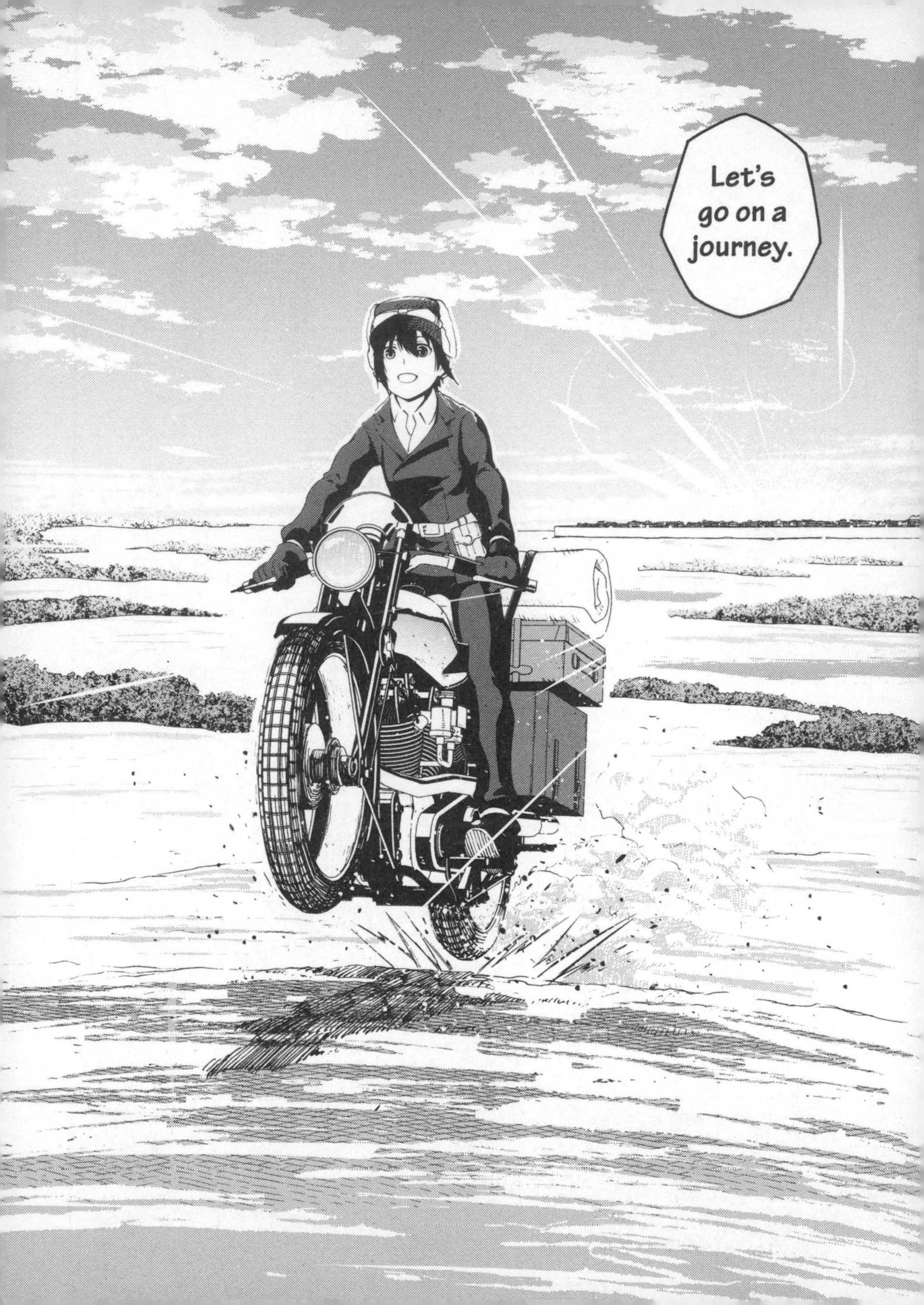
Let's go on a journey.

Chapter 2

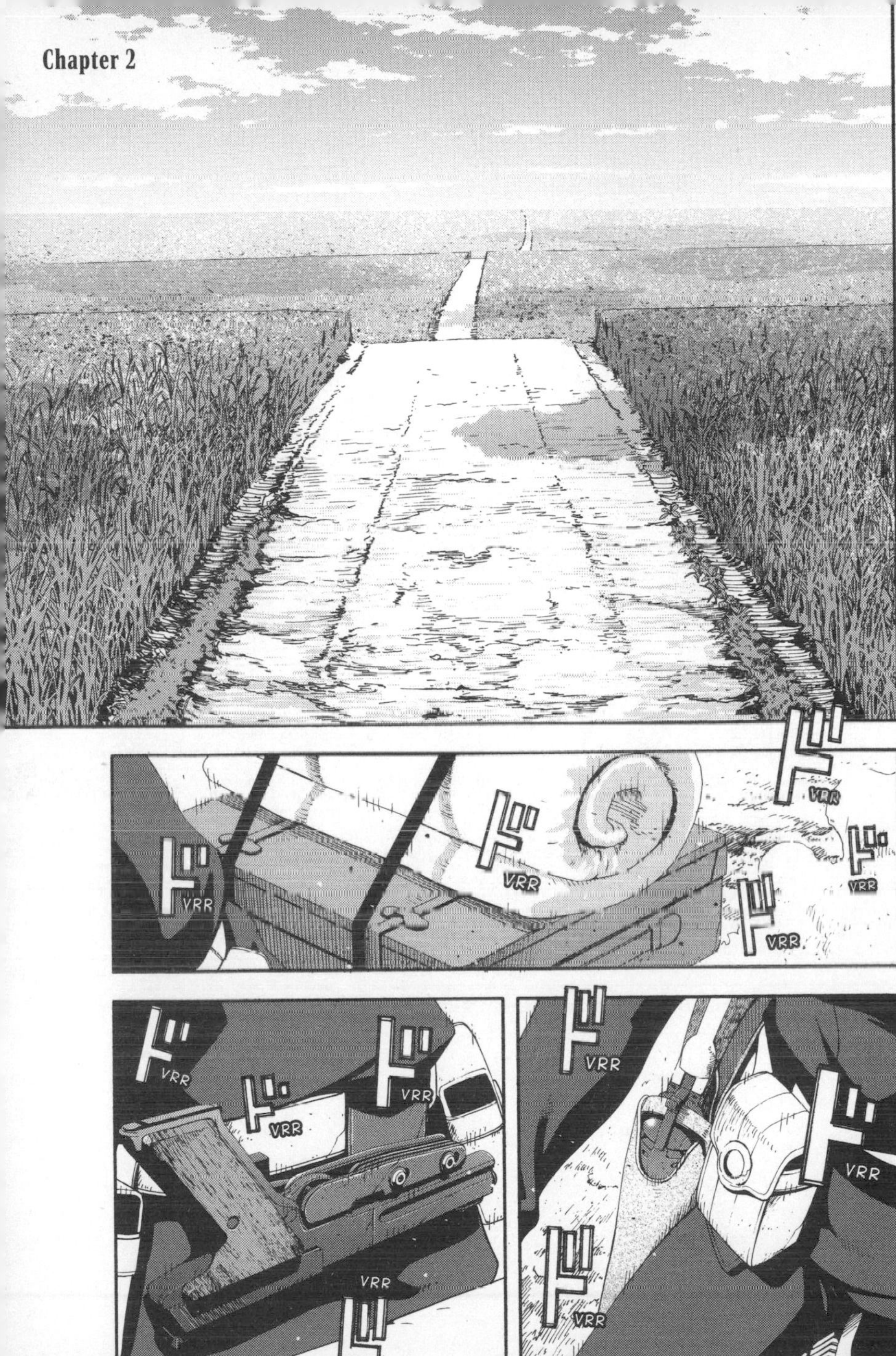
ド VRR
ド VRR
ド VRR
ド VRR
ド VRR
ド VRR
ド VRR
ド VRR
ド VRR
ド VRR
ド VRR
VRR ド

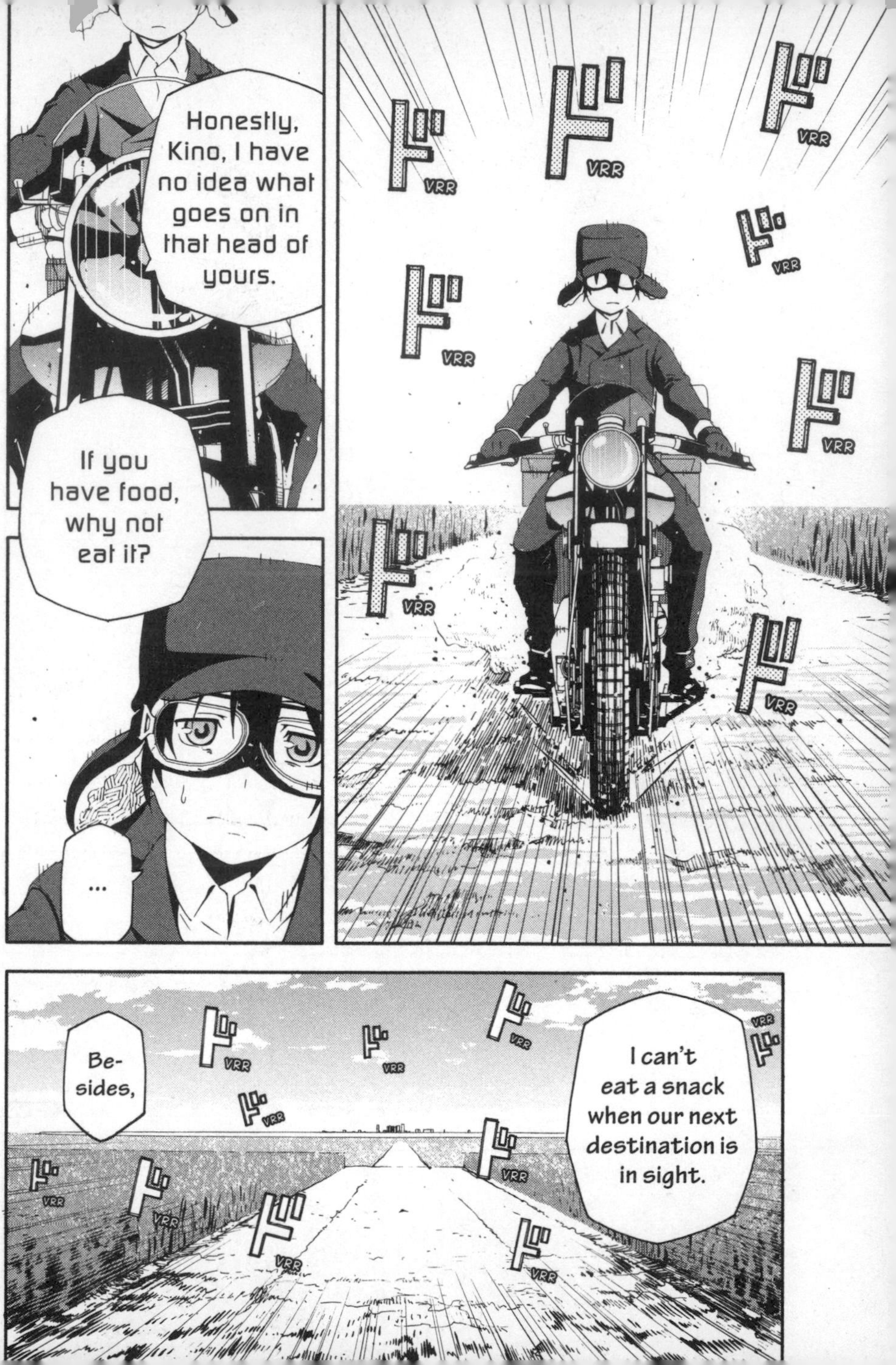

ド VRR
Honestly, Kino, I have no idea what goes on in that head of yours.
If you have food, why not eat it?
...
ド VRR
Be-sides,
I can't eat a snack when our next destination is in sight.

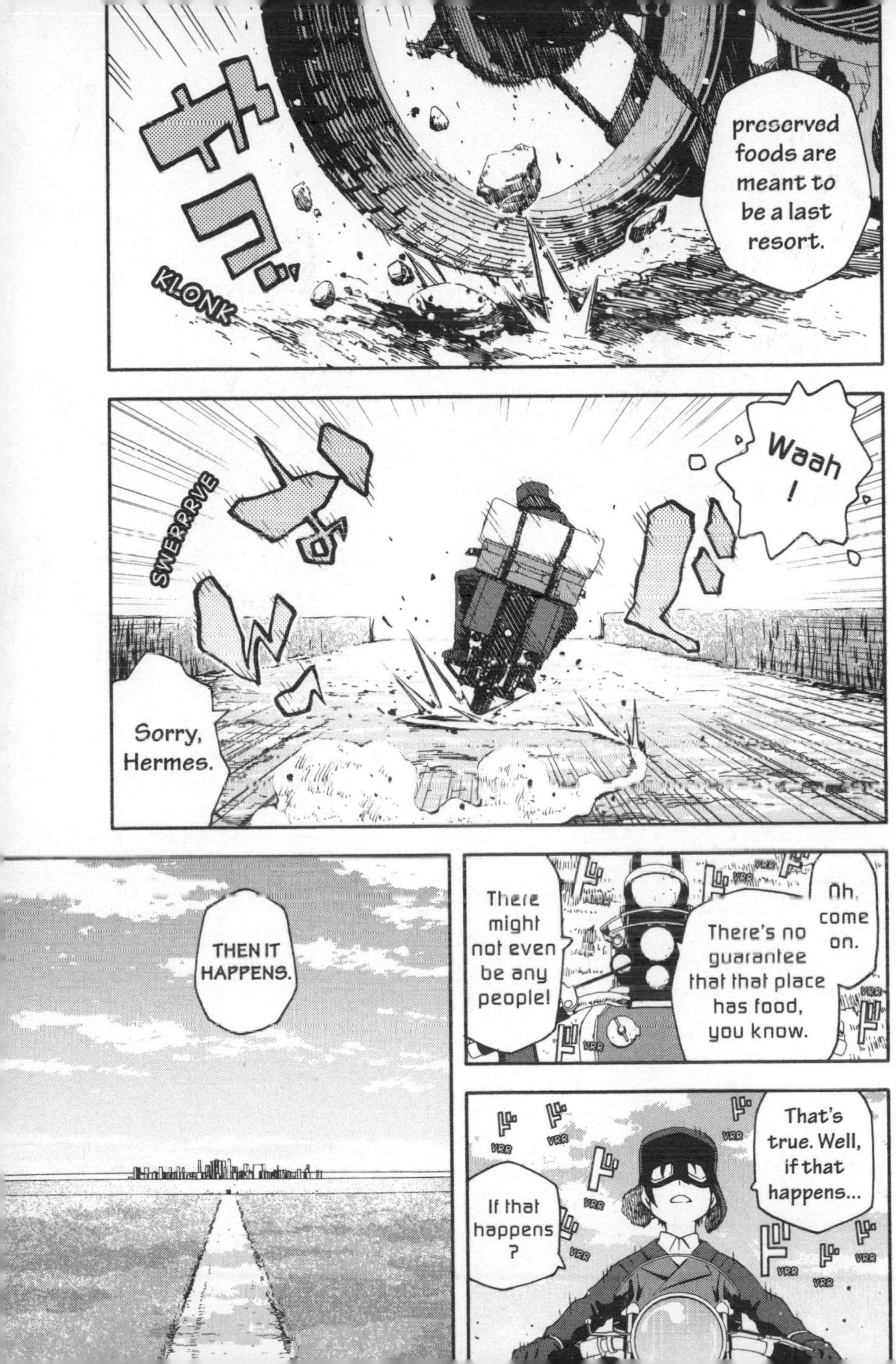
preserved foods are meant to be a last resort.
KLONK
Waah!
SWERRRVE
Sorry, Hermes.
Oh, come on.
There's no guarantee that that place has food, you know.
There might not even be any people!
VRR
That's true. Well, if that happens...
If that happens?
VRR
THEN IT HAPPENS.

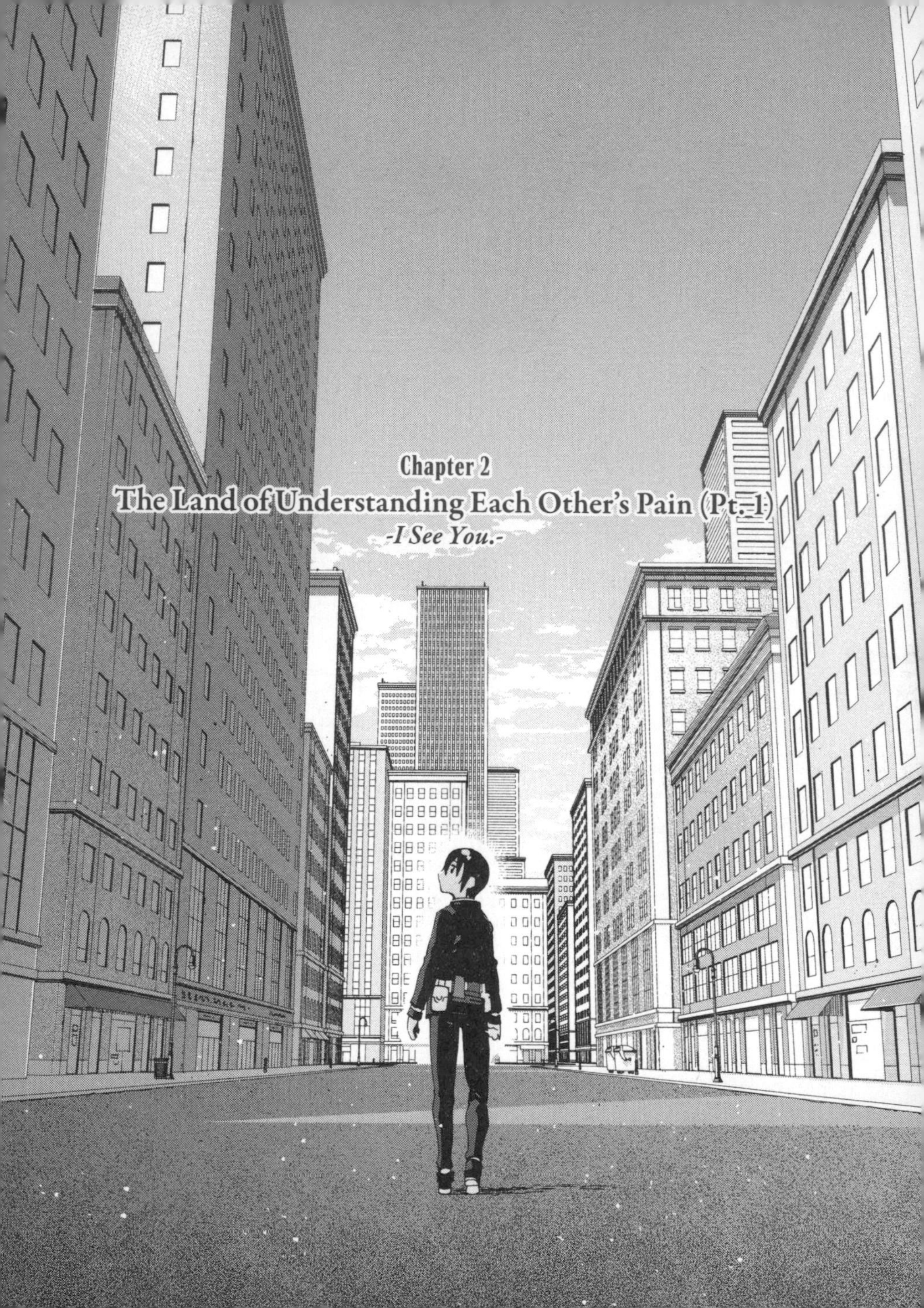
Chapter 2
The Land of Understanding Each Other's Pain (Pt. 1)
-I See You.-

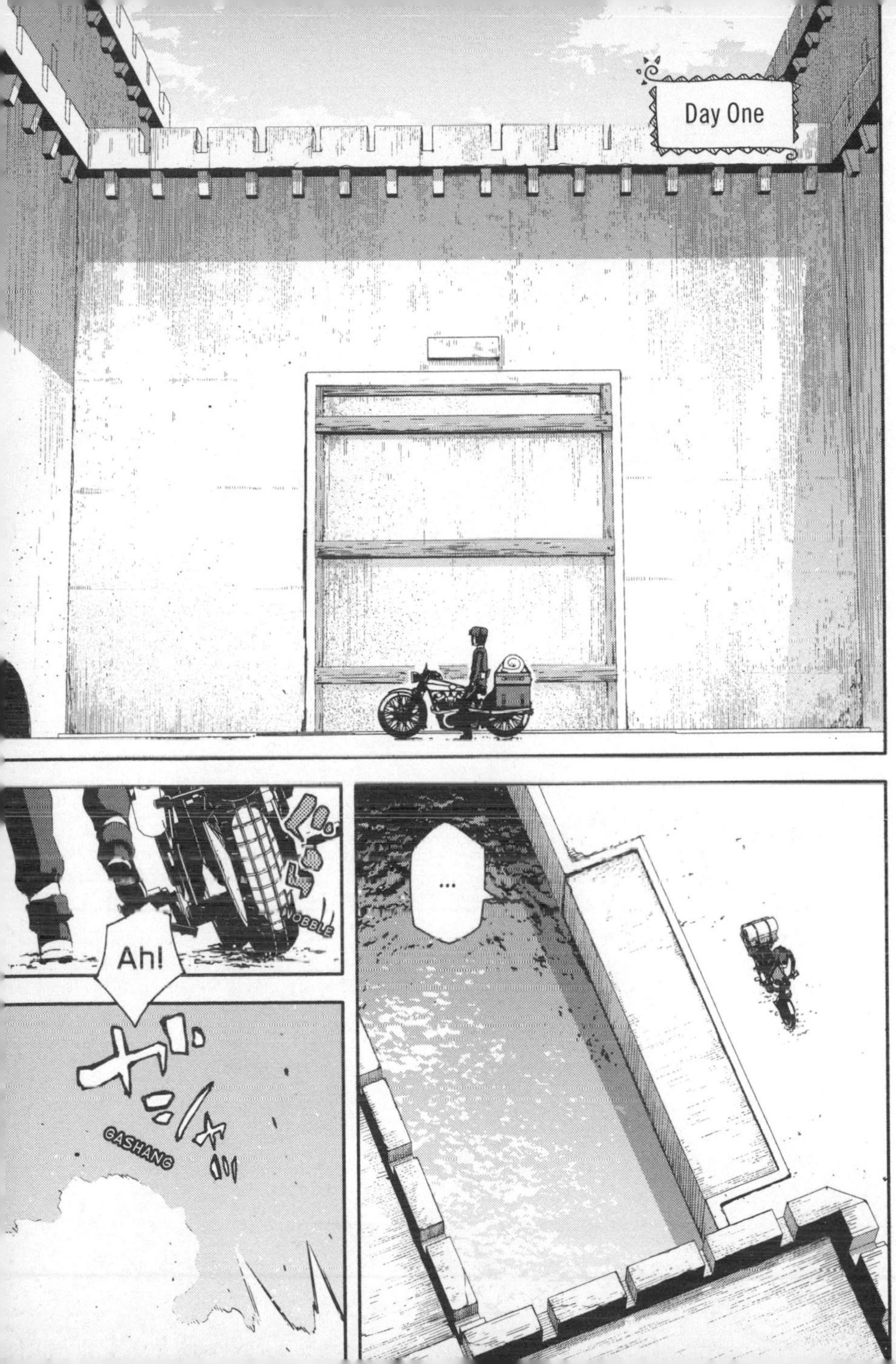
Day One
...
WOBBLE
Ah!
GASHANG

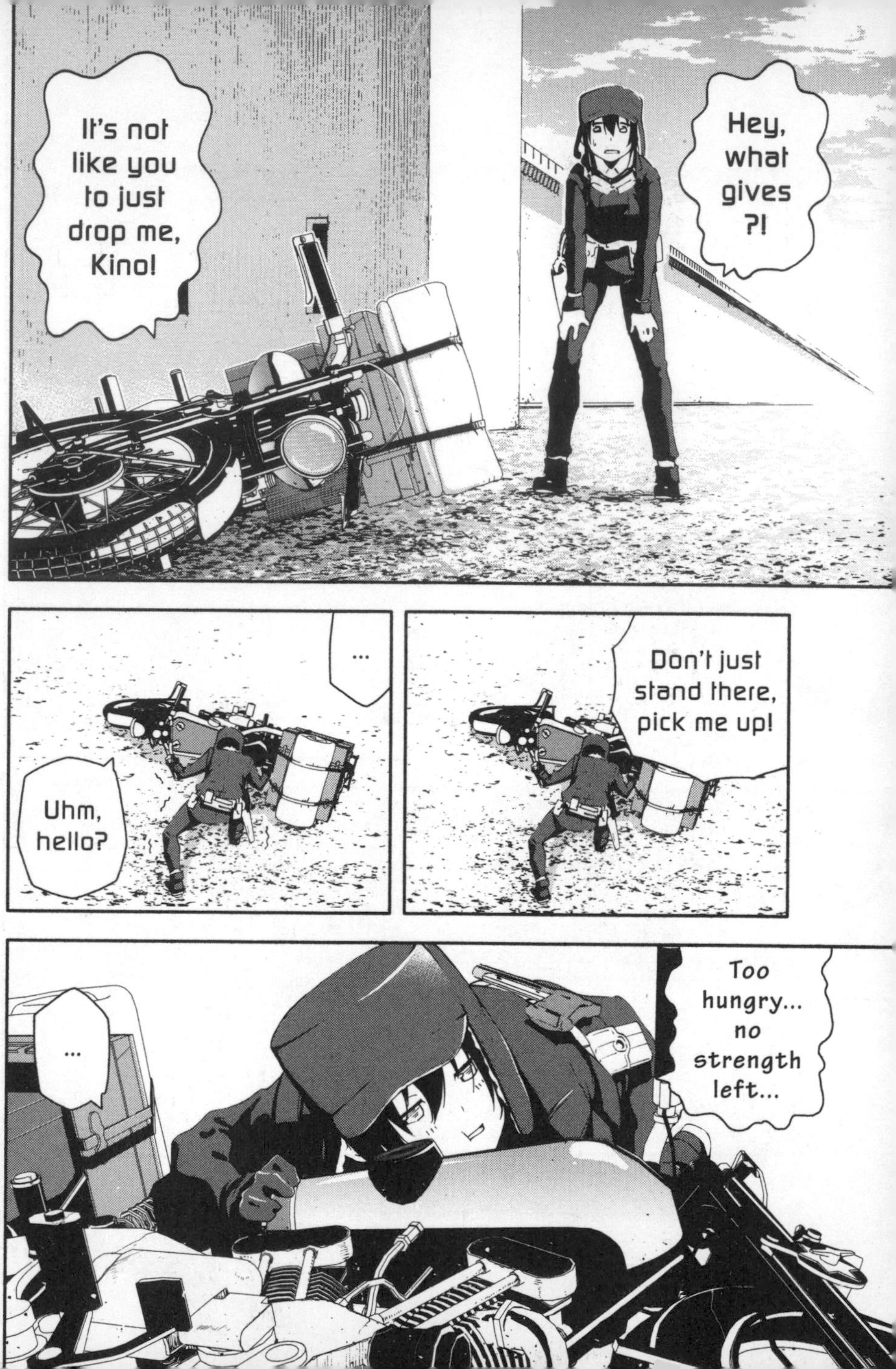
Hey, what gives ?!
It's not like you to just drop me, Kino!
Don't just stand there, pick me up!
...
Uhm, hello?
Too hungry... no strength left...
...

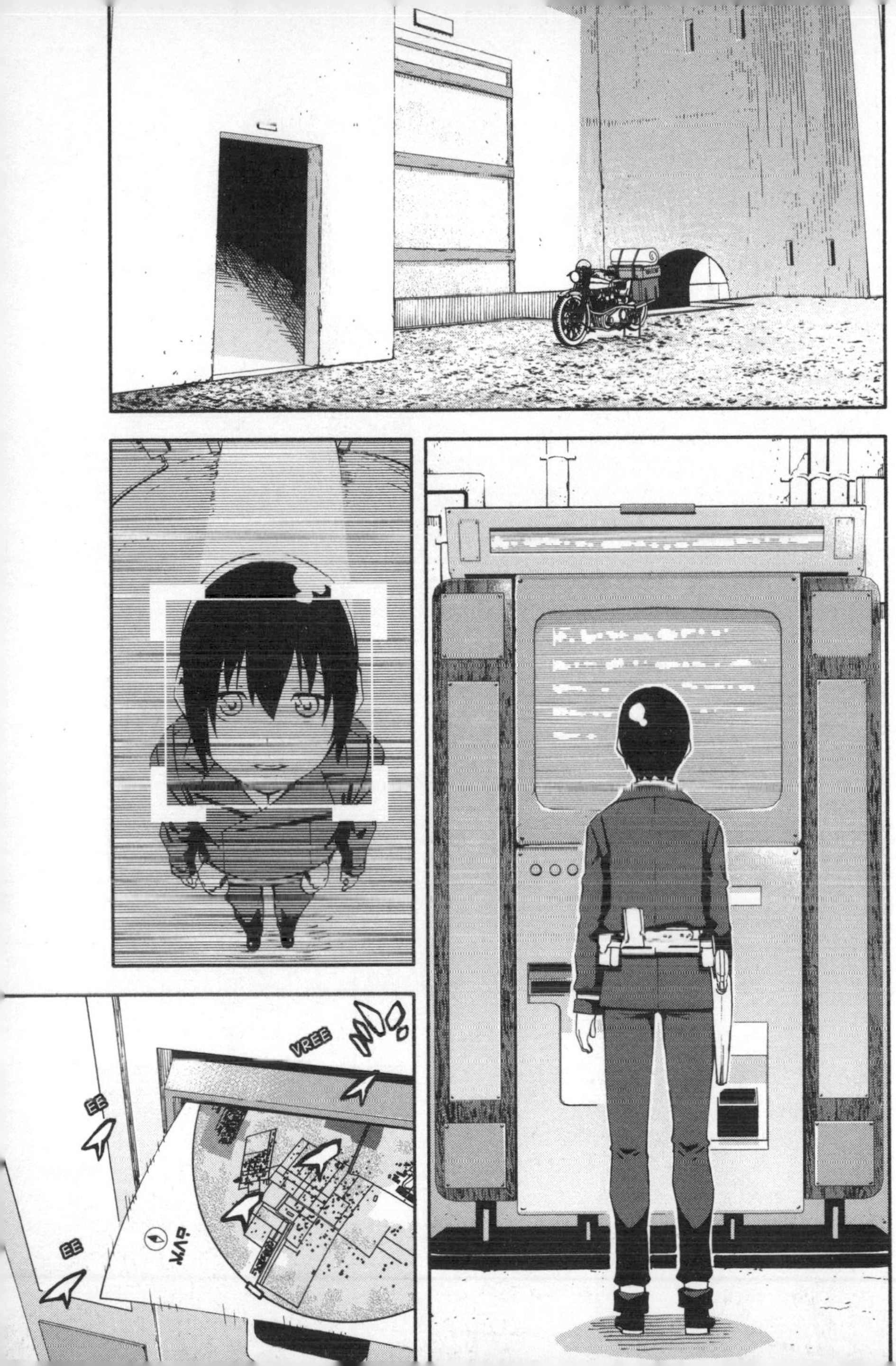
VREE
EE
EE

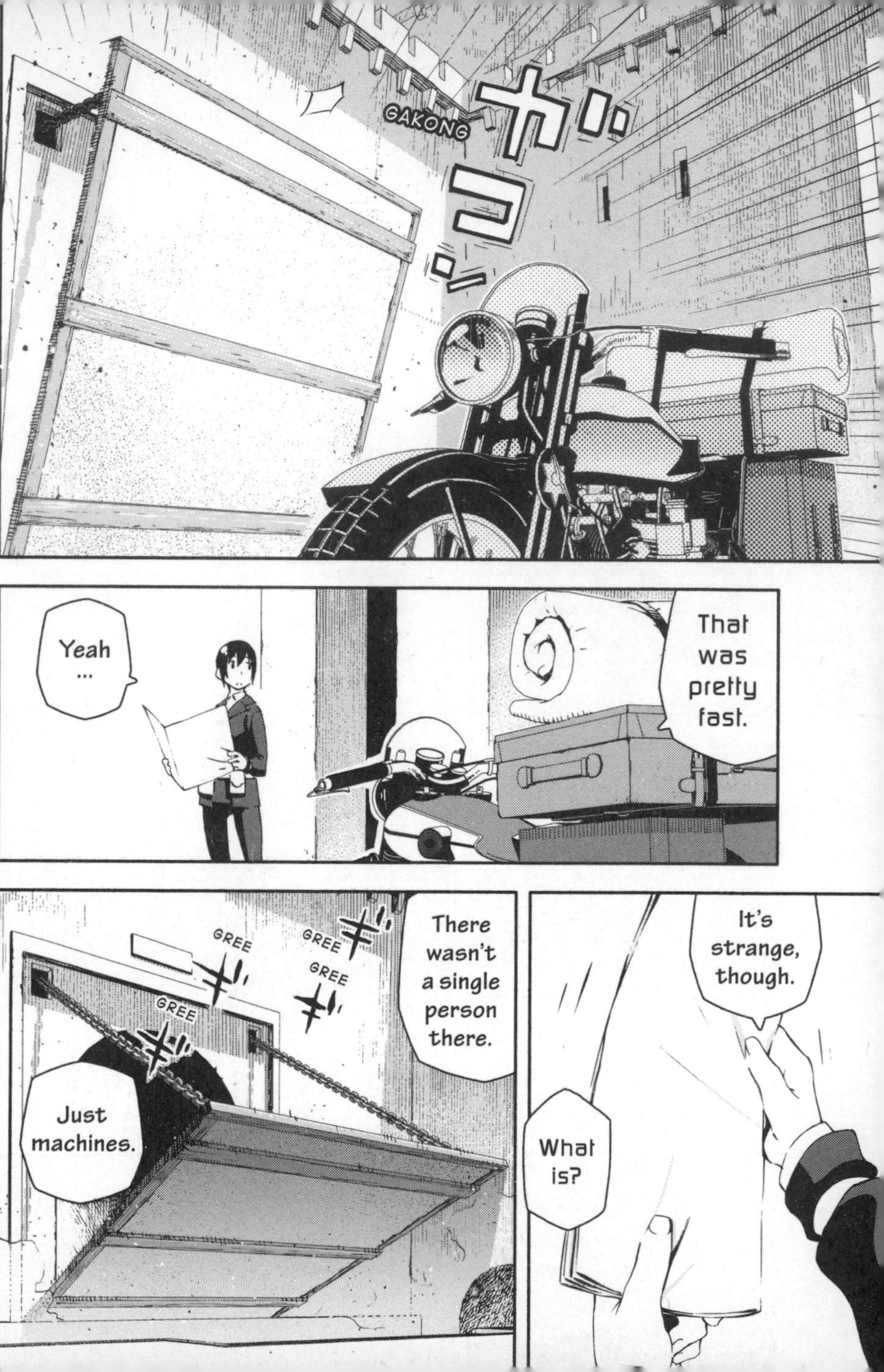
GAKONG
That was pretty fast.
Yeah ...
It's strange, though.
What is?
There wasn't a single person there.
GREE
GREE
GREE
GREE
Just machines.

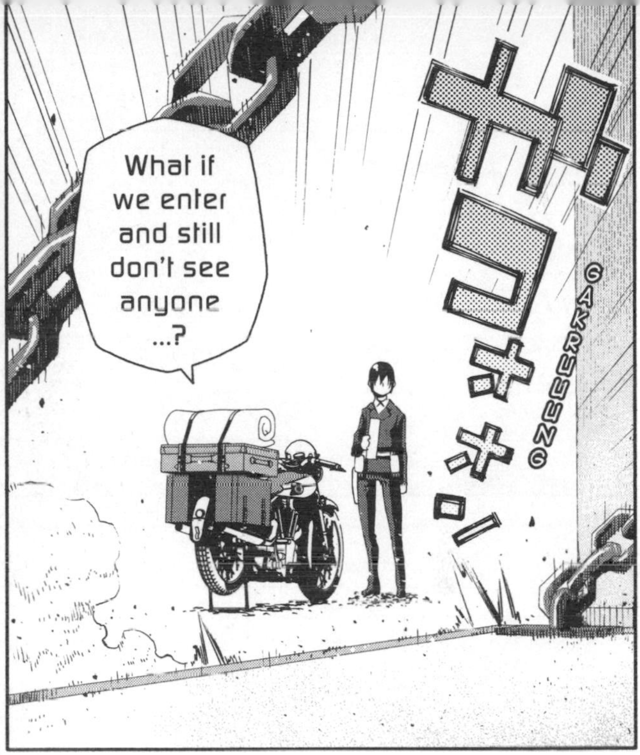
What if we enter and still don't see anyone ...?
GAKRUUUUNG
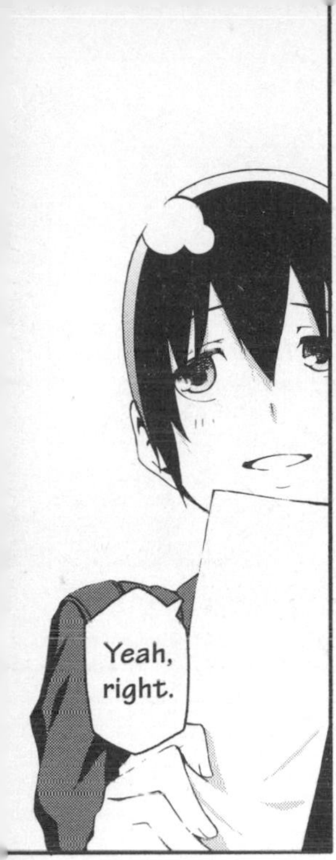
Yeah, right.
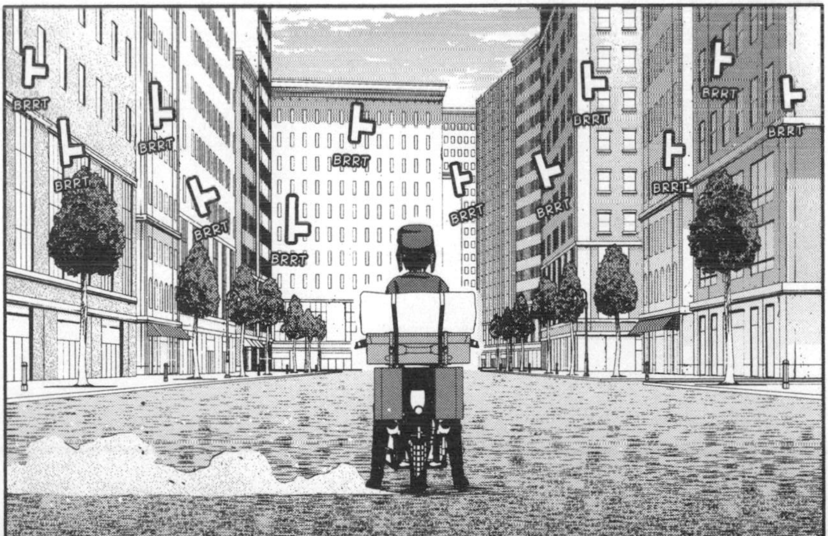
BRRT
BRRT
BRRT
BRRT
BRRT
BRRT
BRRT
BRRT
BRRT
BRRT
BRRT
BRRT

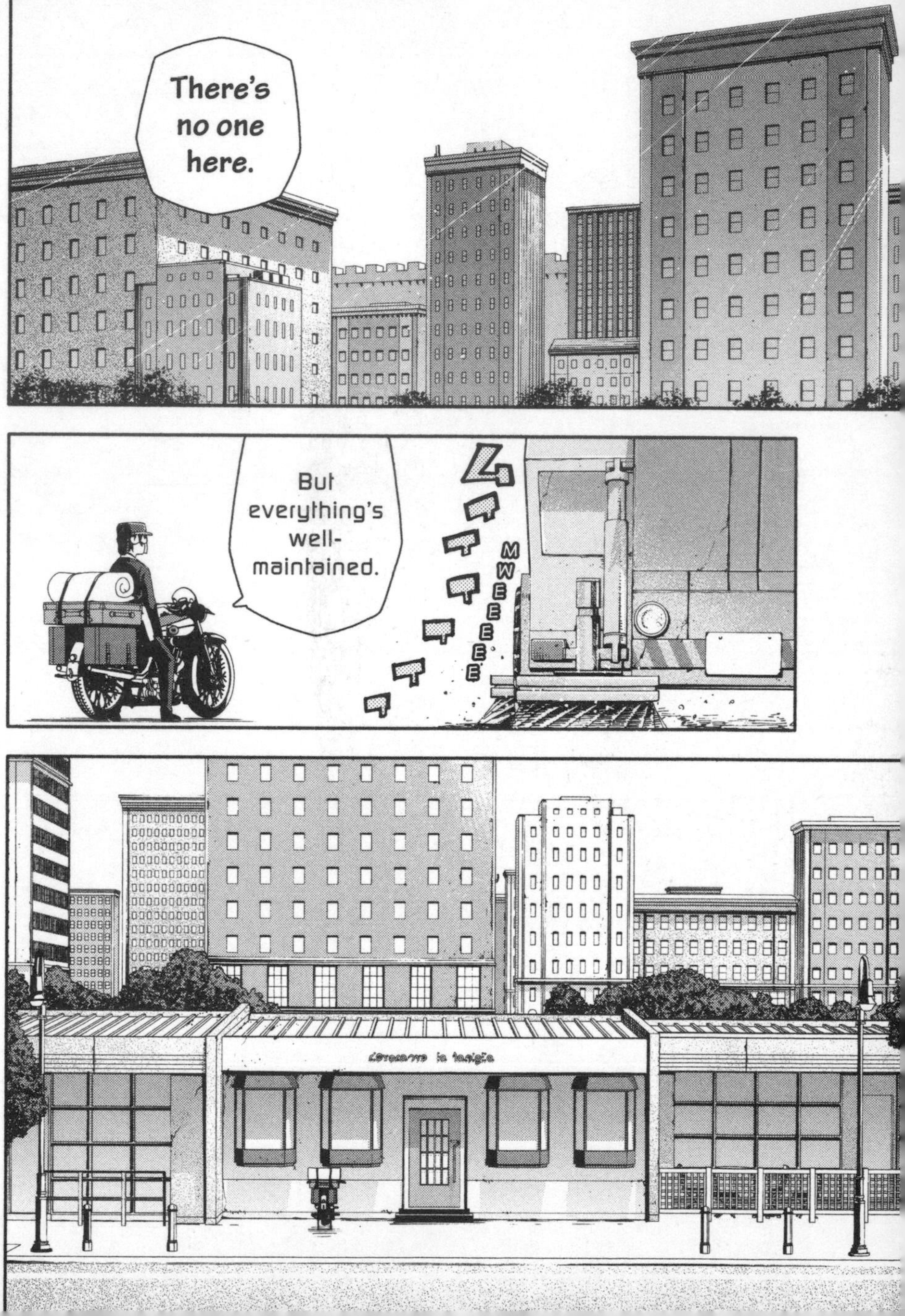
There's no one here.
But everything's well-maintained.
MWEEEEEE

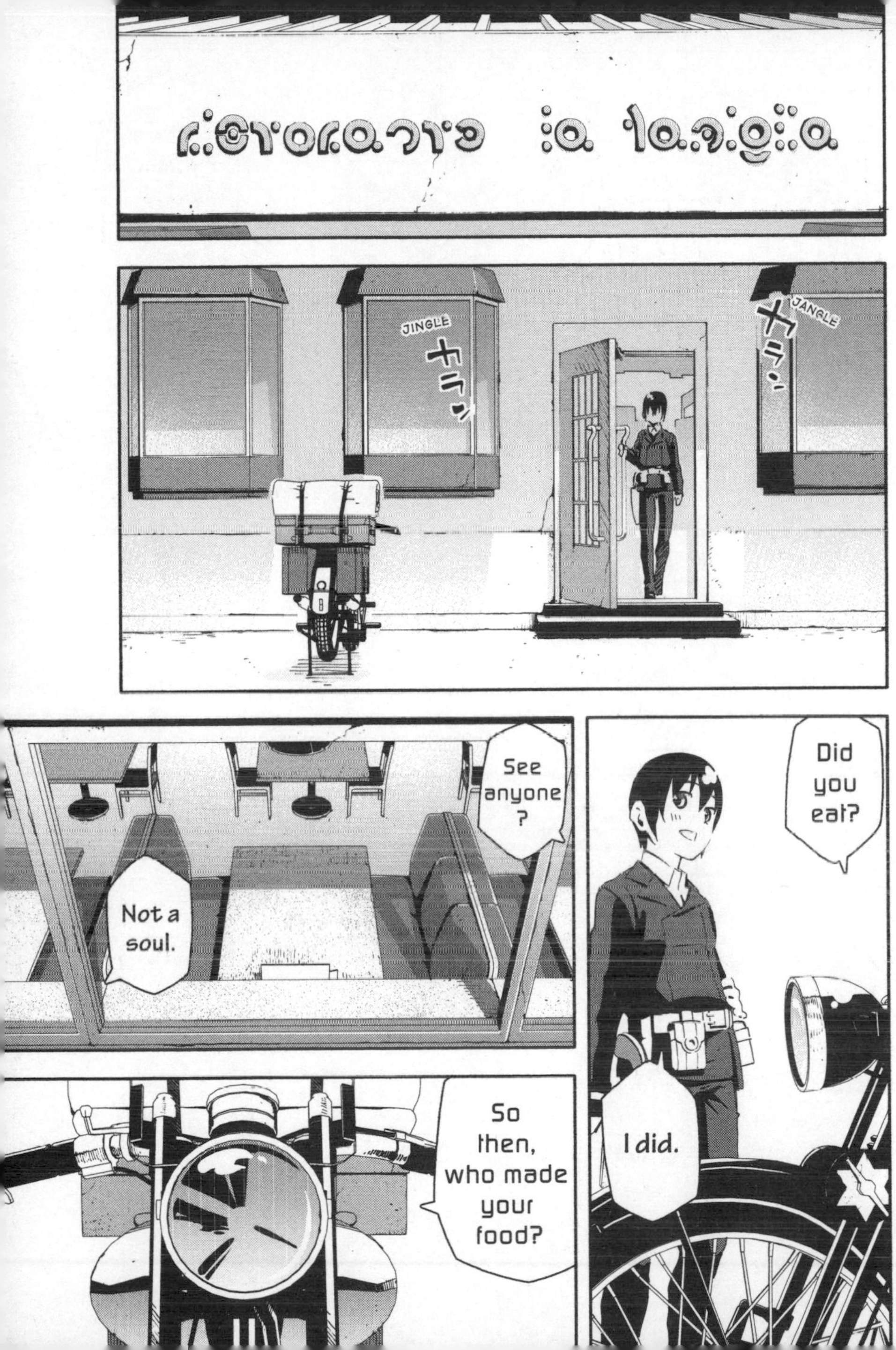
JANGLE
JINGLE
Did you eat?
I did.
See anyone?
Not a soul.
So then, who made your food?

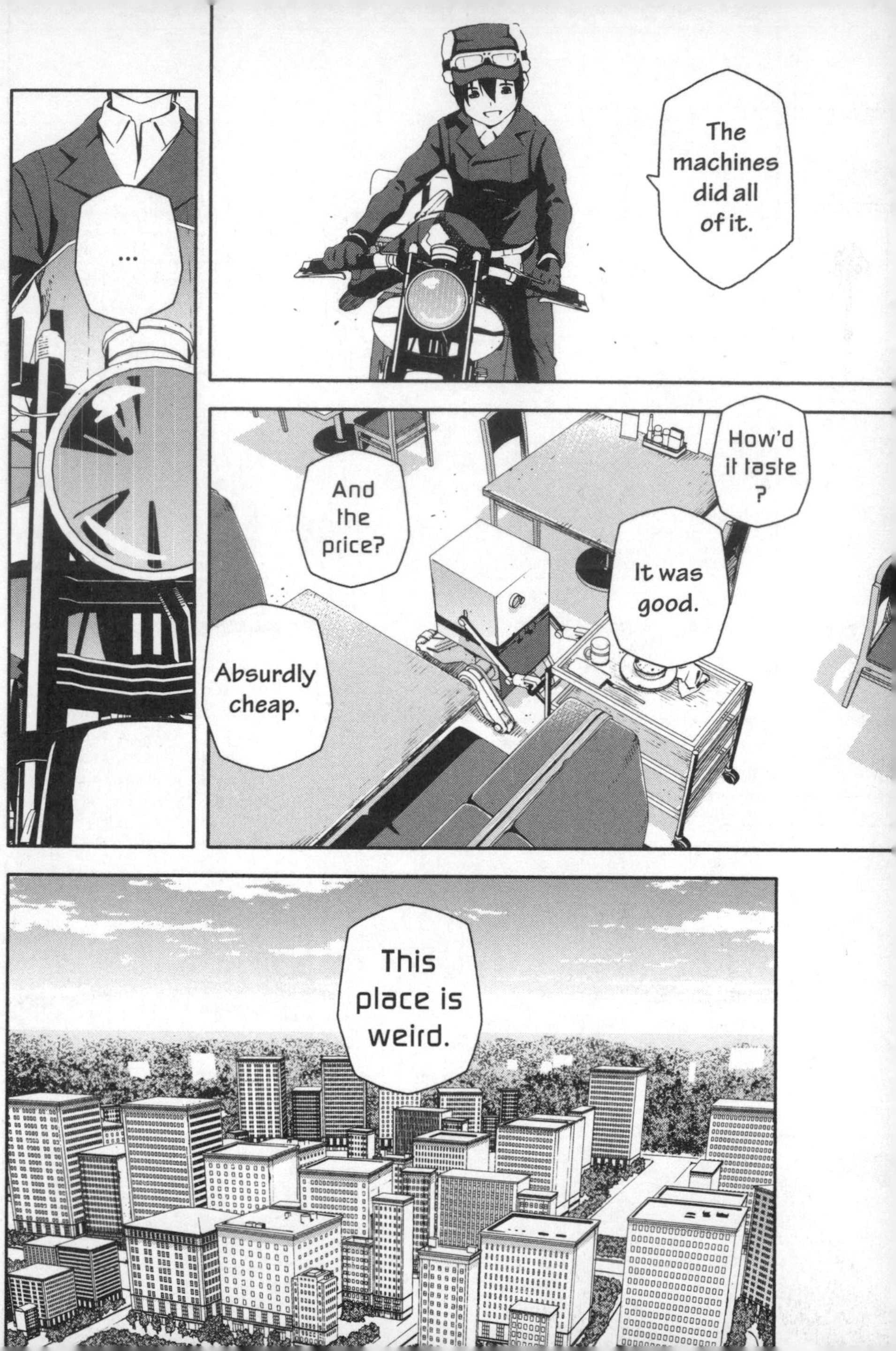
The machines did all of it.
How'd it taste?
It was good.
And the price?
Absurdly cheap.
...
This place is weird.

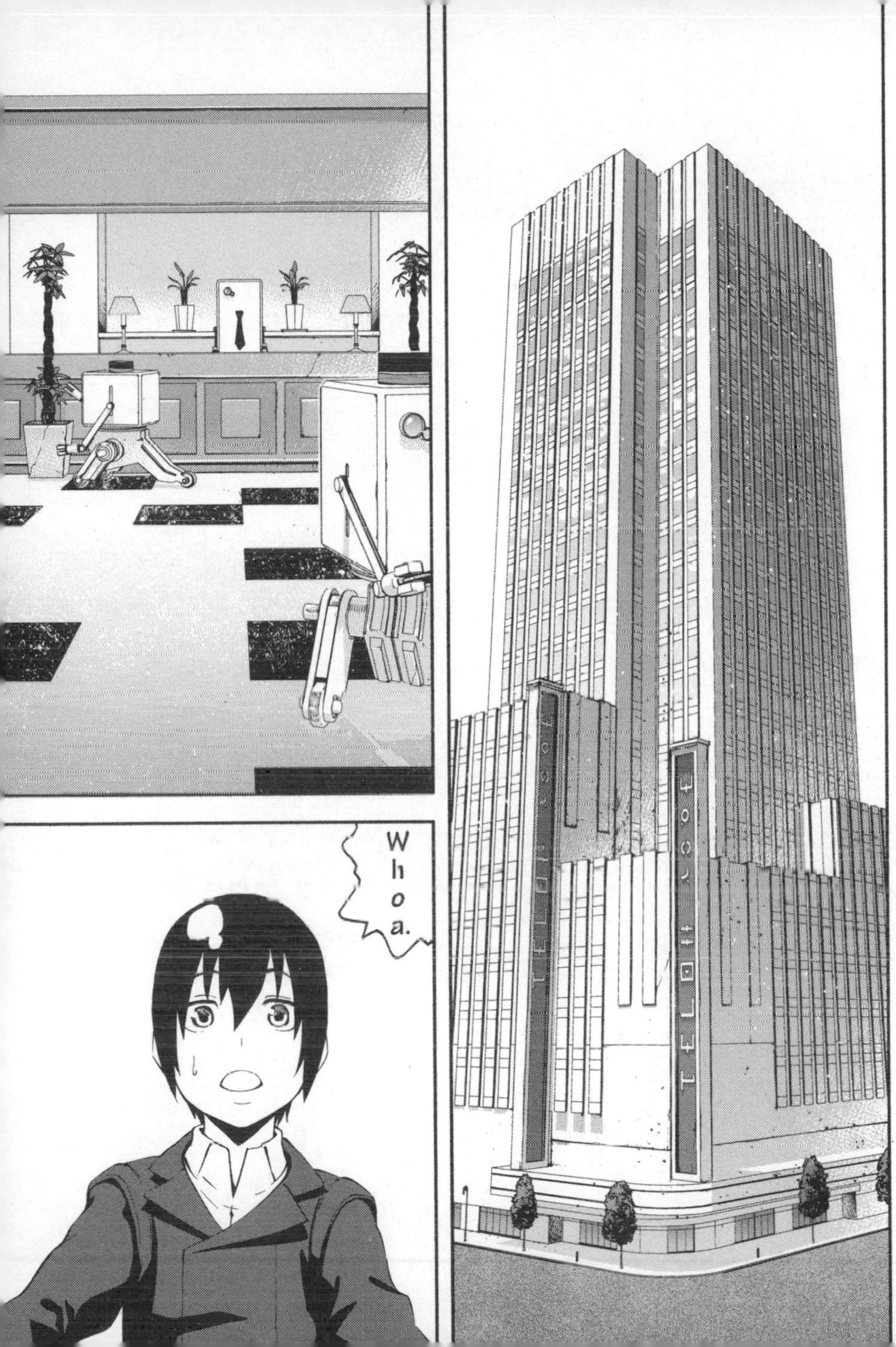
Whoa.

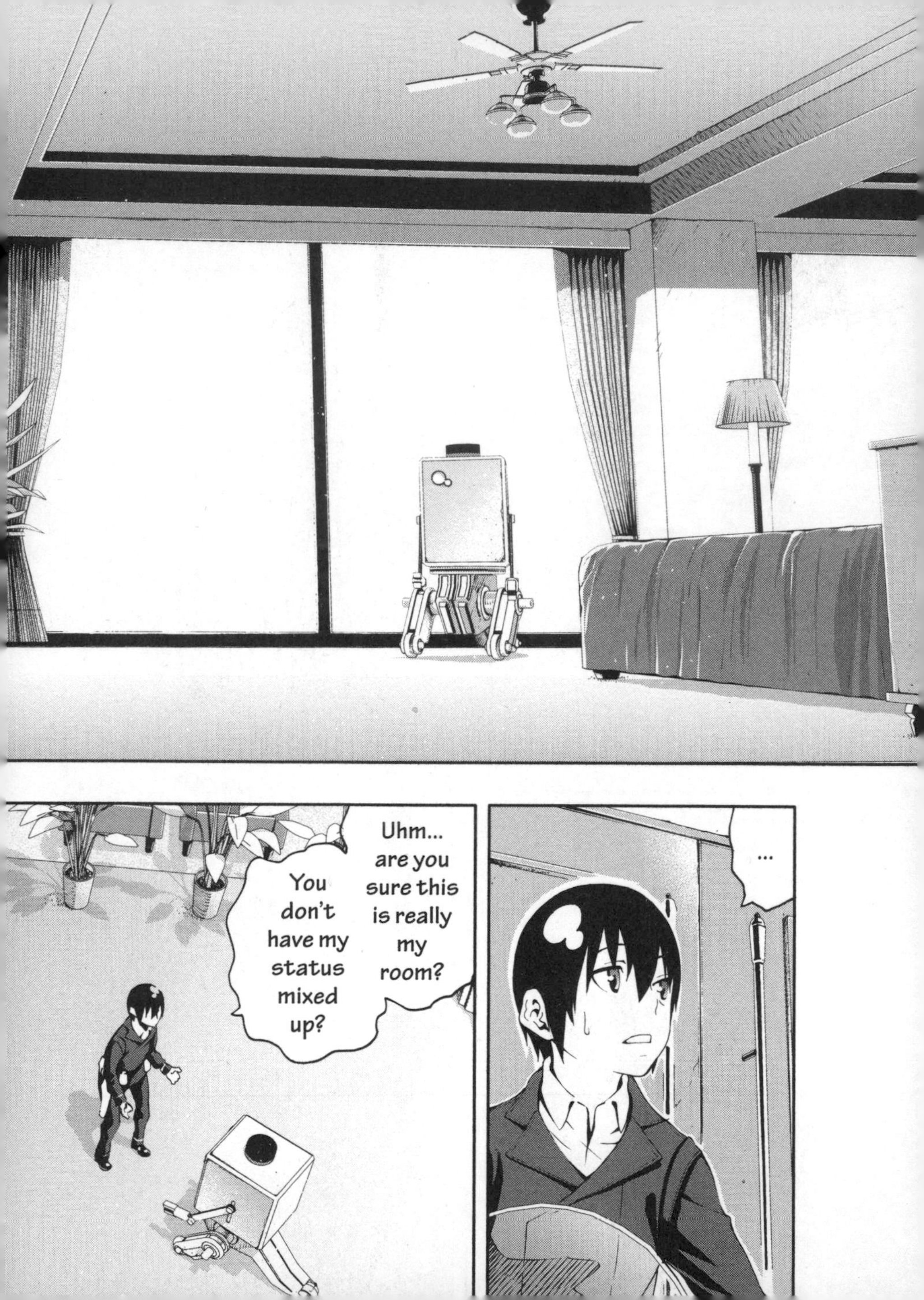
...
Uhm... are you sure this is really my room?
You don't have my status mixed up?

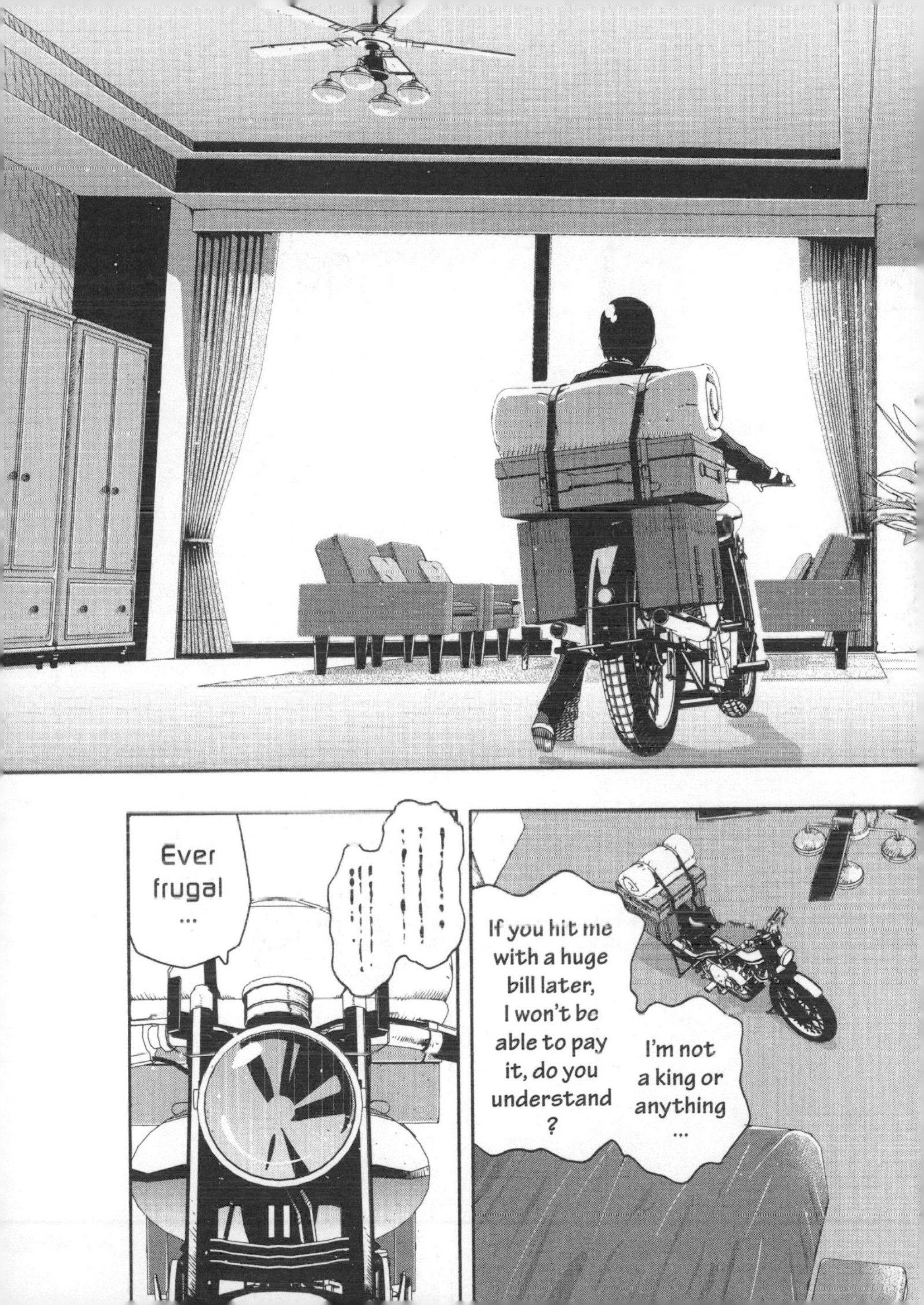
I'm not a king or anything ...
If you hit me with a huge bill later, I won't be able to pay it, do you understand ?
Ever frugal ...

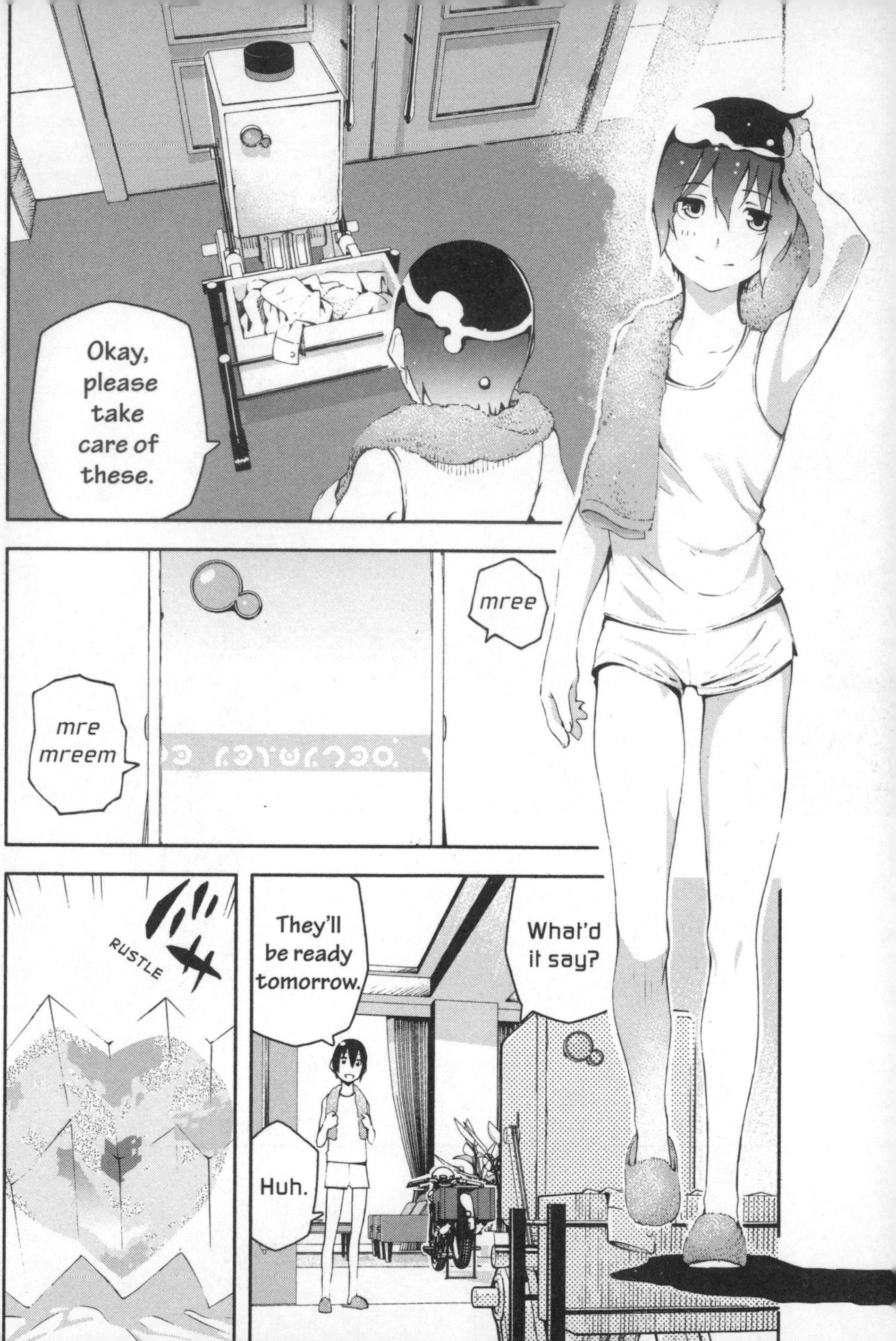
Okay, please take care of these.
mree
mre mreem
What'd it say?
They'll be ready tomorrow.
Huh.
RUSTLE

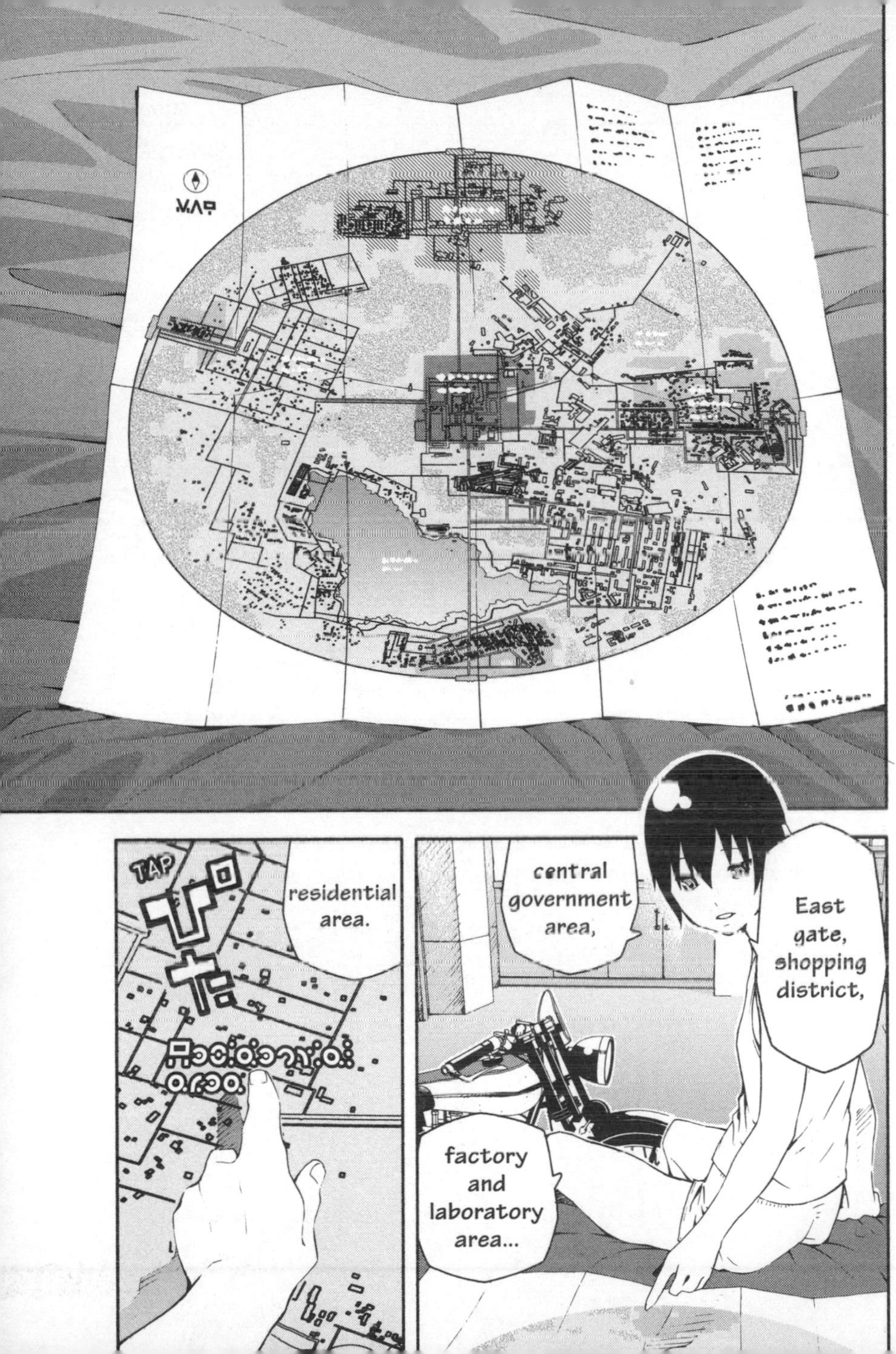
East gate, shopping district,
central government area,
factory and laboratory area...
TAP
residential area.

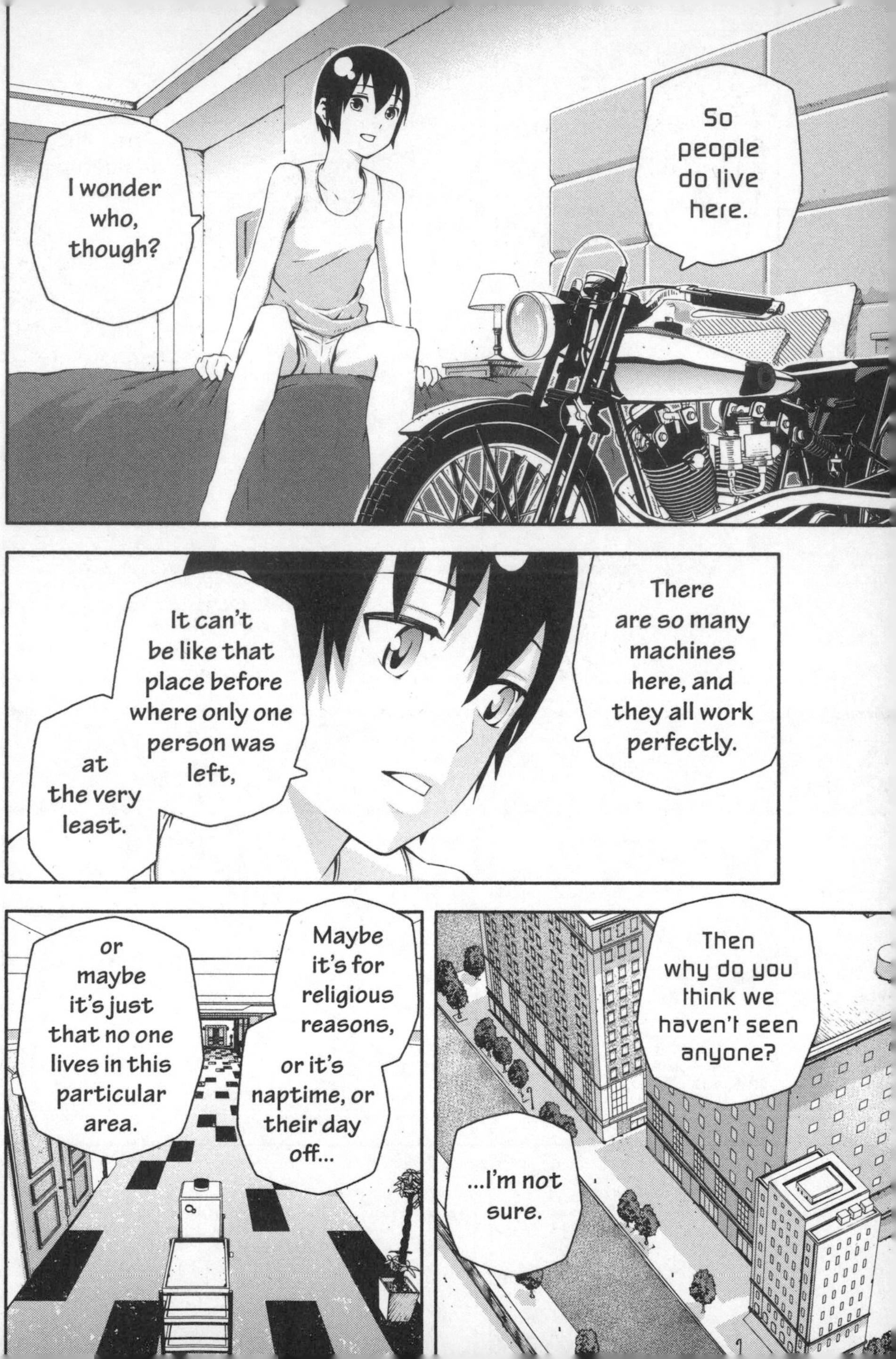
So people do live here.
I wonder who, though?
There are so many machines here, and they all work perfectly.
It can't be like that place before where only one person was left,
at the very least.
Then why do you think we haven't seen anyone?
...I'm not sure.
Maybe it's for religious reasons,
or it's naptime, or their day off...
or maybe it's just that no one lives in this particular area.

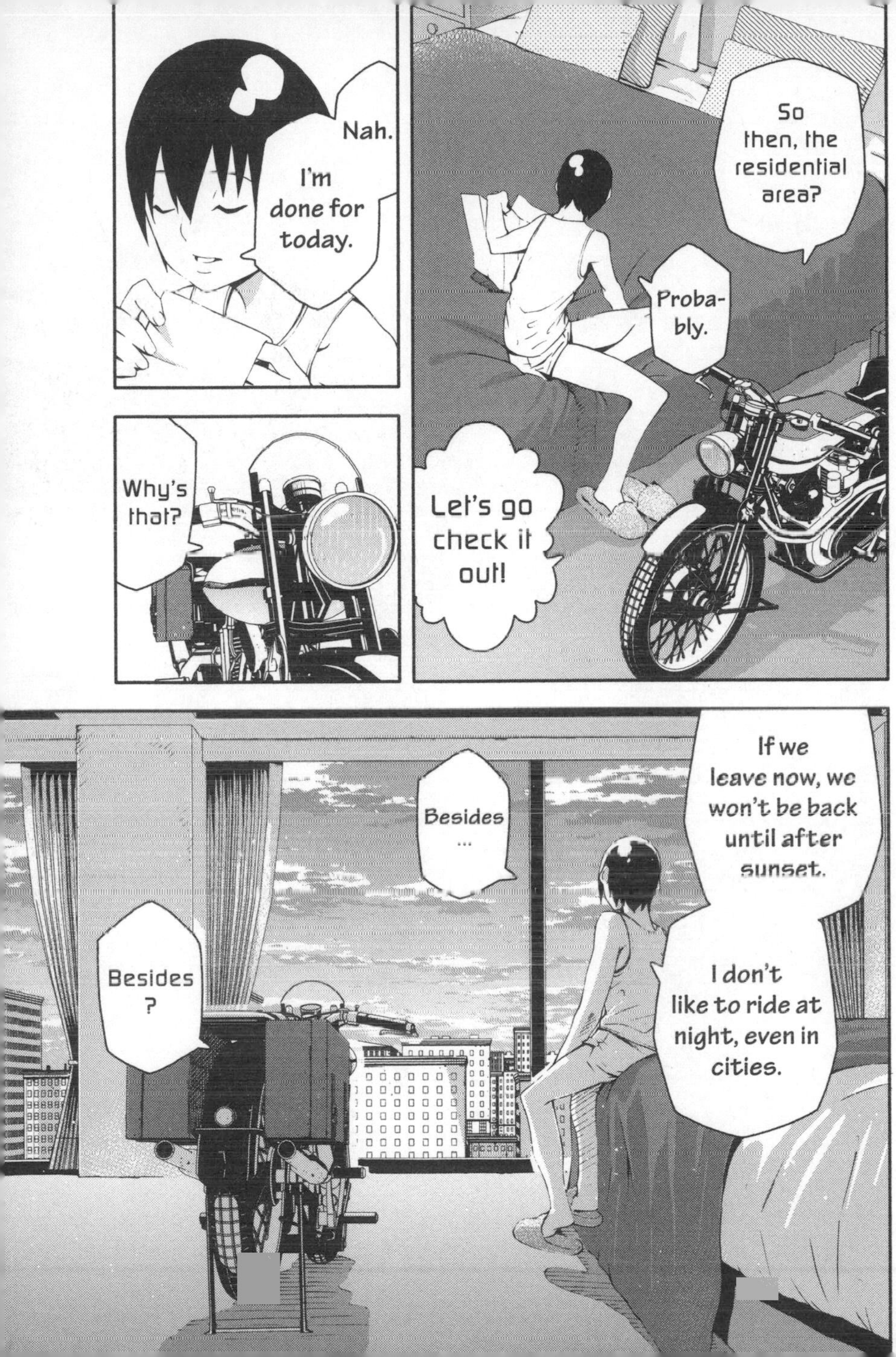
So then, the residential area?
Proba-bly.
Let's go check it out!
Nah. I'm done for today.
Why's that?
If we leave now, we won't be back until after sunset.
Besides ...
Besides ?
I don't like to ride at night, even in cities.

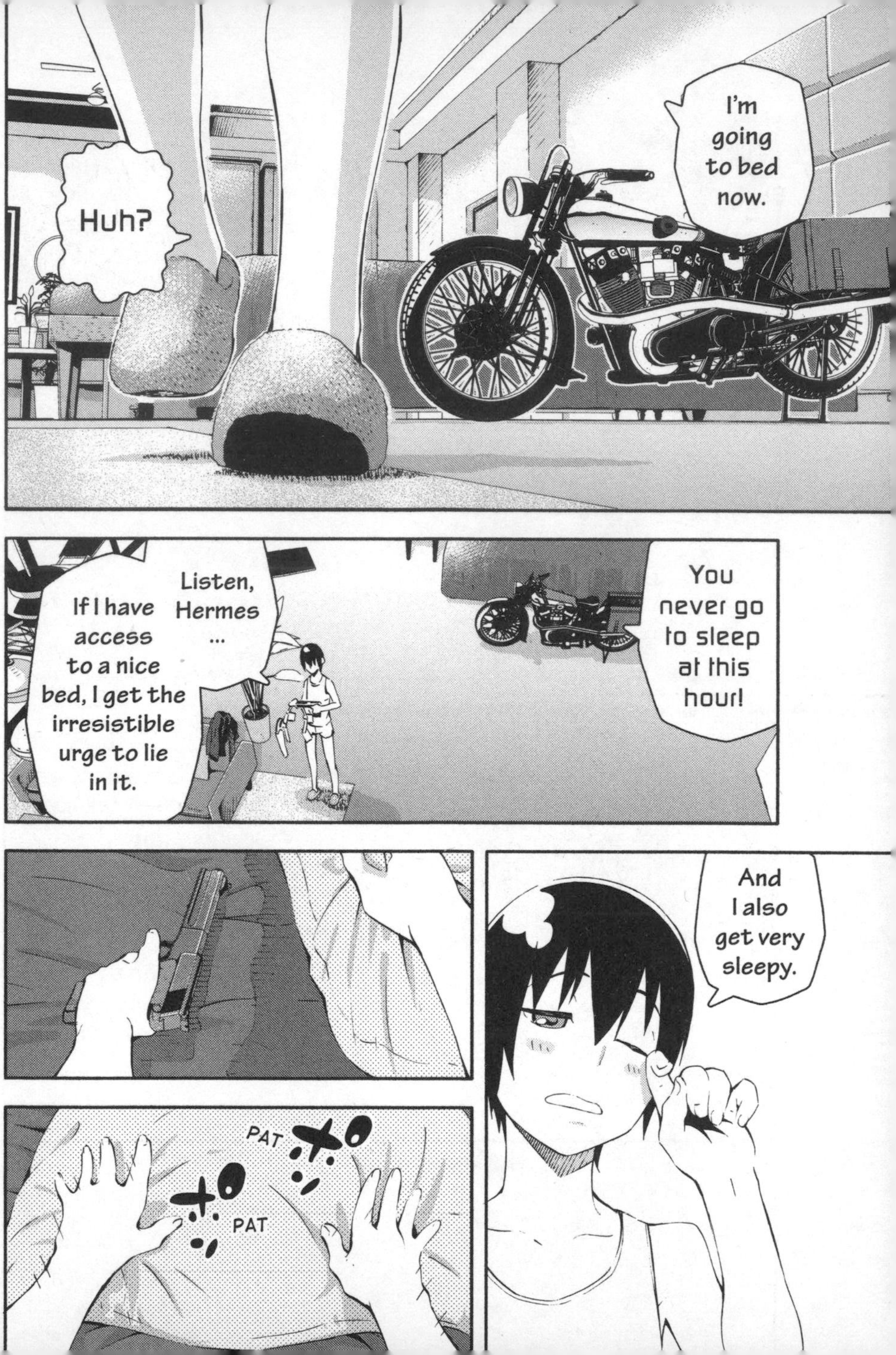
I'm going to bed now.
Huh?
You never go to sleep at this hour!
Listen, Hermes ...
If I have access to a nice bed, I get the irresistible urge to lie in it.
And I also get very sleepy.
PAT
PAT

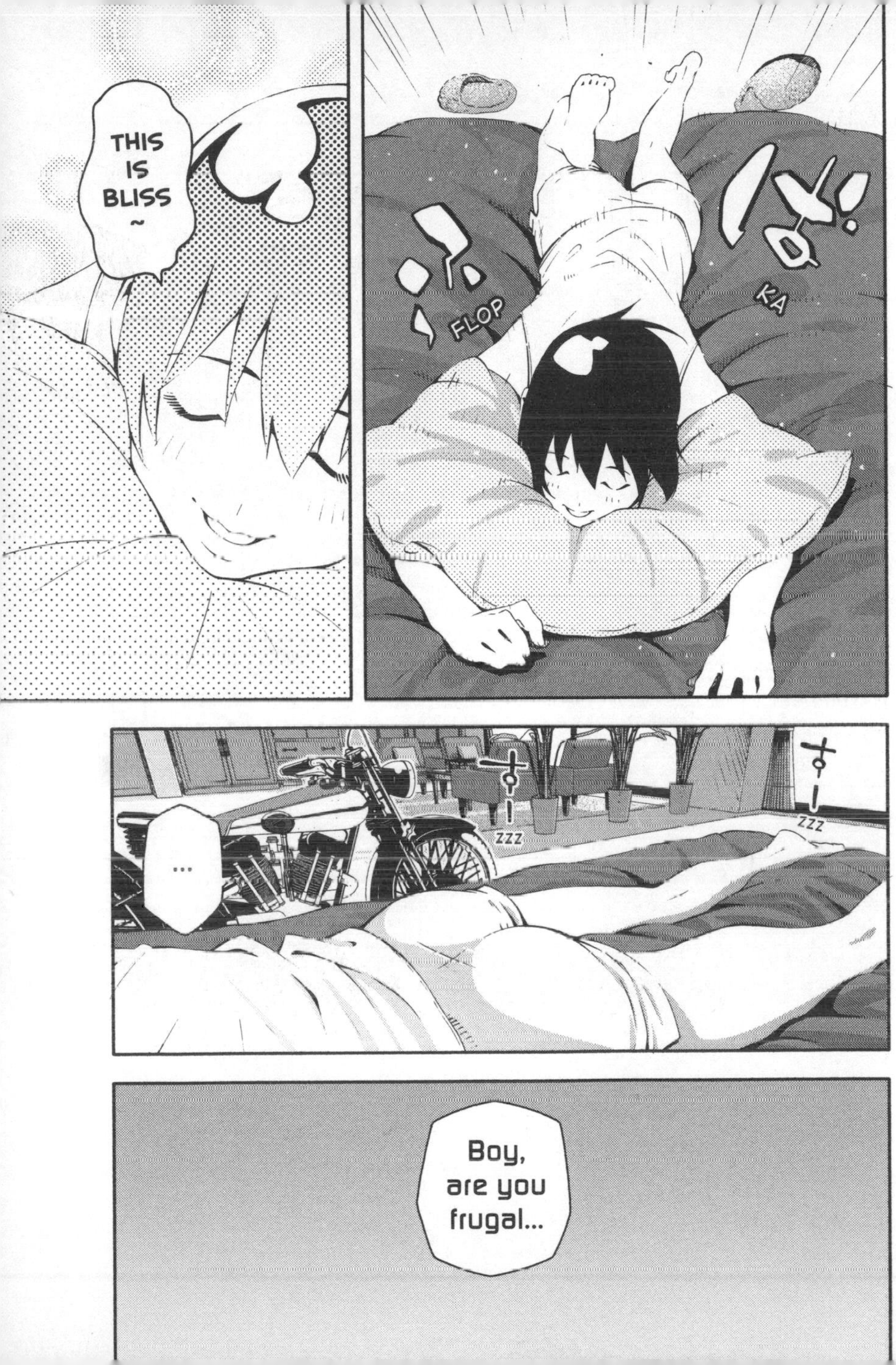
FLOP
KA
THIS IS BLISS ~
zzz
zzz
...
Boy, are you frugal...

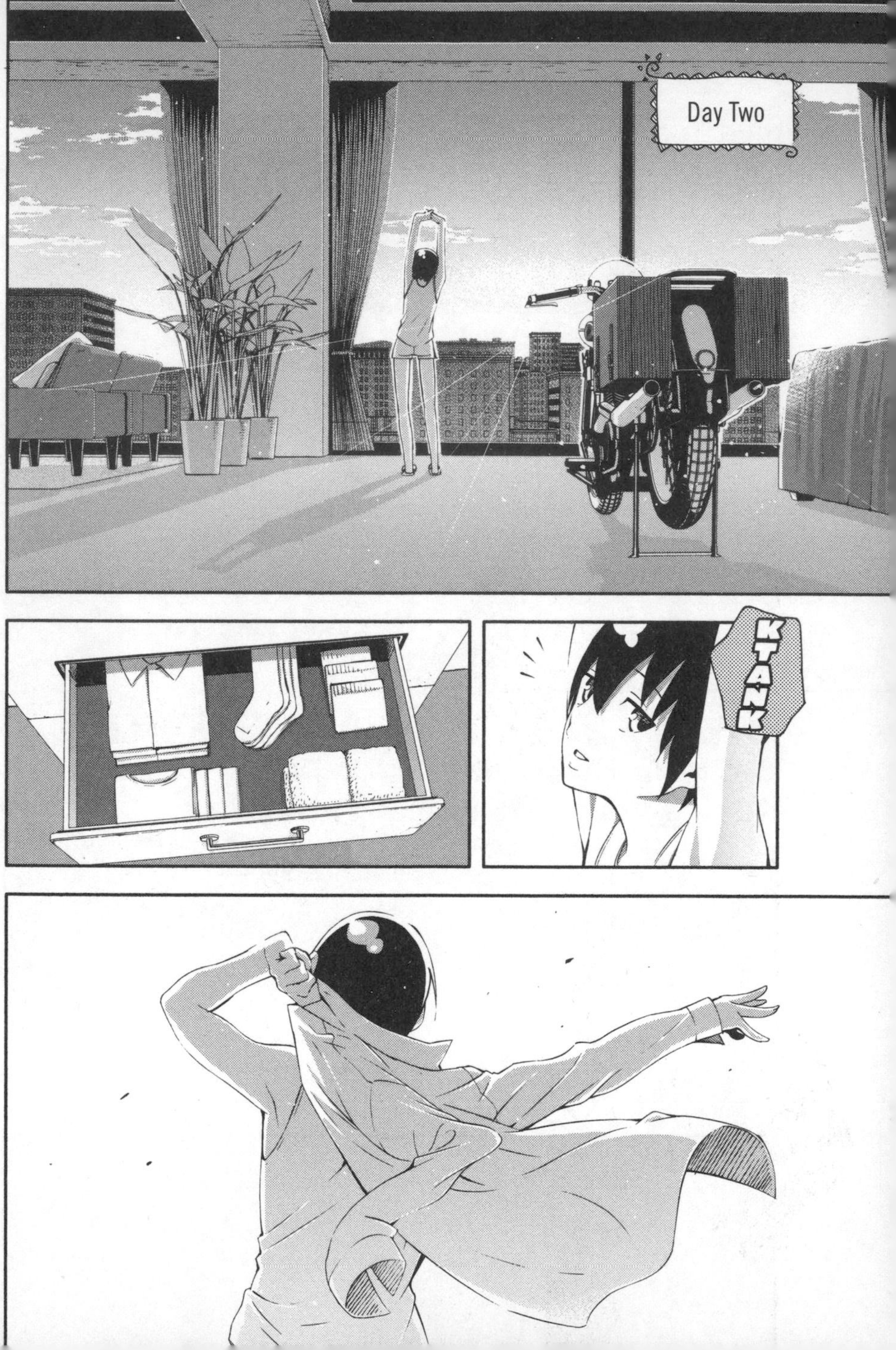
Day Two
KTANK

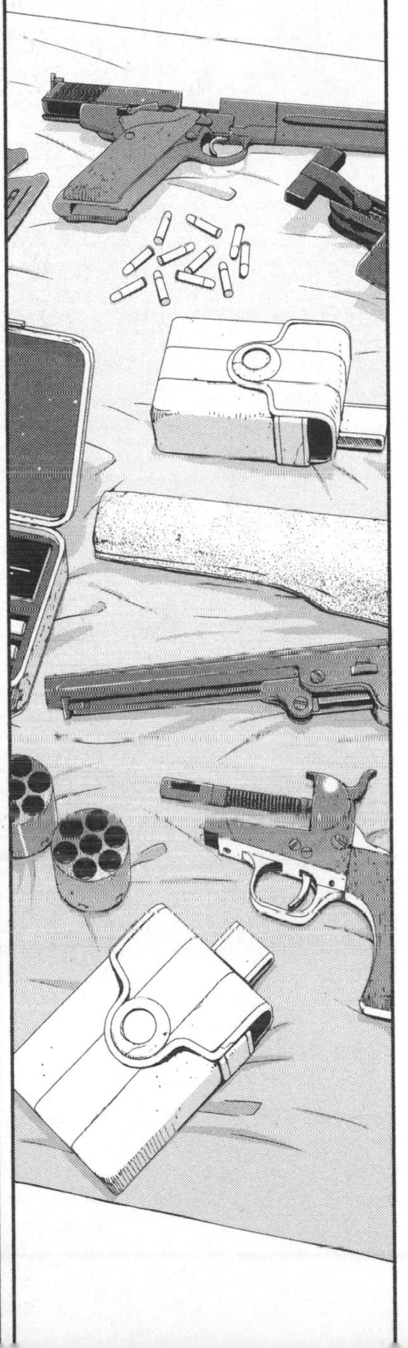

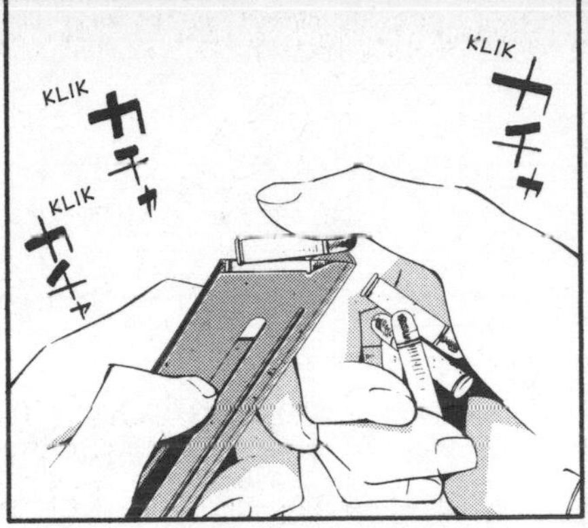
KLIK
カチャ
KLIK
カチャ

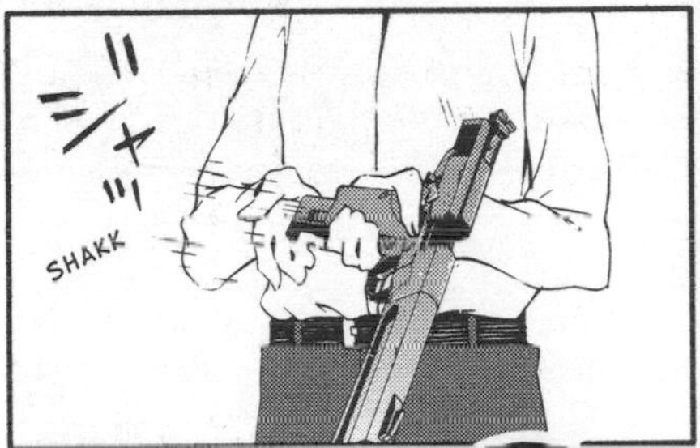
ジャッ
SHAKK

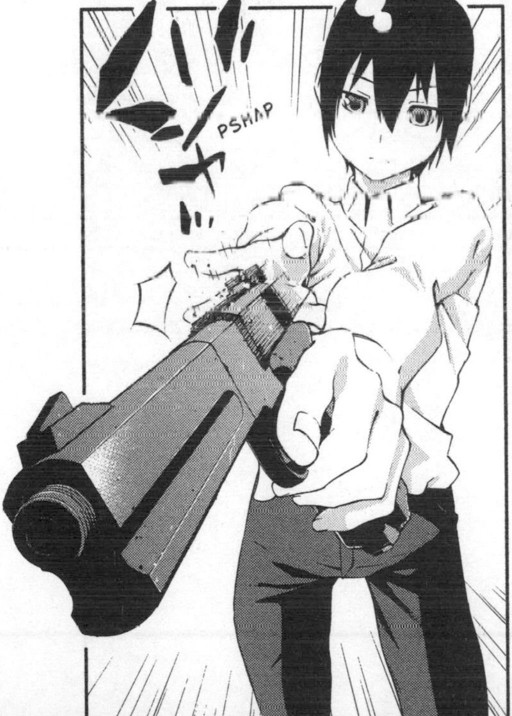
バシャッ
PSHAP

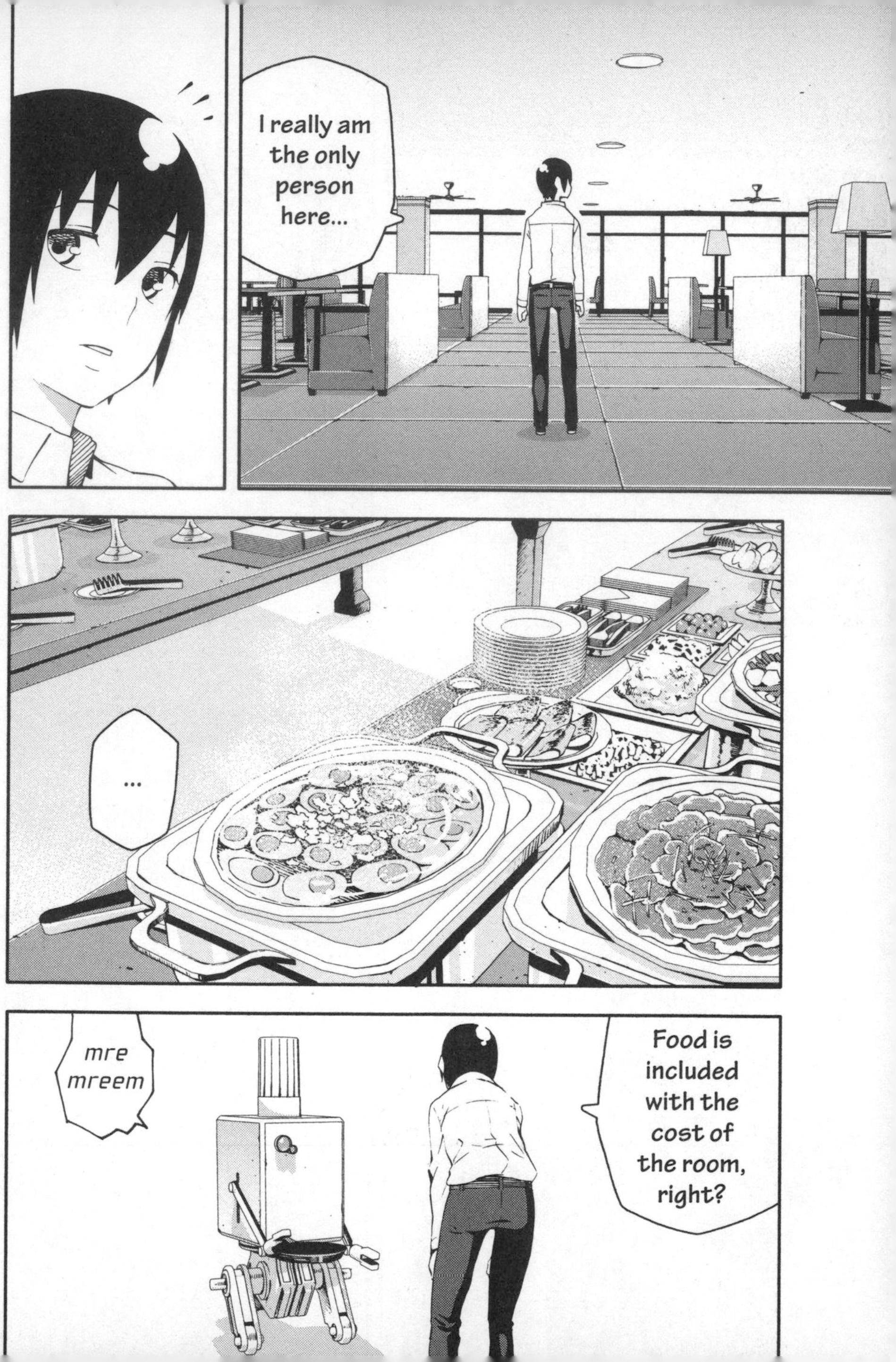
I really am the only person here...
...
Food is included with the cost of the room, right?
mre mreem

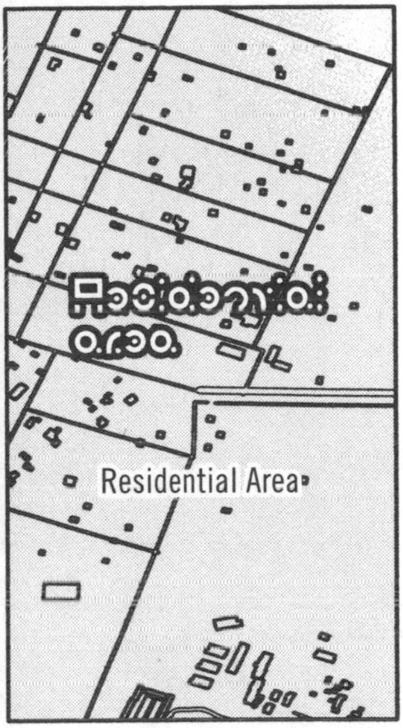
Residential Area
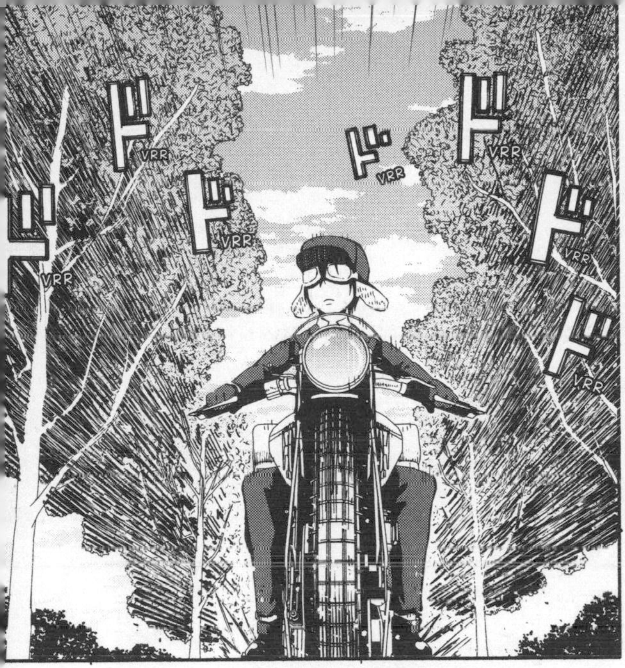
ド VRR
ド VRR
ド VRR
ド VRR
ド VRR
ド VRR
ド VRR
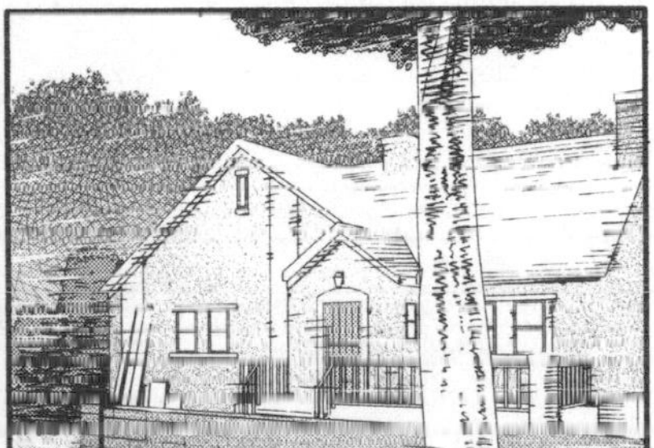
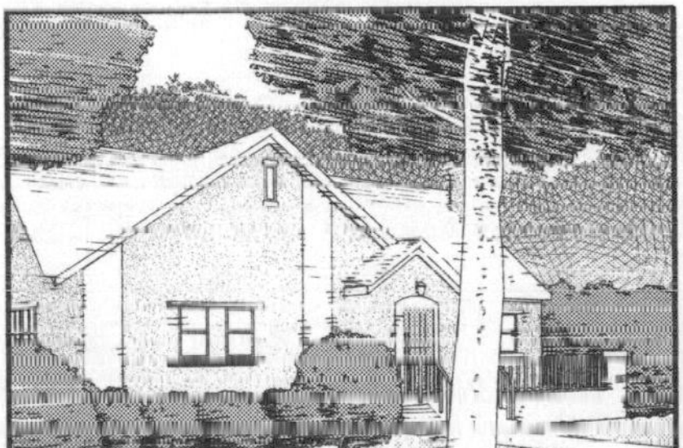
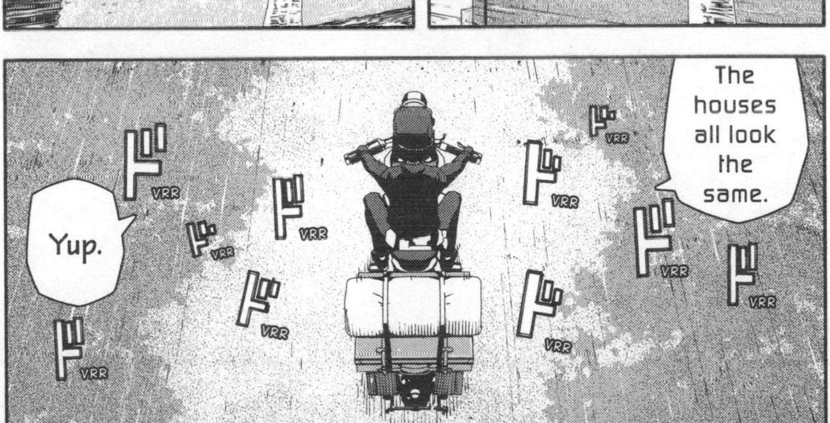
The houses all look the same.
Yup.
ド VRR
ド VRR
ド VRR
ド VRR
ド VRR
ド VRR
ド VRR
ド VRR
ド VRR
ド VRR

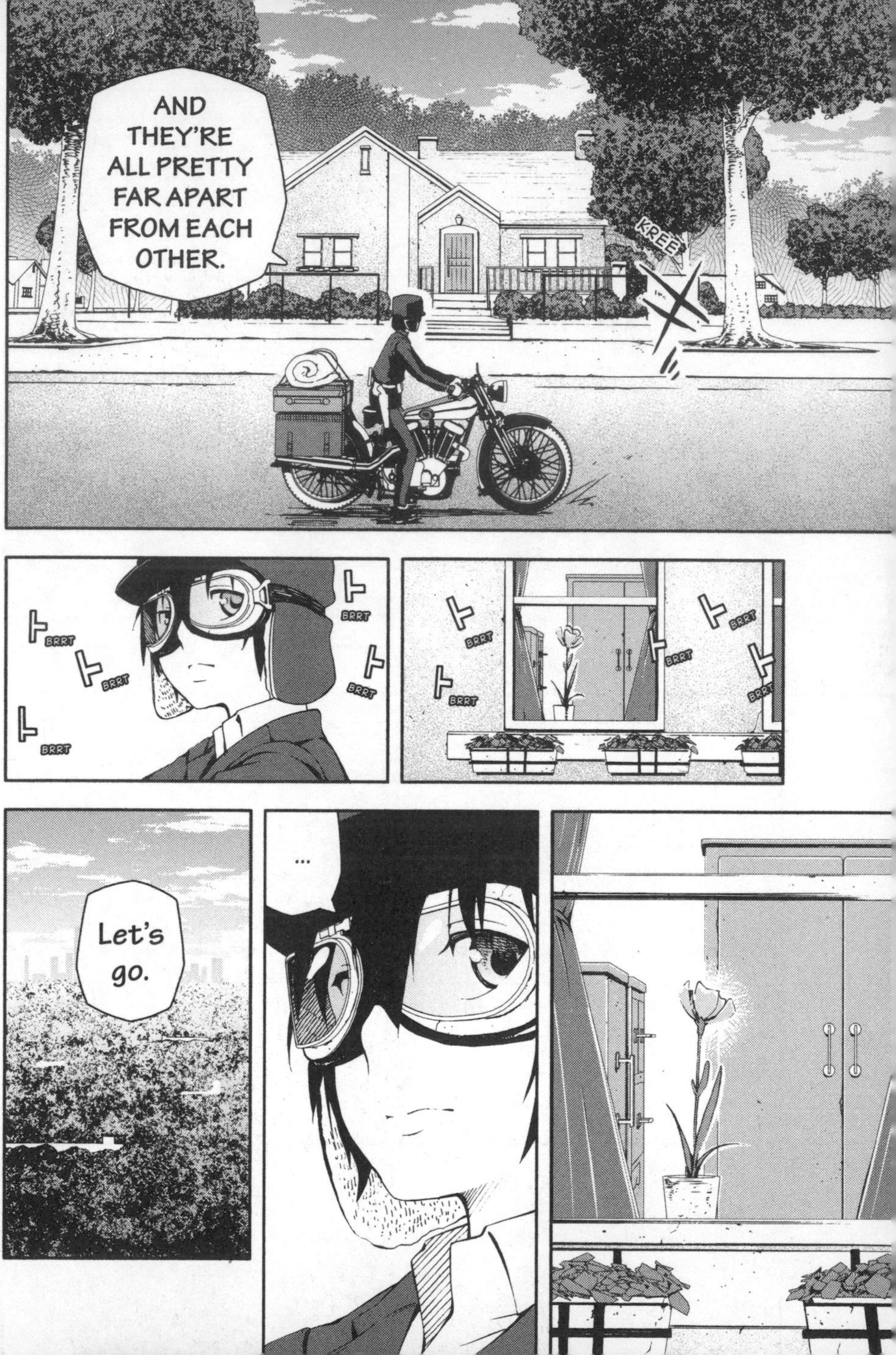
AND THEY'RE ALL PRETTY FAR APART FROM EACH OTHER.
KREE
BRRT
BRRT
BRRT
BRRT
BRRT
BRRT
BRRT
BRRT
BRRT
...
Let's go.

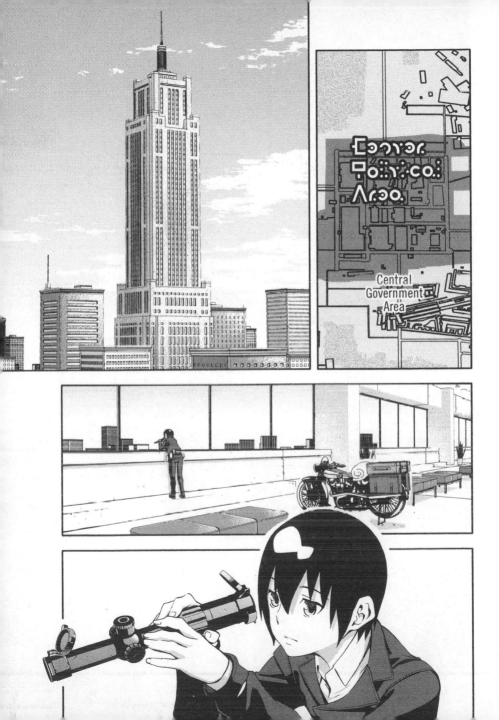

Central
Government
Area

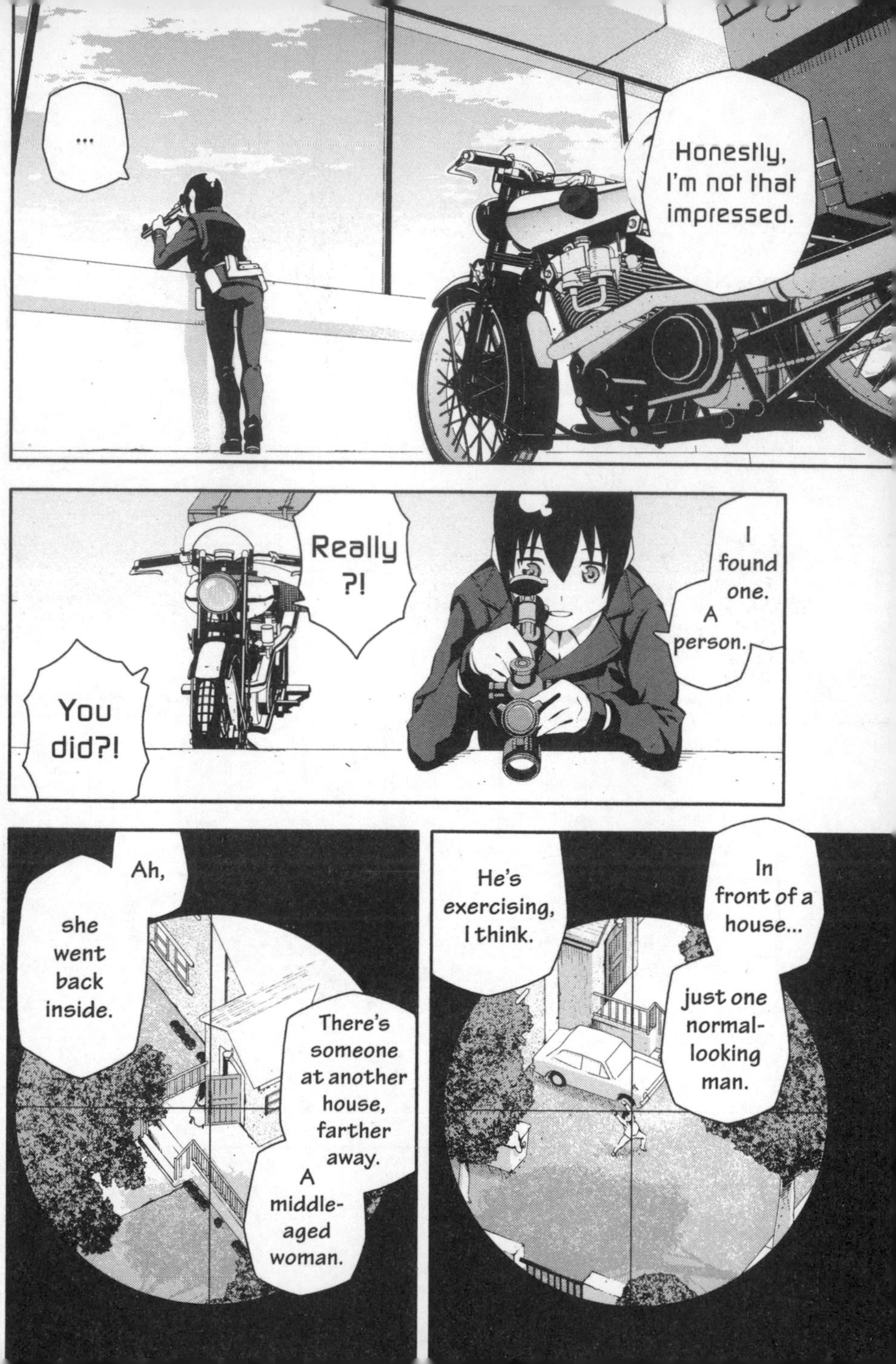
Honestly, I'm not that impressed.
...
I found one. A person.
Really?!
You did?!
In front of a house...
He's exercising, I think.
just one normal-looking man.
Ah, she went back inside.
There's someone at another house, farther away. A middle-aged woman.

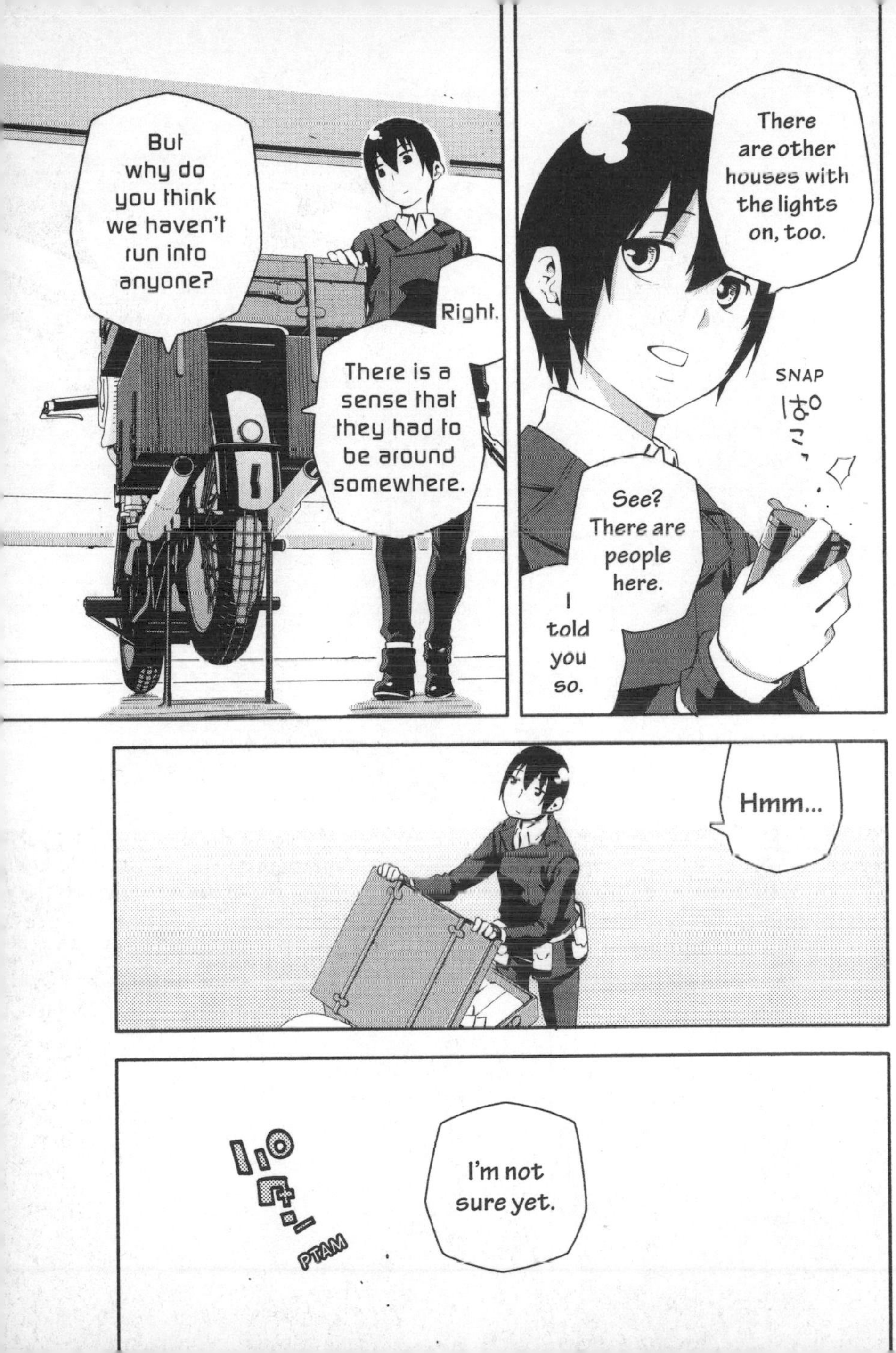
There are other houses with the lights on, too.
SNAP
See? There are people here.
I told you so.
But why do you think we haven't run into anyone?
Right.
There is a sense that they had to be around somewhere.
Hmm...
I'm not sure yet.
PTAM

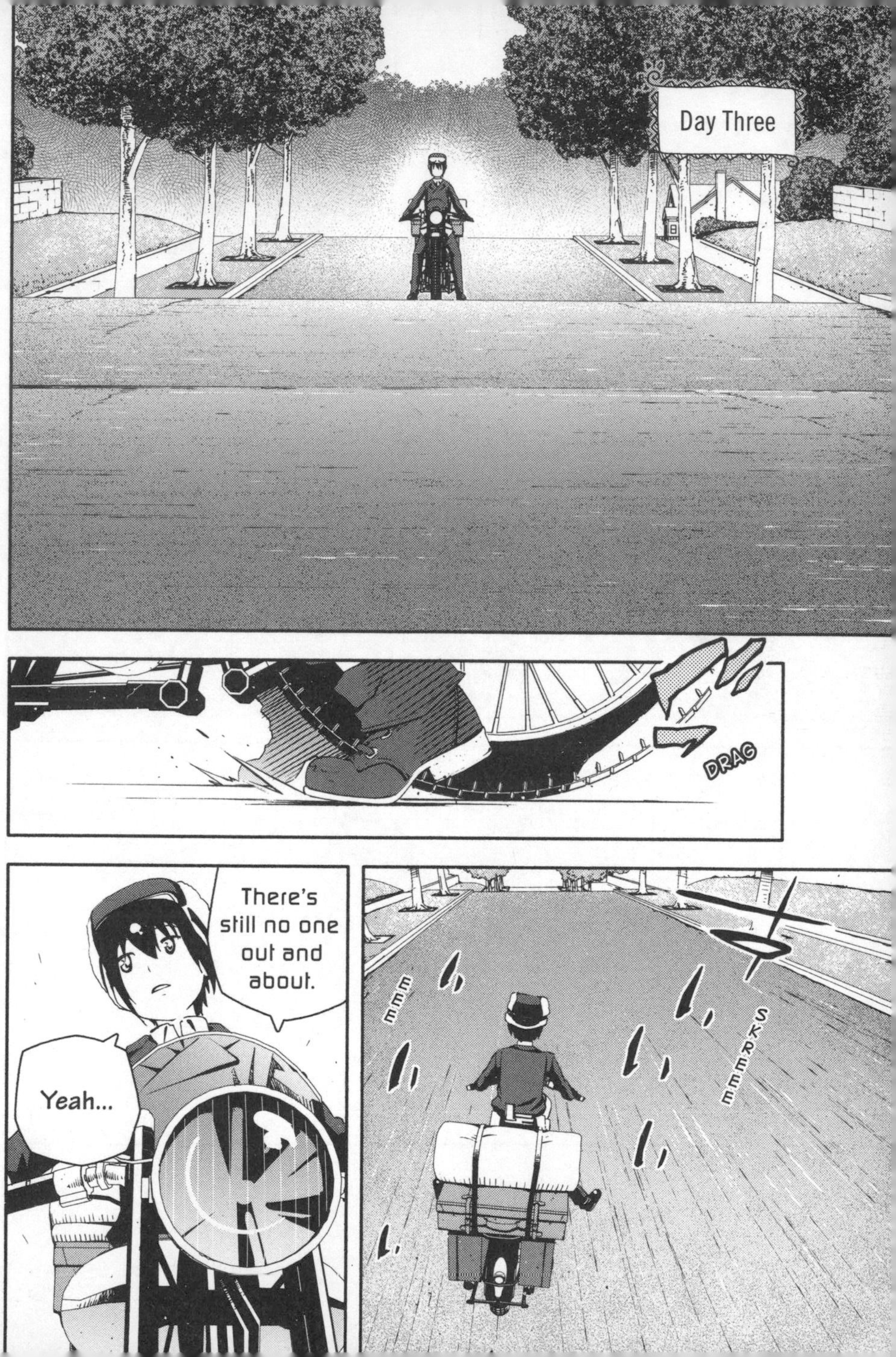
Day Three
DRAG
SKREEE
EEE
There's still no one out and about.
Yeah...

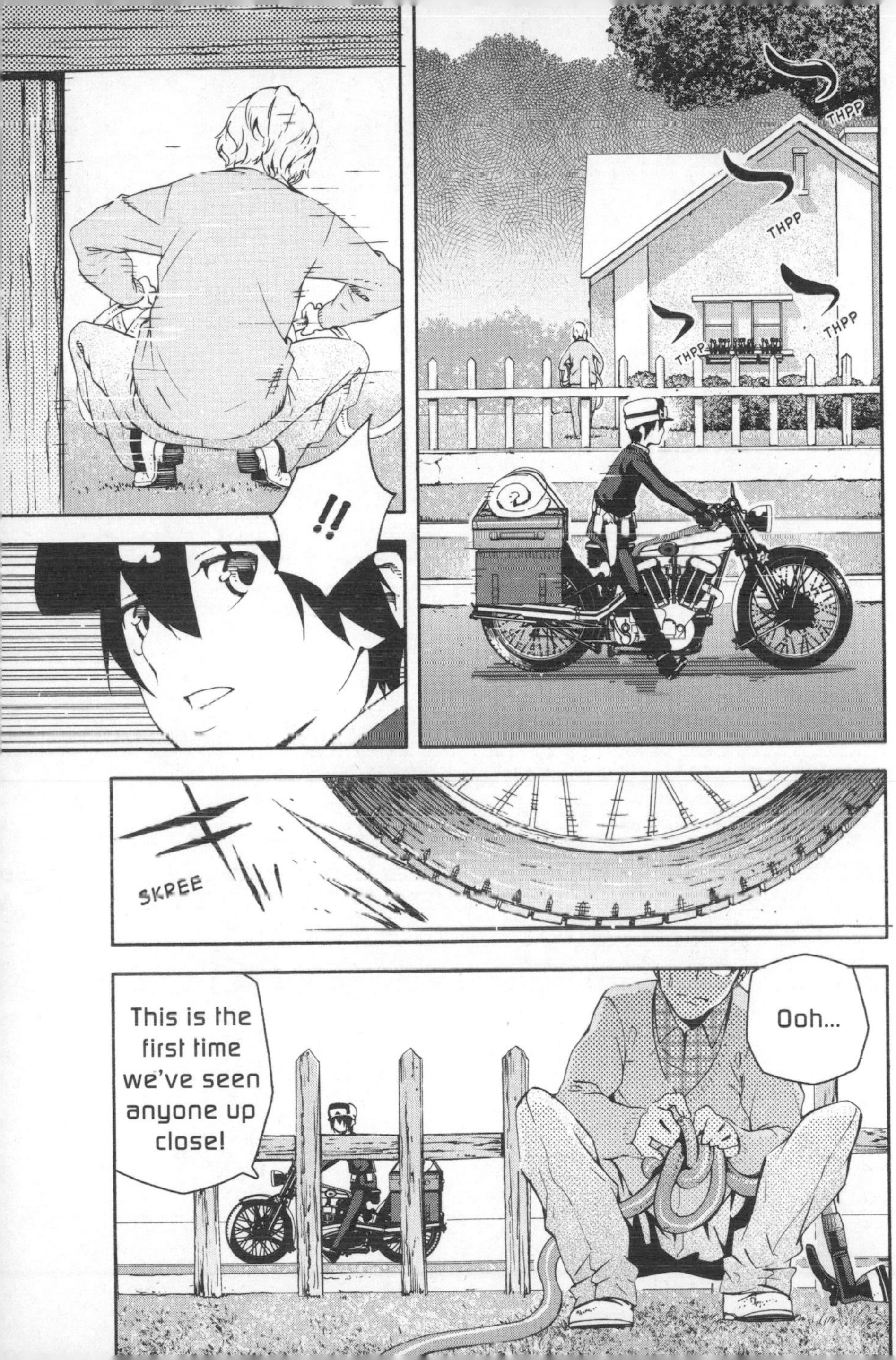
THPP
THPP
THPP
THPP
!!
SKREE
Ooh...
This is the first time we've seen anyone up close!

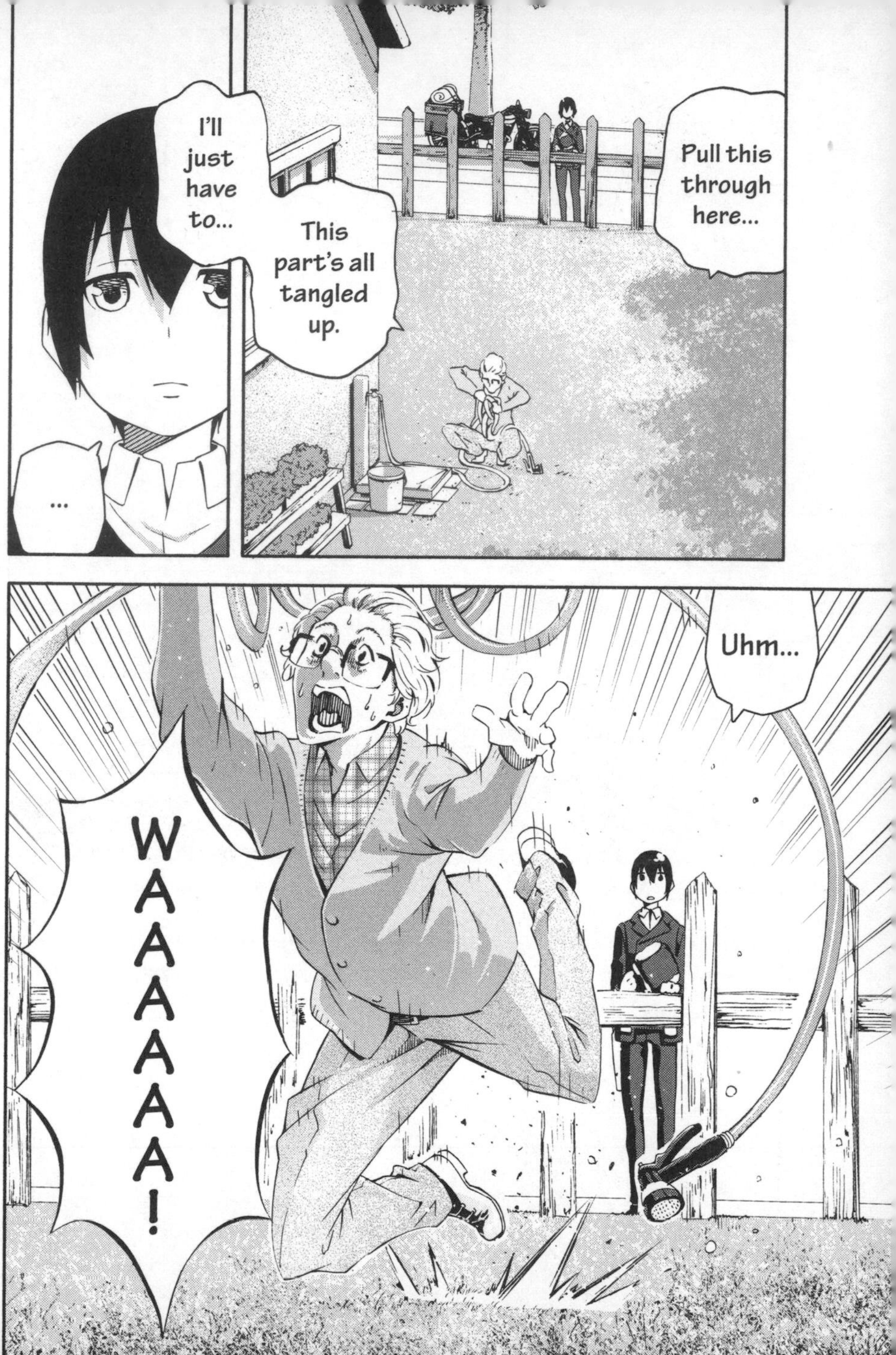
Pull this through here...
This part's all tangled up.
I'll just have to...
...
Uhm...
WAAAAAA!

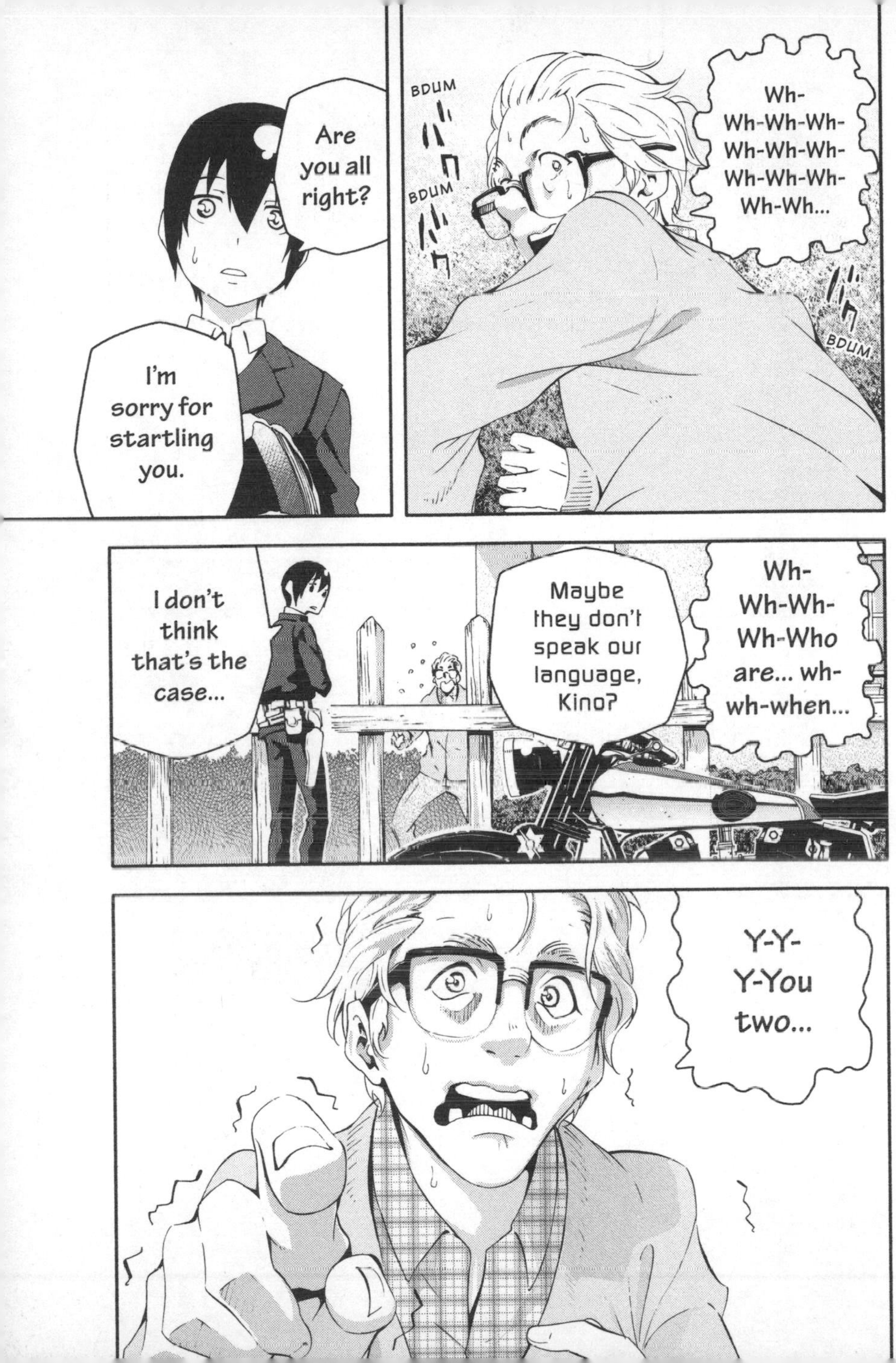
Wh-
Wh-Wh-Wh-
Wh-Wh-Wh-
Wh-Wh-Wh-
Wh-Wh...
BDUM
BDUM
BDUM
Are you all right?
I'm sorry for startling you.
Wh-
Wh-Wh-
Wh-Who
are... wh-
wh-when...
Maybe they don't speak our language, Kino?
I don't think that's the case...
Y-Y-
Y-You
two...

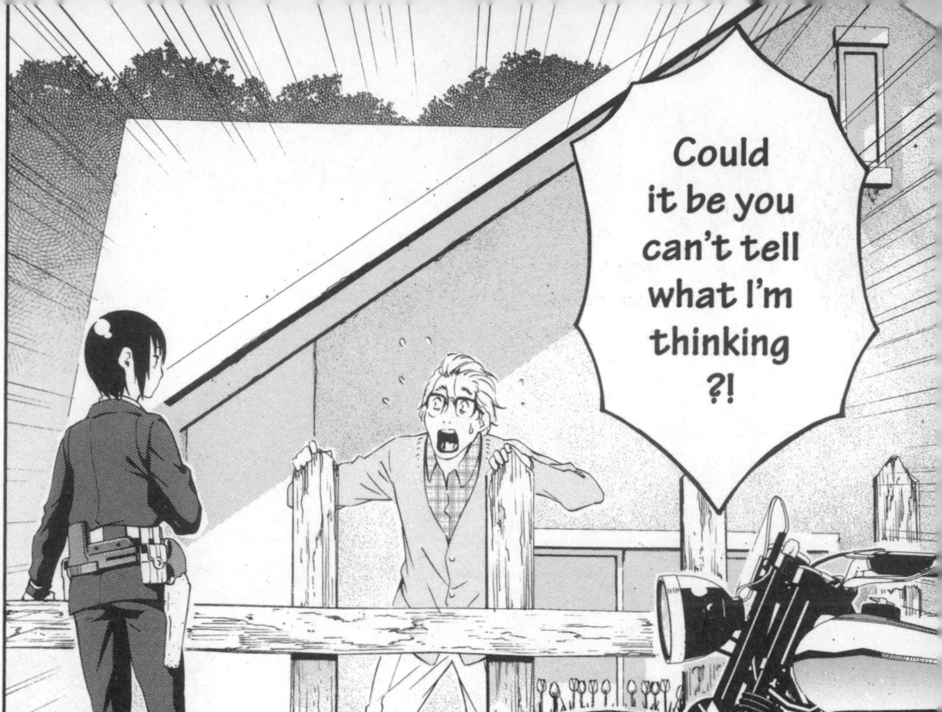
Could it be you can't tell what I'm thinking ?!
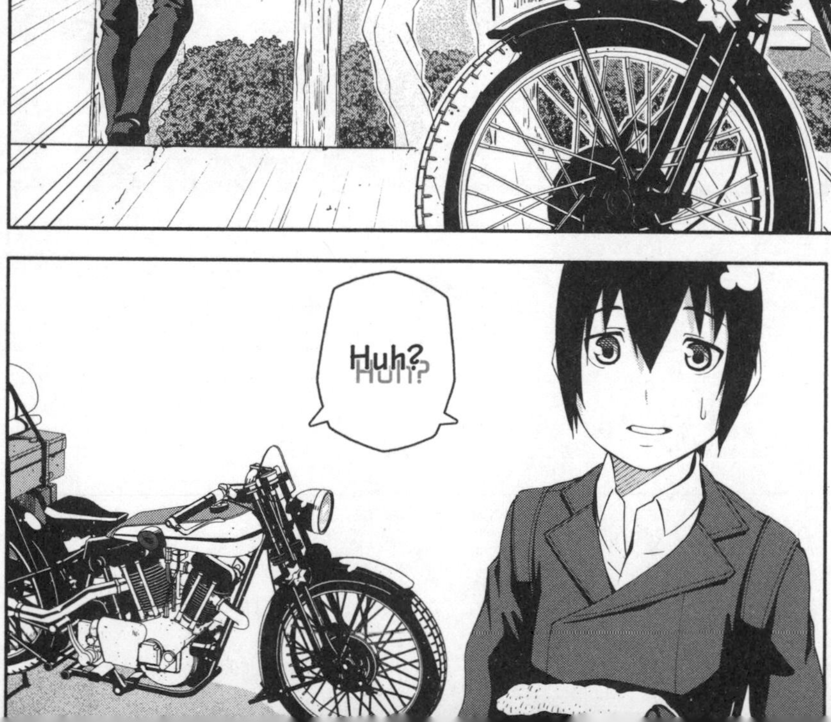
Huh? Huh?

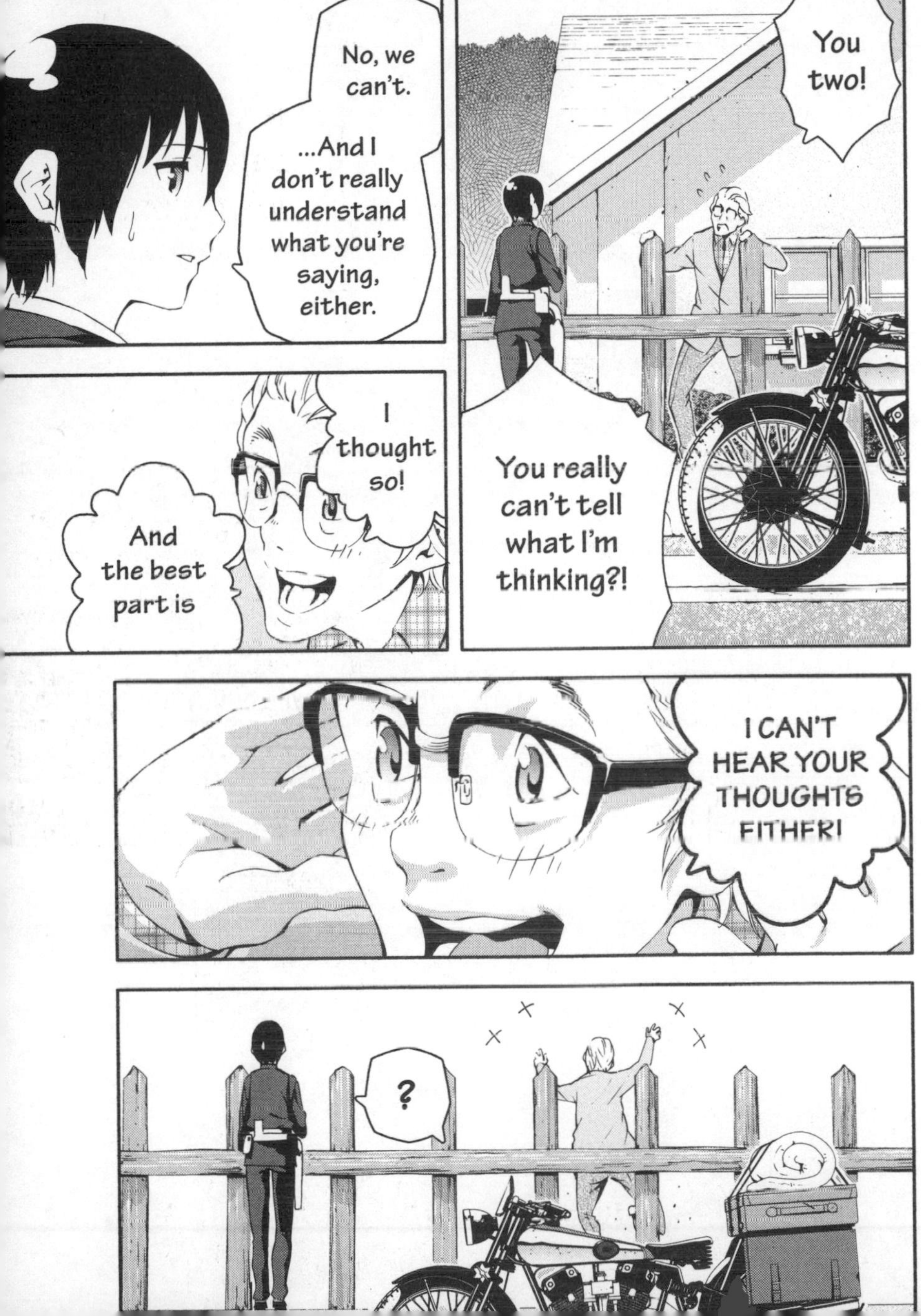
You two!
You really can't tell what I'm thinking?!
No, we can't.
...And I don't really understand what you're saying, either.
I thought so!
And the best part is
I CAN'T HEAR YOUR THOUGHTS EITHER!
?

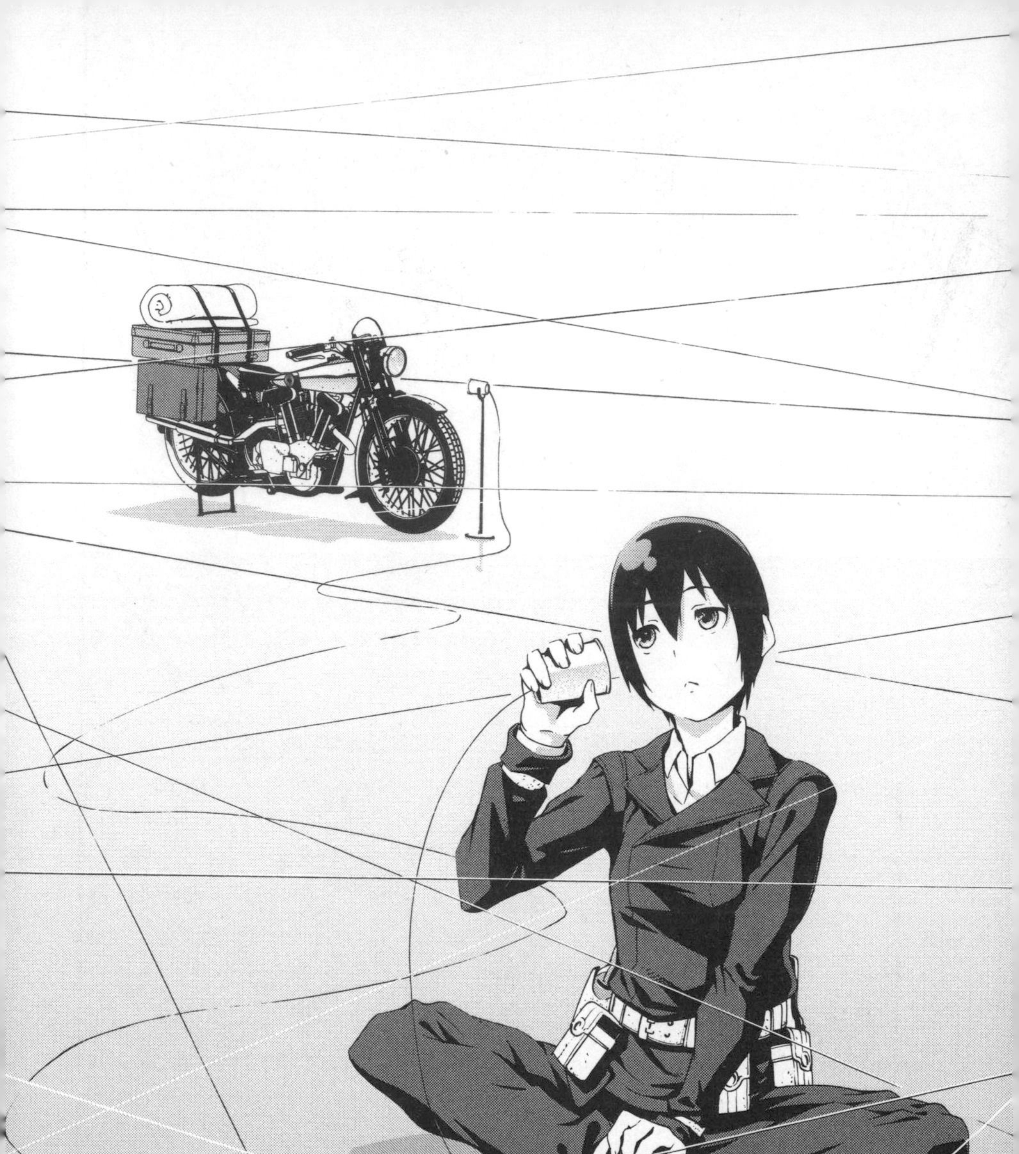

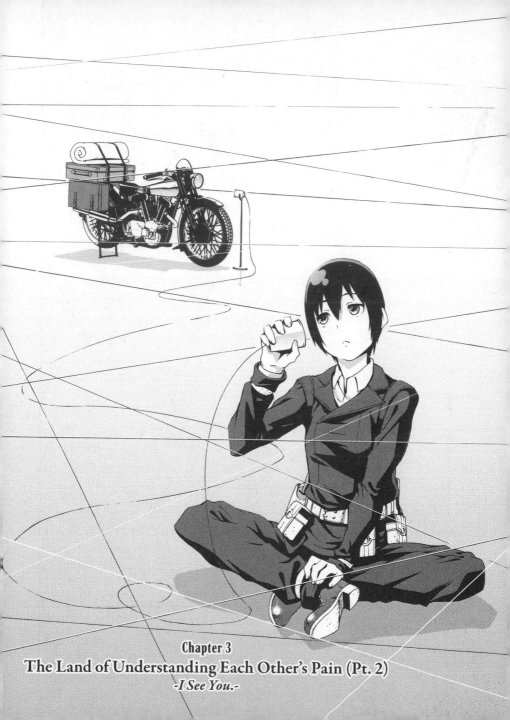

Chapter 3
The Land of Understanding Each Other's Pain (Pt. 2)
-I See You.-

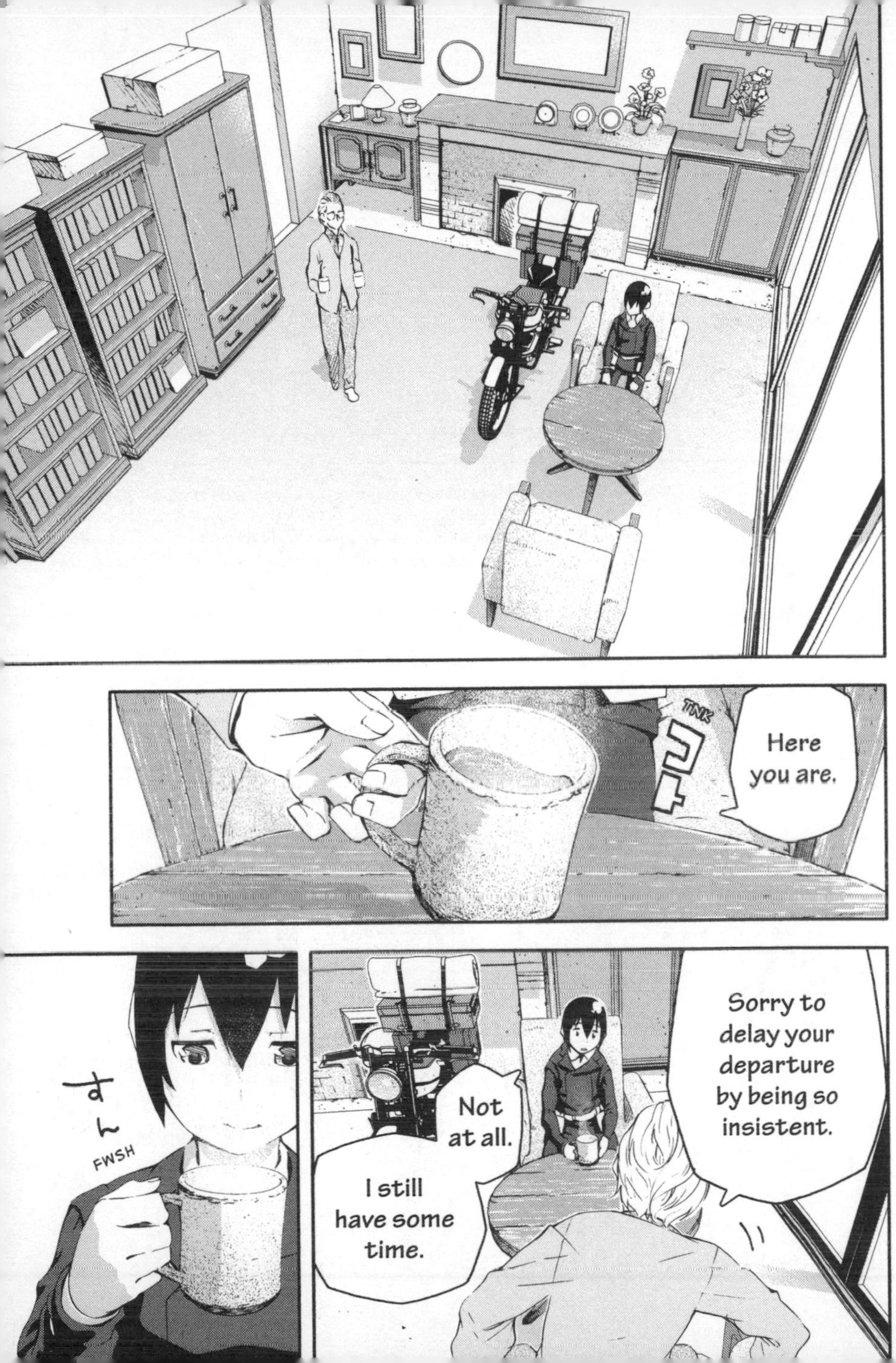
Here you are.
コト
TNK
Sorry to delay your departure by being so insistent.
Not at all.
I still have some time.
すん
FWSH

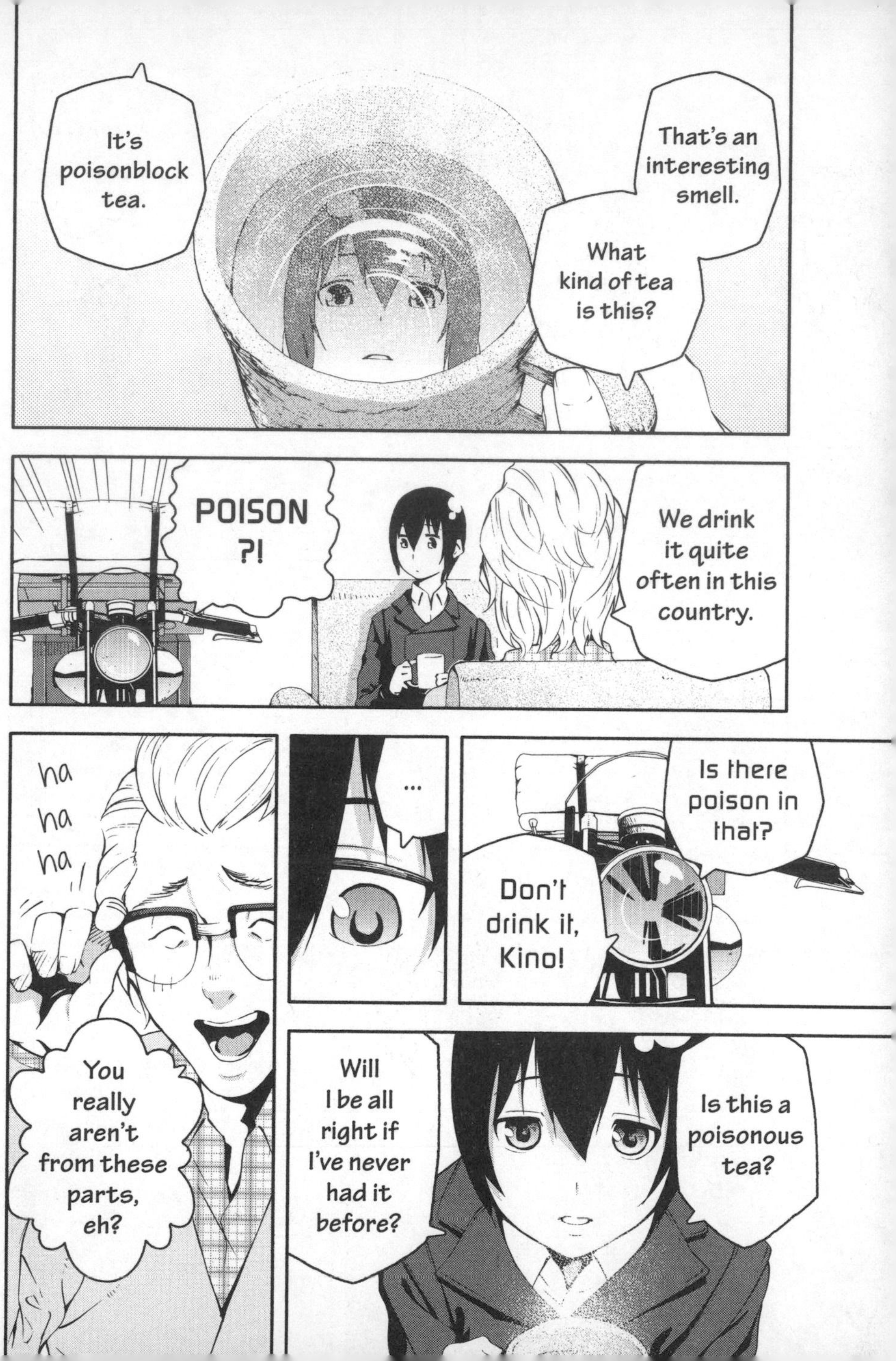
That's an interesting smell.
What kind of tea is this?
It's poisonblock tea.
We drink it quite often in this country.
POISON ?!
Is there poison in that?
Don't drink it, Kino!
...
Is this a poisonous tea?
Will I be all right if I've never had it before?
ha ha ha
You really aren't from these parts, eh?

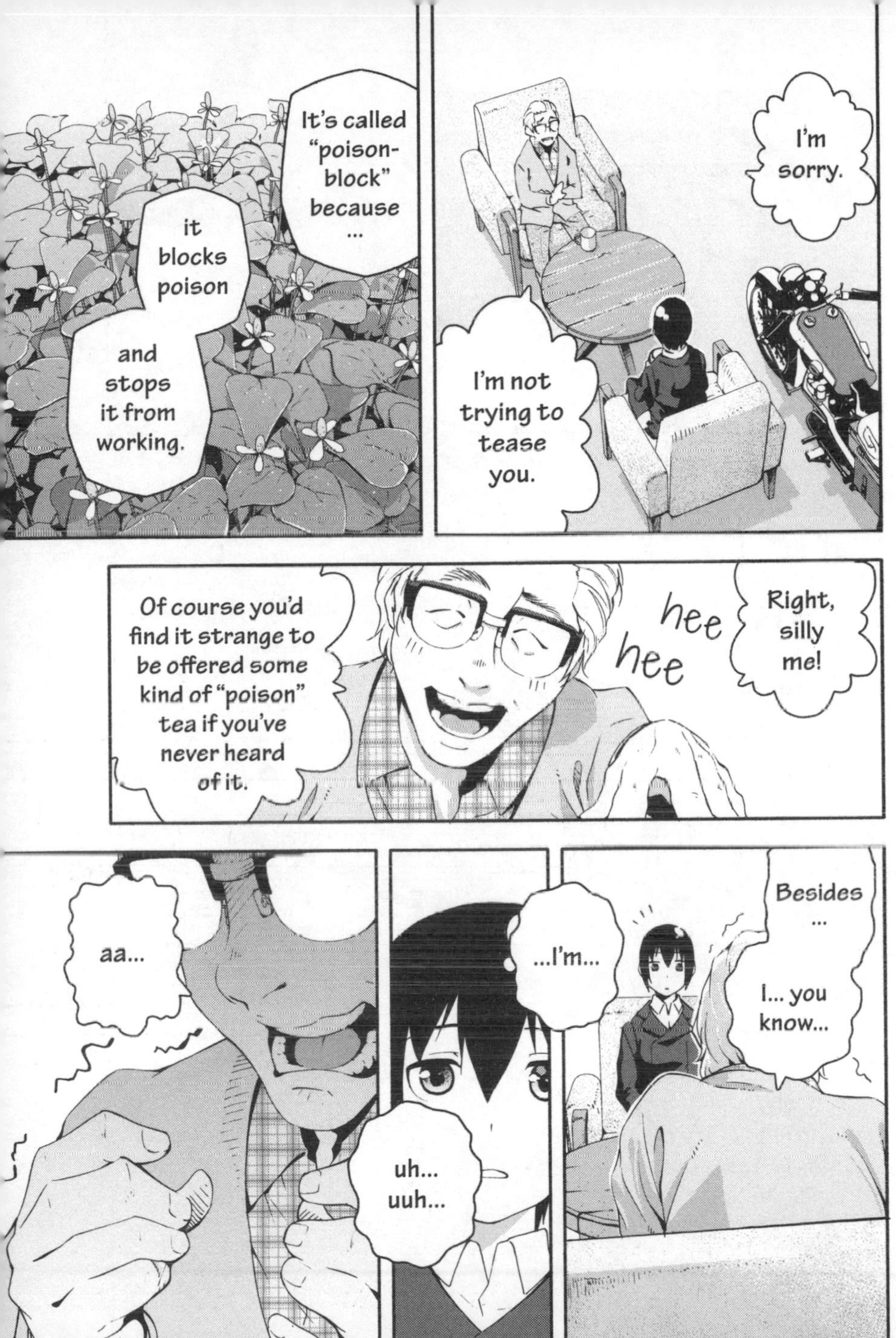
I'm sorry.
I'm not trying to tease you.
It's called "poison-block" because ...
it blocks poison
and stops it from working.
Right, silly me!
hee hee
Of course you'd find it strange to be offered some kind of "poison" tea if you've never heard of it.
Besides ...
I... you know...
...I'm...
uh... uuh...
aa...

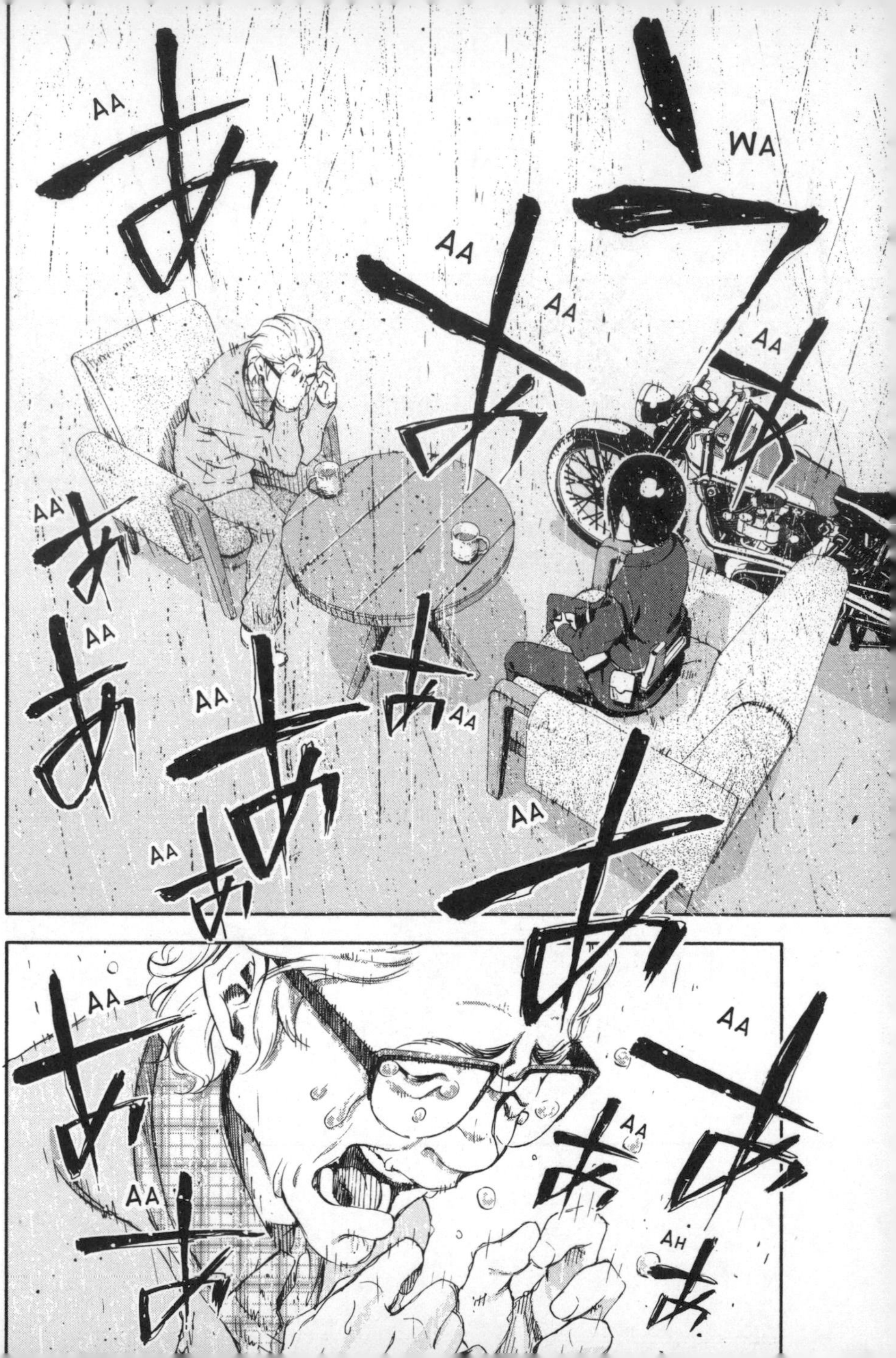
WA
AA
AA
AA
AA
AA
AA
AA
AA
AA
AA
AA
AA
AH
AA
AA-
AA

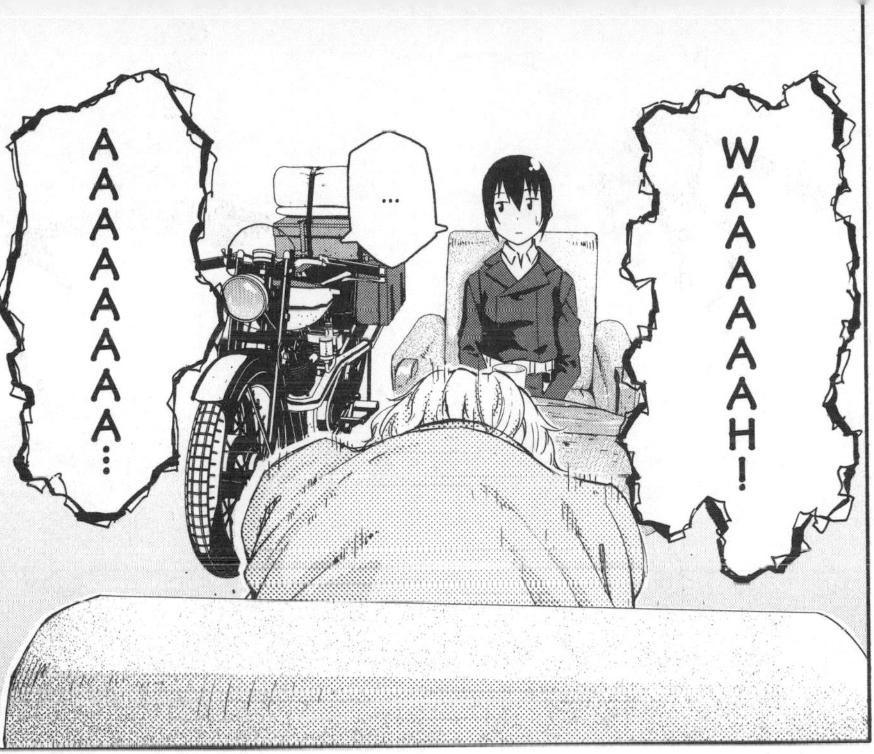
WAAAAAAAH!
...
AAAAAAAAA...

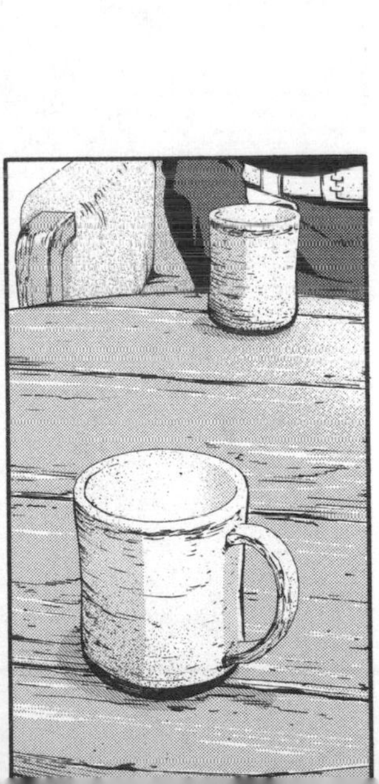

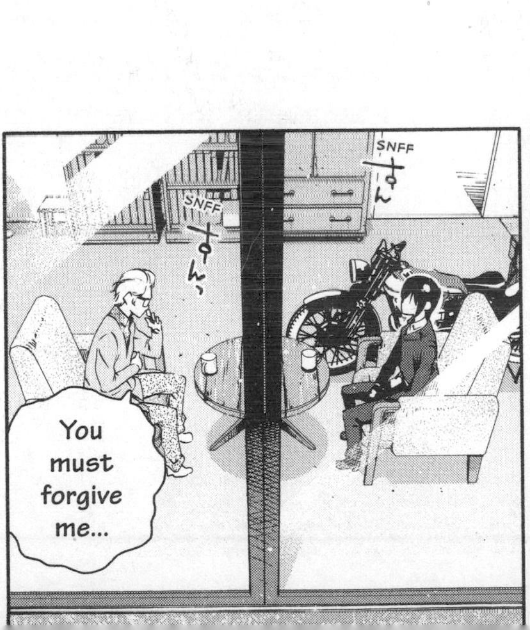
SNFF
SNFF
You must forgive me...

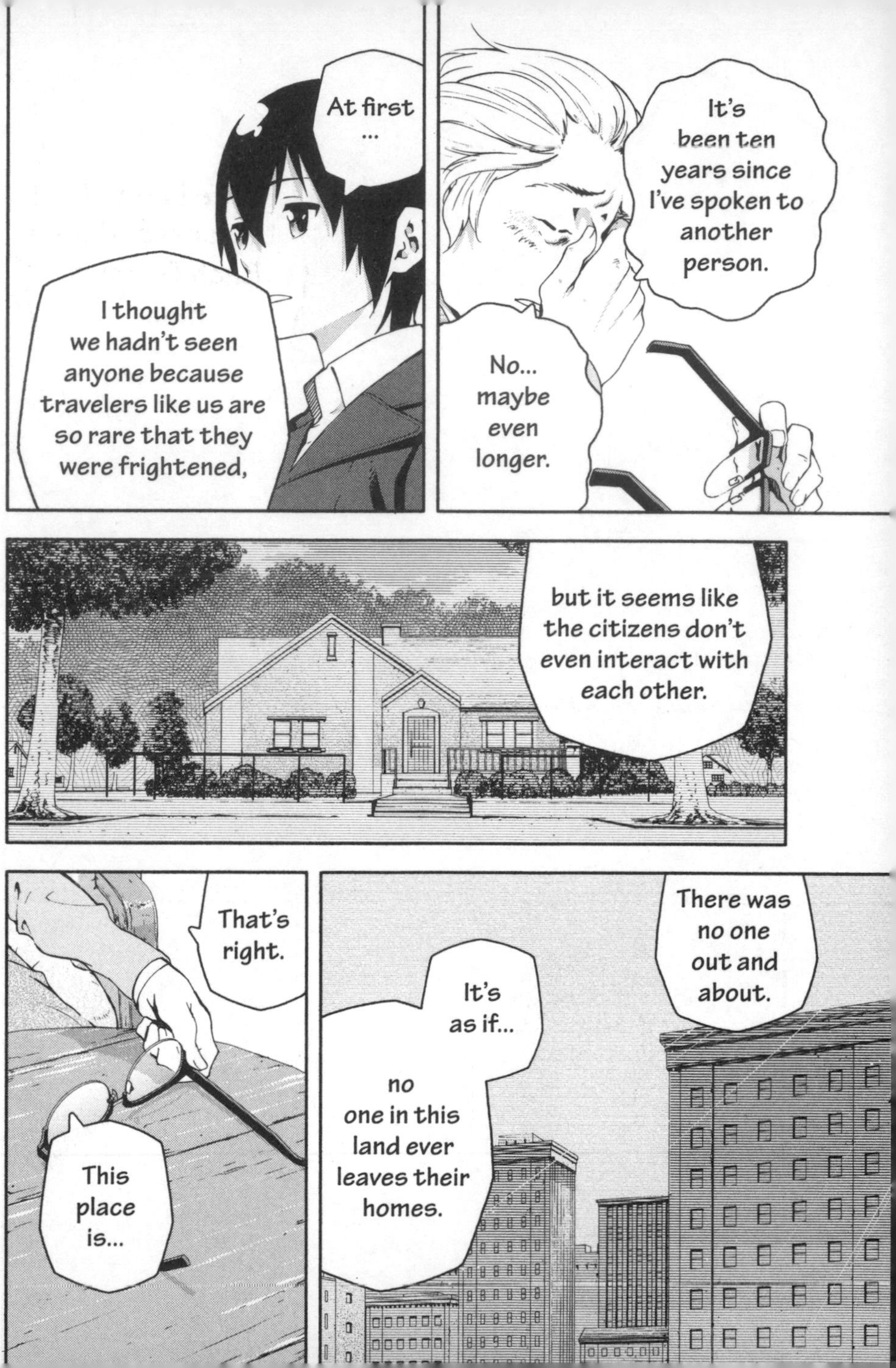

It's been ten years since I've spoken to another person.
No... maybe even longer.
At first ...
I thought we hadn't seen anyone because travelers like us are so rare that they were frightened,
but it seems like the citizens don't even interact with each other.
There was no one out and about.
It's as if...
no one in this land ever leaves their homes.
That's right.
This place is...

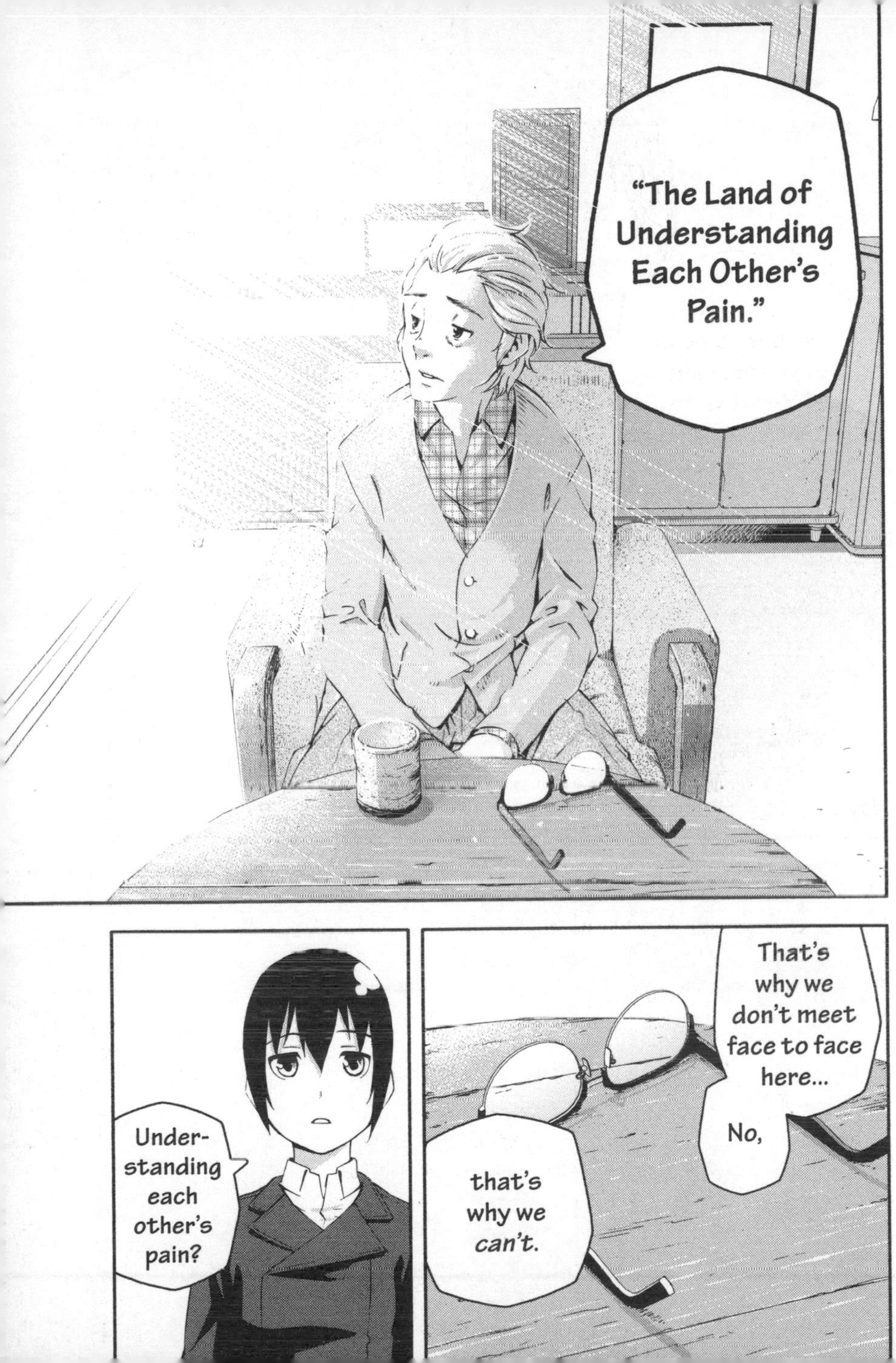
"The Land of Understanding Each Other's Pain."
That's why we don't meet face to face here...
No,
that's why we *can't.*
Under-standing each other's pain?

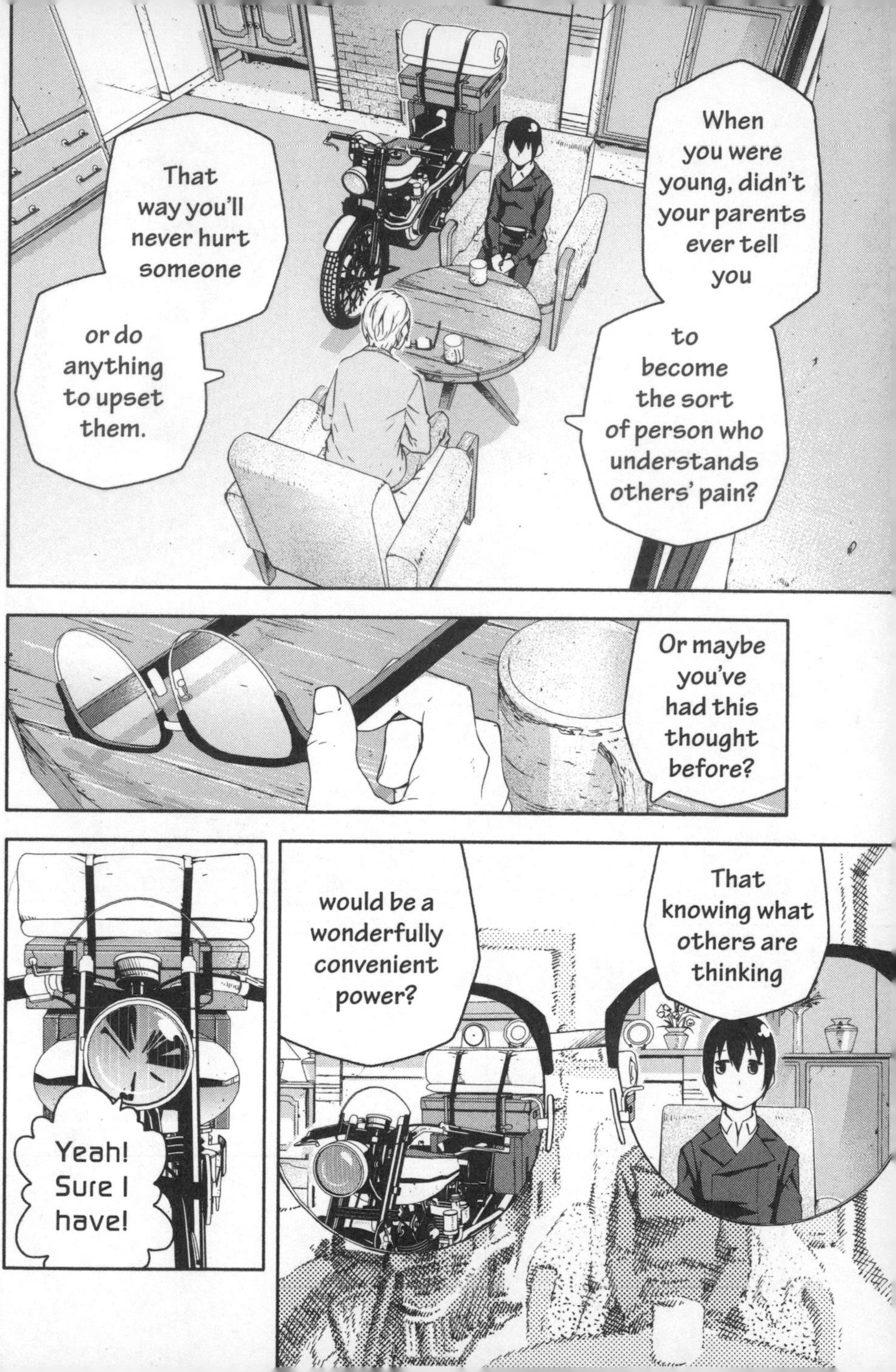
When you were young, didn't your parents ever tell you
to become the sort of person who understands others' pain?
That way you'll never hurt someone
or do anything to upset them.
Or maybe you've had this thought before?
That knowing what others are thinking
would be a wonderfully convenient power?
Yeah! Sure I have!

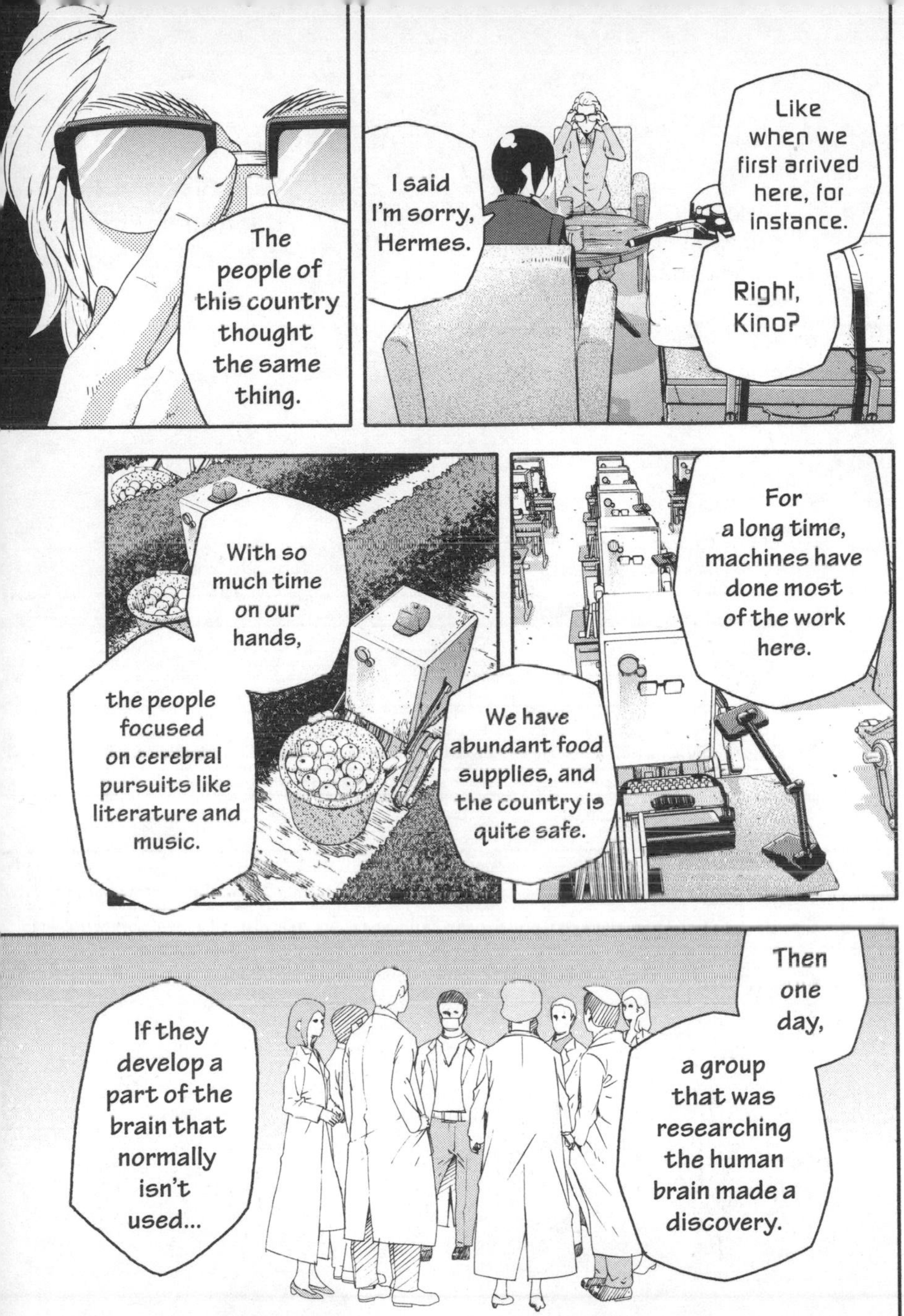
Like when we first arrived here, for instance.
Right, Kino?
I said I'm sorry, Hermes.
The people of this country thought the same thing.
For a long time, machines have done most of the work here.
We have abundant food supplies, and the country is quite safe.
With so much time on our hands,
the people focused on cerebral pursuits like literature and music.
Then one day,
a group that was researching the human brain made a discovery.
If they develop a part of the brain that normally isn't used...

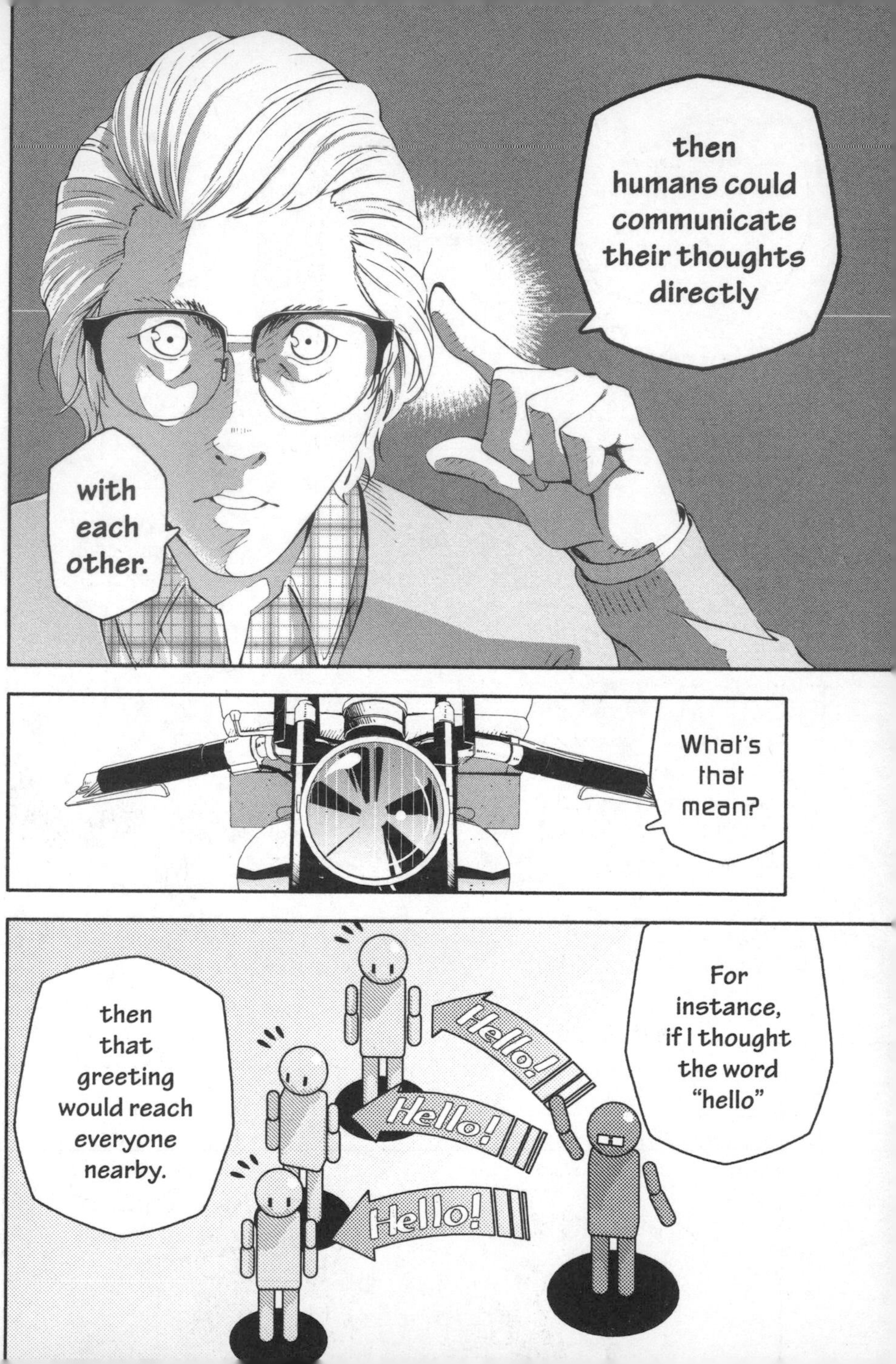
then humans could communicate their thoughts directly
with each other.
What's that mean?
For instance, if I thought the word "hello"
Hello!
Hello!
Hello!
then that greeting would reach everyone nearby.

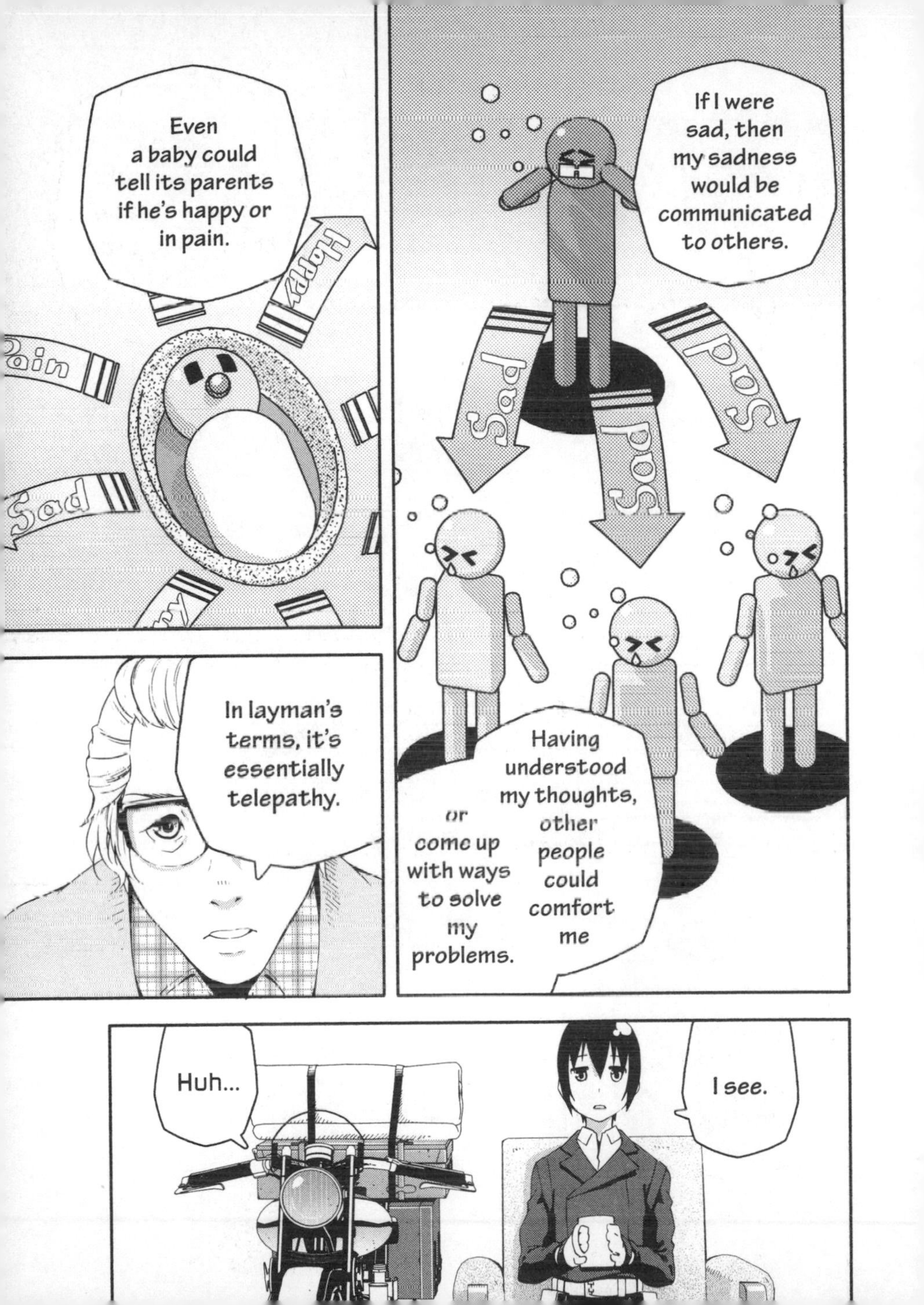
If I were sad, then my sadness would be communicated to others.
Sad
Sad
Sad
Having understood my thoughts, other people could comfort me
or come up with ways to solve my problems.
Even a baby could tell its parents if he's happy or in pain.
Happy
Pain
Sad
In layman's terms, it's essentially telepathy.
I see.
Huh...

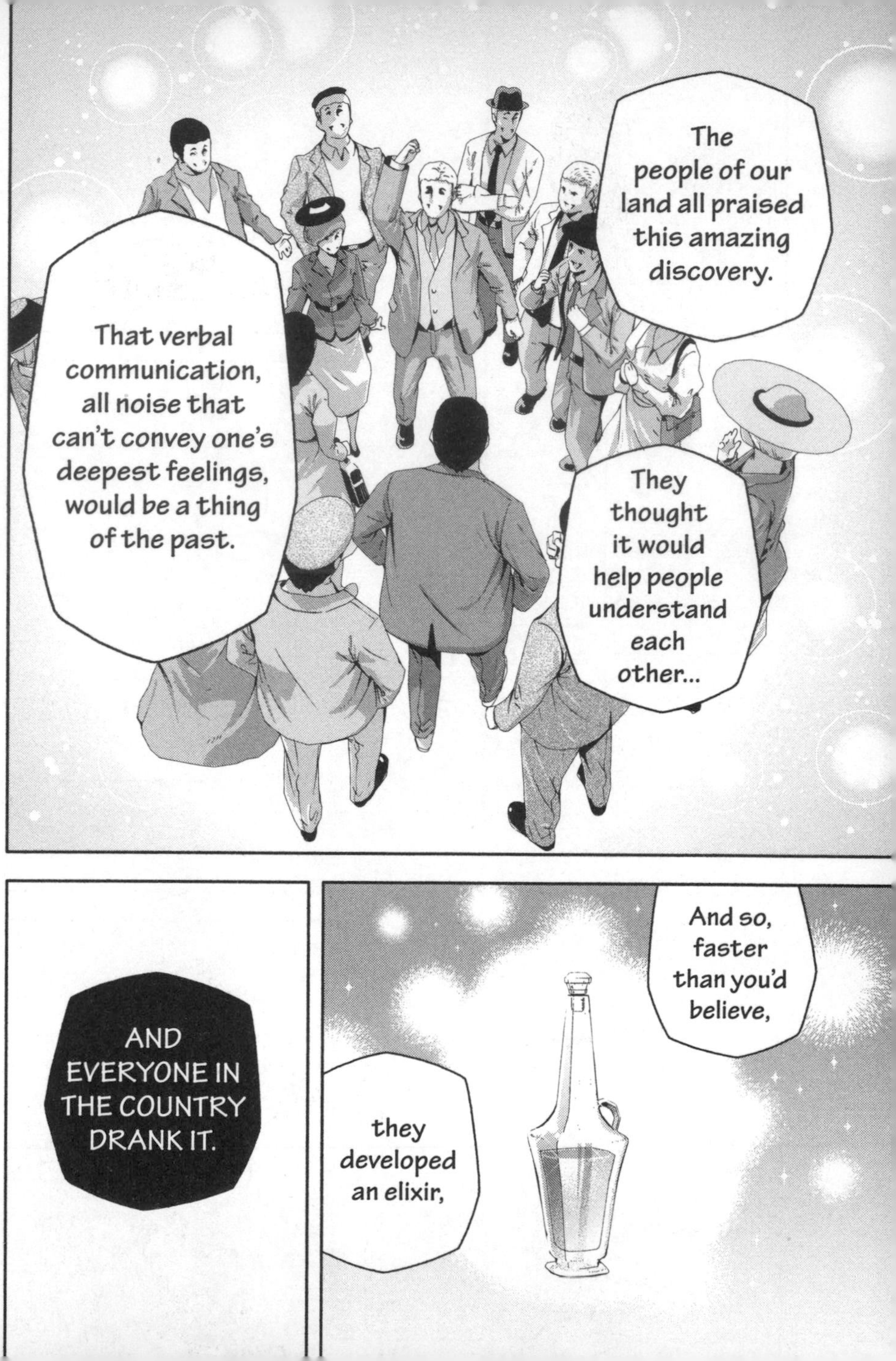
The people of our land all praised this amazing discovery.
That verbal communication, all noise that can't convey one's deepest feelings, would be a thing of the past.
They thought it would help people understand each other...
And so, faster than you'd believe,
they developed an elixir,
AND EVERYONE IN THE COUNTRY DRANK IT.

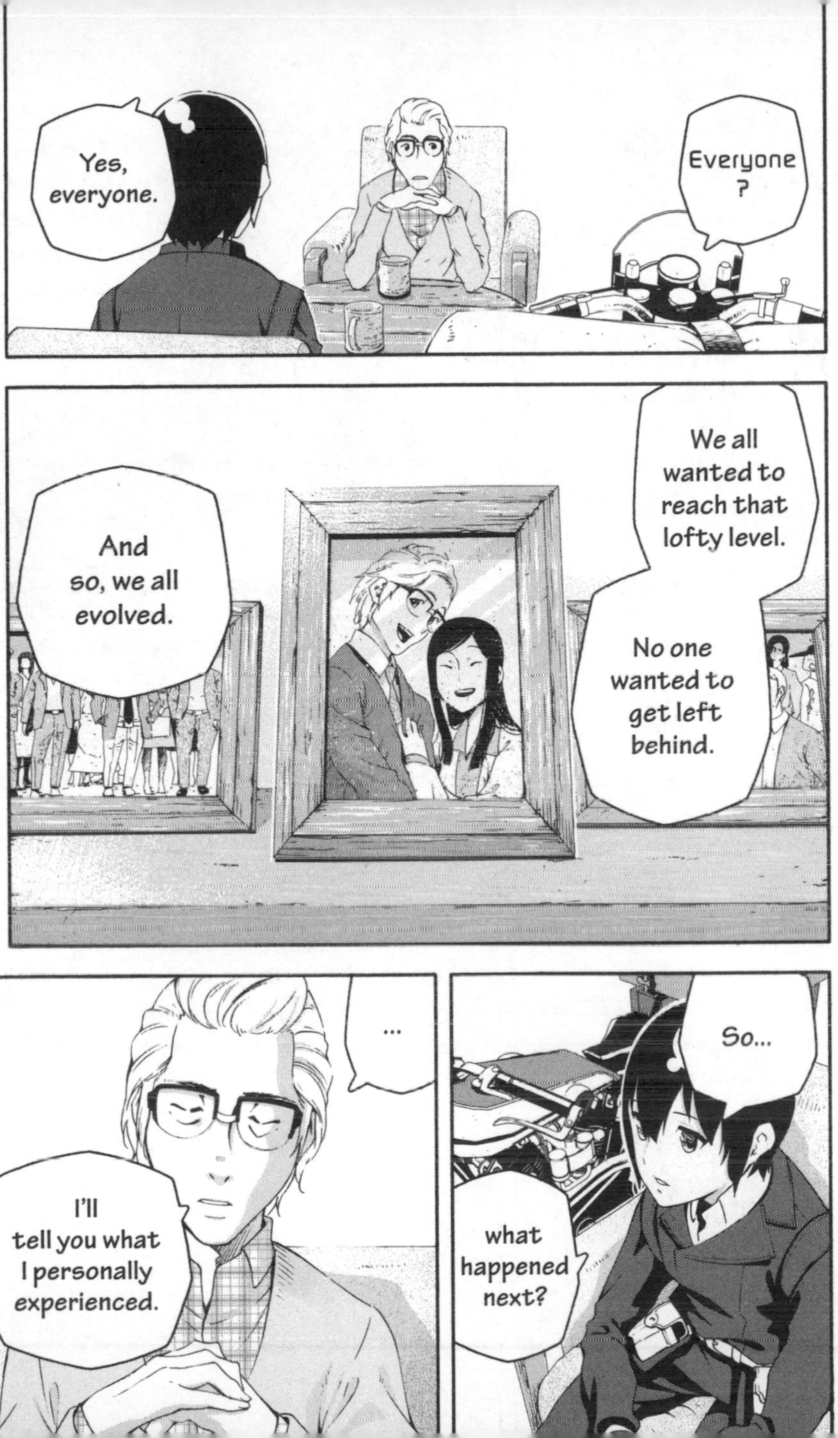
Everyone ?
Yes, everyone.
We all wanted to reach that lofty level.
No one wanted to get left behind.
And so, we all evolved.
So...
what happened next?
...
I'll tell you what I personally experienced.

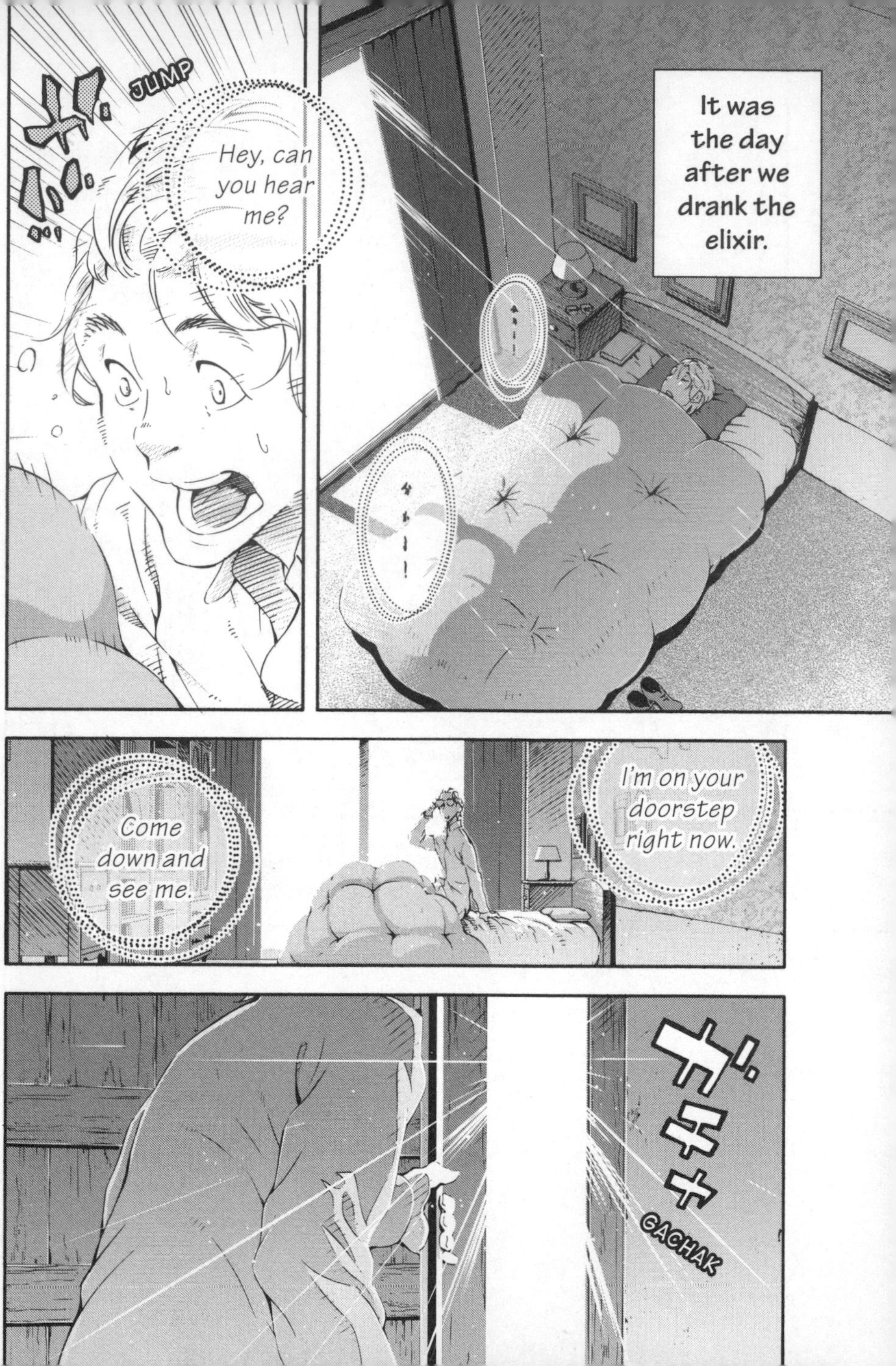
It was the day after we drank the elixir.
Hey, can you hear me?
JUMP
I'm on your doorstep right now.
Come down and see me.
GACHAK

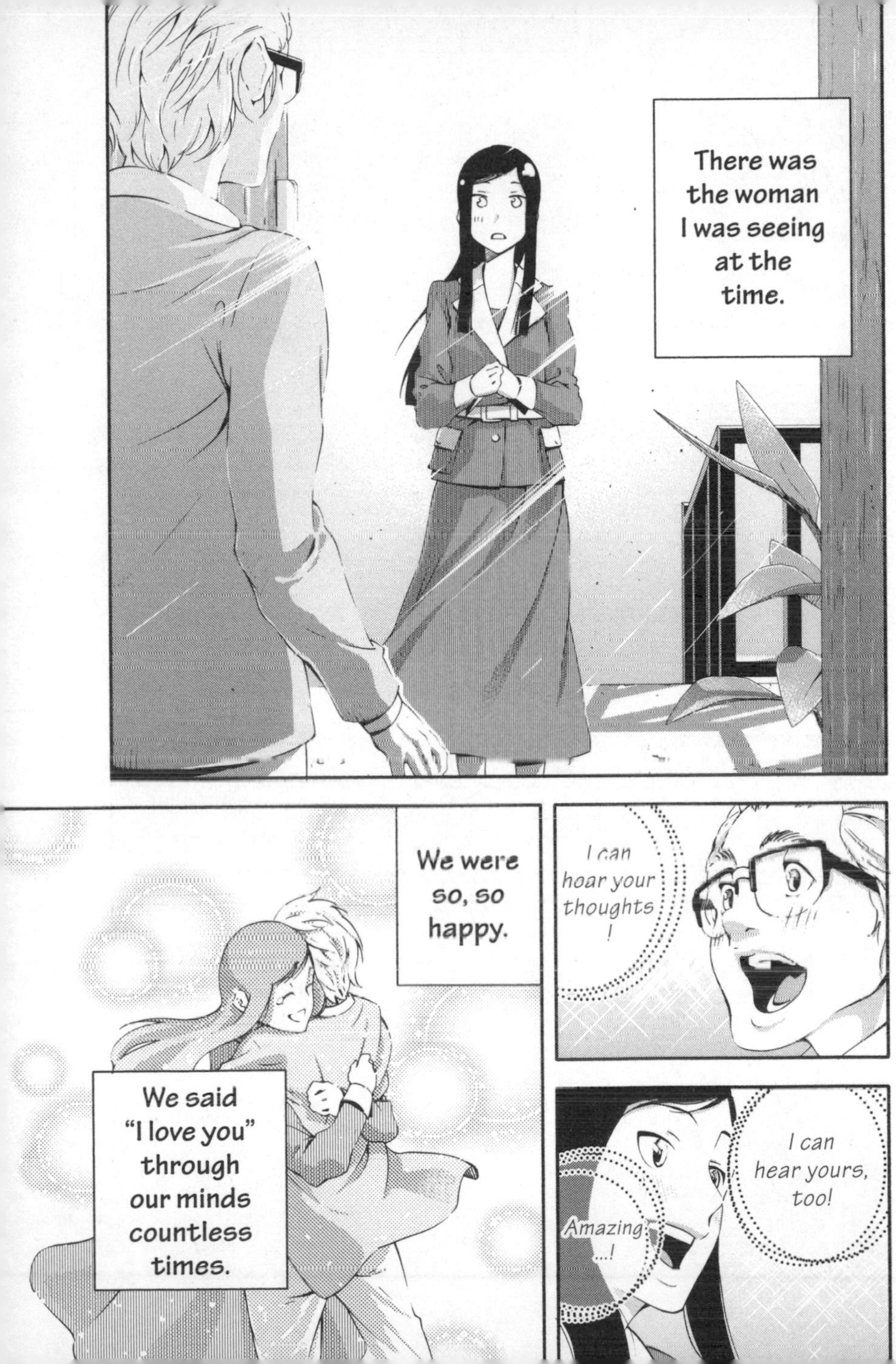
There was the woman I was seeing at the time.
I can hear your thoughts!
I can hear yours, too!
Amazing...!
We were so, so happy.
We said "I love you" through our minds countless times.

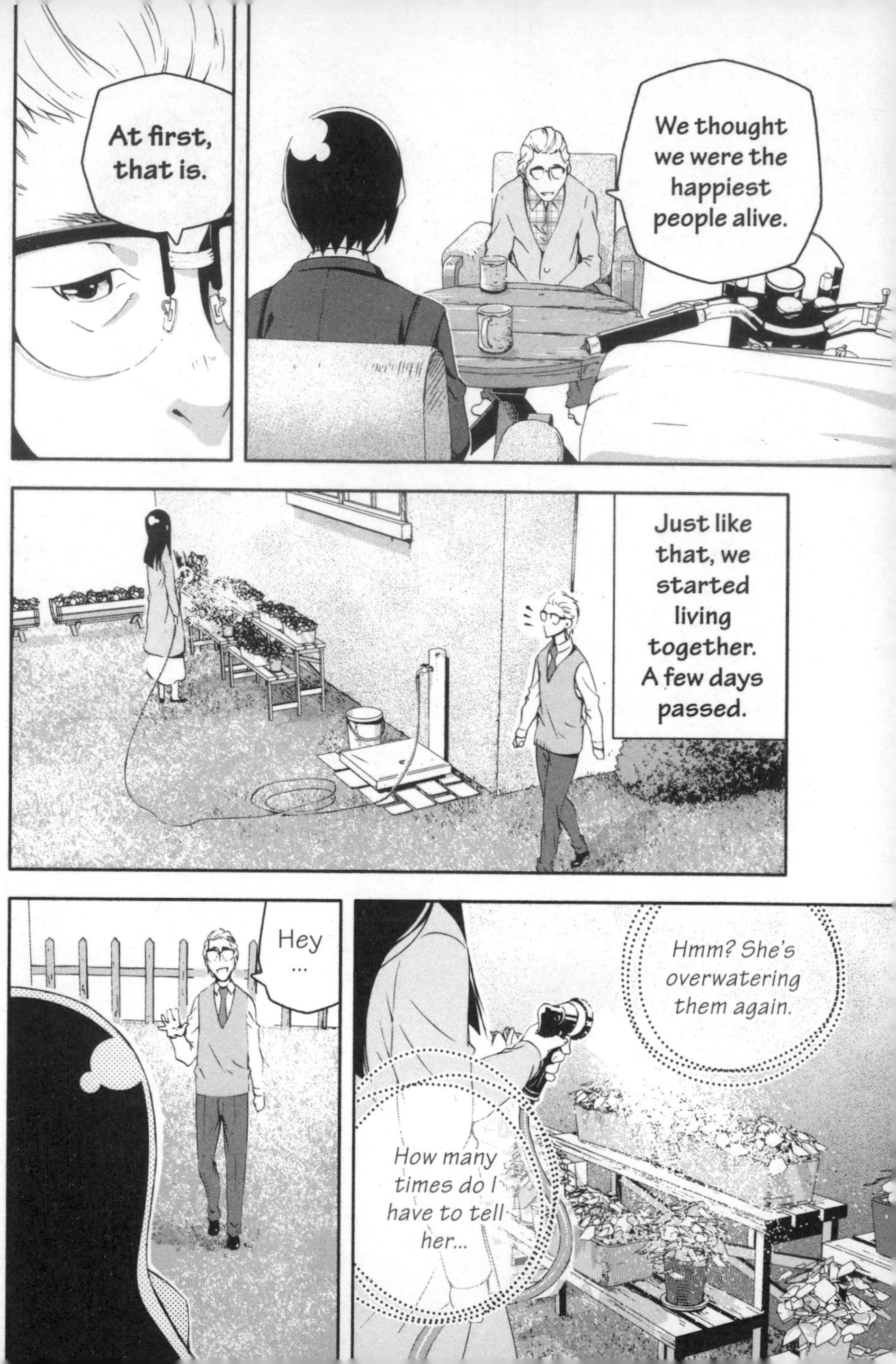
We thought we were the happiest people alive.
At first, that is.
Just like that, we started living together. A few days passed.
Hmm? She's overwatering them again.
How many times do I have to tell her...
Hey ...

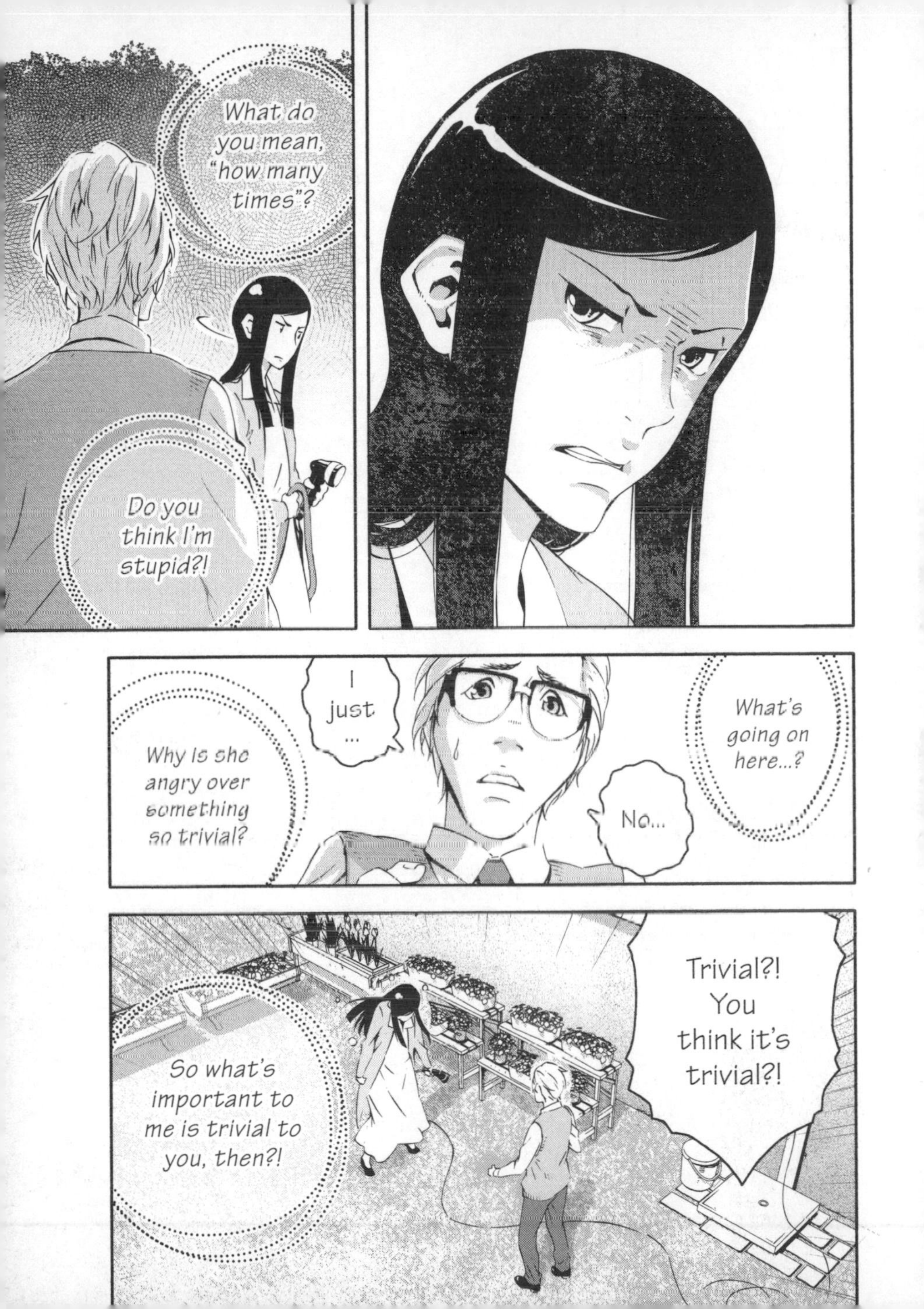
What do you mean, "how many times"?
Do you think I'm stupid?!
What's going on here...?
No...
I just ...
Why is she angry over something so trivial?
Trivial?! You think it's trivial?!
So what's important to me is trivial to you, then?!

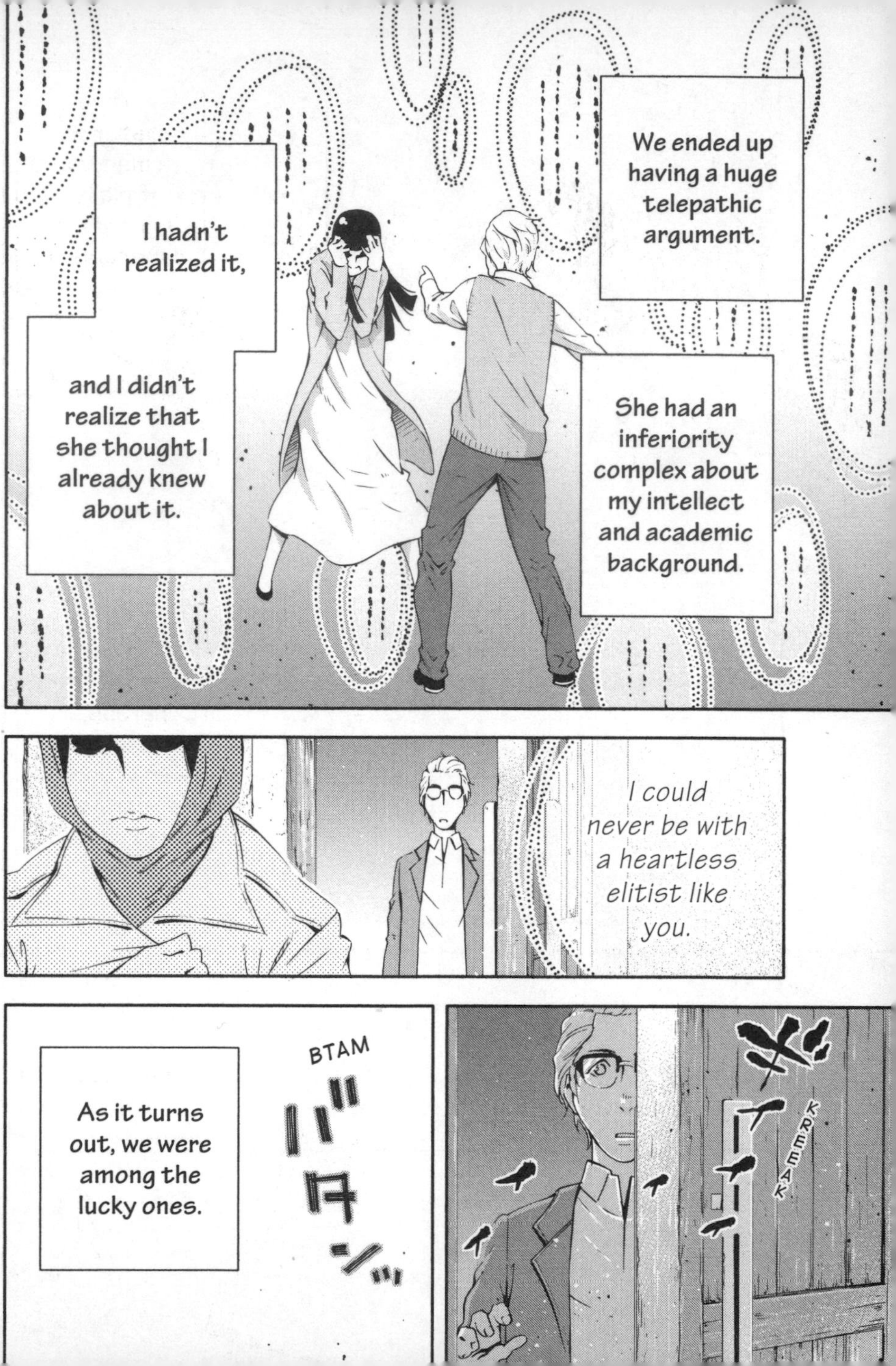
We ended up having a huge telepathic argument.
She had an inferiority complex about my intellect and academic background.
I hadn't realized it,
and I didn't realize that she thought I already knew about it.
I could never be with a heartless elitist like you.
KREEAK
BTAM
As it turns out, we were among the lucky ones.

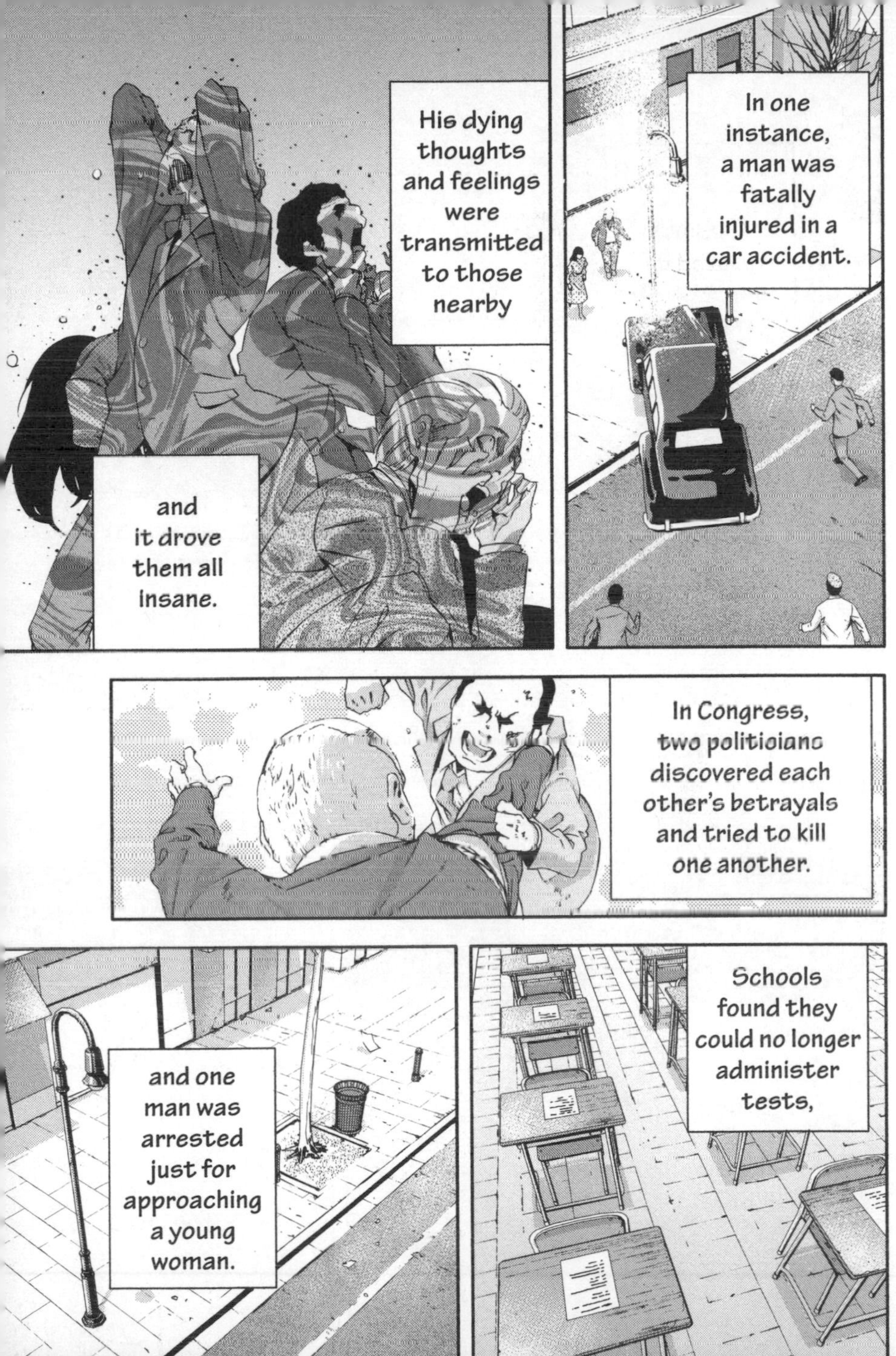
In one instance, a man was fatally injured in a car accident.
His dying thoughts and feelings were transmitted to those nearby
and it drove them all insane.
In Congress, two politicians discovered each other's betrayals and tried to kill one another.
Schools found they could no longer administer tests,
and one man was arrested just for approaching a young woman.

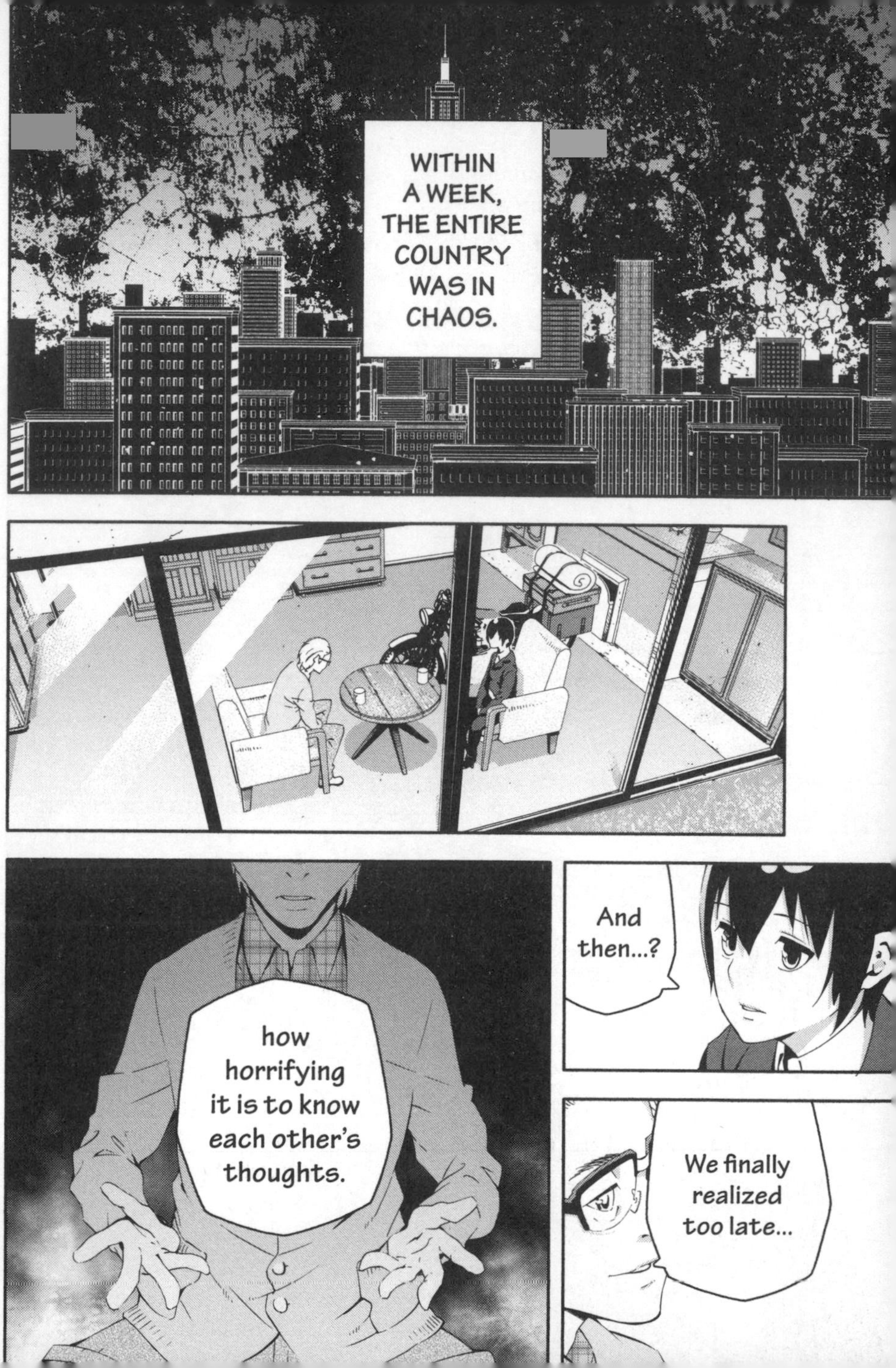
WITHIN A WEEK, THE ENTIRE COUNTRY WAS IN CHAOS.
And then...?
We finally realized too late...
how horrifying it is to know each other's thoughts.

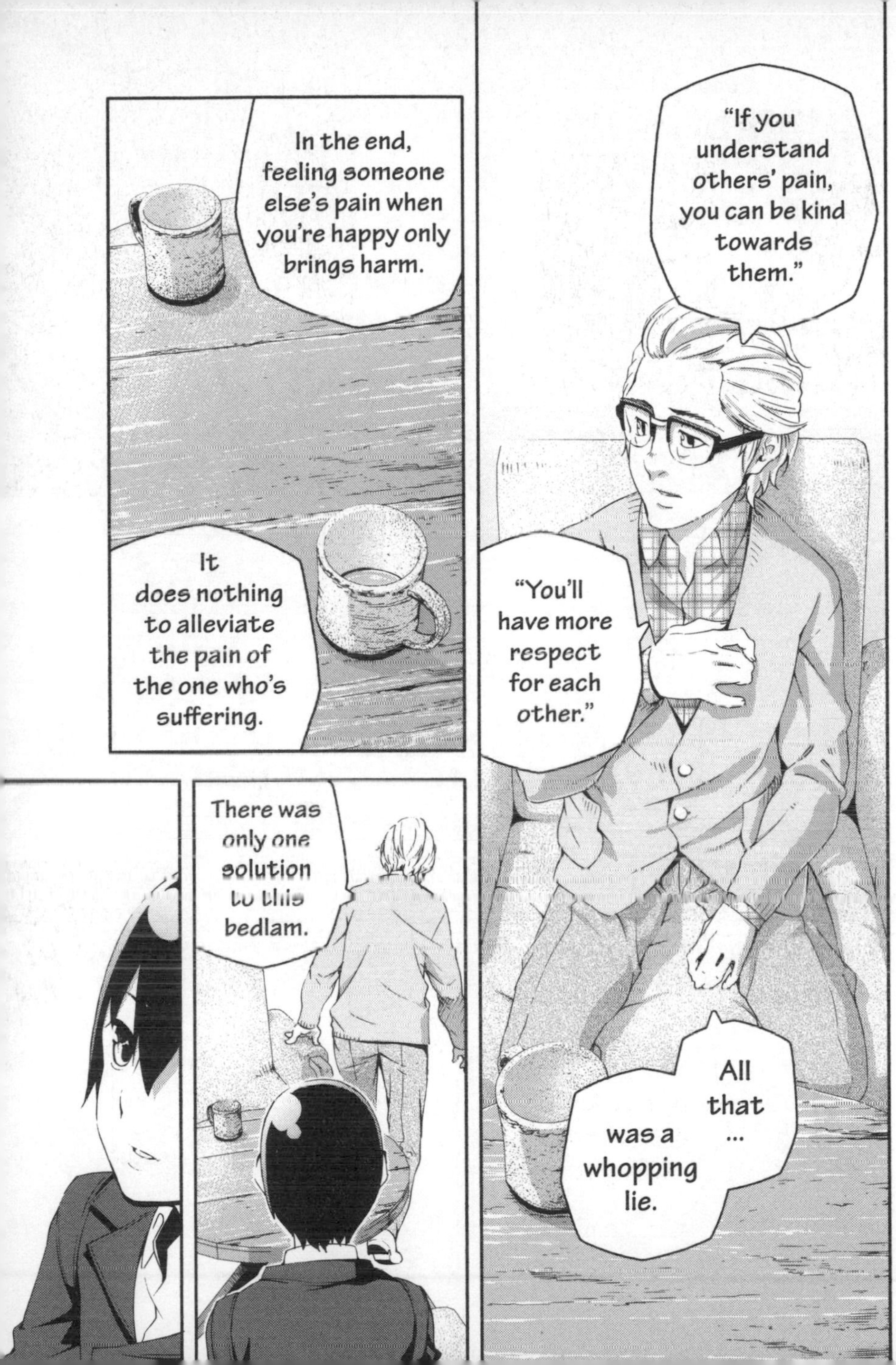
"If you understand others' pain, you can be kind towards them."
"You'll have more respect for each other."
All that ... was a whopping lie.
In the end, feeling someone else's pain when you're happy only brings harm.
It does nothing to alleviate the pain of the one who's suffering.
There was only one solution to this bedlam.

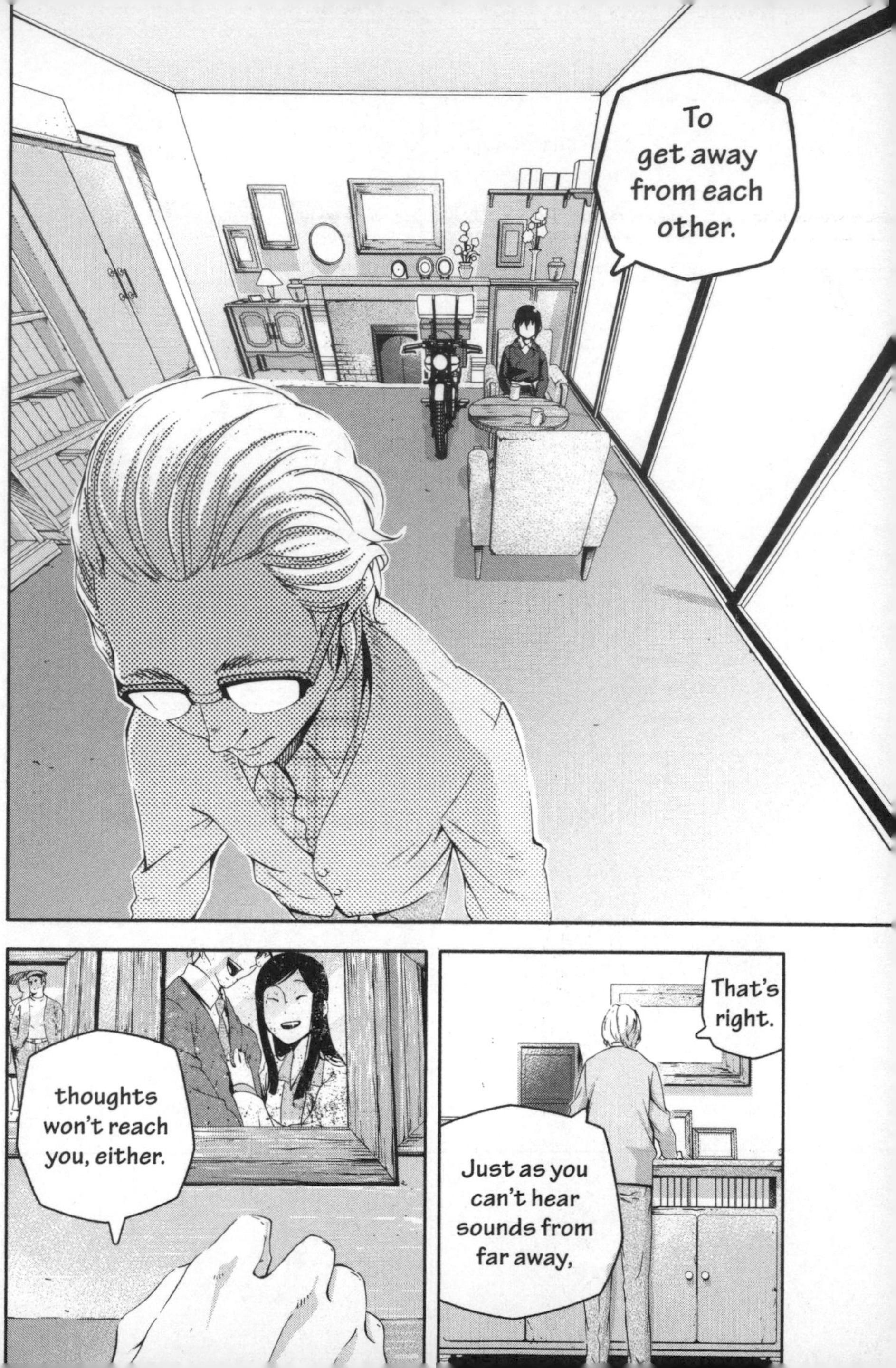
To get away from each other.
That's right.
Just as you can't hear sounds from far away,
thoughts won't reach you, either.

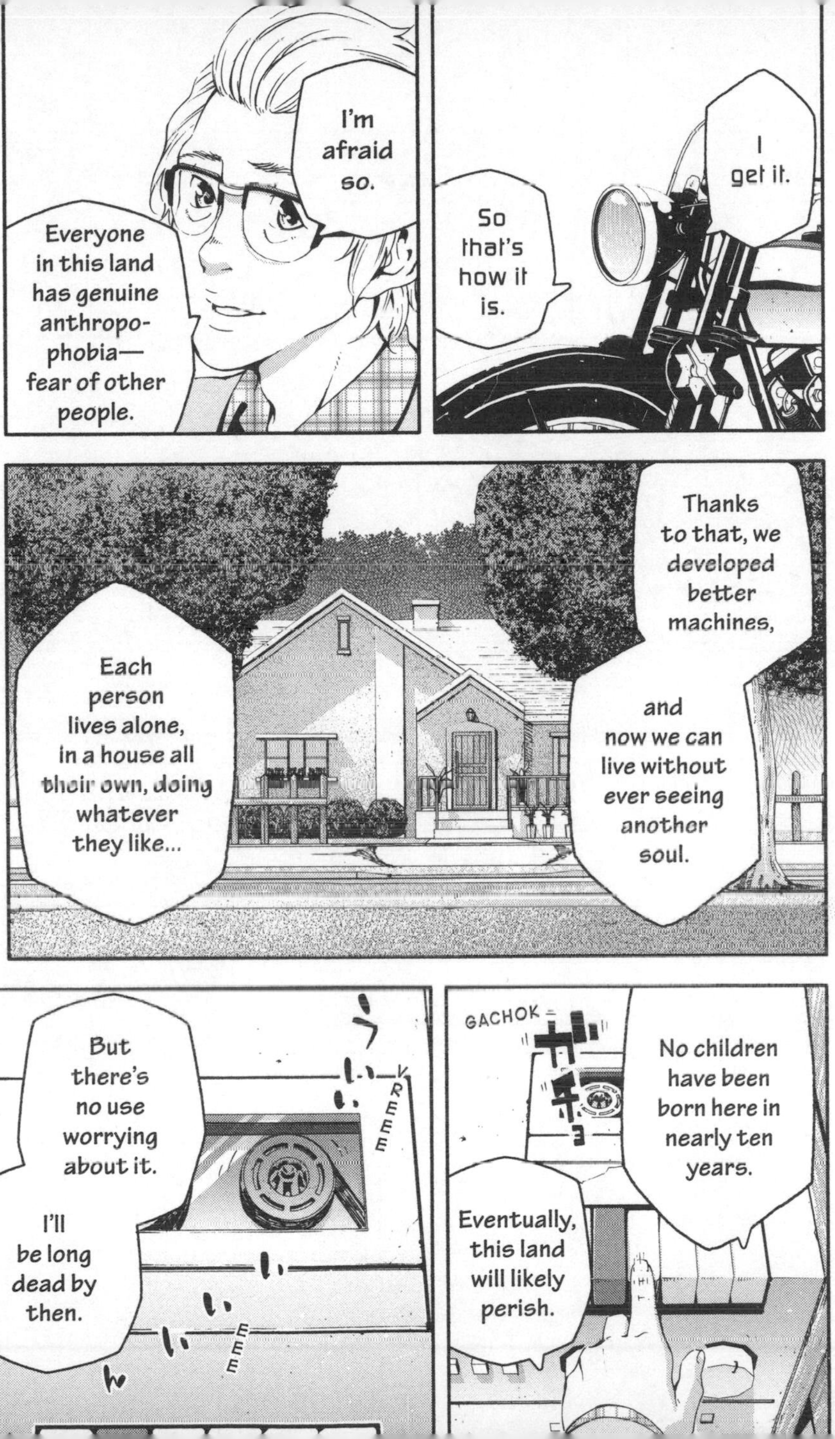
I get it.
So that's how it is.
I'm afraid so.
Everyone in this land has genuine anthropophobia—fear of other people.
Thanks to that, we developed better machines,
and now we can live without ever seeing another soul.
Each person lives alone, in a house all their own, doing whatever they like...
GACHOK
No children have been born here in nearly ten years.
Eventually, this land will likely perish.
VREEEE
But there's no use worrying about it.
I'll be long dead by then.
EEE

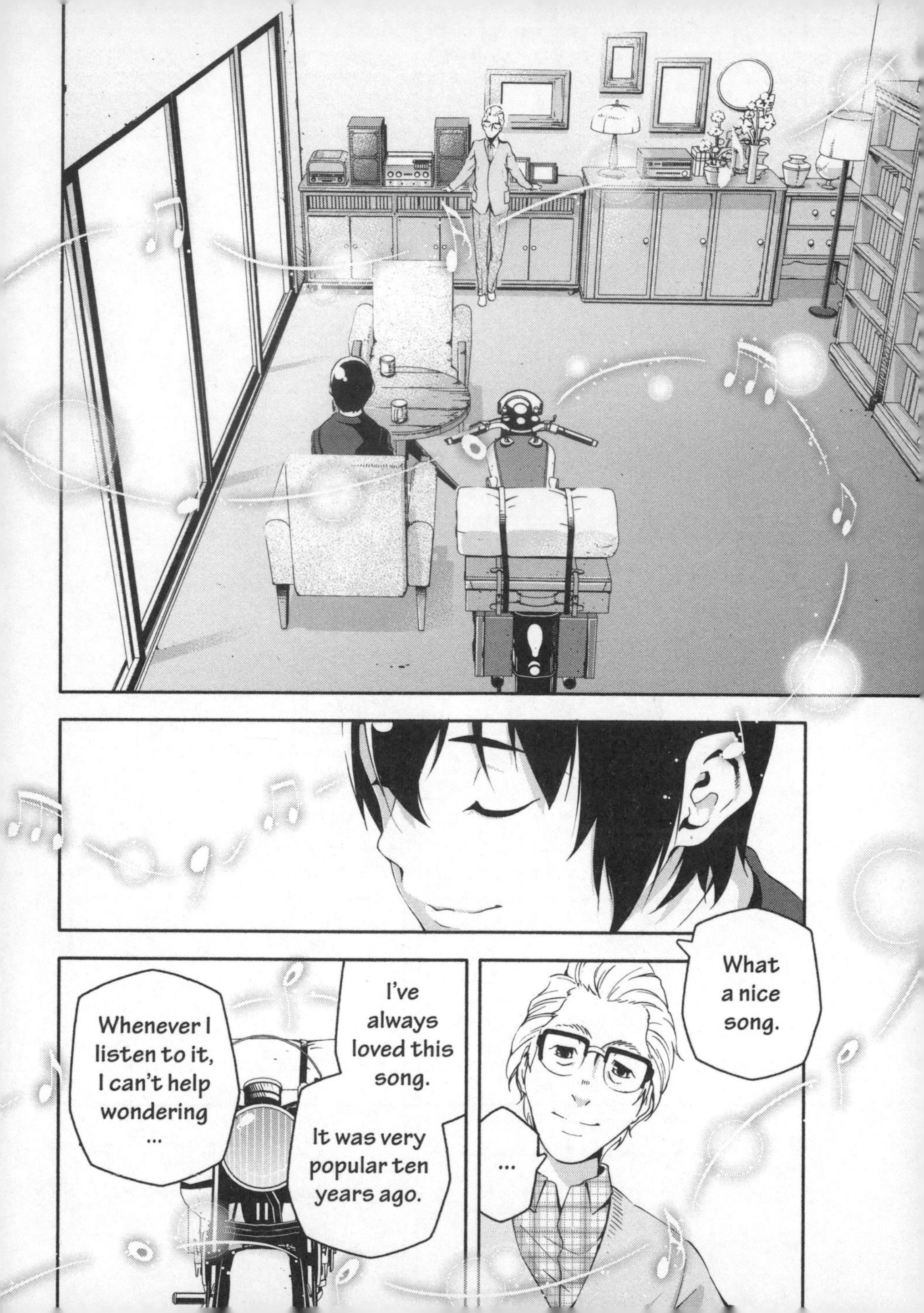
What a nice song.
...
I've always loved this song.
It was very popular ten years ago.
Whenever I listen to it, I can't help wondering ...

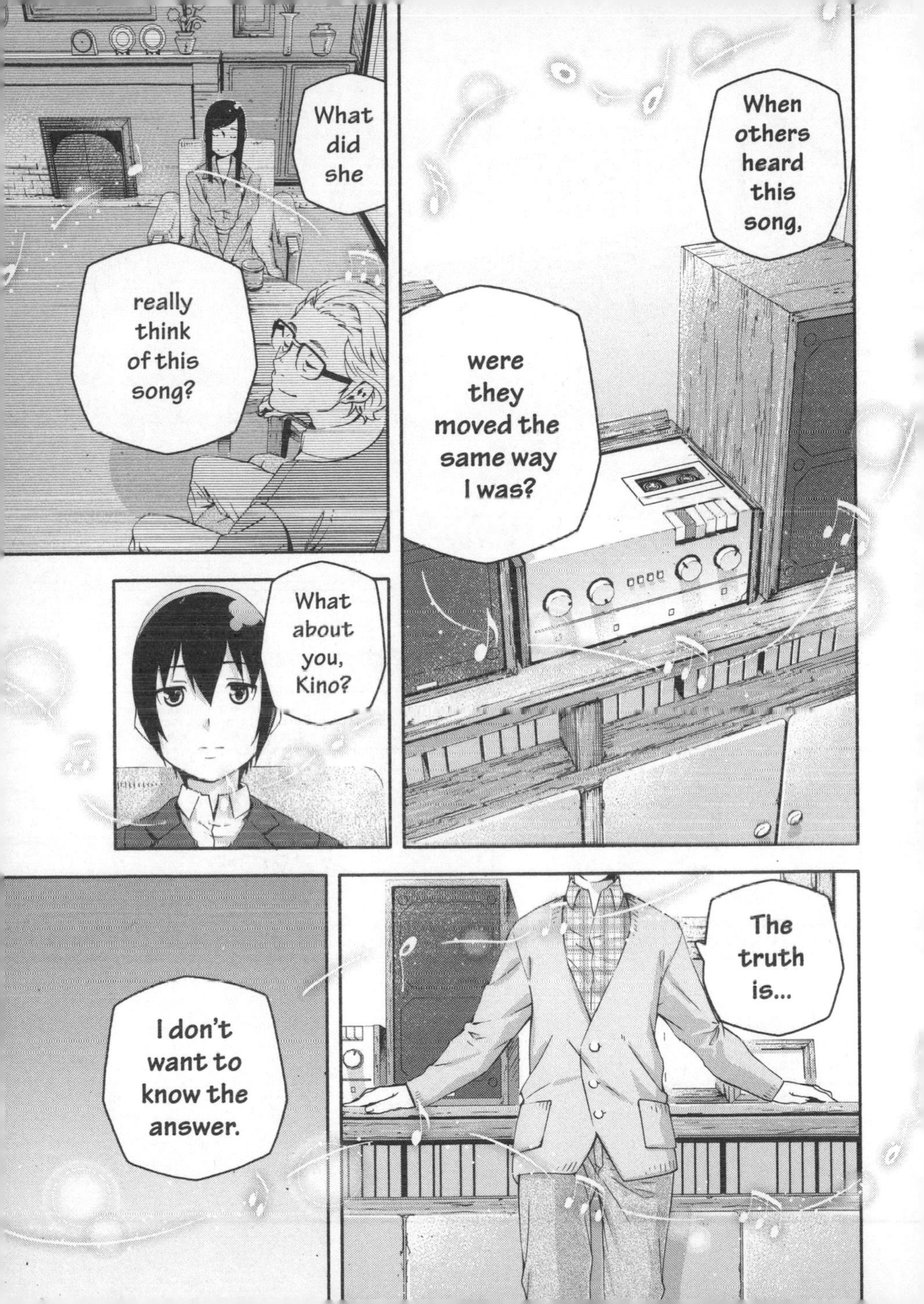
When others heard this song,
were they moved the same way I was?
What did she
really think of this song?
What about you, Kino?
The truth is...
I don't want to know the answer.

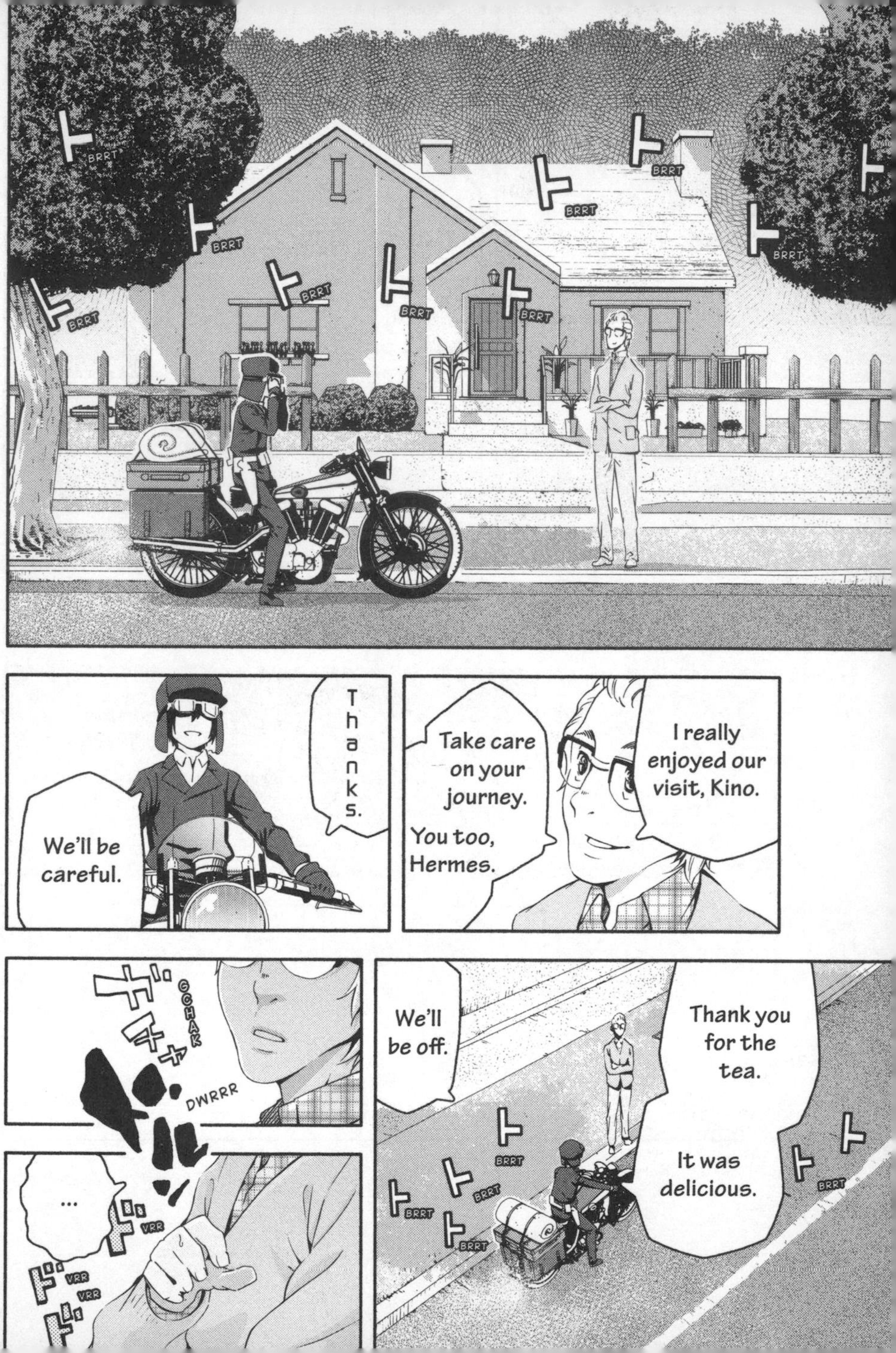
BRRT
BRRT
BRRT
BRRT
BRRT
BRRT
BRRT
BRRT
I really enjoyed our visit, Kino.
Take care on your journey.
You too, Hermes.
Thanks.
We'll be careful.
Thank you for the tea.
We'll be off.
It was delicious.
BRRT
BRRT
BRRT
BRRT
BRRT
GCHAK
DWRRR
...
VRR
VRR
VRR

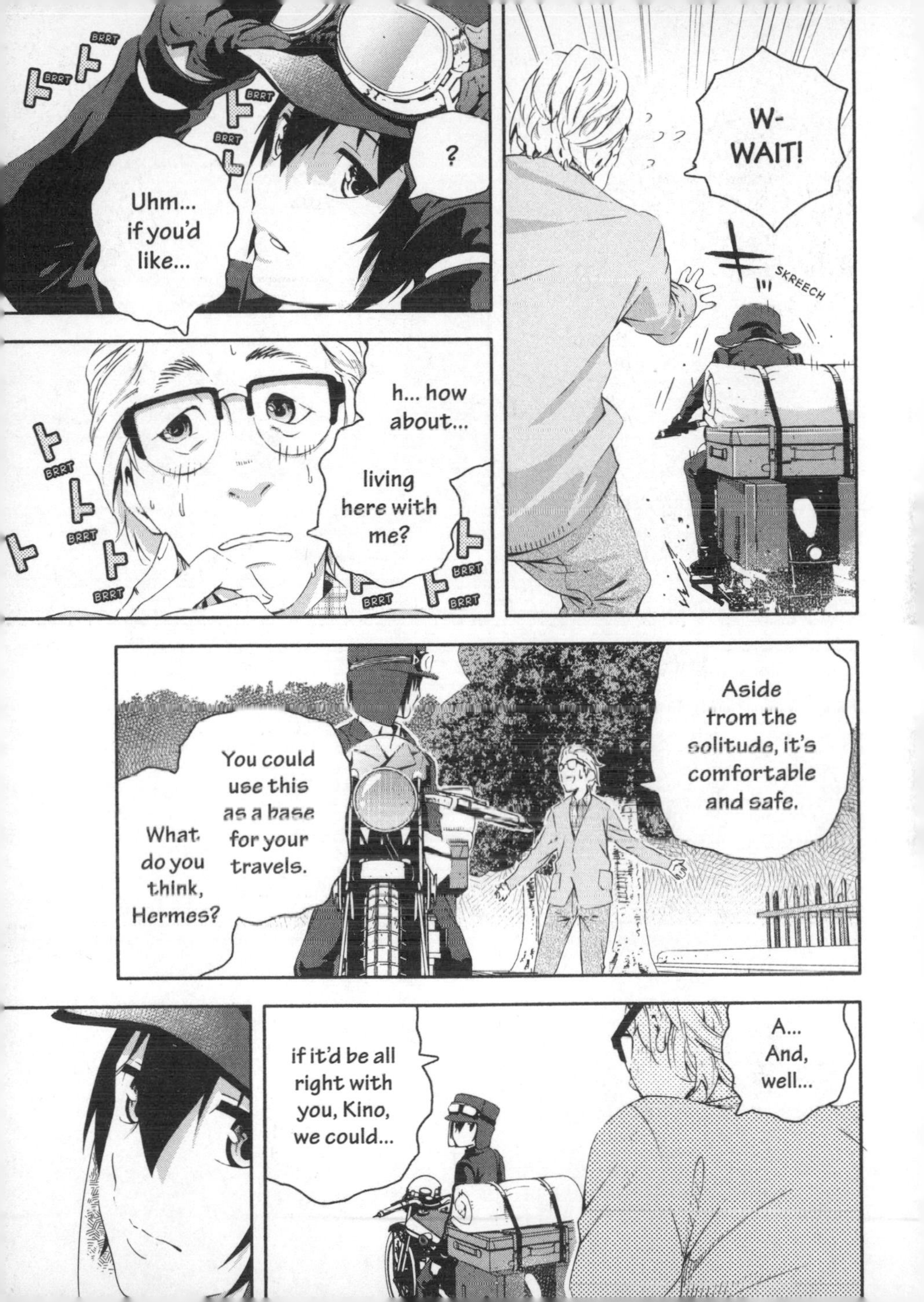
W-
WAIT!
SKREECH
BRRT
BRRT
BRRT
BRRT
?
Uhm... if you'd like...
h... how about...
living here with me?
BRRT
BRRT
BRRT
BRRT
BRRT
BRRT
Aside from the solitude, it's comfortable and safe.
You could use this as a base for your travels.
What do you think, Hermes?
A... And, well...
if it'd be all right with you, Kino, we could...

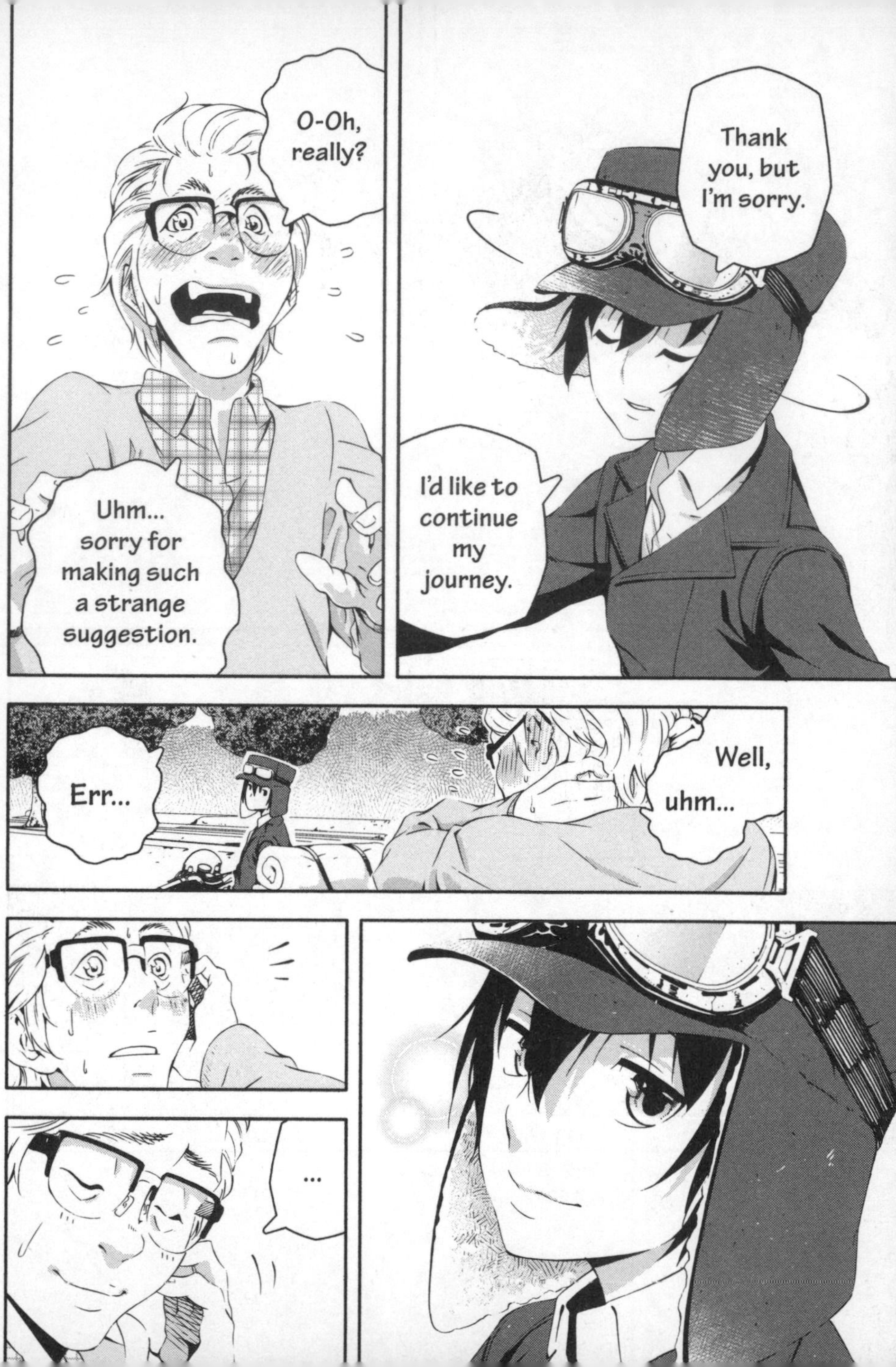
Thank you, but I'm sorry.
I'd like to continue my journey.
O-Oh, really?
Uhm... sorry for making such a strange suggestion.
Well, uhm...
Err...
...

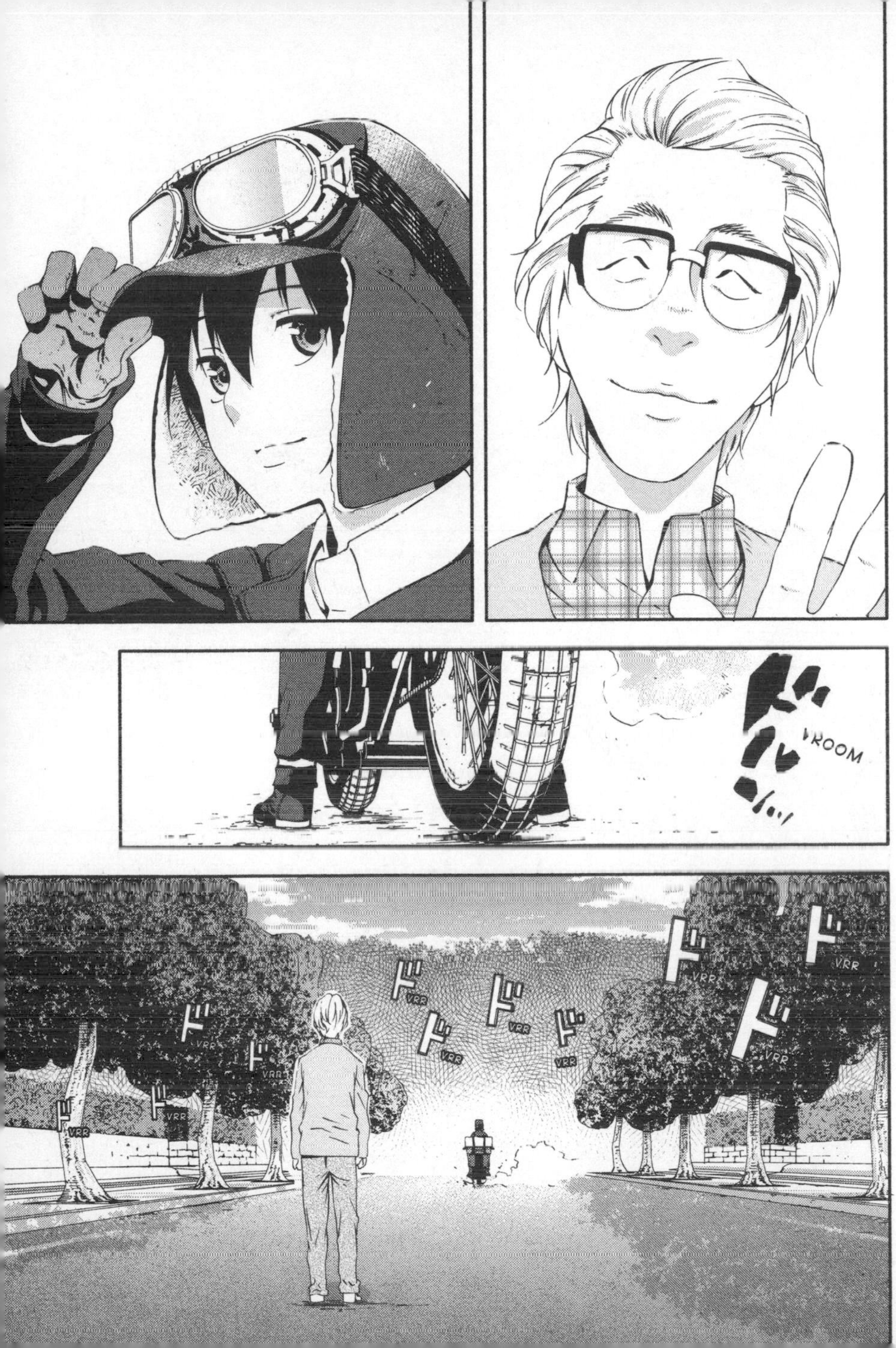
VROOM
ド
VRR
ド
VRR
ド
VRR
ド
VRR
ド
VRR
ド
VRR
ド
VRR
ド
VRR
ド
VRR
ド
VRR
ド
VRR

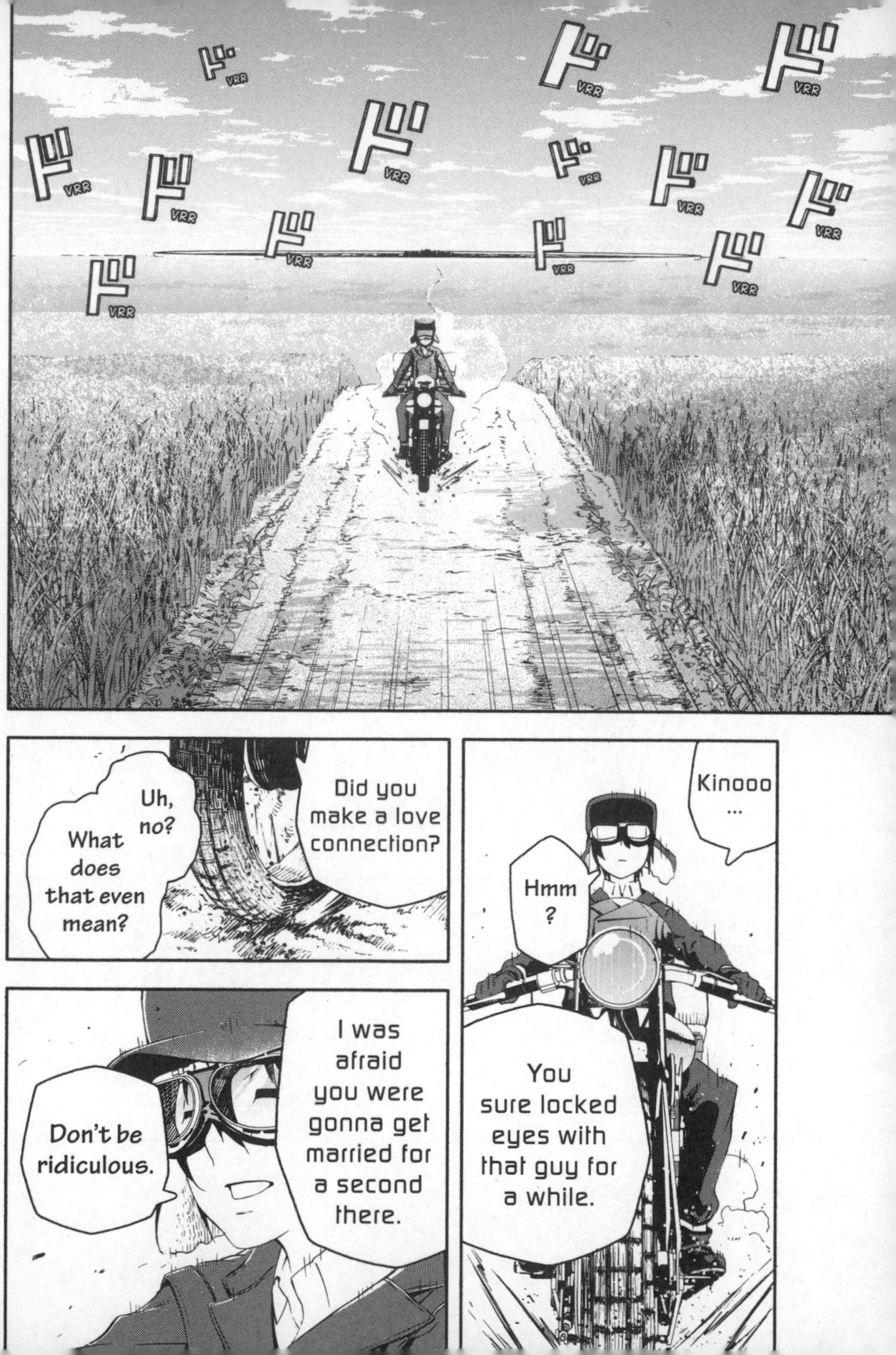
ド VRR
ド VRR
ド VRR
ド VRR
ド VRR
ド VRR
ド VRR
ド VRR
ド VRR
ド VRR
ド VRR
ド VRR
ド VRR
Kinooo...
Hmm?
You sure locked eyes with that guy for a while.
Did you make a love connection?
Uh, no? What does that even mean?
I was afraid you were gonna get married for a second there.
Don't be ridiculous.

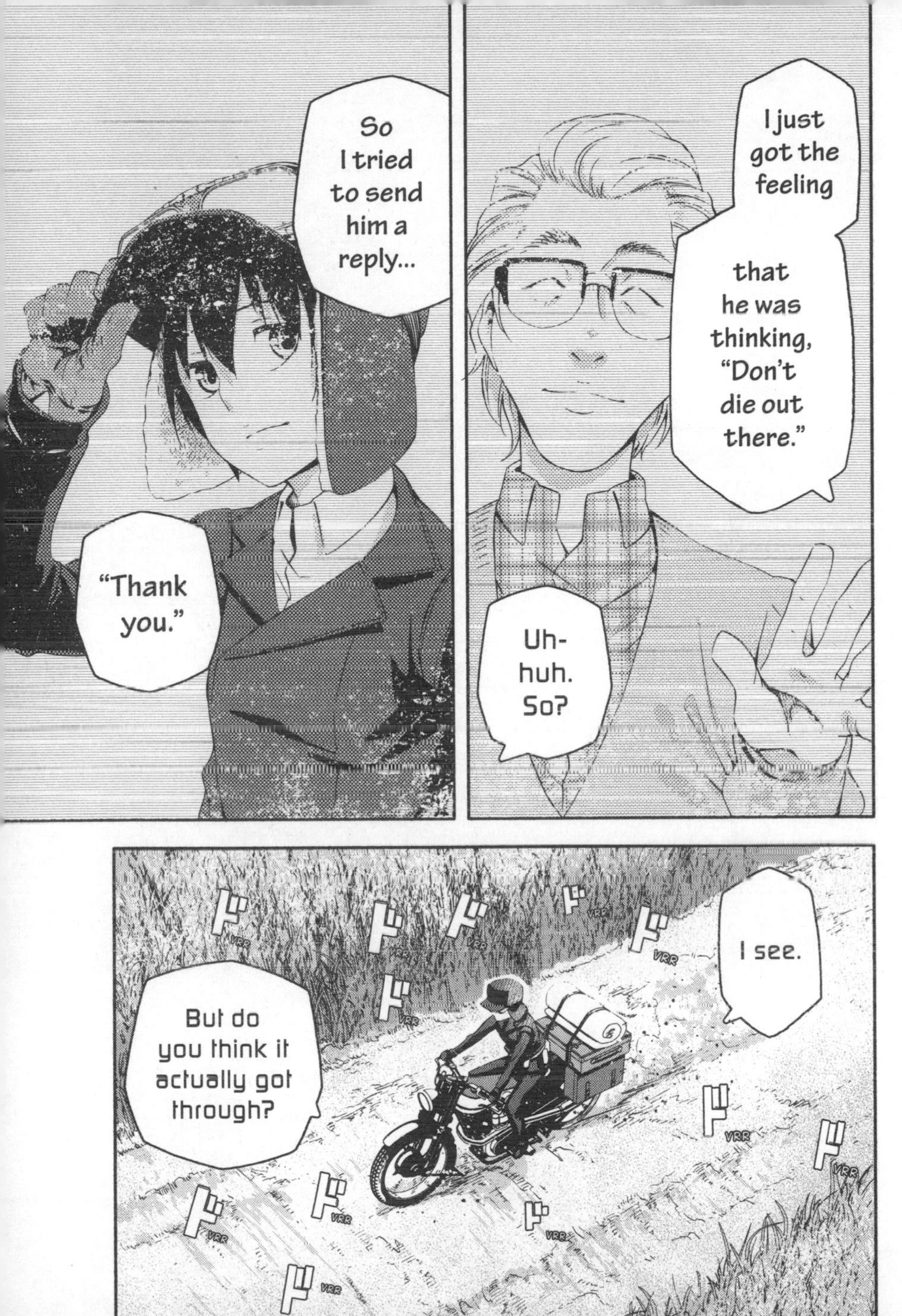
I just got the feeling
that he was thinking, “Don't die out there.”
Uh-huh. So?
So I tried to send him a reply...
“Thank you.”
I see.
But do you think it actually got through?
ド VRR

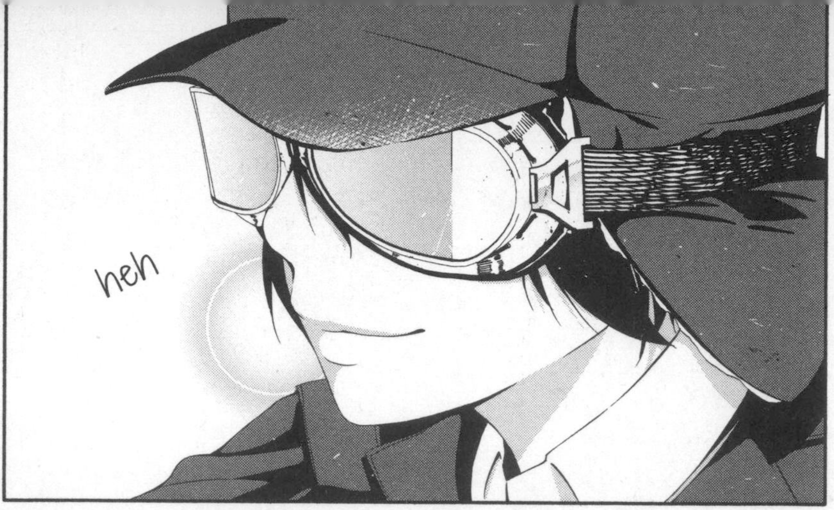
heh
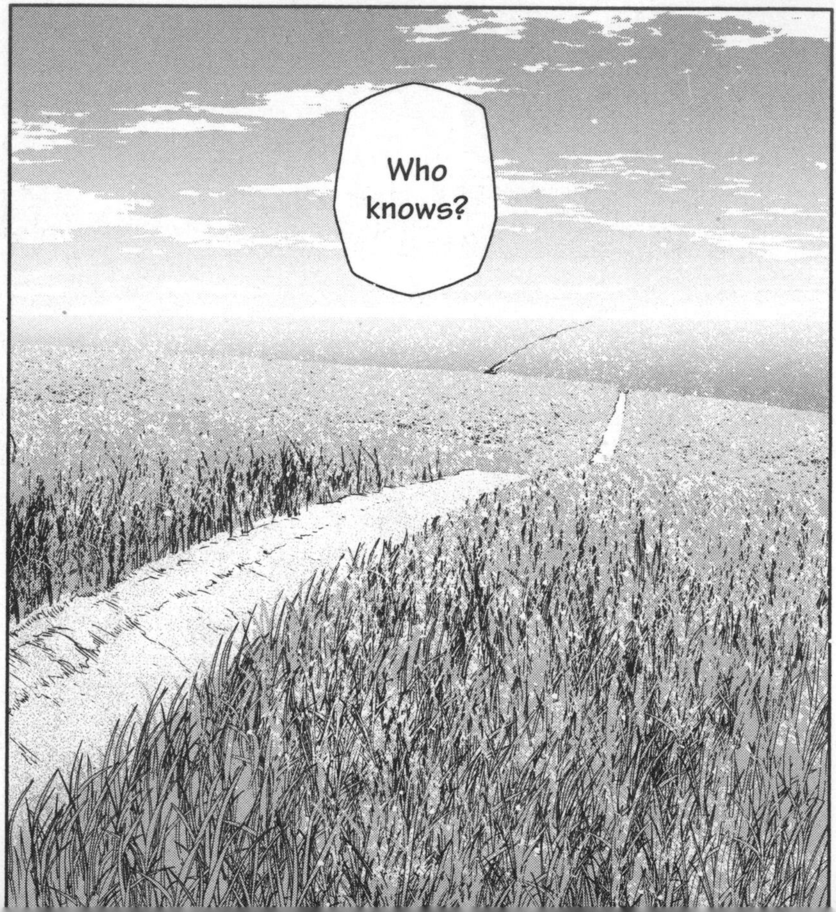
Who knows?

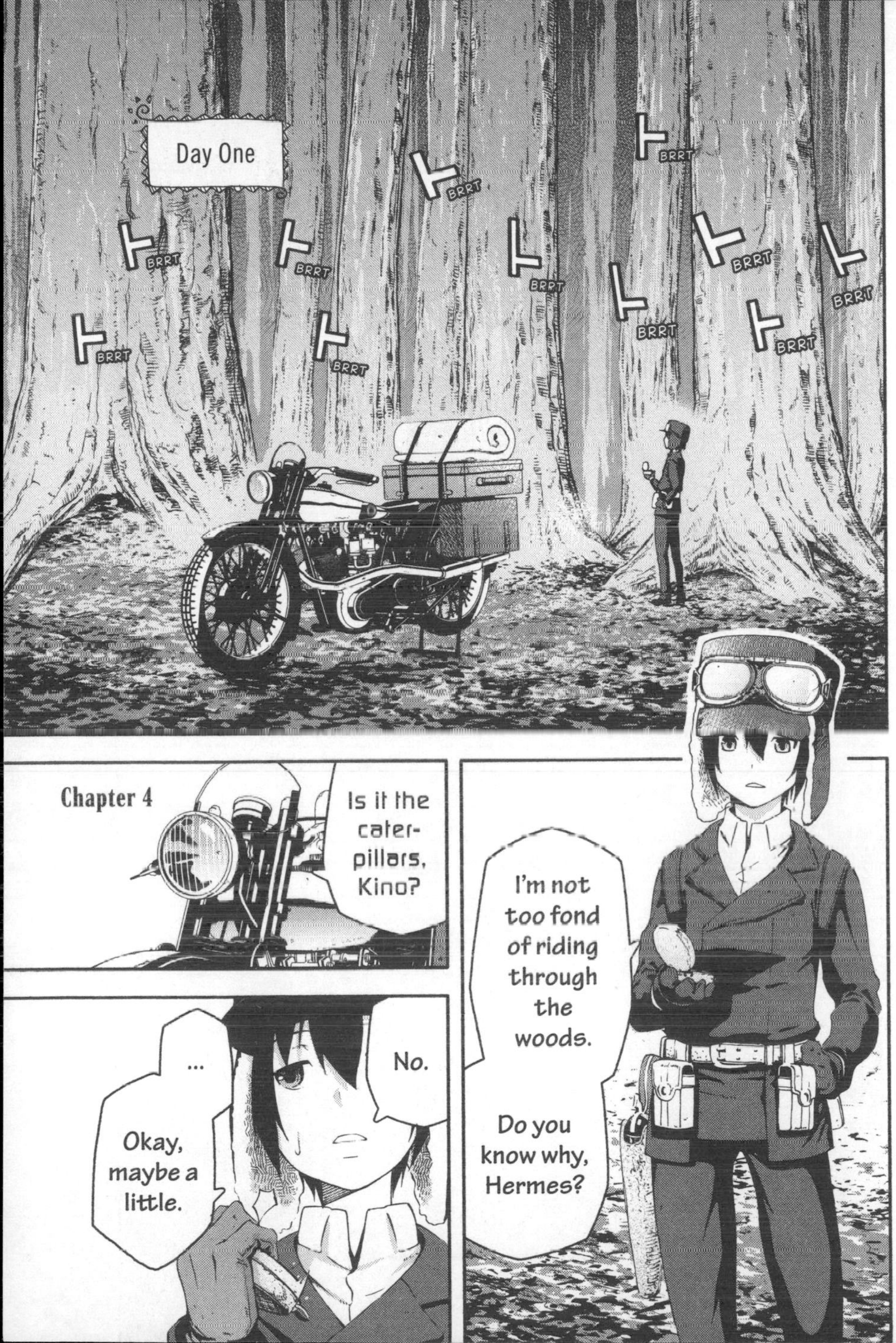
Day One
ト BRRT
ト BRRT
ト BRRT
ト BRRT
ト BRRT
ト BRRT
ト BRRT
ト BRRT
ト BRRT
ト BRRT
ト BRRT
I'm not too fond of riding through the woods.
Do you know why, Hermes?
Chapter 4
Is it the cater-pillars, Kino?
No.
...
Okay, maybe a little.

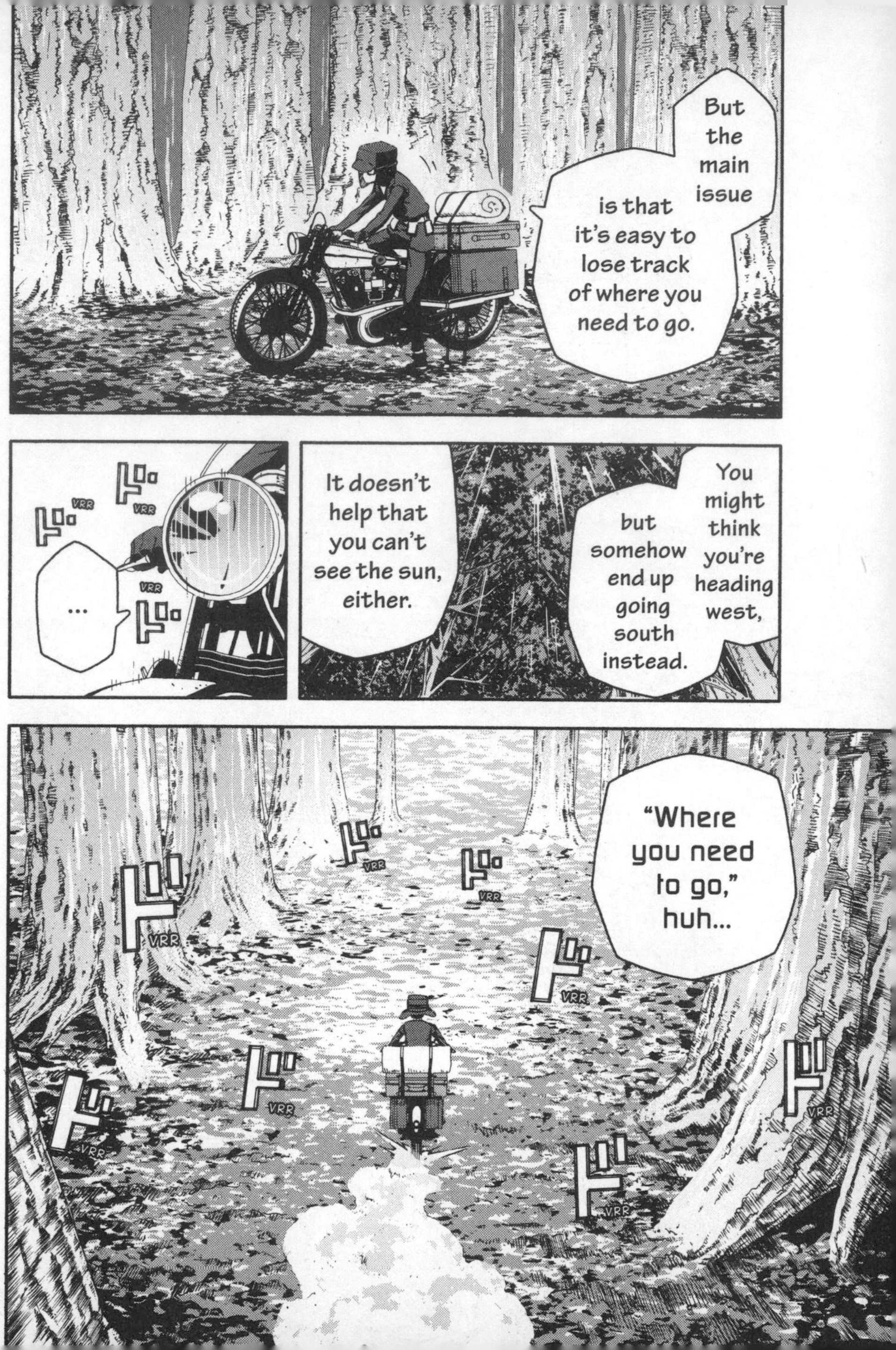
But the main issue is that it's easy to lose track of where you need to go.
You might think you're heading west, but somehow end up going south instead.
It doesn't help that you can't see the sun, either.
VRR
VRR
VRR
...
"Where you need to go," huh...
VRR
VRR
VRR
VRR
VRR
VRR
VRR
VRR

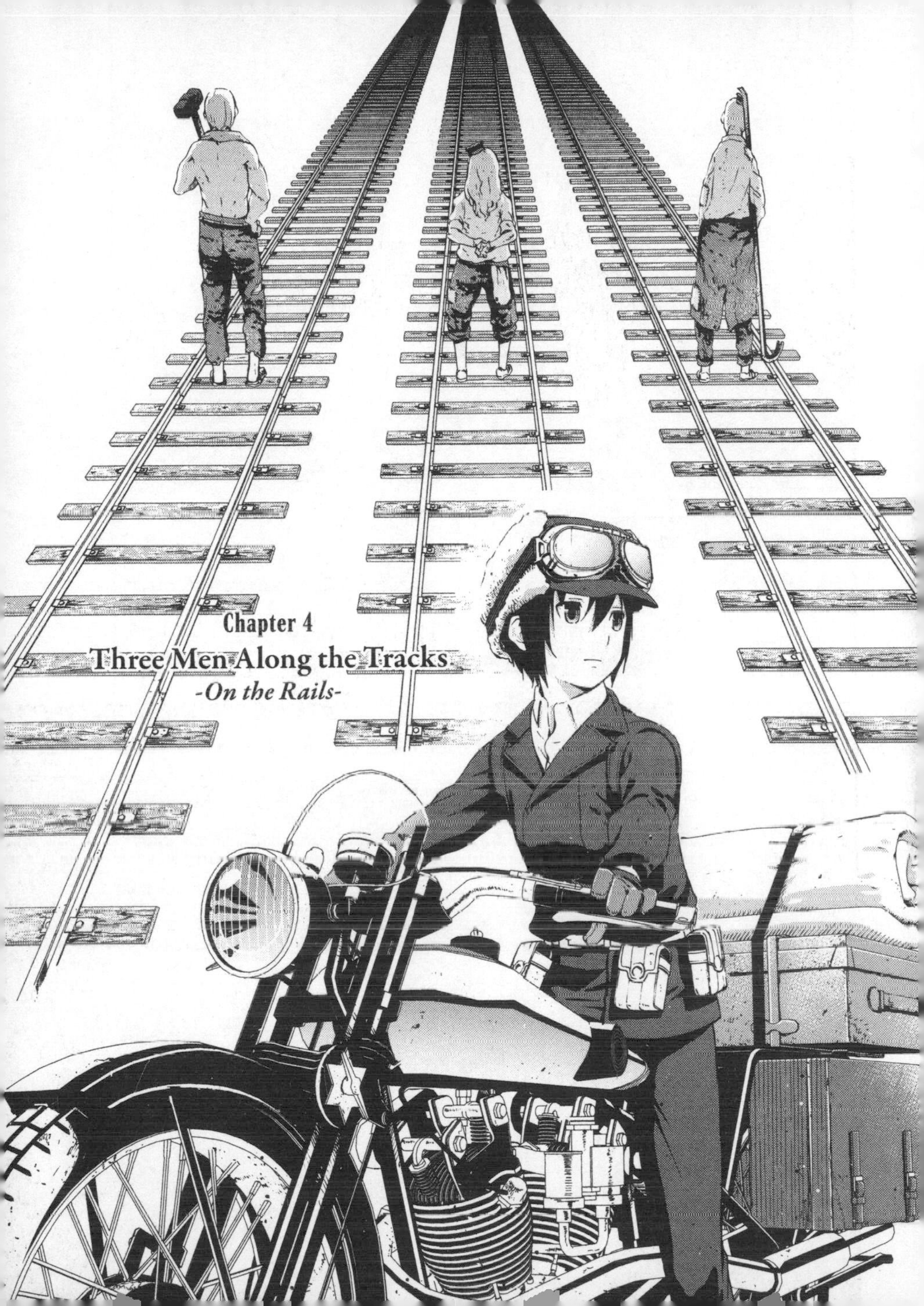
Chapter 4
Three Men Along the Tracks
-On the Rails-

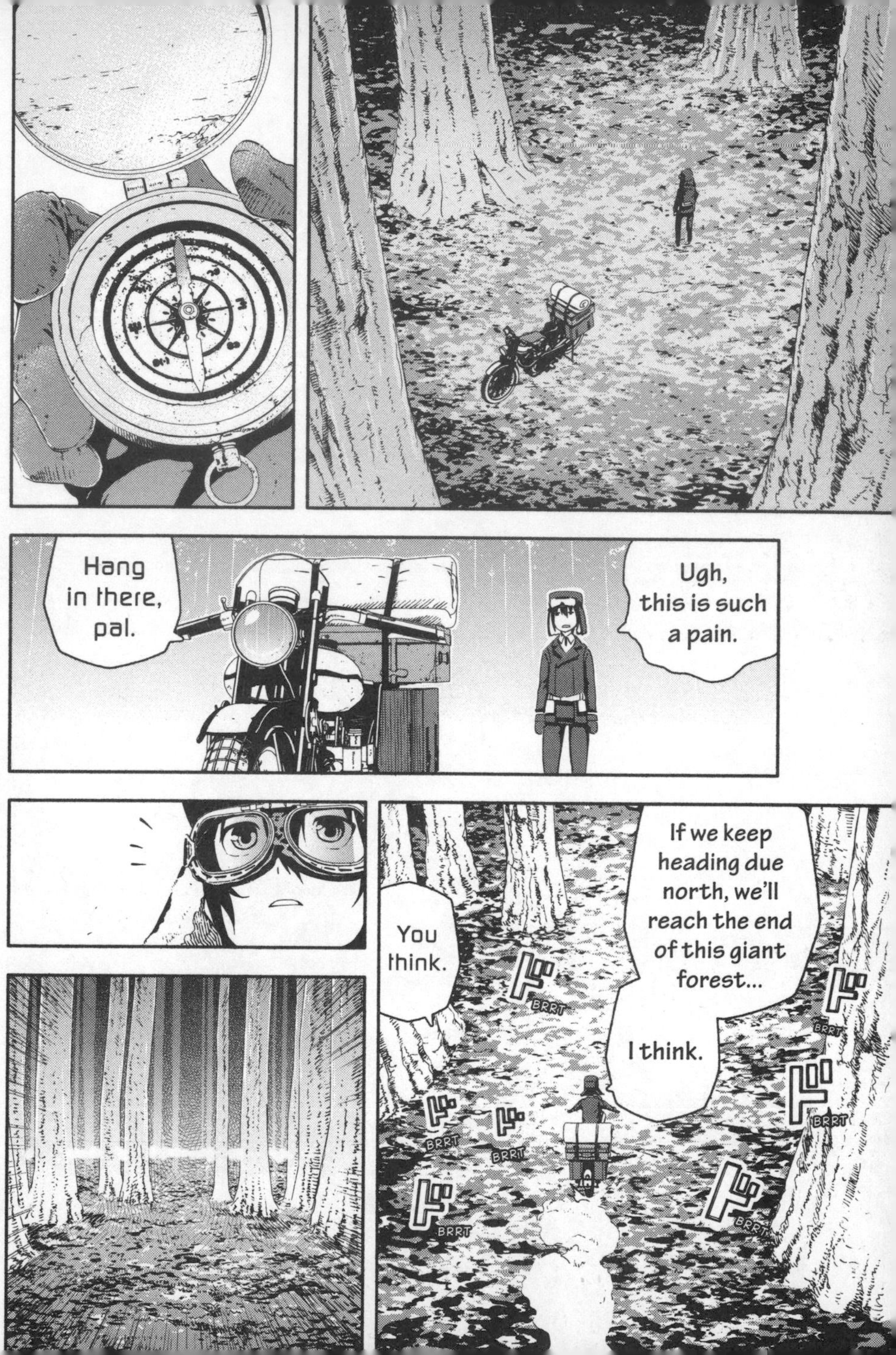
Ugh, this is such a pain.
Hang in there, pal.
If we keep heading due north, we'll reach the end of this giant forest...
I think.
You think.
BRRT
BRRT
BRRT
BRRT
BRRT
BRRT
BRRT

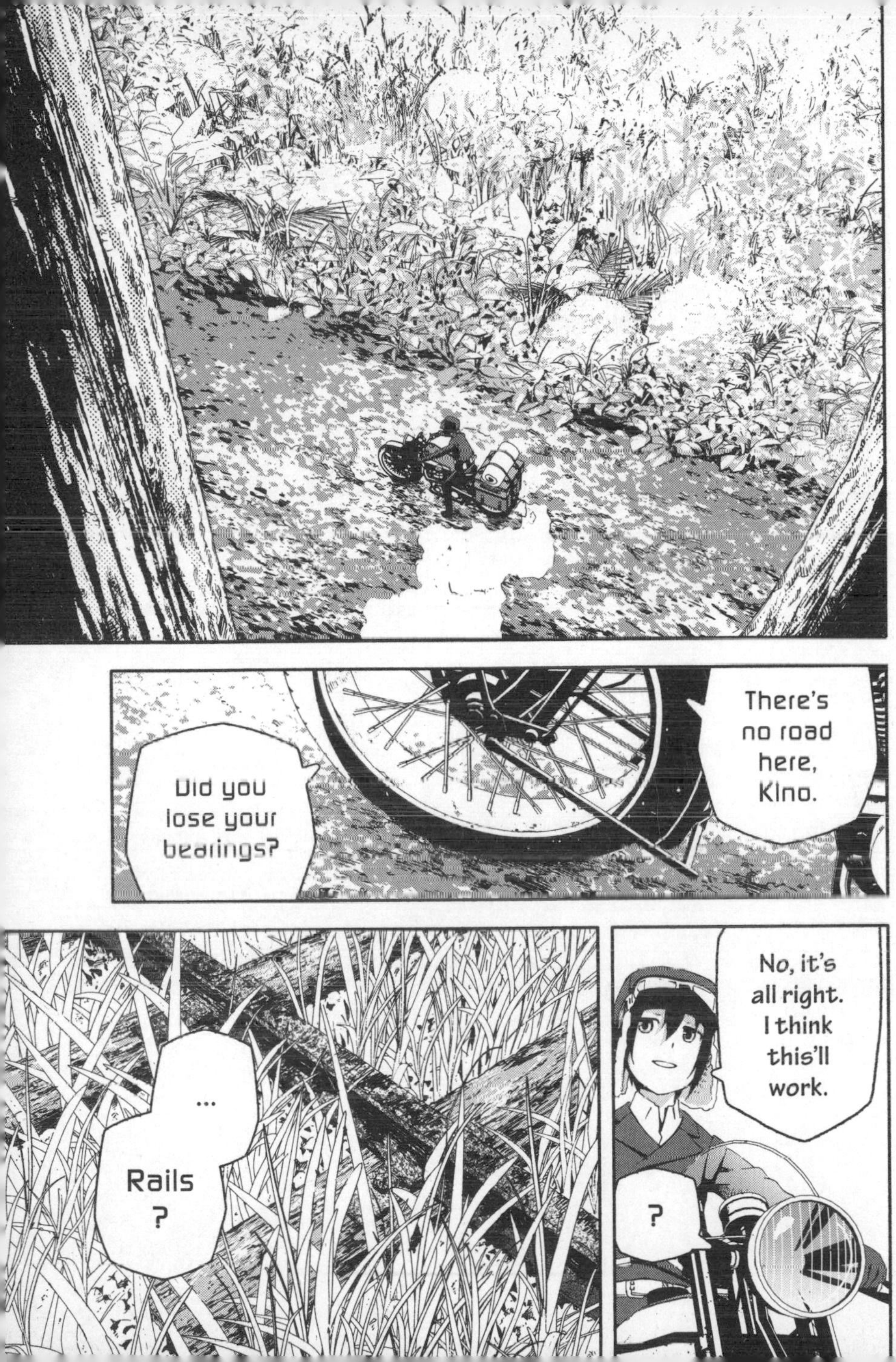
There's no road here, Kino.
Did you lose your bearings?
No, it's all right. I think this'll work.
?
...
Rails ?

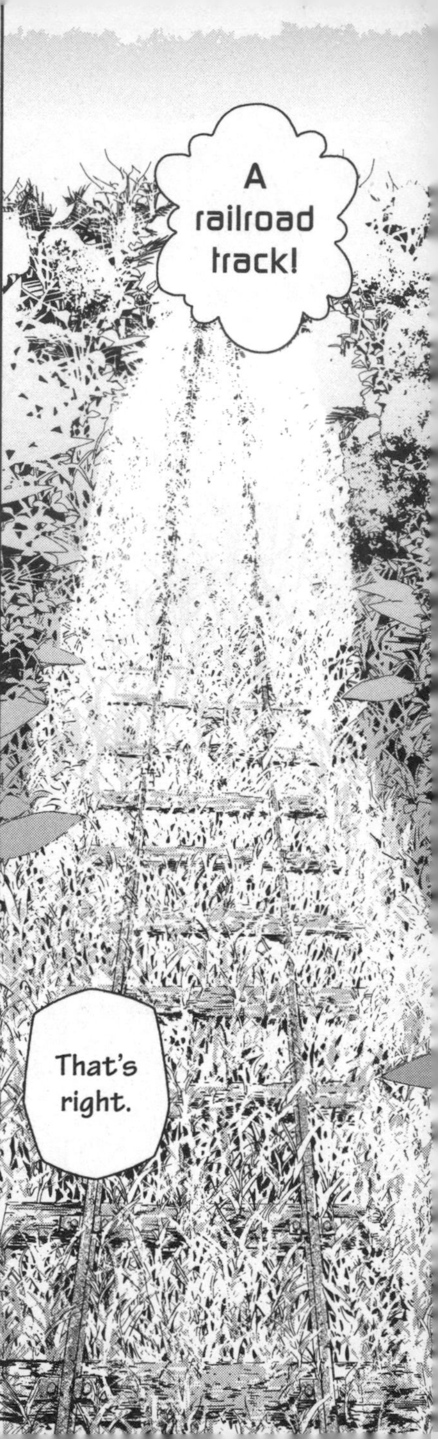
A railroad track!
That's right.
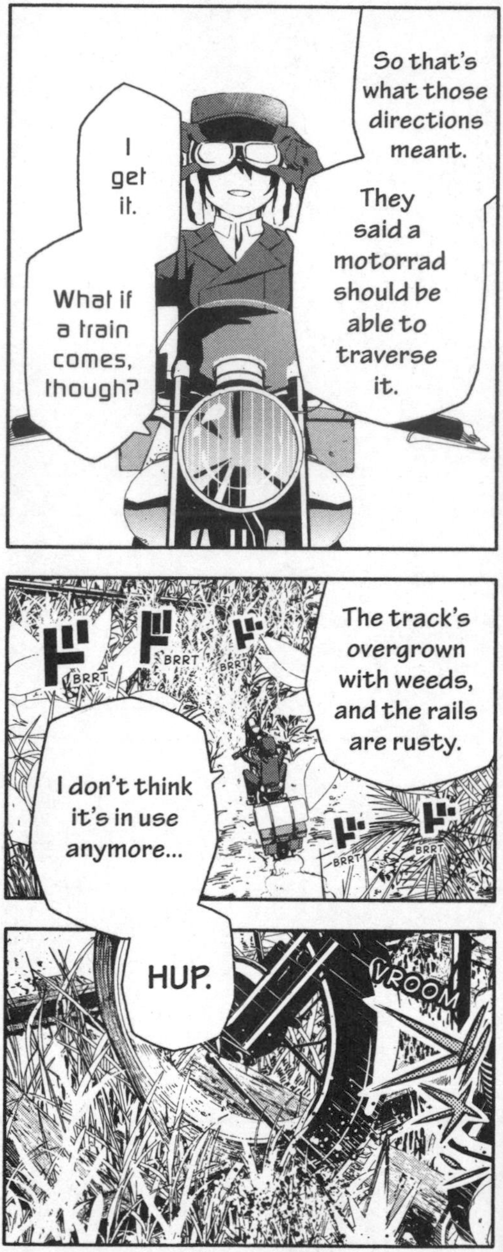
So that's what those directions meant.
They said a motorrad should be able to traverse it.
I get it.
What if a train comes, though?
The track's overgrown with weeds, and the rails are rusty.
ド BRRT
ド BRRT
ド BRRT
I don't think it's in use anymore...
ド BRRT
ド BRRT
VROOM
HUP.

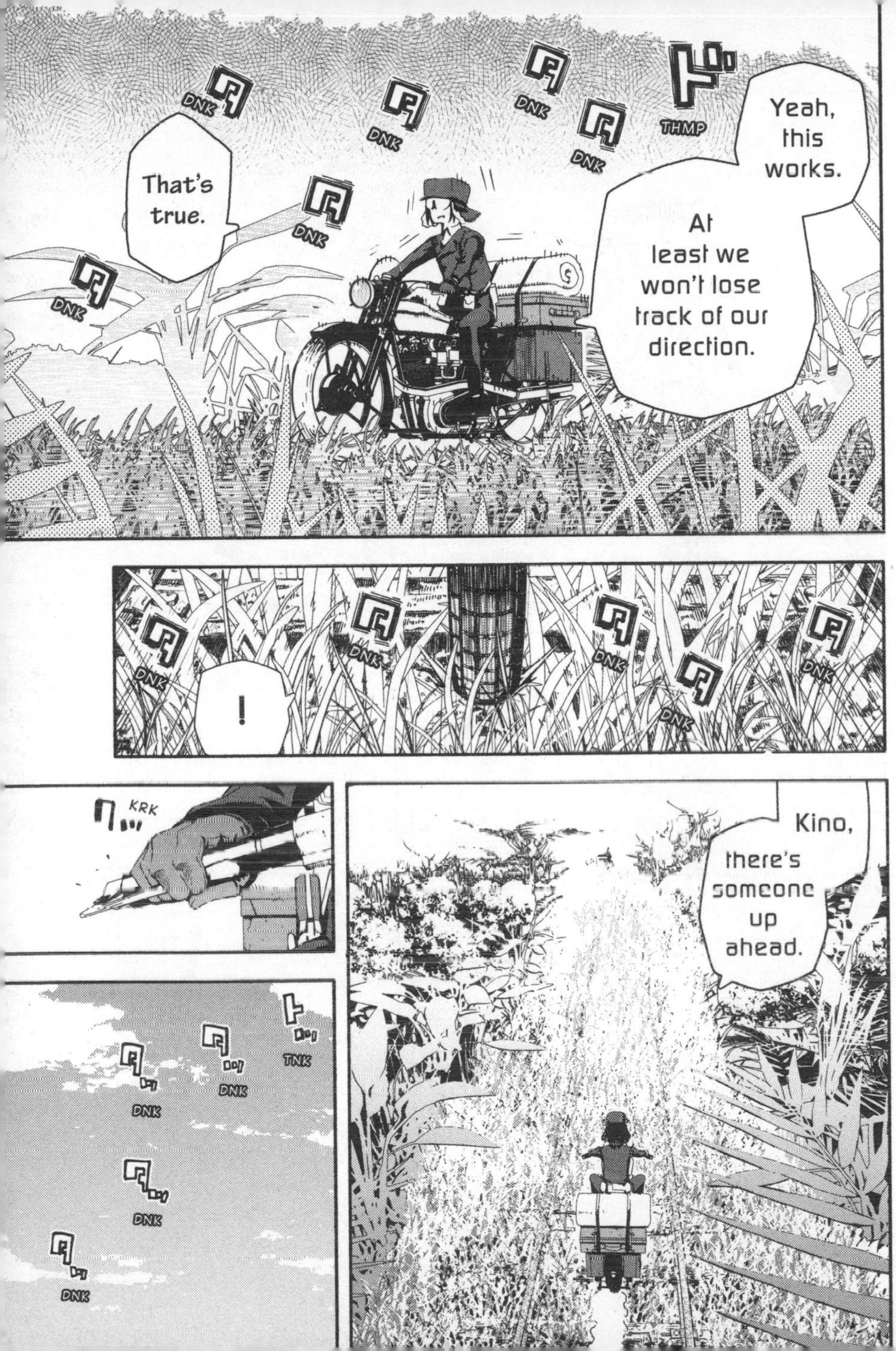
THMP
Yeah, this works.
At least we won't lose track of our direction.
DNK
DNK
DNK
DNK
That's true.
DNK
DNK
DNK
DNK
DNK
!
DNK
Kino, there's someone up ahead.
KRK
TNK
DNK
DNK
DNK
DNK

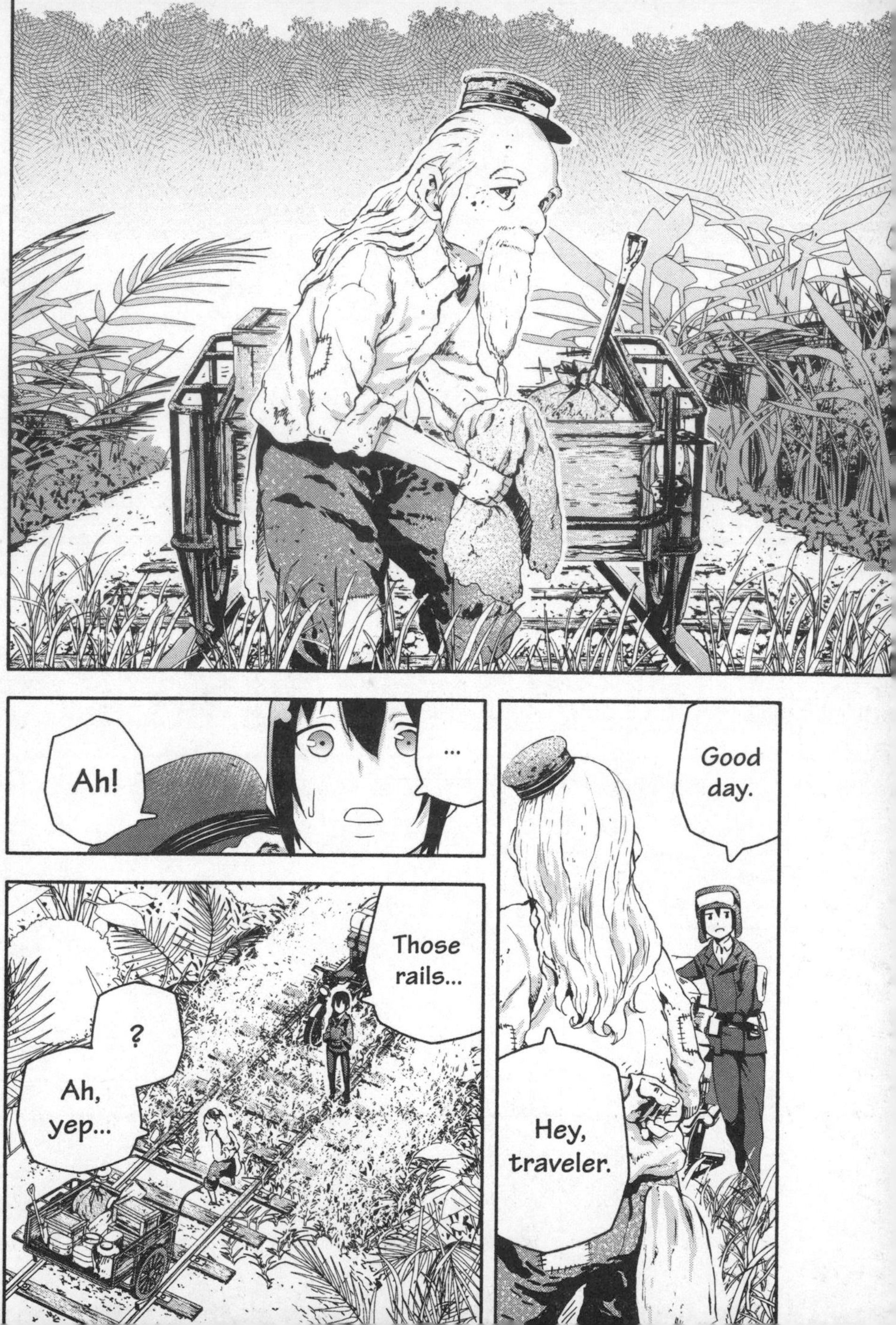
Good day.
...
Ah!
Hey, traveler.
Those rails...
?
Ah, yep...

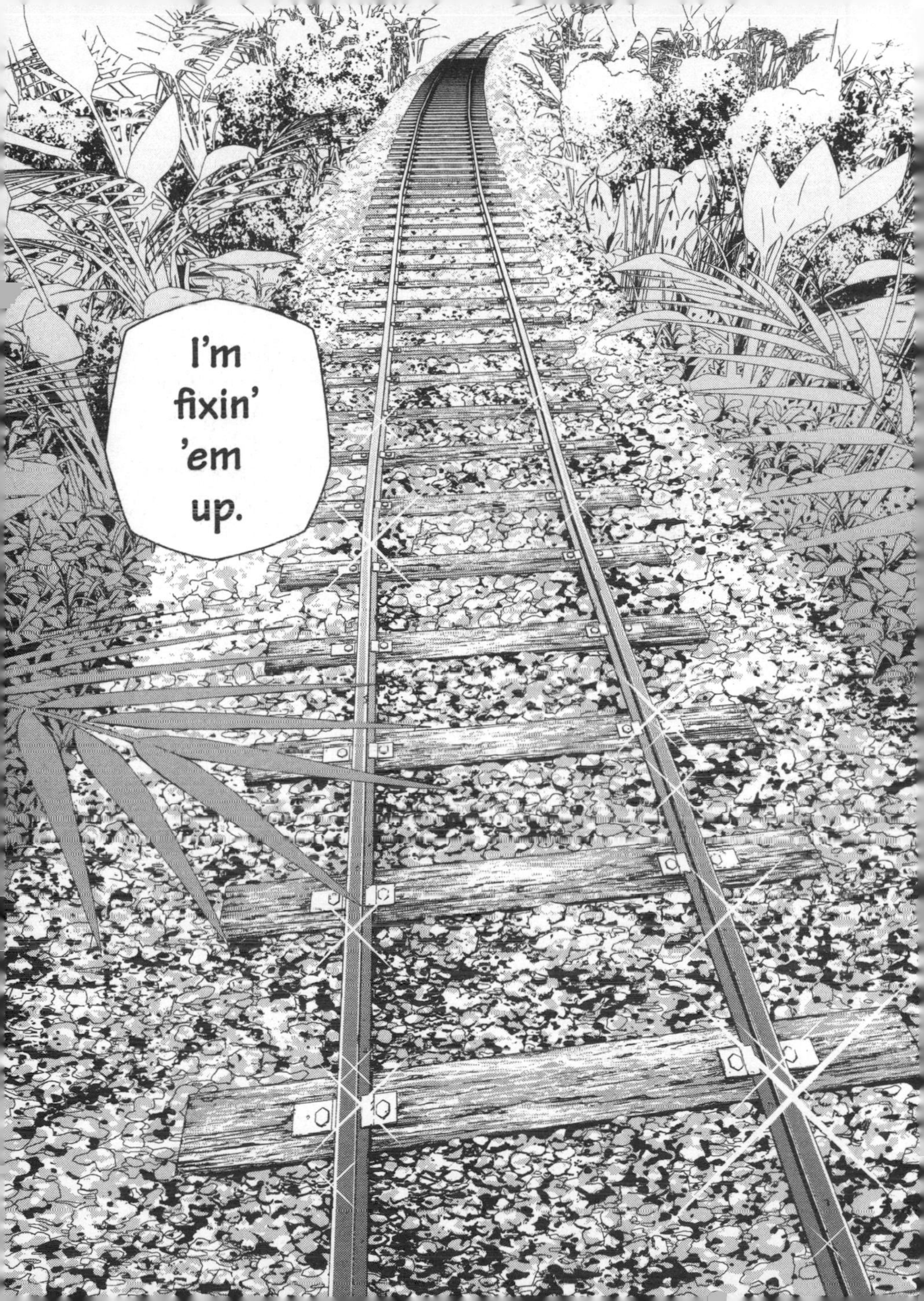
I'm fixin' 'em up.

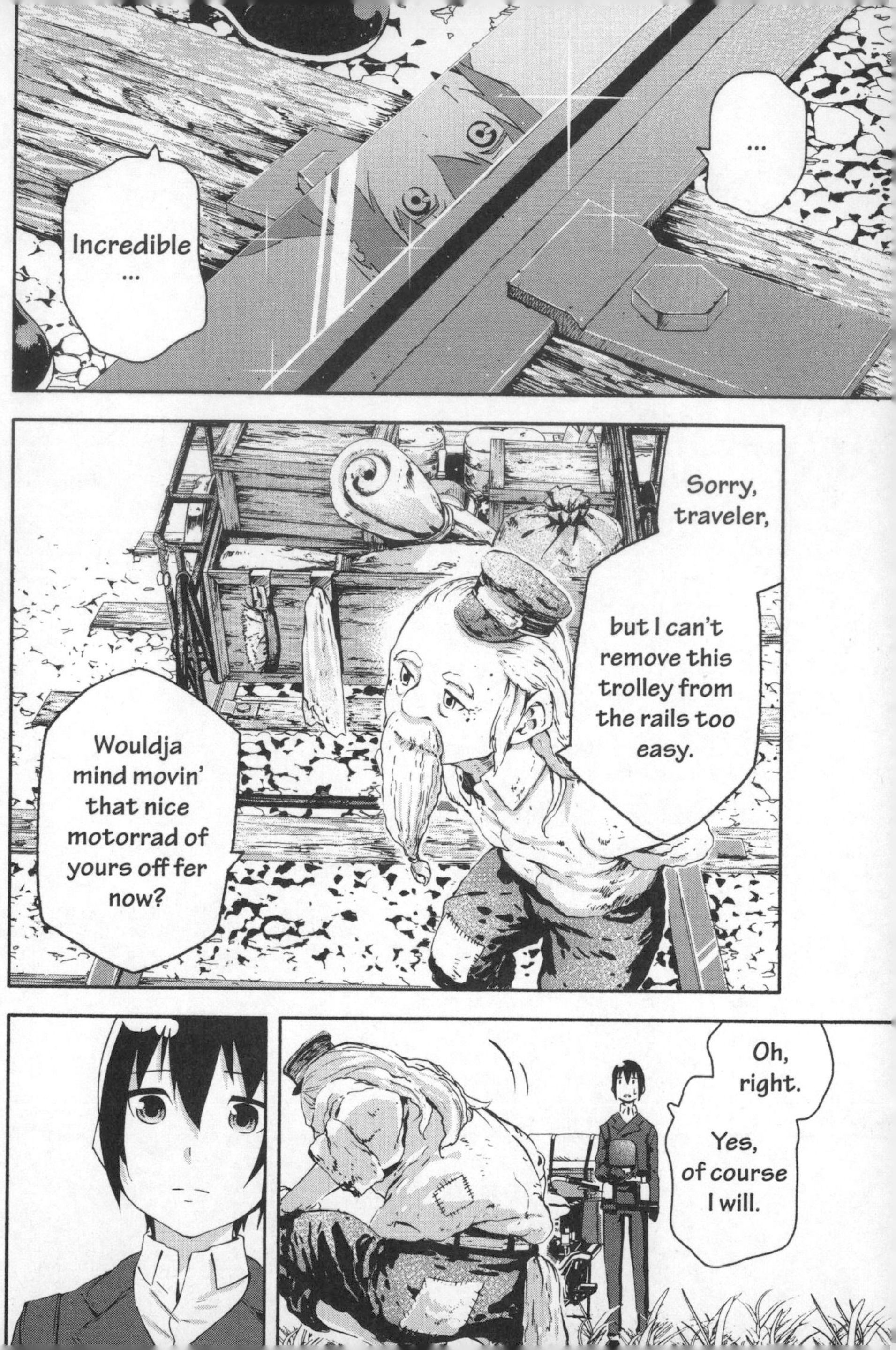
...
Incredible ...
Sorry, traveler,
but I can't remove this trolley from the rails too easy.
Wouldja mind movin' that nice motorrad of yours off fer now?
Oh, right.
Yes, of course I will.

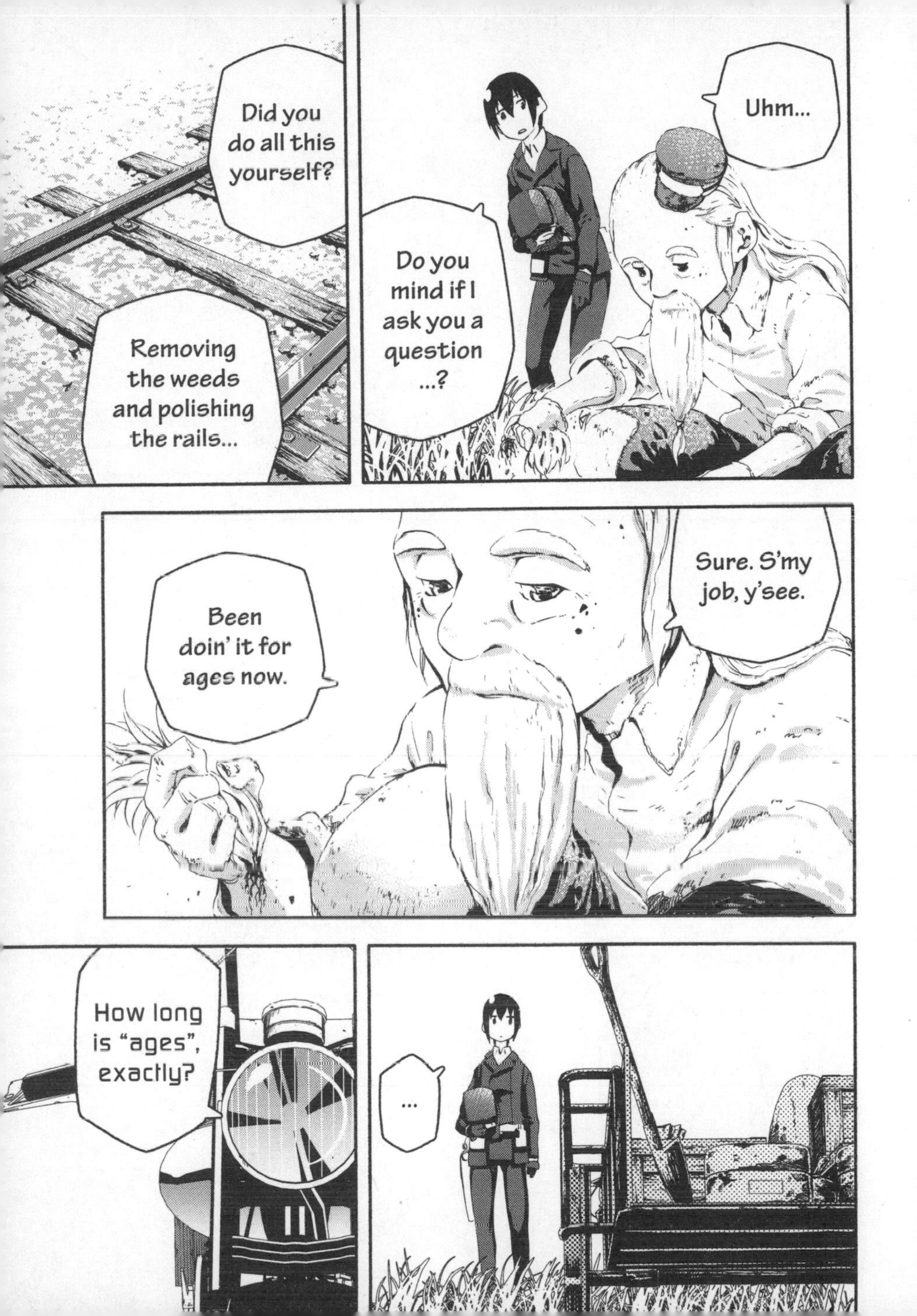

Uhm...
Do you mind if I ask you a question ...?
Did you do all this yourself?
Removing the weeds and polishing the rails...
Sure. S'my job, y'see.
Been doin' it for ages now.
...
How long is "ages", exactly?

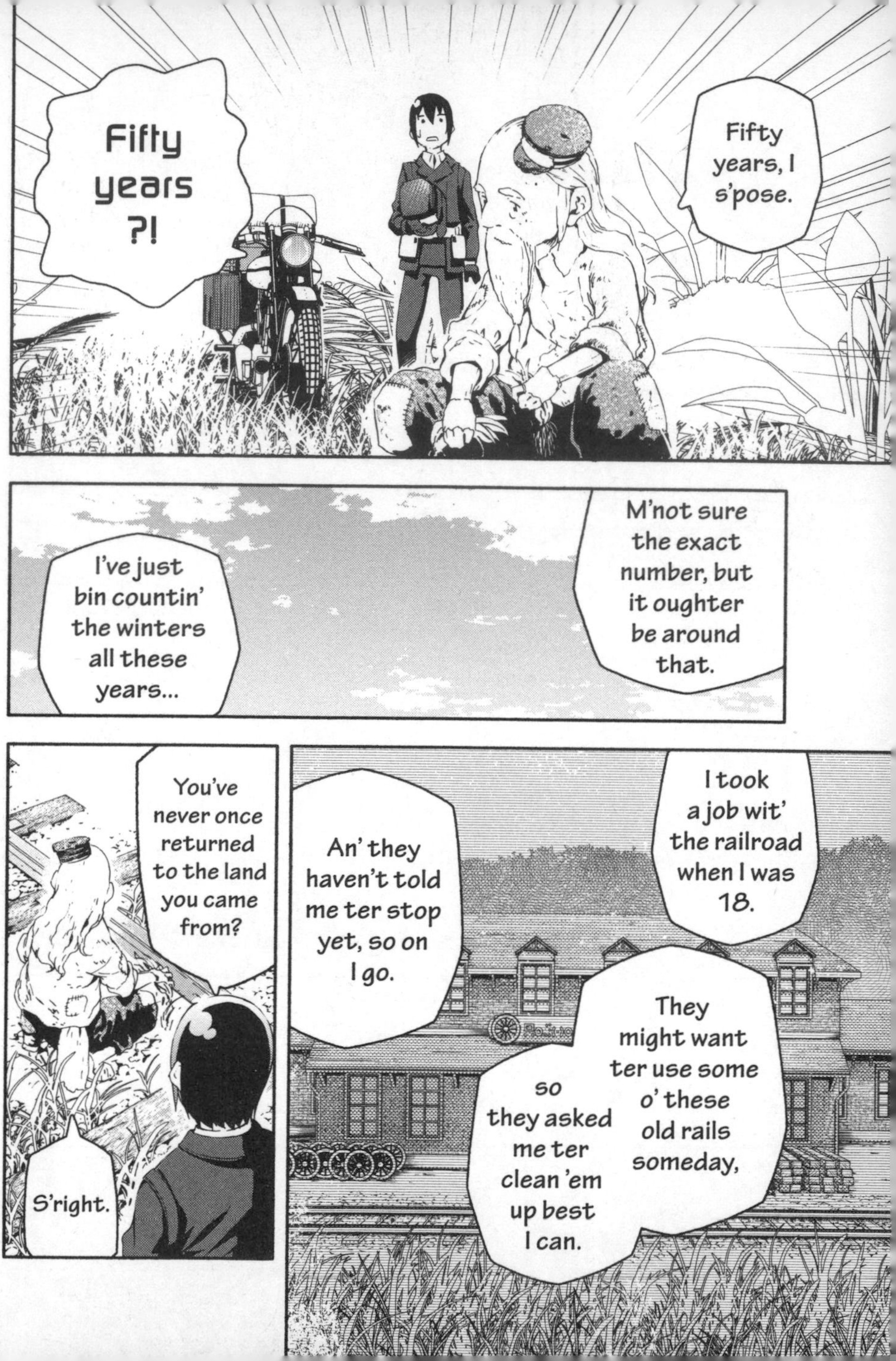
Fifty years, I s'pose.
Fifty years ?!
M'not sure the exact number, but it oughter be around that.
I've just bin countin' the winters all these years...
I took a job wit' the railroad when I was 18.
An' they haven't told me ter stop yet, so on I go.
They might want ter use some o' these old rails someday,
so they asked me ter clean 'em up best I can.
You've never once returned to the land you came from?
S'right.

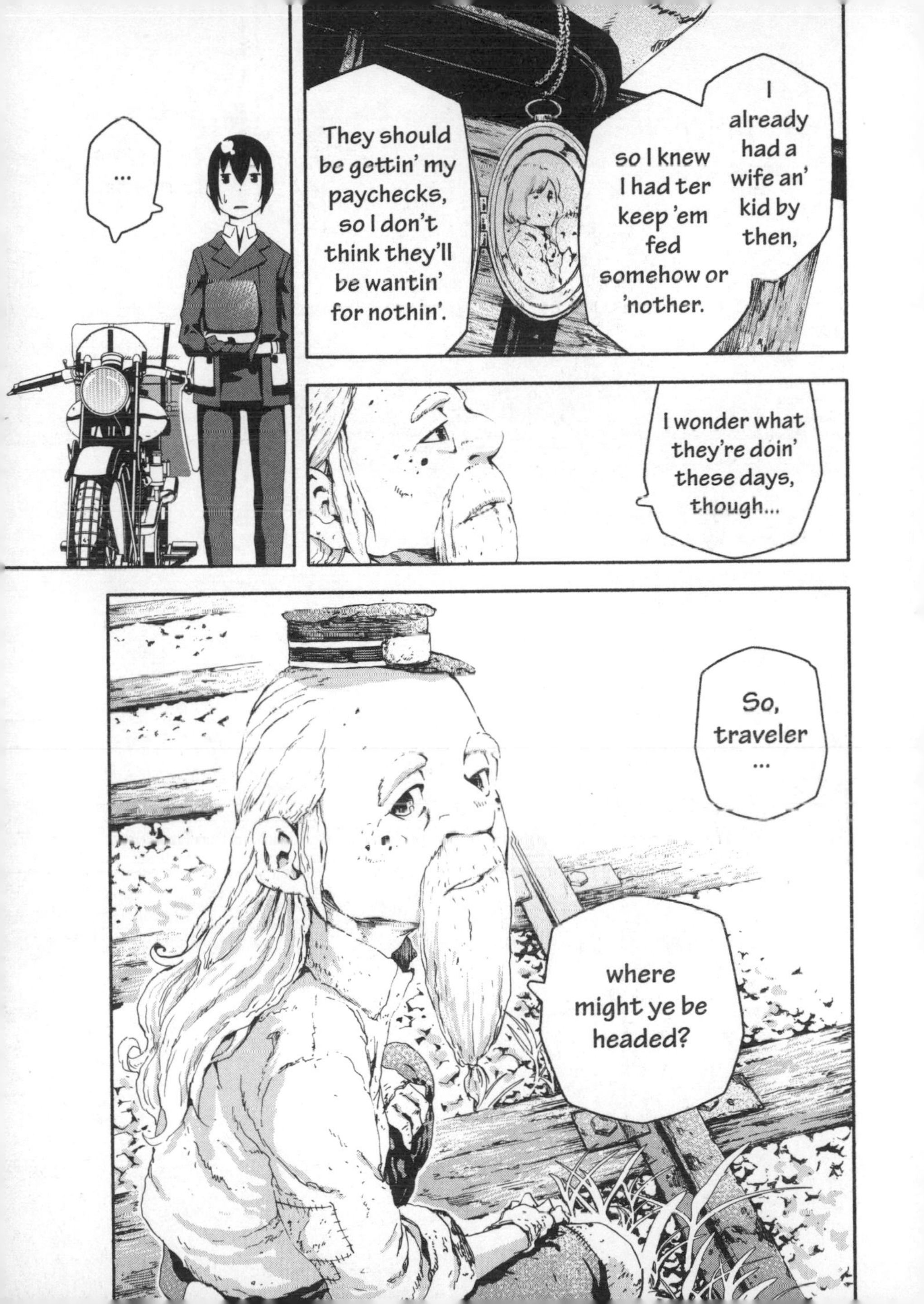
I already had a wife an' kid by then,
so I knew I had ter keep 'em fed somehow or 'nother.
They should be gettin' my paychecks, so I don't think they'll be wantin' for nothin'.
I wonder what they're doin' these days, though...
...
So, traveler ...
where might ye be headed?

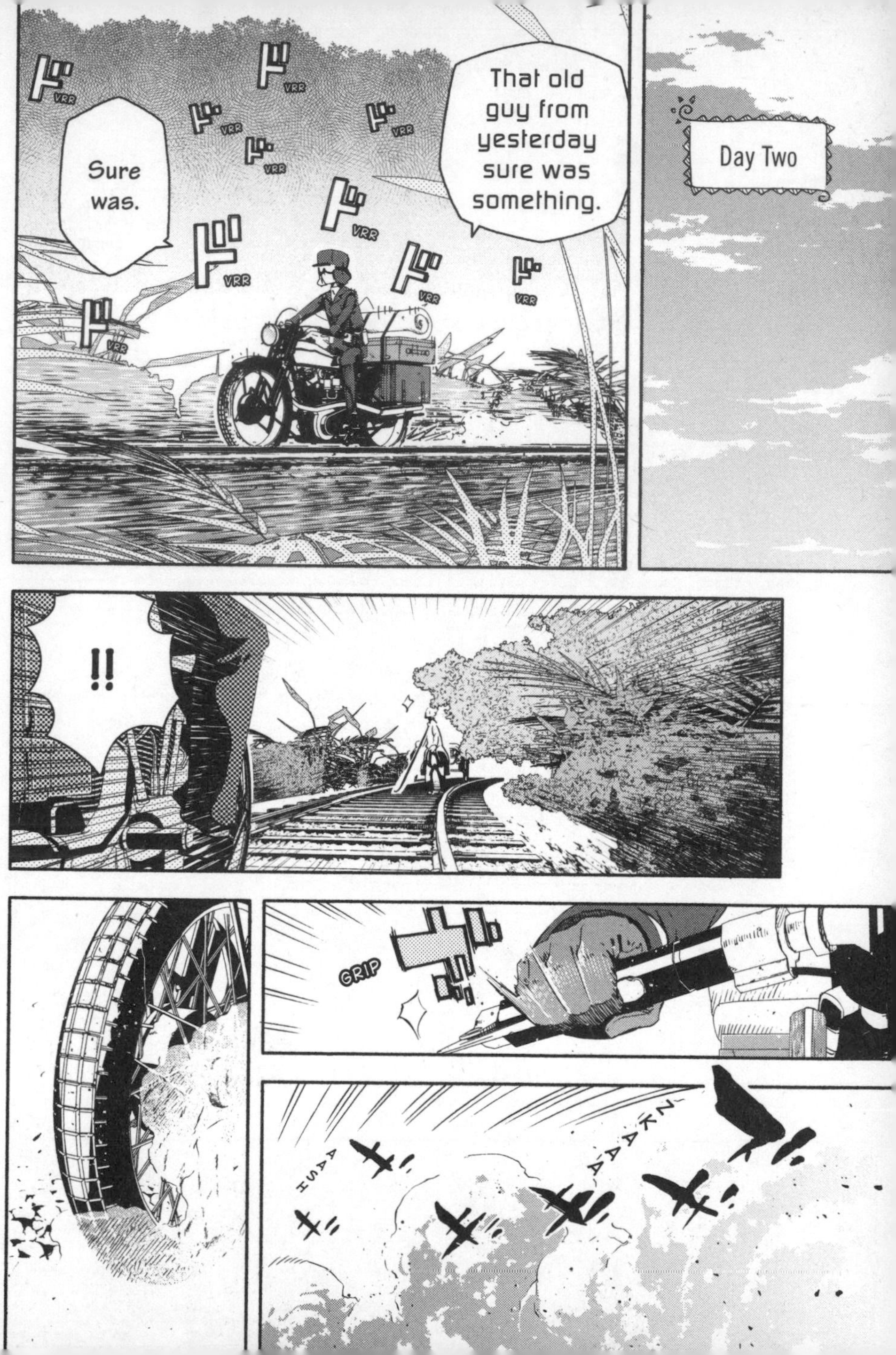
Day Two
That old guy from yesterday sure was something.
Sure was.
VRR
!!
GRIP

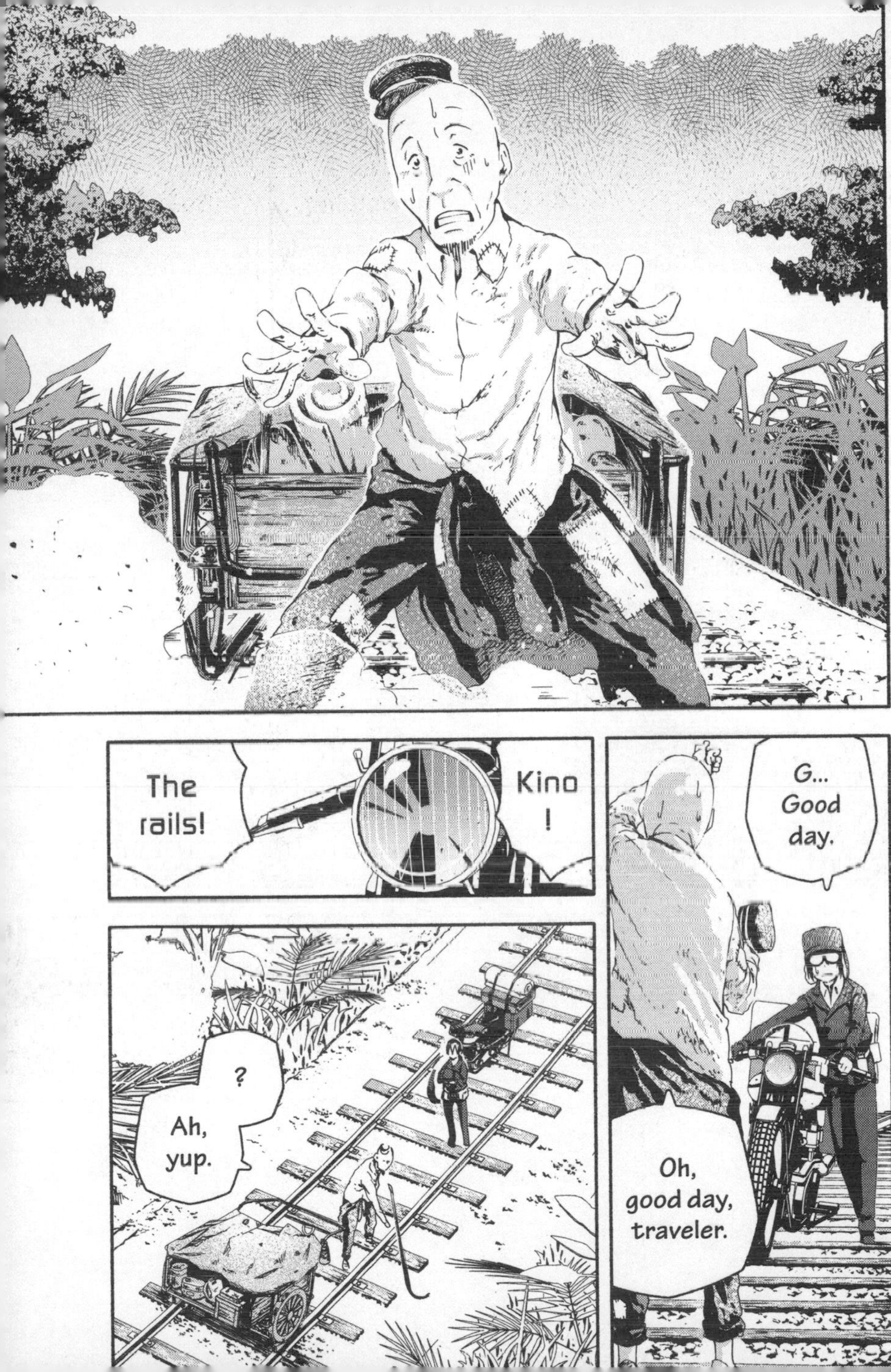
G... Good day.
Oh, good day, traveler.
Kino!
The rails!
?
Ah, yup.

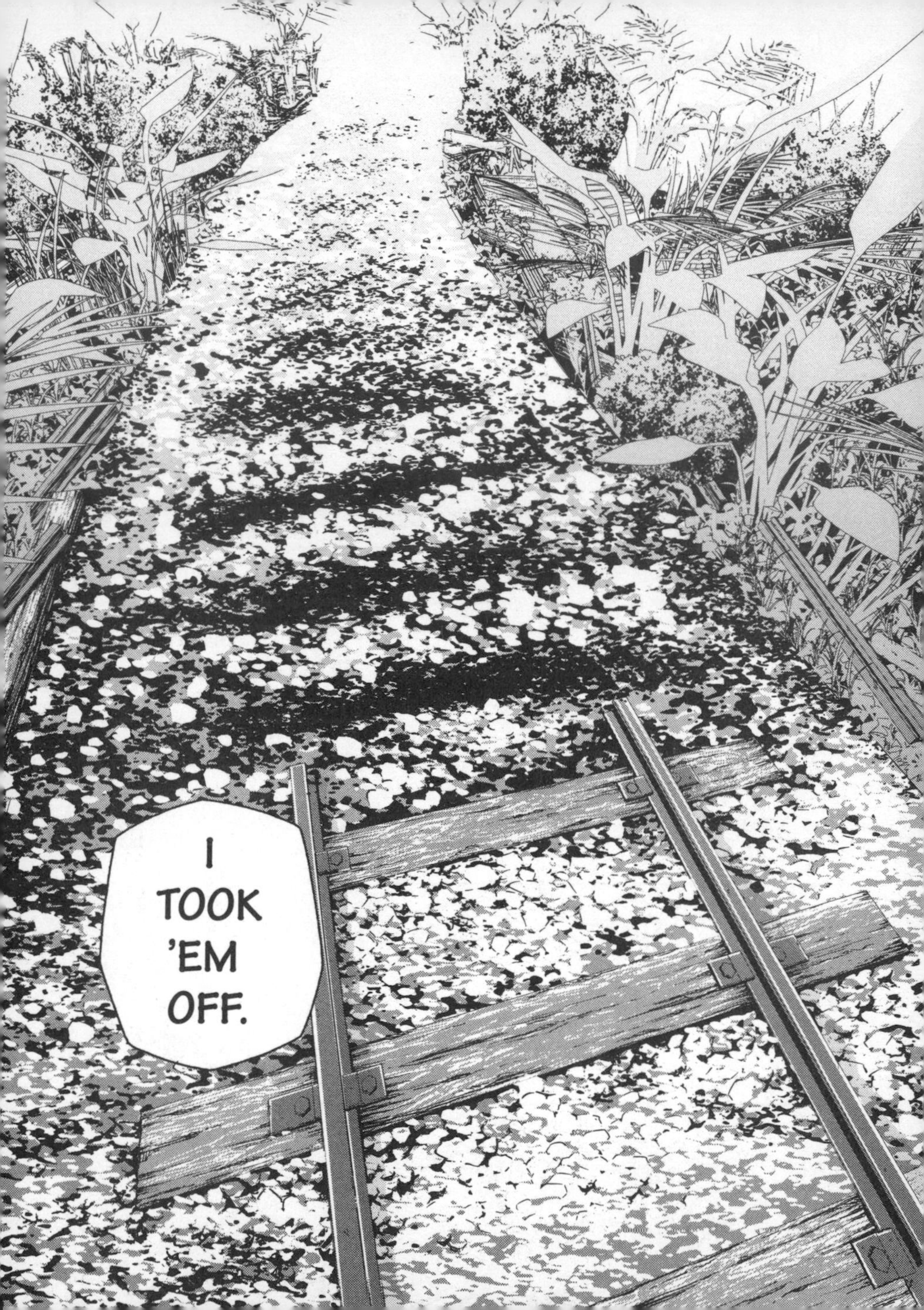
I TOOK 'EM OFF.

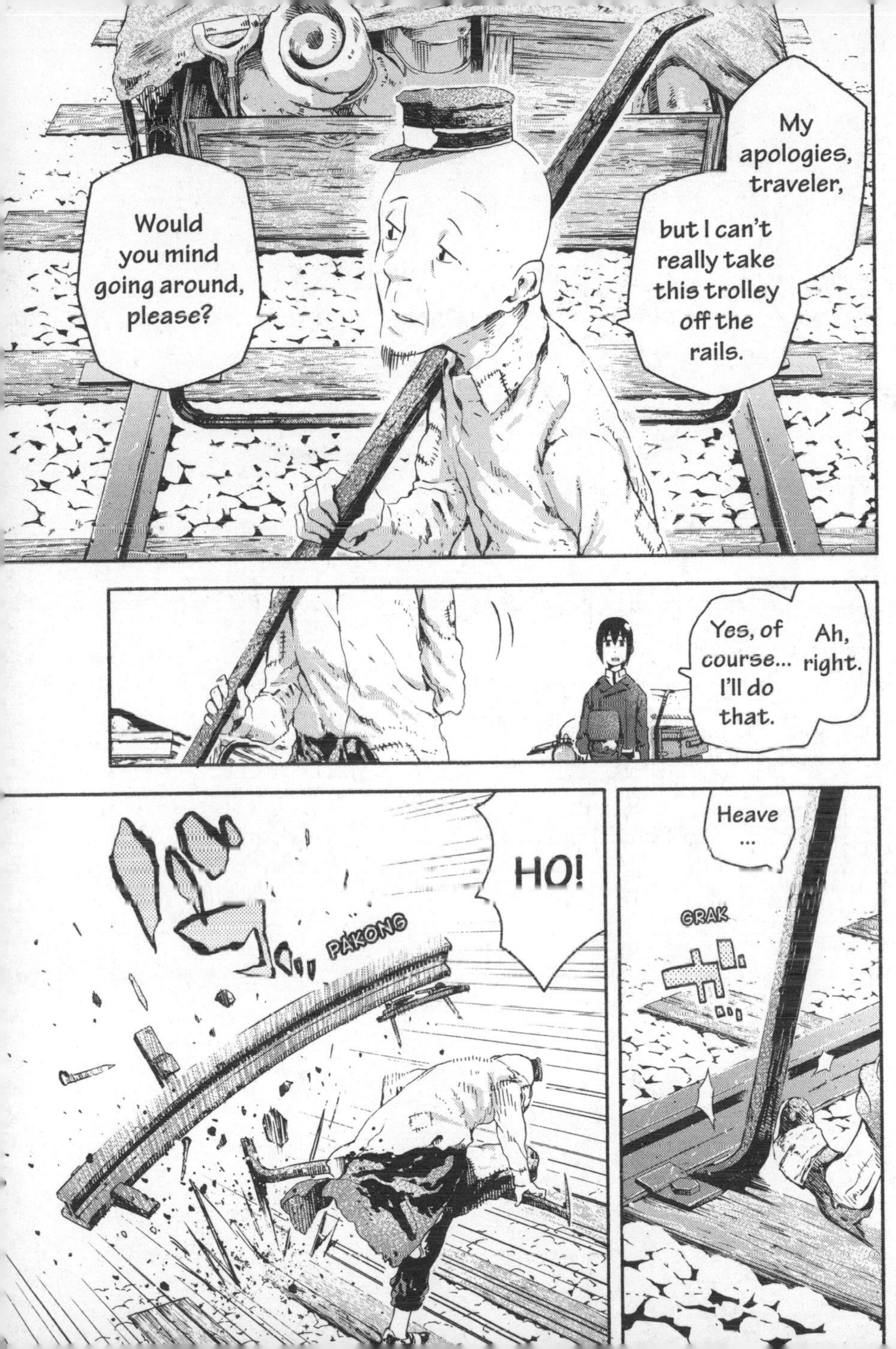
My apologies, traveler,
but I can't really take this trolley off the rails.
Would you mind going around, please?
Ah, right.
Yes, of course... I'll do that.
Heave ...
GRAK
HO!
PAKONG

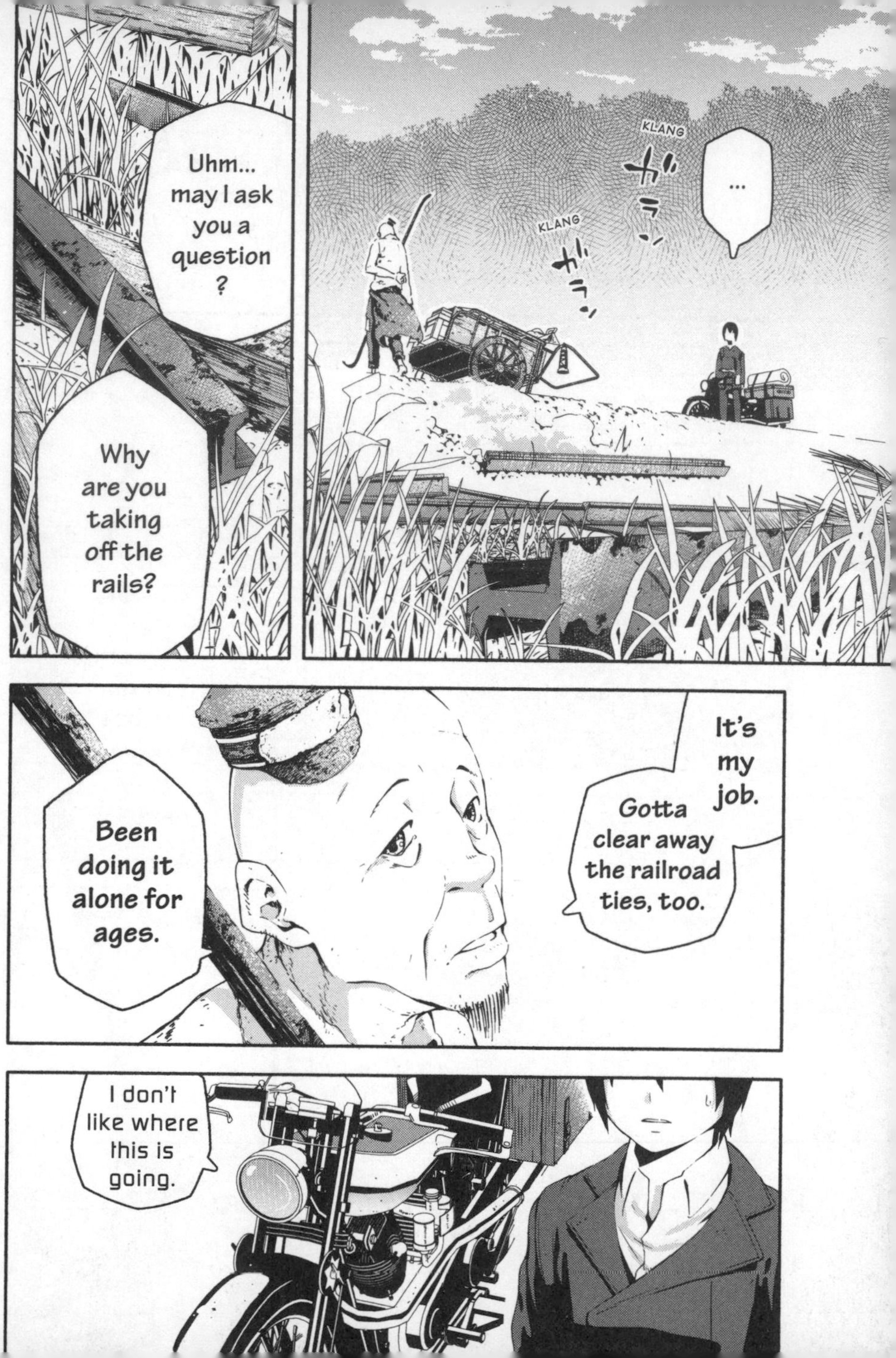
KLANG
ガラン
KLANG
ガラン
...
Uhm... may I ask you a question?
Why are you taking off the rails?
It's my job.
Gotta clear away the railroad ties, too.
Been doing it alone for ages.
I don't like where this is going.

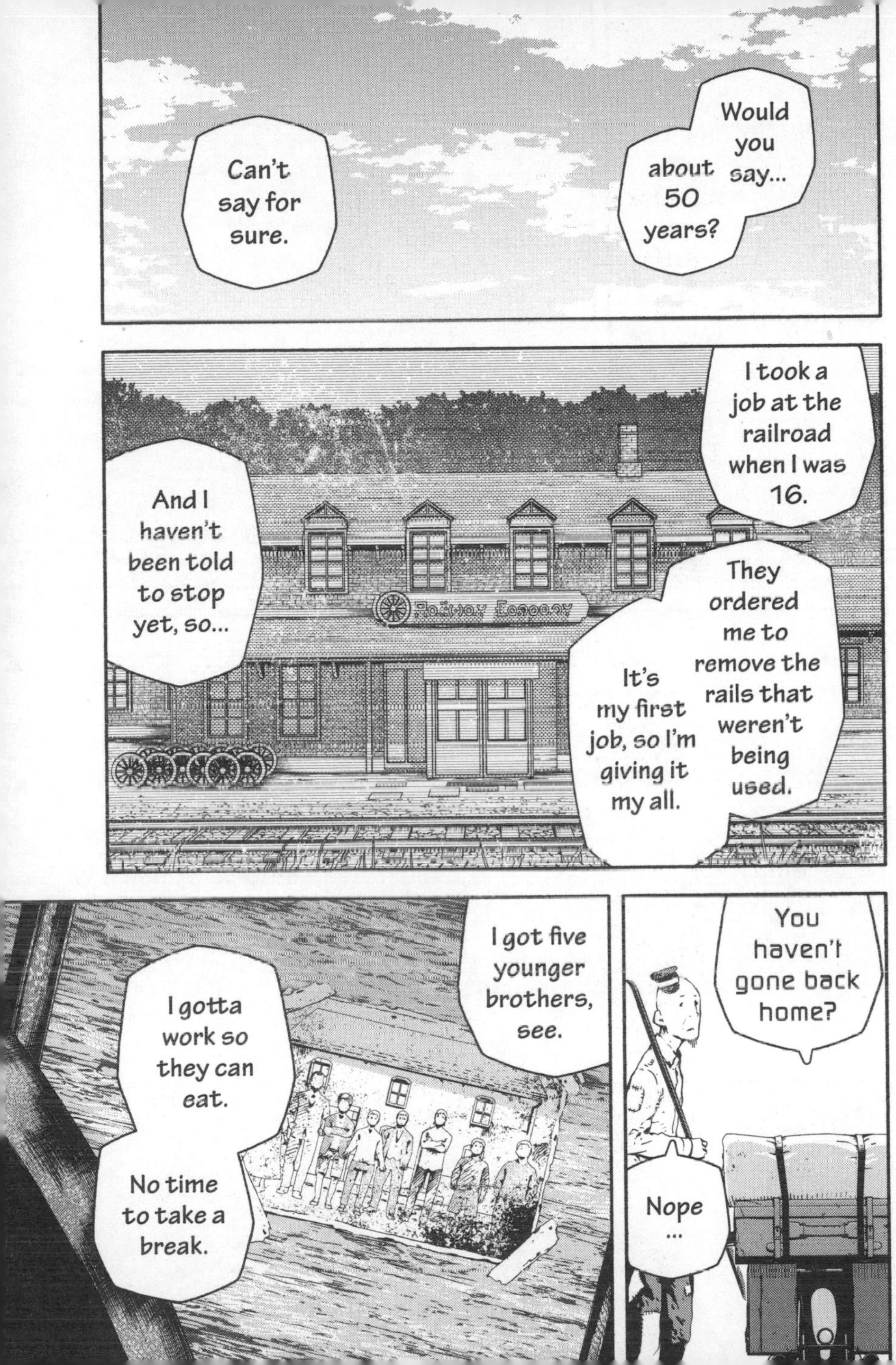
Would you say... about 50 years?
Can't say for sure.
I took a job at the railroad when I was 16.
They ordered me to remove the rails that weren't being used.
It's my first job, so I'm giving it my all.
And I haven't been told to stop yet, so...
You haven't gone back home?
Nope...
I got five younger brothers, see.
I gotta work so they can eat.
No time to take a break.

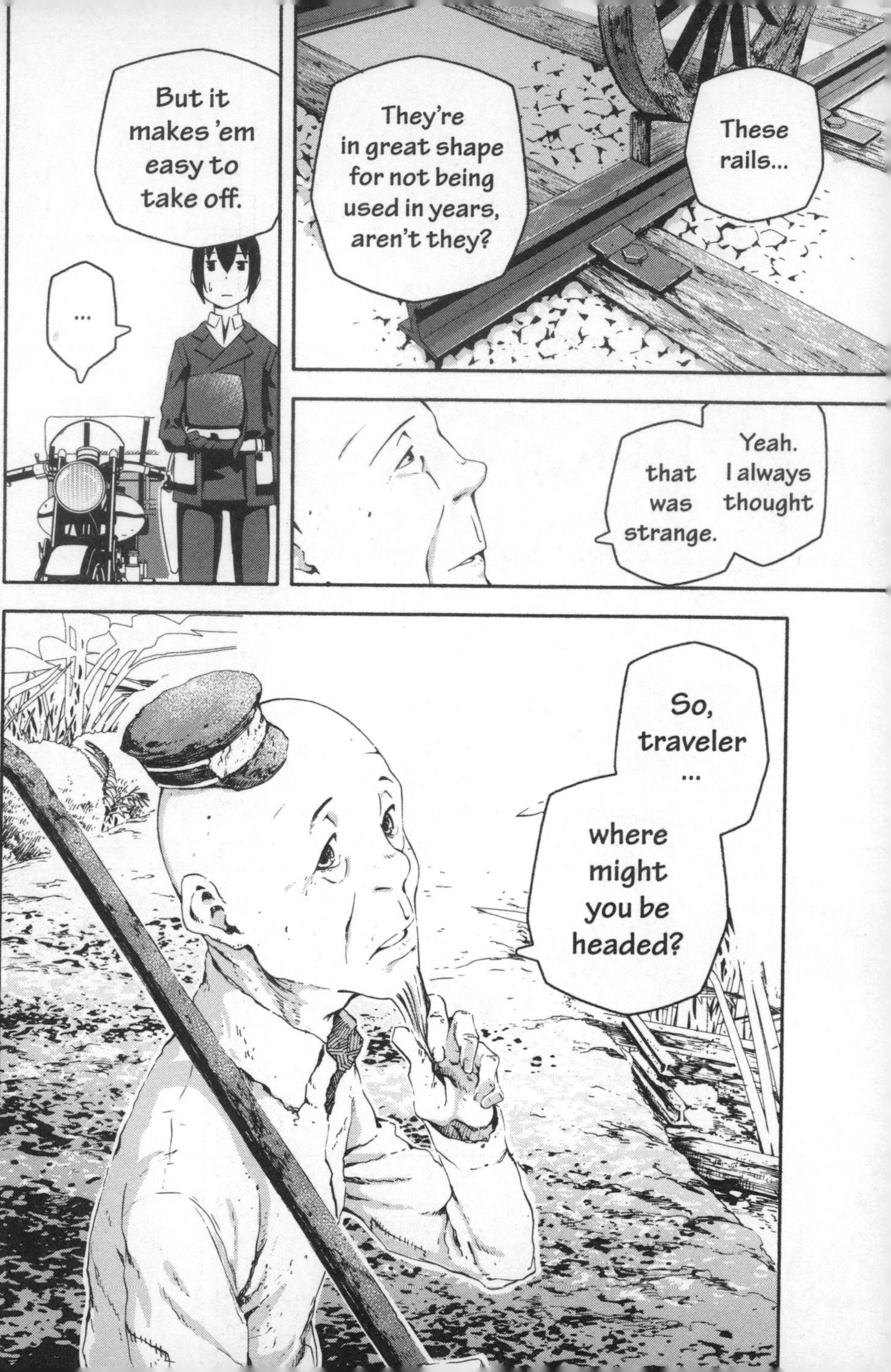
These rails...
They're in great shape for not being used in years, aren't they?
Yeah. I always thought that was strange.
But it makes 'em easy to take off.
...
So, traveler ...
where might you be headed?

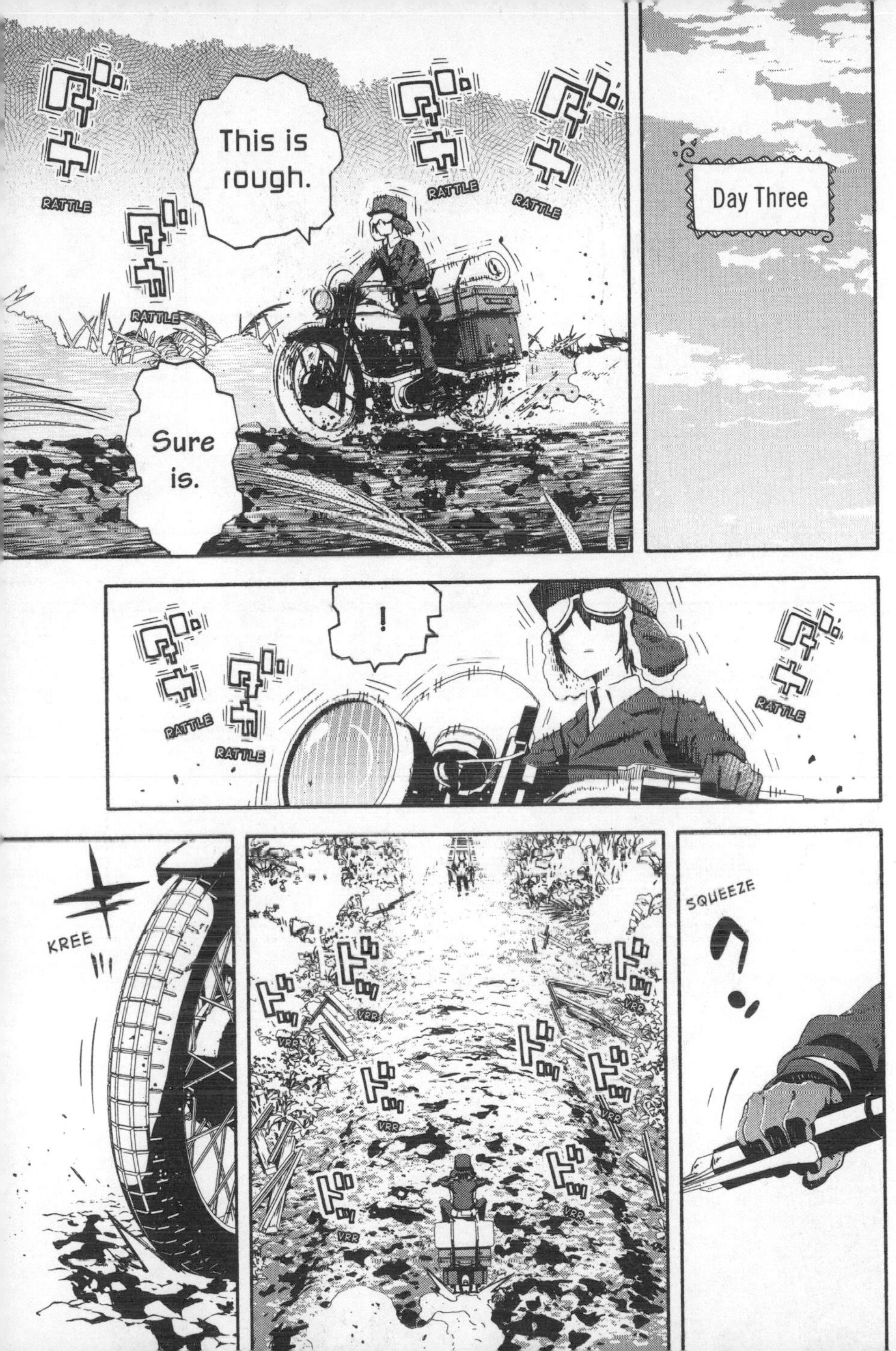
Day Three
RATTLE
RATTLE
This is rough.
RATTLE
RATTLE
Sure is.
RATTLE
!
RATTLE
RATTLE
SQUEEZE
VRR
VRR
VRR
VRR
VRR
KREE

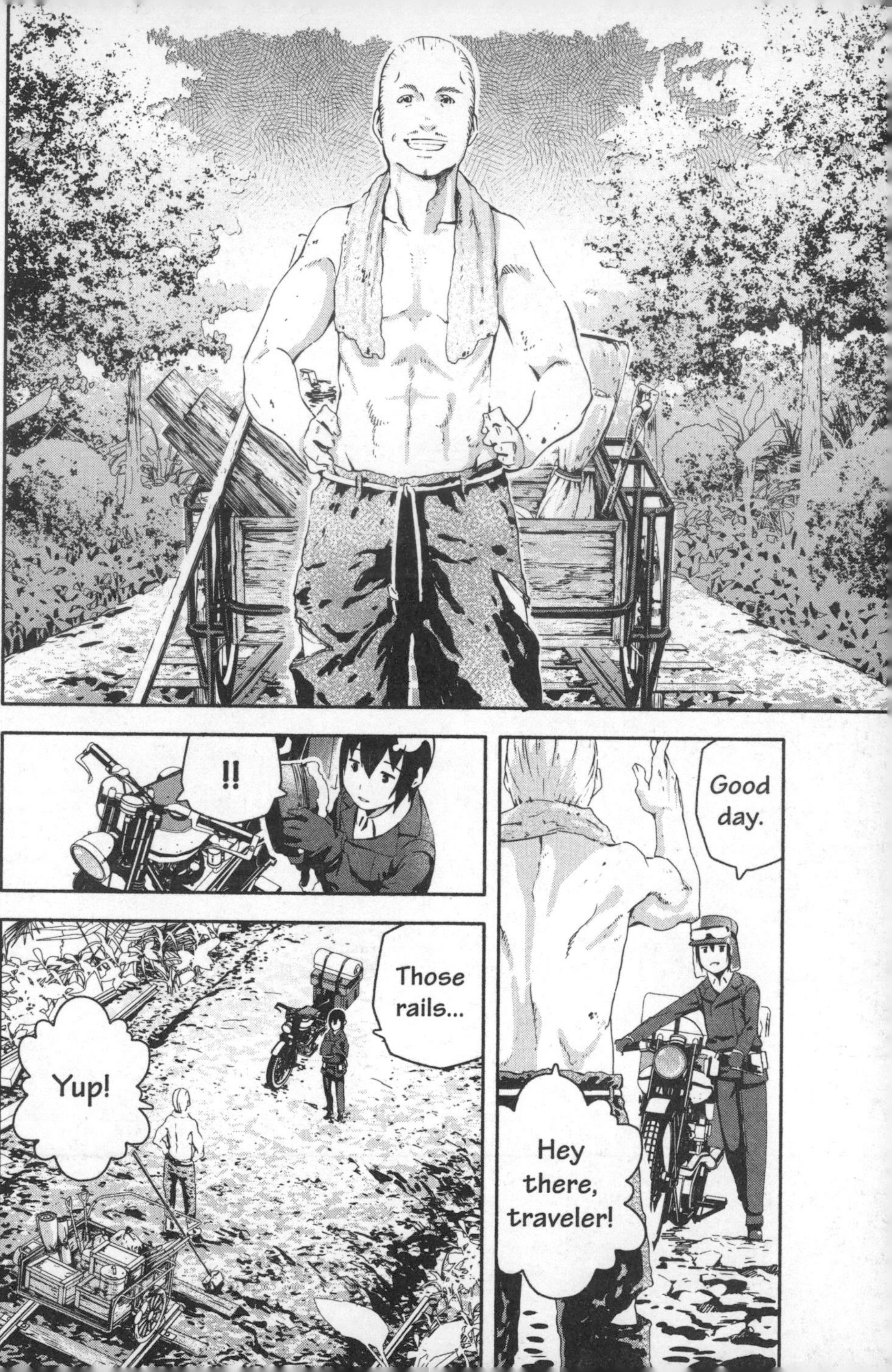
Good day.
Hey there, traveler!
!!
Those rails...
Yup!

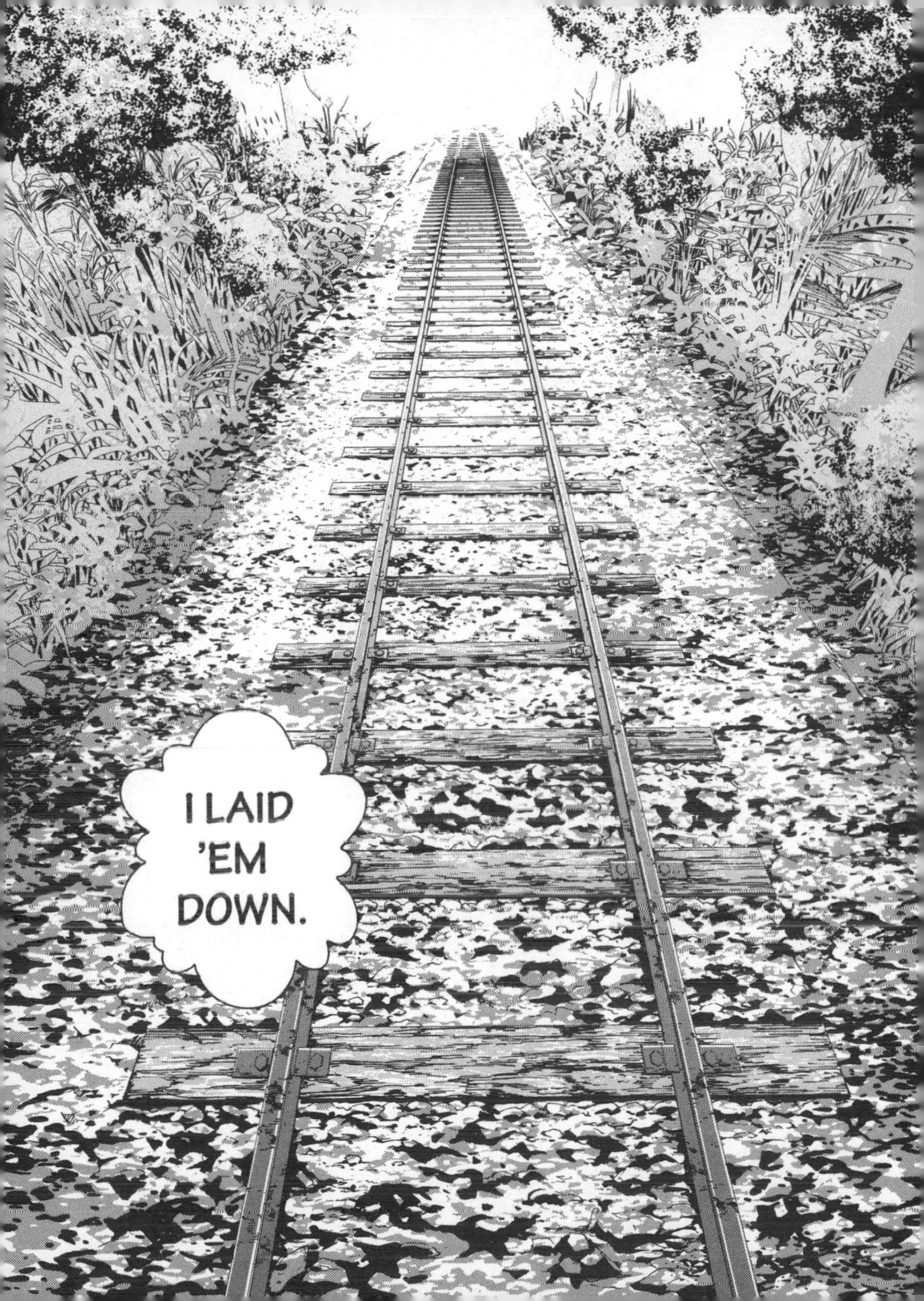
I LAID 'EM DOWN.

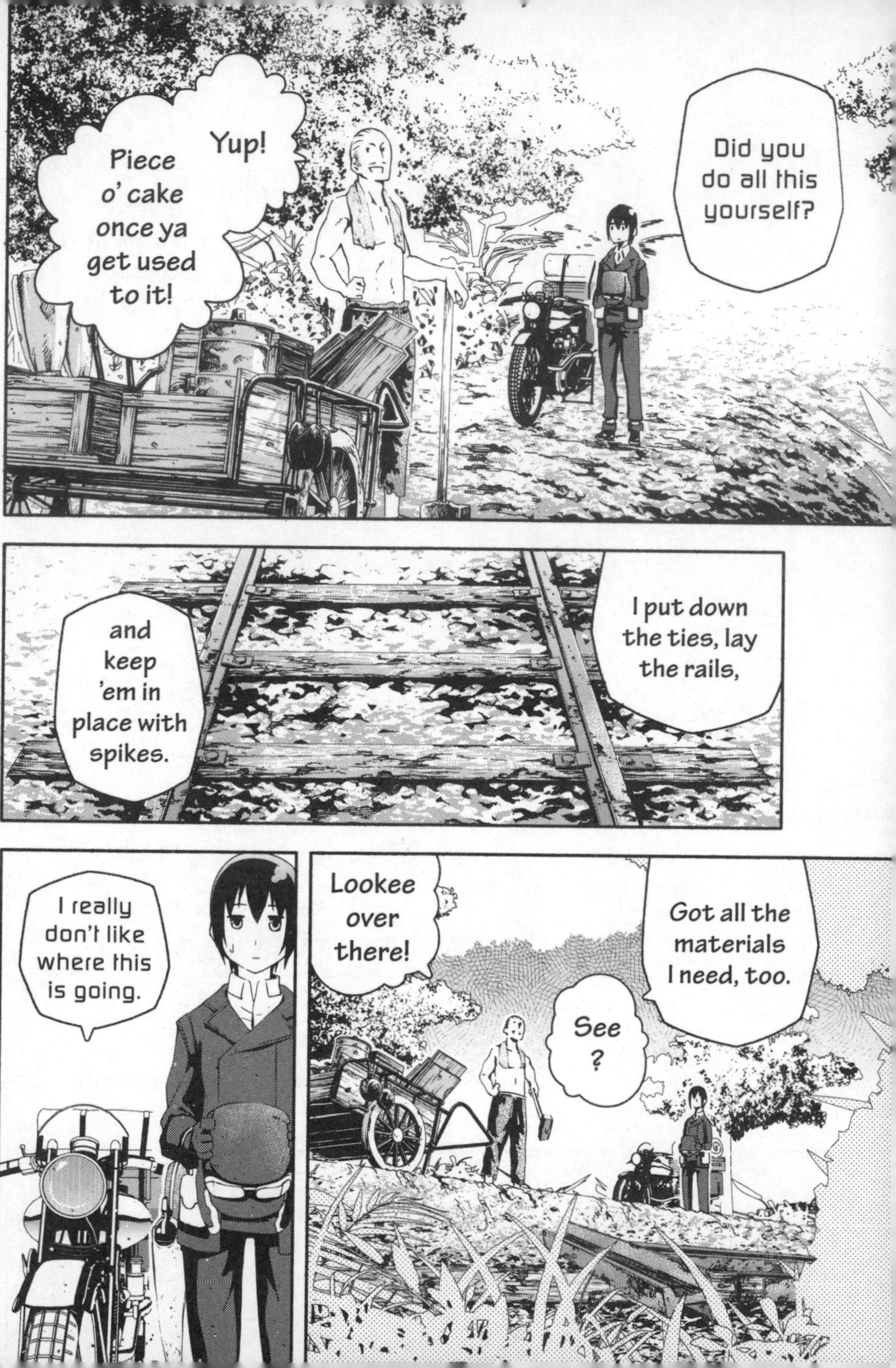
Did you do all this yourself?
Yup!
Piece o' cake once ya get used to it!
I put down the ties, lay the rails,
and keep 'em in place with spikes.
Got all the materials I need, too.
Lookee over there!
See?
I really don't like where this is going.

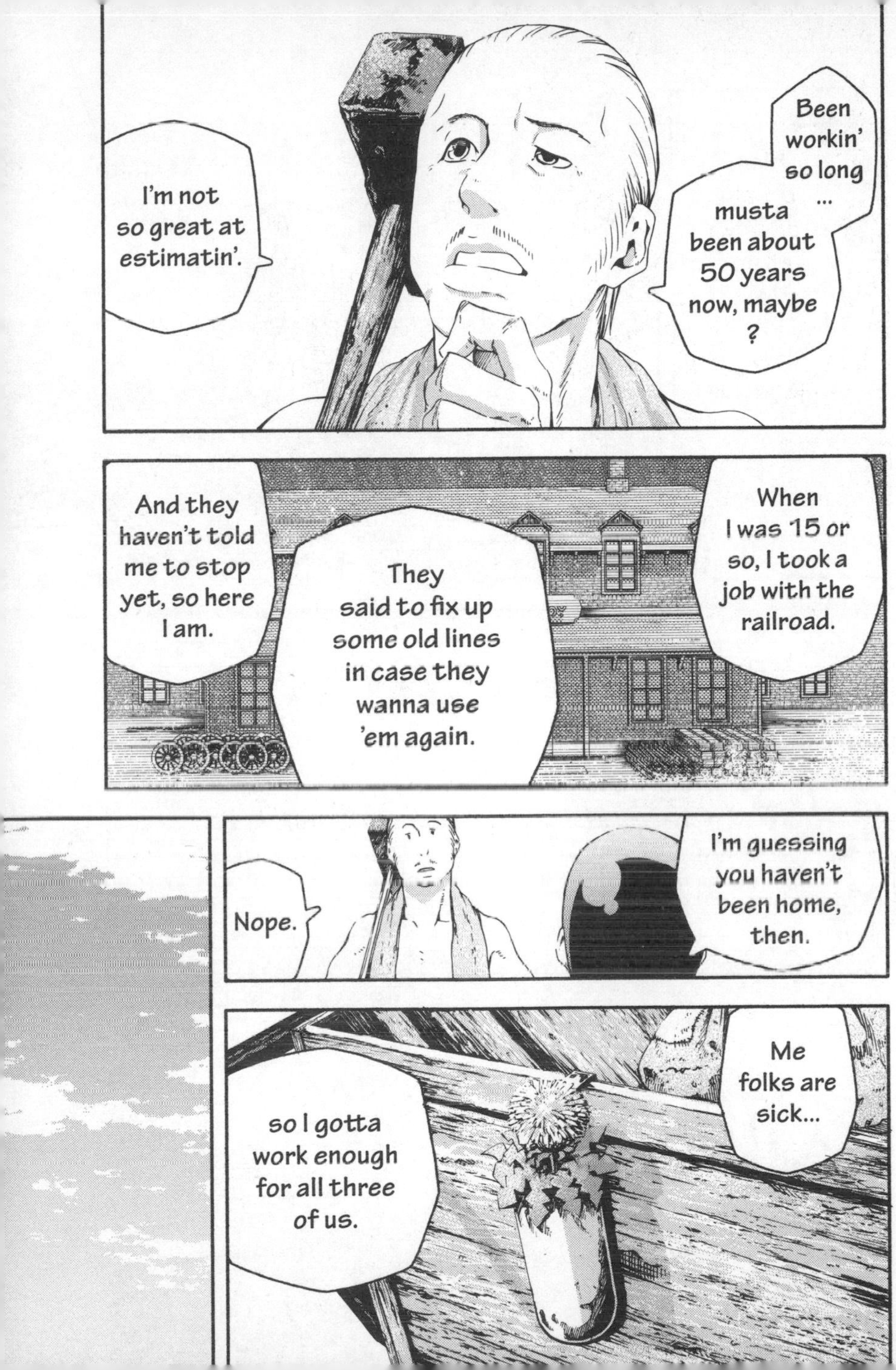
Been workin' so long ... musta been about 50 years now, maybe ?
I'm not so great at estimatin'.
When I was 15 or so, I took a job with the railroad.
They said to fix up some old lines in case they wanna use 'em again.
And they haven't told me to stop yet, so here I am.
I'm guessing you haven't been home, then.
Nope.
Me folks are sick...
so I gotta work enough for all three of us.

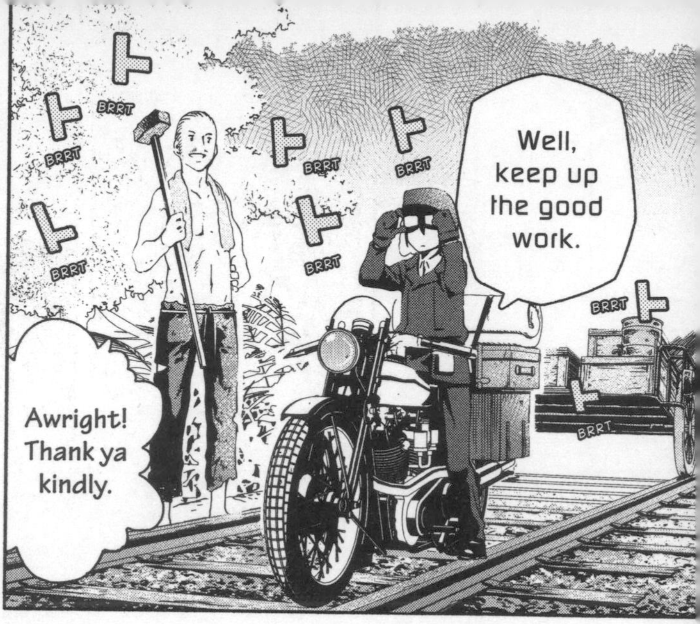
BRRT
BRRT
BRRT
BRRT
BRRT
Well, keep up the good work.
BRRT
BRRT
BRRT
Awright! Thank ya kindly.

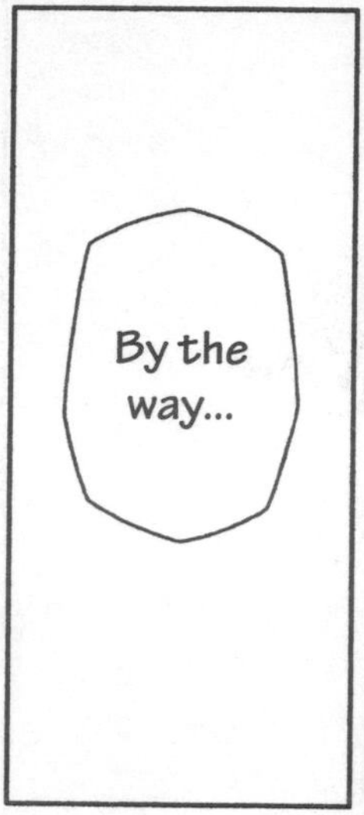
By the way...

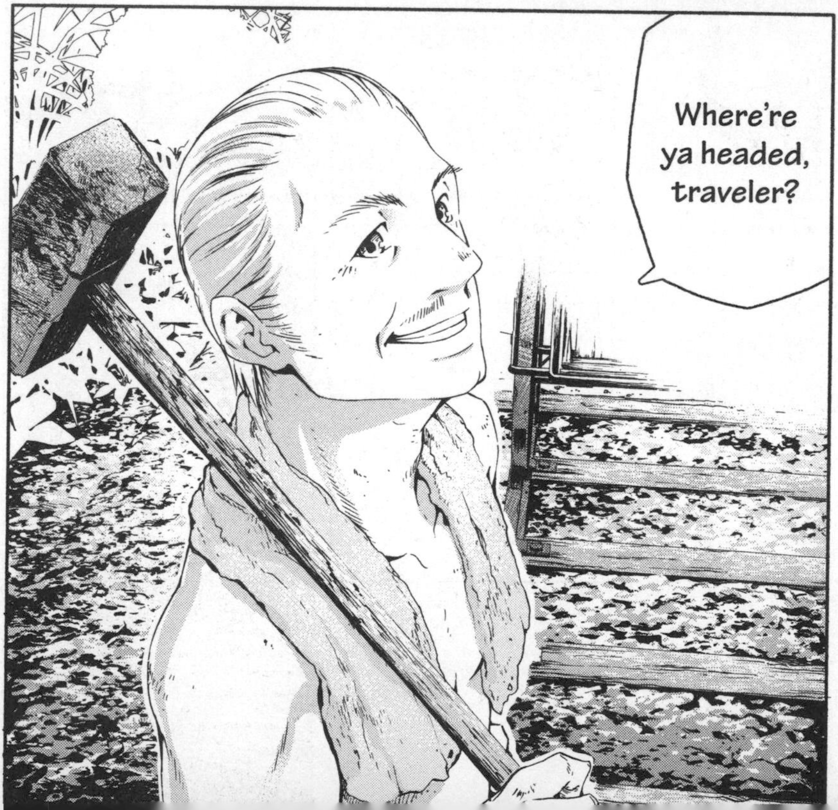
Where're ya headed, traveler?

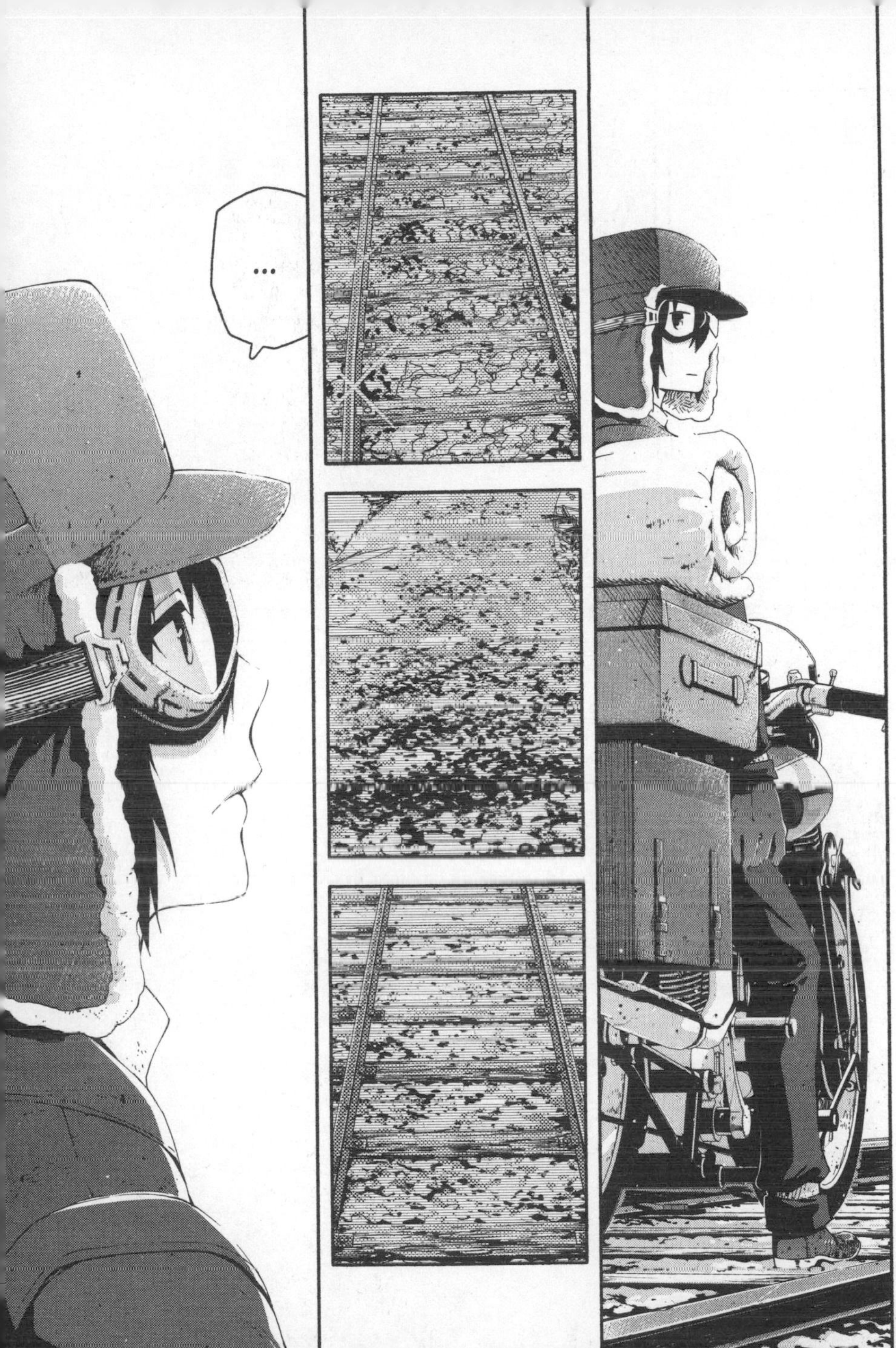
...

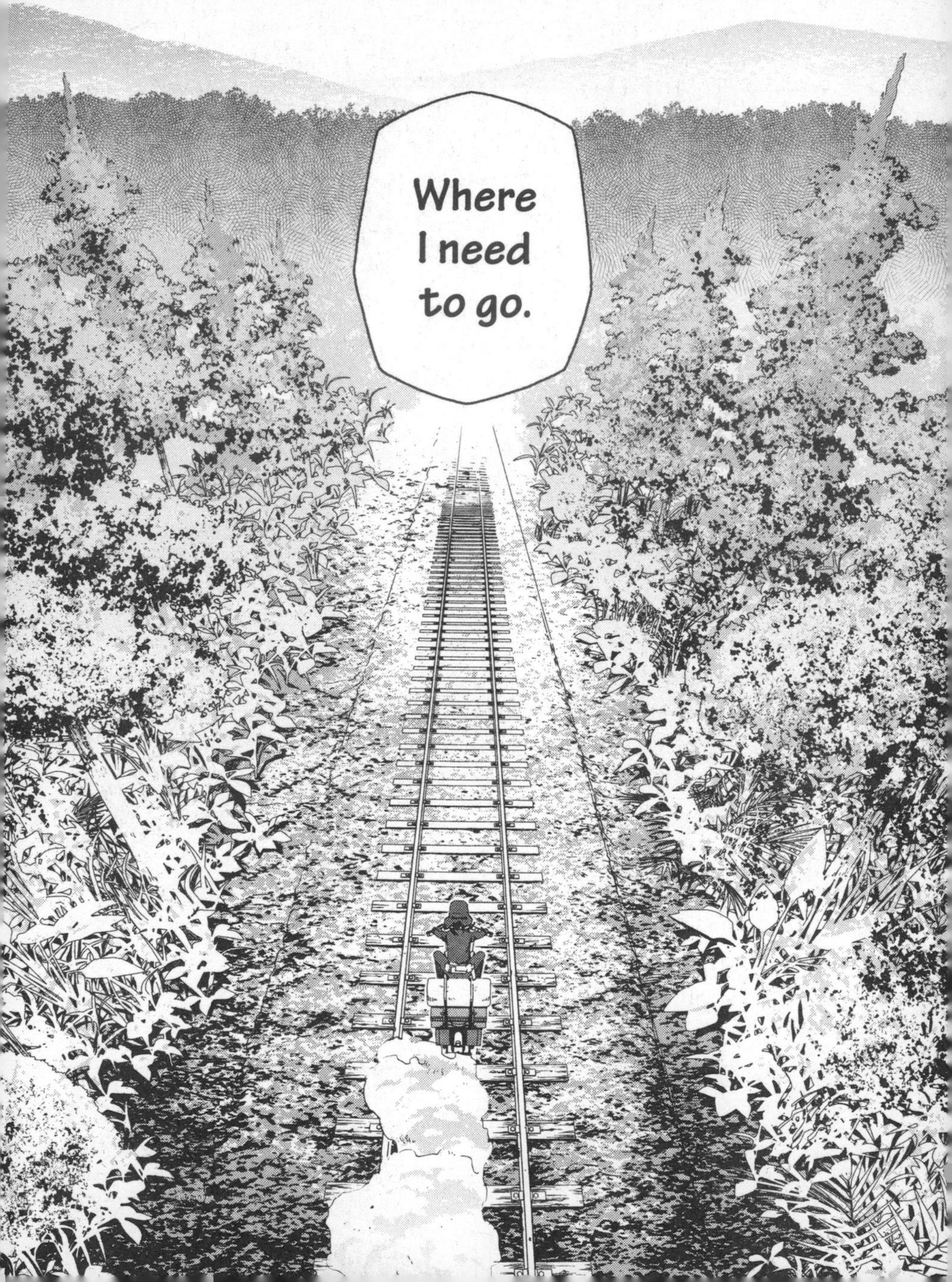
Where I need to go.

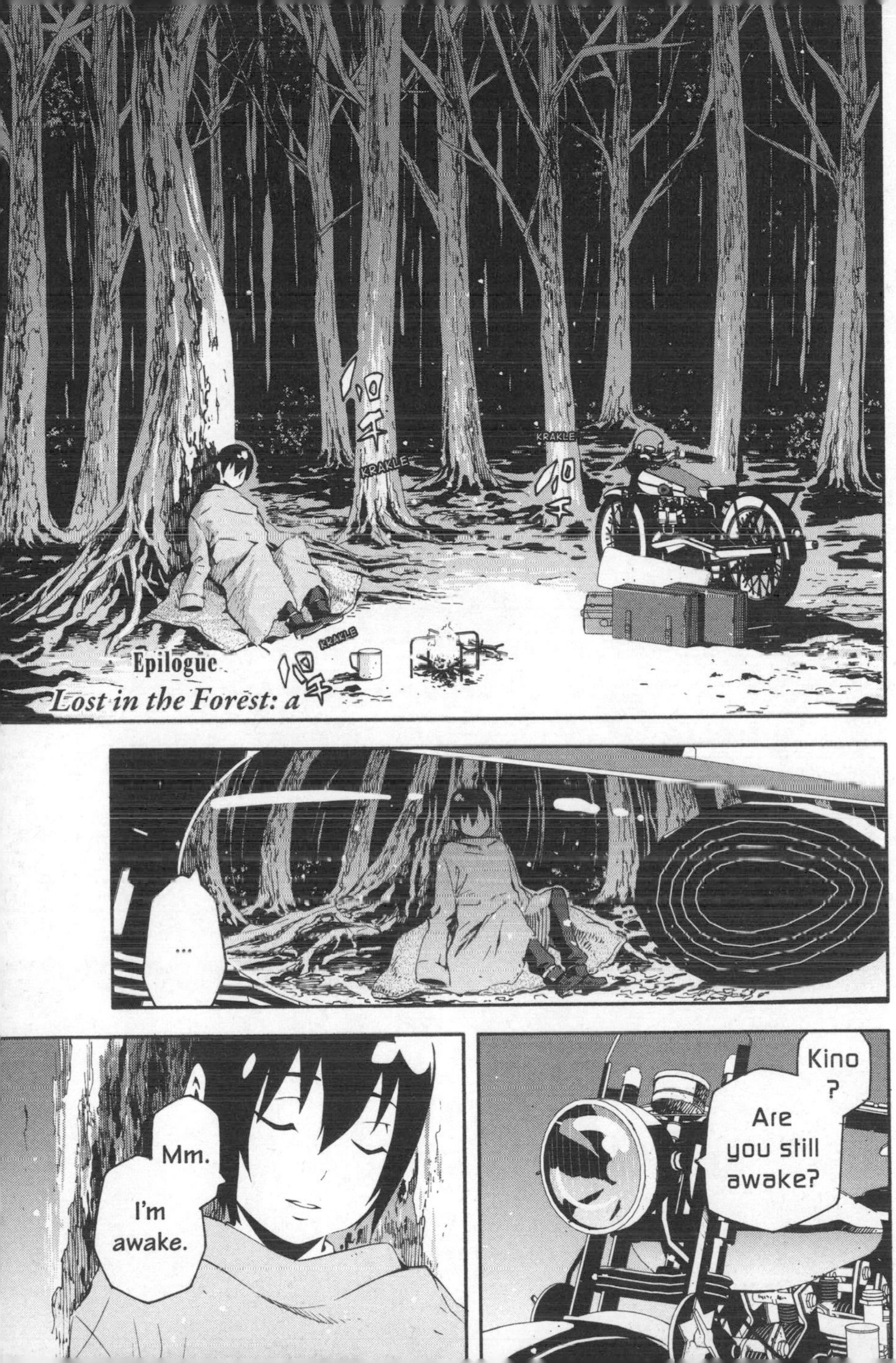
KRAKLE
KRAKLE
KRAKLE
Epilogue
Lost in the Forest: a
...
Kino?
Are you still awake?
Mm.
I'm awake.

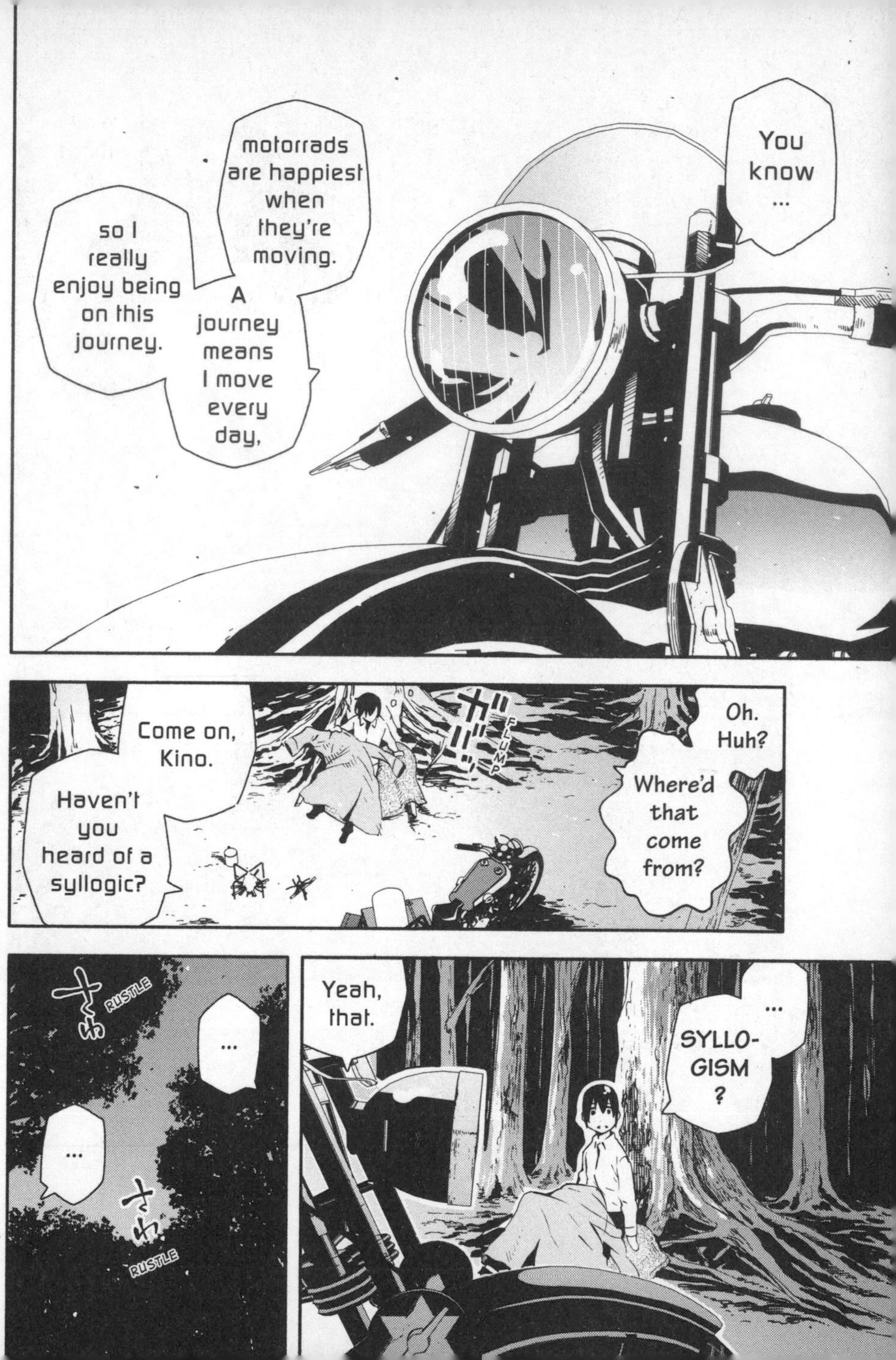
You know ...
motorrads are happiest when they're moving.
A journey means I move every day,
so I really enjoy being on this journey.
Oh. Huh?
Where'd that come from?
FLUMP
Come on, Kino.
Haven't you heard of a syllogic?
... SYLLO-GISM ?
Yeah, that.
RUSTLE
...
...
RUSTLE

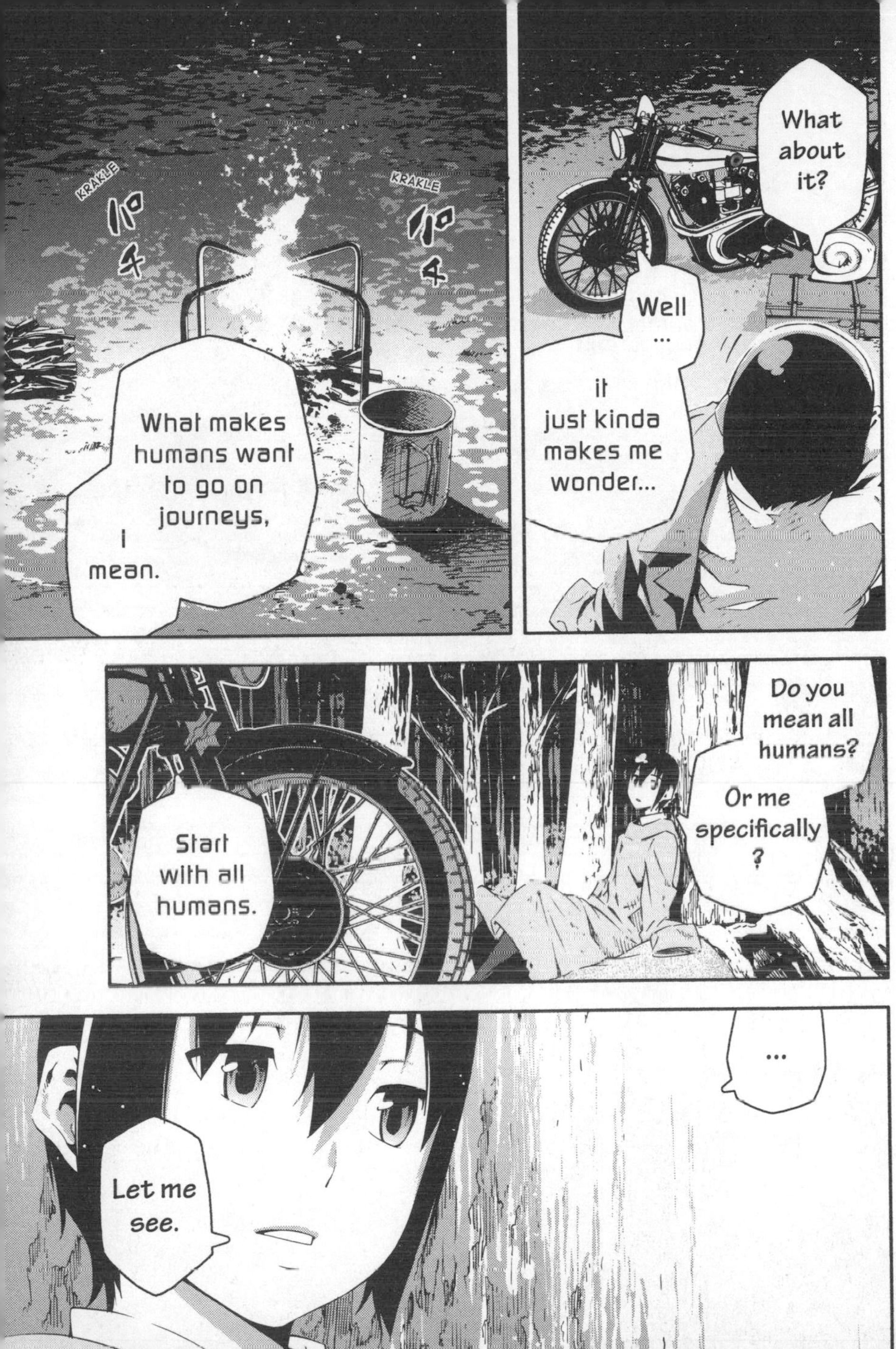
What about it?
Well ...
it just kinda makes me wonder...
KRAKLE
パチ
KRAKLE
パチ
What makes humans want to go on journeys, I mean.
Do you mean all humans?
Or me specifically?
Start with all humans.
...
Let me see.

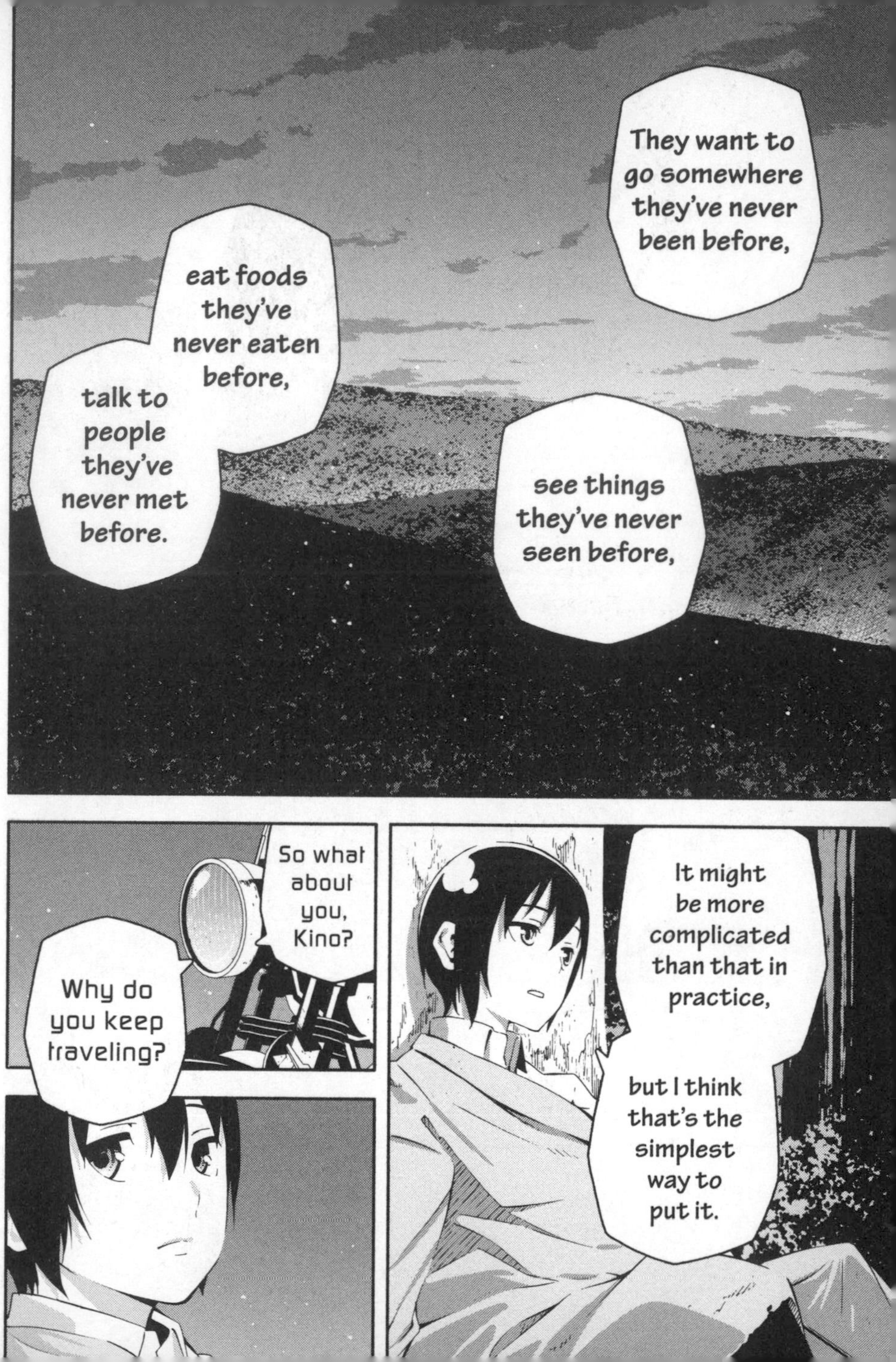
They want to go somewhere they've never been before,
see things they've never seen before,
eat foods they've never eaten before,
talk to people they've never met before.
It might be more complicated than that in practice,
but I think that's the simplest way to put it.
So what about you, Kino?
Why do you keep traveling?

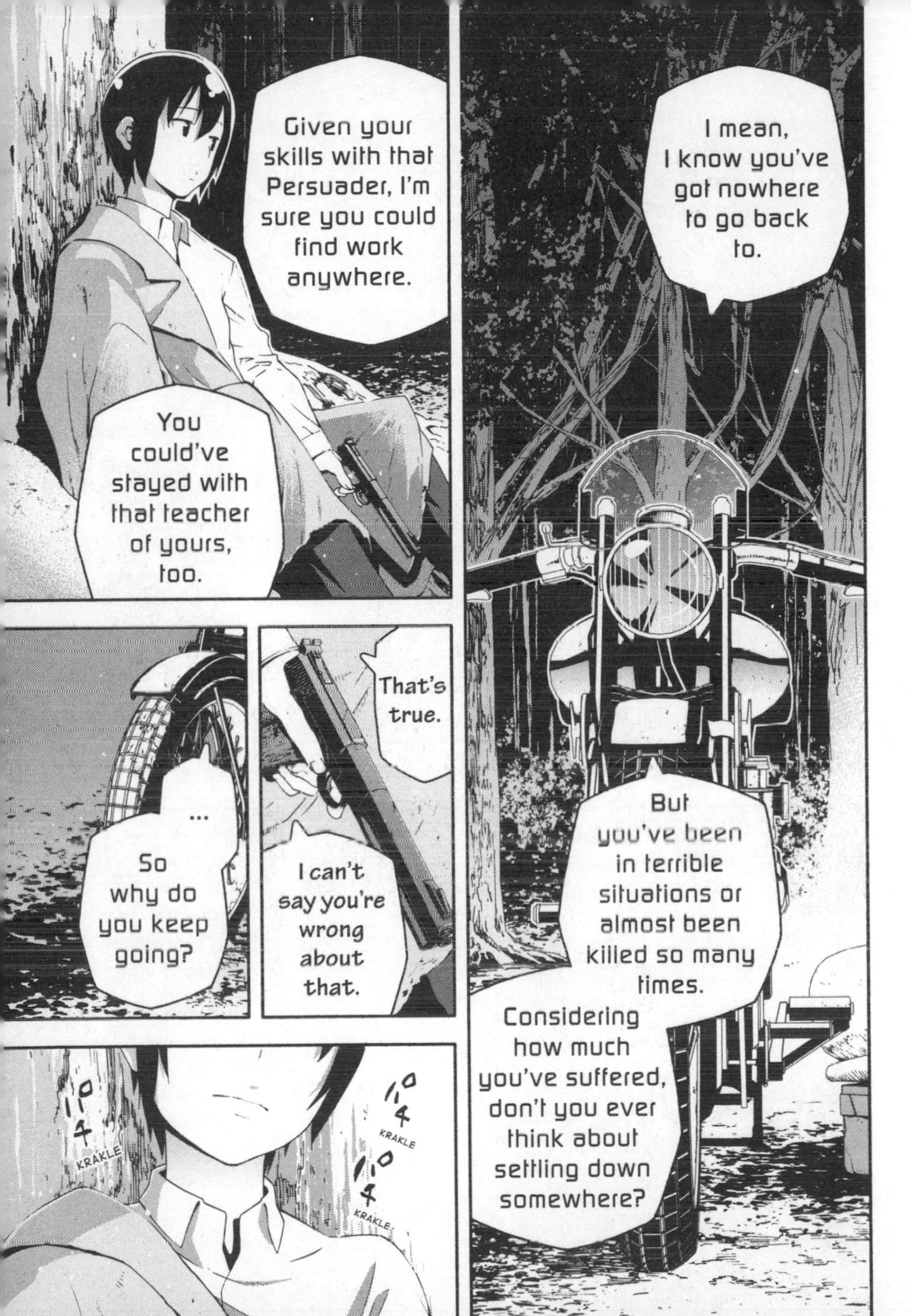
I mean, I know you've got nowhere to go back to.
But you've been in terrible situations or almost been killed so many times.
Considering how much you've suffered, don't you ever think about settling down somewhere?
Given your skills with that Persuader, I'm sure you could find work anywhere.
You could've stayed with that teacher of yours, too.
That's true.
I can't say you're wrong about that.
...
So why do you keep going?
KRAKLE
KRAKLE
KRAKLE

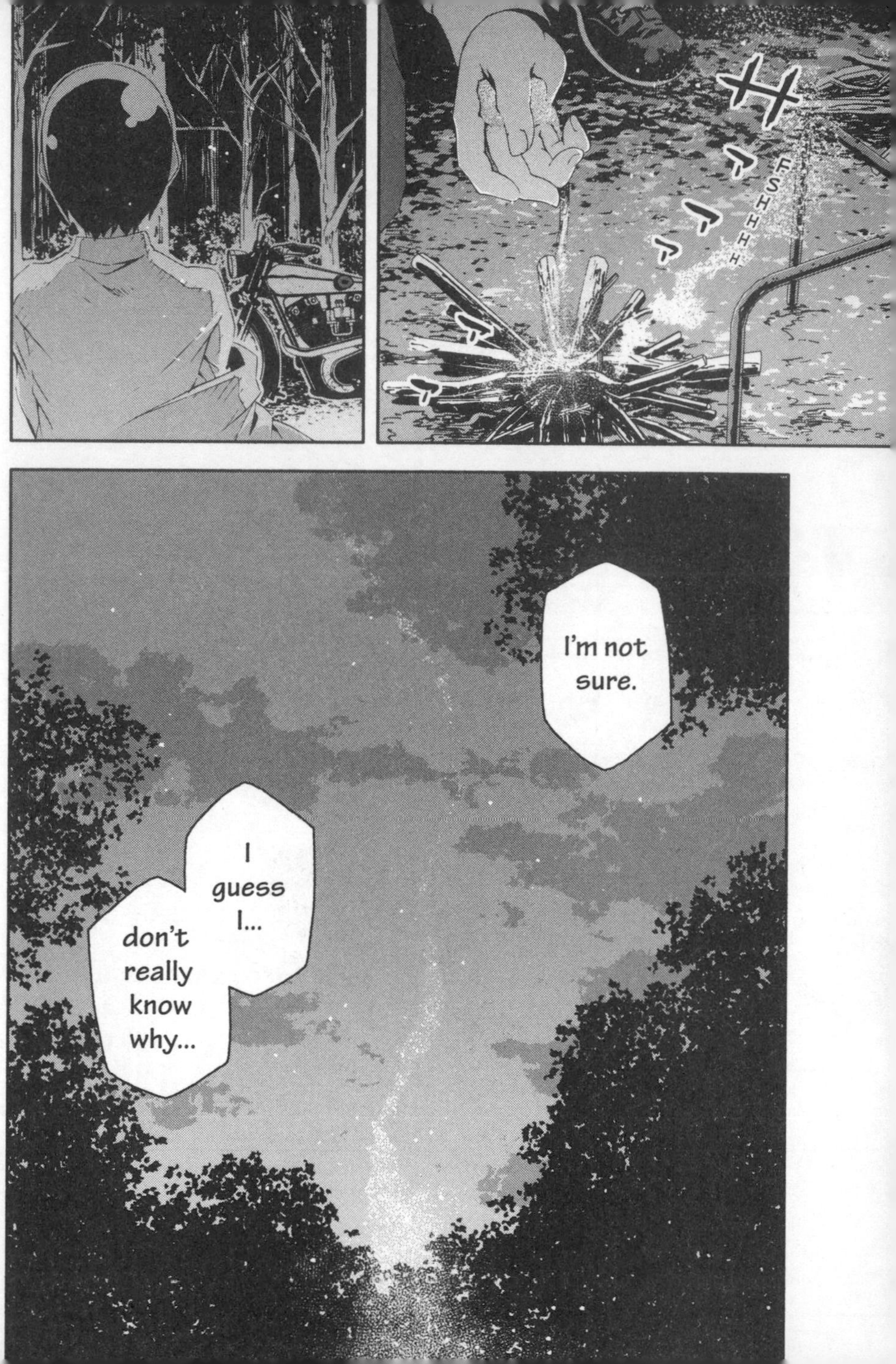
FSHHHH
I'm not sure.
I guess I...
don't really know why...

Art Assistant

Taku Umemoto

3D Assistants

yubikitax
Jeri

It's a miracle. The curse has finally been broken!

As far as the quality of the adaptation, I only have one word for my feelings: "Excited!" and "Gratified!" I'm sorry, that was two words.

Iruka Shiomiya's version of Kino is so sharp and stylish, and I can't get enough of the occasional cute expressions. The grin on my face as I read the finished manuscript must never be shared on social media.

Hermes looks very gallant and cool rendered in 3DCG, full of mechanical charm. I made a ridiculous amount of notes and retakes on the design (more than Kino's, in fact), and Shiomiya kindly went along with all of them. I don't have the words to fully express my gratitude.

I'll probably get in trouble if I don't wrap this up soon, so let me end by expressing my feelings.

The journey of our manga serialization is only just beginning, as is the journey of collecting them into tankobon volumes.

I hope that you will enjoy this journey with the manga version of Kino and Hermes. Will it lead to a fluffy bed with clean white sheets, or perhaps...?

Well, until we meet again in the next volume!

July 2017   Keiichi Sigsawa

Afterword!

Hello, dear reader of *Kino's Journey: The Beautiful World*! I'm the author of the original light novels, Keiichi Sigsawa (Note: An author. Cannot fly).

I've been given the honor of writing the afterword this time, to my great pleasure. Hopefully I don't write so much that the text ends up having to be really small!

As is often the case with paperback afterwords, I'll be sure to avoid spoiling the contents of the book, so it's all right to read this first, if you like!

Now, with the release of this first volume, I can hardly contain my happiness. I'm so thrilled, I feel like flying through the sky! I can't actually fly, though.

Kino's Journey was my debut as an author and is also my most well-known work, and while it's even been made into anime, games, and so on, this is the first time it's been adapted into a manga. That's quite unusual these days, when most multi-media projects start with a manga.

Of course, the plans for a manga version have been in the works for a long time, but it kept falling through for one reason or another.

"Could it be that *Kino's Journey* is cursed to never become a manga...?" Naturally, I was starting to seriously worry. Maybe I did something wrong in a previous life? If anyone knows, please tell me via telepathy.

At any rate, this year (2017), seventeen years after the original book was released, Kodansha has made the manga version a reality!

Kino's Journey
The Beautiful World
volume 1

A Vertical Comics Edition

Translation: Jenny McKeon
Production: Grace Lu
        Anthony Quintessenza

First published in Japan in 2017 by Kodansha, Ltd., Tokyo
Publication for this English edition arranged through Kodansha, Ltd., Tokyo
English language version produced by Vertical, Inc.

Translation provided by Vertical Comics, 2019
Published by Vertical Comics, an imprint of Vertical, Inc., New York

Originally published in Japanese as *Kino no Tabi the Beautiful World 1* by Kodansha, Ltd.
Kino no Tabi the Beautiful World 1 first serialized in *Shonen Magazine Edge*,
Kodansha, Ltd., 2017-

This is a work of fiction.

ISBN: 978-1-947194-35-9

Manufactured in Canada

First Edition

Vertical, Inc.
451 Park Avenue South
7th Floor
New York, NY 10016
www.vertical-comics.com

Vertical books are distributed through Penguin-Random House Publisher Services.